Praise for the First Edition

"Glenn [Fleishman] and his co-author, Adam Engst, have written **a great primer for anyone who wants to get connected to the Internet wirelessly.**" —*Peter Lewis, technology editor,* Fortune *magazine*

"…a year or two after the 802.11b/WiFi revolution took all geekdom by storm, I have finally joined the bandwagon—with a little help from **a book I'm happy to recommend,** Adam Engst and Glenn Fleishman's *Wireless Networking Starter Kit.* (Engst's *Internet Starter Kit* was the book I used to put my Macintosh on the Net back in 1994, so this all felt right.)"—*Scott Rosenberg, Salon.com*

"[This book] is **an ideal way to get up to speed** on designing, installing, and troubleshooting Wi-Fi hot spots and other devices."—*Brian Livingston,* InfoWorld

"If you've been holding out on getting some Wi-Fi gear because you weren't sure what to do with it once you got it home, **this book would be an excellent choice** to assist you in deciding what to buy and how to use it."—*LockerGnome Windows Daily*

"…This book is a great introduction to wireless networking and covers the hardware and software you need to start surfing while sipping that espresso double latte."—*Andrew King, Webreference.com*

"[This] is **the best book so far** for the average reader on Wi-Fi/AirPort/ 802.11b networking. If you want to cut the (Ethernet) cord, start by reading this book!"—*David Weeks, MyMac.com*

"**The authors' comfortable, reassuring tone** helps the reader feel at ease with this technology. Their detailed coverage of all the issues affecting this form of networking ensures that network administrators, who may be discovering wireless networking, fully understand how to design and optimize their networks."—*Kirk McElhearn, ATPM*

"Finally, **here's a smart, accessible, comprehensive guide** to the often incomprehensible world of wireless….Adam and Glenn are two tech journalists who know how to make even the most complex and arcane subjects understandable— and fun to boot."—*J.D. Lasica, technology journalist*

"Your book is **the best resource I've found** for when people want to learn the basics of wireless technology."—*Linda Rosewood Hooper, University of California at Santa Cruz*

The Wireless Networking Starter Kit

Second Edition

The practical guide to Wi-Fi networks for Windows and Macintosh

By **Adam Engst** and **Glenn Fleishman**

 Peachpit Press

The Wireless Networking Starter Kit
Second Edition
The practical guide to Wi-Fi networks for Windows and Macintosh
By Adam Engst and Glenn Fleishman

Peachpit Press
1249 Eighth Street
Berkeley, CA 94710
510/524-2178
800/283-9444
510/524-2221 (fax)

Find us on the World Wide Web at: www.peachpit.com
Find the book's Web site at: www.wireless-starter-kit.com
To report errors, please send a note to errata@peachpit.com
Peachpit Press is a division of Pearson Education

Editor: Nancy Davis
Production Coordinator: Lupe Edgar
Copyeditor: Tonya Engst
Proofreaders: Ted Waitt and Jason Silvis
Indexer: Caroline Parks
Cover illustration and design: Jeff Tolbert
Interior illustrations: Jeff Tolbert
Interior design: David Blatner and Jeff Tolbert

ISBN 0-321-22468-X

9 8 7 6 5 4

Printed and bound in the United States of America

Acknowledgements

Even though our names appear on the cover, we couldn't have written and produced a book about a subject as far-reaching as wireless networking on our own. We stand on the backs of giants, and we offer our heartfelt thanks to the many generous individuals who selflessly share their knowledge.

In particular, we'd like to thank Rob Flickenger and Tim Pozar, whose sites and email have been guideposts for many of us in the wireless networking world. Our discussions with Andy Shiekh about long-range wireless connections were also extremely helpful.

We'd also like to thank the people who helped produce the book: Tonya Engst, whose copyediting remains spot on and Jeff Tolbert, whose cover and interior illustrations were exactly what we had in mind. We're also indebted to the remarkable people at Peachpit Press, including Nancy Davis, whose publishing instincts remain unmatched; Kim Lombardi, whose promotion of the book was invaluable; publisher Nancy Ruenzel; and also Scott Cowlin, Jim Bruce, and Lupe Edgar at Peachpit Press.

Adam: "Writing a book is hard work, but partnering with someone of Glenn's knowledge, enthusiasm, and skill made it not only easier, but also far more enjoyable. I couldn't, and wouldn't, have done it without him. My undying appreciation also to my wife, Tonya, who copyedited the book and helped me find the time I needed to write and edit in the final few weeks."

Glenn: "Adam is the hardest working man in computation, and a great co-author. I enjoyed the bicoastal (him on the East Coast, me on the West Coast) experience of writing with him immensely. Thanks are due to my officemates, colleagues, and friends for their continual support, and above all, I'd like to thank my wife, Lynn, for her constant encouragement."

Photograph and Illustration Credits

Photos of the AirPort Base Station are courtesy of Apple Computer.

Photos of Linksys gateways and bridges are courtesy of Linksys.

The Wi-Fi logo (Figure 2.1) is used with permission of The Wi-Fi Alliance.

Photo of Sony Ericsson T608 phone (Figure 4.2) courtesy of Sony Ericsson.

Photos of Linksys gateways, bridges, cameras (Figure 18.3), print servers (Figure 18.5), media players (18.9), and other gear are courtesy of Linksys.

The photo of the Nikon D2H Pro camera (Figure 18.1) is courtesy of Nikon.

Photos of D-Link cameras (Figure 18.2) are courtesy of D-Link Systems.

The photo of the IQinvision IQeye3 camera (Figure 18.4) is courtesy of IQinvision.

Photos of the Nomad printer (Figure 18.6) are used with permission of Mobile Command Systems.

The photo of the Smart ID WFS-1 Wi-Fi detector (Figure 18.7) is used with permission of Smart ID Technology.

Photos of the WiFiSense handbag (Figure 18.8) are used with permssion of WiFiSense.

The photo of the ViewSonic Airpanel V150p wireless monitor (Figure 18.10) is courtesy of ViewSonic.

The photo of the Vocera Communications Badge (Figure 18.11) is used with permission of Vocera.

The photo of an Proxim Orinoco PC Card (Figure 21.1) is courtesy of Proxim.

KisMAC network scan (Figure 25.6) is courtesy of the developers.

Warchalking cartoon (Figure 25-8) ©2003 Geek Culture, and is used with permission.

The photo of the Sierra Wireless AirCard 555 (Figure 30.9) is used with permission of Sierra Wireless.

The photo of a warchalking symbol (Figure 32.1) is copyright ©2002 Ben Hammersley and is used with permission.

The photo of a Pringles can yagi antenna (Figure 34.8) is copyright ©2001 Rob Flickenger and is used with permission.

Contents

Section III

Building Your Wireless Network... 165

Introduction

Wireless. The word evokes those heady days long ago when radio ruled the entertainment world and families gathered around a console radio the size of a coffee table to marvel at a technology that emitted disembodied voices from far away. Though we now take radio for granted, back then it was pure magic each time words and music came out, without even the need for wires between the receiver and a transmitter that could be miles away.

Fast forward to the present, where a different kind of radio is taking the computer world by storm. These new radios are minuscule chips embedded in credit-card-sized devices that plug into computers themselves not much larger than pads of writing paper. These radios transmit and receive not the scratchy voices and sound effects of a newscast but tiny chunks of zeros and ones—computer data. In the past, radio connected people and made possible the first mass culture; today, radio connects computers with wireless networks and the greater Internet.

What's most amazing about wireless networking is how powerful it is, considering the underlying simplicity. There's nothing all that unique, technologically speaking, in wireless networking, but the combination of different aspects of computing and transmission makes it a compelling choice, and even hints at the roots of social revolution as people communicate with one another in new and ever more mobile ways.

Networks that run over wires have long provided the same types of communication between computers that wireless networks can offer, and, what's more, data generally flows over less-expensive wired networks at much faster speeds. Faster speeds and cheaper hardware turn out not to be the point—what's compelling about wireless networking is the combination of flexibility, network ubiquity, and the distance between network nodes that takes wireless networking far beyond the mundane wired world. Plug in a few inexpensive pieces of gear, fire up a connection, and you can wander around your home or office, go out on the patio, or visit a café, with full network access the entire time. Suddenly you're networking in a way that seemed like science fiction just a decade ago.

Unplug, Tune In, Power Up

Look behind your desktop computer. If it's anything like our computers, there's a rat's nest of wires back there. The monitor and the keyboard connect to the computer, the monitor and computer both plug into electrical sockets in a power strip that itself plugs into a wall outlet, and then there are cables snaking to and from the printer, the mouse, and so on. Now imagine a computer completely freed of cables and wires—the laptop computer, with its integrated screen, keyboard, and mouse, all receiving power from a battery inside. In many ways, the laptop is the future of computing, and as evidence of that, laptop sales have recently outstripped desktop computer sales.

With a laptop, you're free to work wherever you like—in bed, on the couch, on an airplane, or in a coffeehouse. And with today's laptops, which combine speedy processors and beautiful screens in svelte packages weighing only a few pounds, you aren't even making many tradeoffs for your freedom from your desk. But until recently, there was one thing you did give up—Internet access.

We won't go on about how amazing the Internet is because you already know all about the power of exchanging email, browsing the Web, and relying on instant messaging to remain in constant contact with friends and colleagues. But amazing it is—and we've been using and writing about the Internet since well before it became the cultural phenomenon it is today. (In fact, Adam wrote one of the very first books about the Internet back in 1993, and within a few years, hundreds of thousands of people had used his *Internet Starter Kit* series of books to get on the Internet for the first time. And Glenn founded one of the first Web development companies in 1994.) Today's computers are communication devices, and to communicate, they require Internet access.

This need for Internet access hobbled laptops for a while, because while you could work without the laptop plugged in as long as its battery held out, if your work required the Internet, you had to have a modem cable or Ethernet cable tethering your computer to the wall. Enter wireless networking. Suddenly, with the addition of two inexpensive pieces of hardware—a wireless network card to plug into your computer and an access point—you could use your laptop anywhere within range of your access point while enjoying Internet connectivity.

The freedom offered by wireless networking doesn't stop when you leave home. Many offices have jumped on the bandwagon, networking conference rooms and lounges so employees can access shared files and Internet resources no matter where they are. (An added benefit is checking your email during particularly boring meetings, but you didn't hear us say that.) Business travelers have come to expect wireless Internet access in airports, at trade shows, and even in coffeehouses, libraries, and sports arenas.

Wireless networking also has strong grassroots support. Community-minded folk in many cities around the world have put up large wireless networks that cover whole neighborhoods, so if you're in Bryant Park in New York City, or almost anywhere in Ashland, Oregon (home of the annual Oregon Shakespeare Festival), accessing the Internet is merely a matter of opening your laptop, though we're sure you wouldn't do that in the middle of *Romeo and Juliet.*

Put bluntly, wireless networking is one of the most exciting developments in computing in the last few years, not because it makes possible any new technical feats, but because it lets computers fit better into our lives. People weren't meant to sit in the same place, day in and day out, and while those of us who spend our time working on computers have made that sacrifice for years, the combination of a slim laptop and wireless networking providing Internet access wherever we go is tremendously liberating.

It's just freaking cool.

Wireless Networking Roots

So what exactly do we mean when we talk about wireless networking? For the purposes of this book, we're almost always talking about three short-range, unlicensed radio technologies: IEEE *802.11a, 802.11b,* and *802.11g,* known together by the more mellifluous moniker *Wi-Fi* (it's an odd shortening of "wireless fidelity" by a trade association). Although we may occasionally refer to one of the specific technologies for accuracy, we mostly use Wi-Fi throughout the book to avoid confusion. Wi-Fi is by no means the only wireless networking technology, but it's by far the most common.

Let's take a quick spin through the development of wireless networking.

The first wireless network was developed at the University of Hawaii in 1971 to link computers on four islands without using telephone wires. Wireless networking entered the realm of personal computing in the 1980s, when the idea of sharing data between computers was becoming popular. Some of the first wireless networks didn't use radio at all, though, instead relying on infrared transceivers. Unfortunately, infrared never took off because infrared radiation can't penetrate most physical objects. Thus, it required a clear line of sight at all times, a tricky thing to accomplish in most offices, and something that could engender office hostility—"Hey, move it! You're blocking the network!" Infrared also wasn't very fast, and even modern infrared is still quite low bandwidth, when it works.

Radio-based wireless networks started to gain momentum in the early 1990s as chip processing power became sufficient to manage data transmitted and received over radio connections. However, these early implementations were expensive and proprietary—they couldn't communicate with one another. Incompatible networks are doomed to failure, so in the mid-1990s, attention coalesced around the fledgling IEEE 802.11 standard for wireless communication. Early generations of 802.11, ratified in 1997, were relatively slow, running at 1 and then 2 megabits per second (Mbps). They were often used in logistics: warehouses and inventory operations where wires weren't feasible or would be enormously expensive to maintain.

It was clear that the technology could be pushed much farther, and in 1999 the IEEE finalized the 2.4 GHz 802.11b standard, increasing the throughput of wireless networks to 11 Mbps (to compare, standard 10Base-T wired Ethernet runs at 10 Mbps). Although many companies were involved in creating the 802.11b specification, Lucent Technologies and Apple Computer led the way in producing affordable wireless network devices for the consumer market. (Other companies like BreezeCOM and Aironet Wireless Communications were already selling expensive equipment aimed at the corporate market.)

The turning point for wireless networking came in July of 1999, with Apple's release of its AirPort technology. AirPort was an industry-standard compliant version of IEEE 802.11b, and Apple jumpstarted the market by charging only $100 for a wireless network card that fit inside different models of the Macintosh and $300 for an access point (which Apple called an AirPort Base Station). It took more than a year for other companies to drop their prices to the level Apple set, but by introducing wireless networking to the much-larger PC market, these other companies were able to continue lowering prices. As we write the second edition of this book, the cost to equip a single PC or Mac with a Wi-Fi card is between $50 and $100, and an access point costs less than $150.

Although the IEEE actually ratified the 802.11a standard first, technical and political realities delayed its development such that the first 802.11a gear shipped in the middle of 2002. 802.11a significantly outperforms 802.11b in terms of speed, with a raw throughput of 54 Mbps compared to 802.11b's 11 Mbps. However, 802.11a equipment isn't compatible with 802.11b hardware because 802.11a runs in the 5 GHz band. This lack of compatibility slowed 802.11a's acceptance.

At the very end of 2002, another standard appeared on the scene, further hurting 802.11a's chances to take over from the slower 802.11b. This new standard, 802.11g, uses the same 2.4 GHz band as 802.11b, provides full backward compatibility with all 802.11b hardware, and matches the 54 Mbps speed of 802.11a. Interestingly, when a few companies started selling 802.11g hardware—most notably Apple, with its AirPort Extreme devices—the formal specification hadn't yet been ratified. But within six months, the IEEE had signed off on the 802.11g draft, and all the equipment manufacturers scrambled to release firmware updates that brought their gear up to full compatibility.

Throughout the last few years, capabilities have increased as prices have dropped, and ease of use has improved so anyone who can set up a computer can also set up a wireless network, complete with a shared Internet connection. We've come a long way in a short time, and with the popularity of wireless networking, the future looks as bright as the recent past.

Who Should Read This Book?

We had a particular audience in mind when we wrote this book. You'll get the most out of the book if you can hear yourself asking questions along the lines of some of these:

- I've just bought a laptop, and I want to share my desktop computer's Internet connection. How can I share that connection cheaply and easily?

- I have a small wired network to share files and an Internet connection between two desktop computers, but now I want to add my laptop to the mix without needing any network cables. What should I buy to add my laptop to the network?

- I've just moved, and running Ethernet cables where I need network access is too expensive and too much work. I want all my computers to share an Internet connection without pulling cable. Will wireless networking solve my problems?

- I have a wireless network in place and working, but I can't receive the signal in some rooms. How can I extend my network's range?

- I bought everything I need, and I set up my wireless network, but I can't make the darn thing work with my Internet connection. Can this book tell me what I did wrong?

- I travel a lot. What do I need in terms of hardware, software, and accounts to get wireless Internet access wherever I go?

- I can't get DSL (Digital Subscriber Line) or cable-modem access to the Internet, but I've heard that I might be able to get high-speed wireless access to the Internet in my location. How do I make this happen?

- I'm trying to understand how wireless networking works so I can advise my department on whether or not we should invest in the technology. Can this book explain the basics of wireless networking, tell me what's coming up, and point to useful Web sites where I can learn more?

- My friends and colleagues turn to me as their Internet and computer guru, and they're all interested in wireless networking. What information do I need to start setting up networks for home users?

- I'm worried about crackers tapping into my wireless network and stealing my company's sensitive product plans. How do I ensure that my network is secure?

We're confident that if your needs are along the lines of these questions, you'll find the information you need in this book. Or, in the event that something has changed since the book was published, we may have covered the topic on the book's Web site at www.wireless-starter-kit.com, on our Apple AirPort Weblog at www.wireless-starter-kit.com/airportblog/, or on Glenn's Wi-Fi Networking News site, at www.wifinetnews.com.

Our goal is to provide practical information and advice for anyone trying to work with a wireless network, although we should note that this book isn't for complete novices. If you don't yet know the basics of using Windows or a Macintosh, for instance, we recommend reading an appropriate beginner's book first—Peachpit Press offers a number of good ones—and then coming back to this book.

On the other end of the spectrum, we don't examine wireless networking at the protocol level, dissect packet headers, discuss the detailed physics involved with radio reception, or handle any other truly deep technical topic. (If you need that level of detail, we recommend Matthew Gast's *802.11 Wireless Networks: The Definitive Guide*.) That sort of information is primarily useful to those few people designing wireless networking hardware, writing wireless software, or setting up community-wide mesh networks, and we want to focus this book on practical issues experienced by large numbers of people.

Who We Are

Before we get into the nuts and bolts of wireless networking (so to speak), we'd like to tell you where we're coming from so you can see that we're not just armchair technologists—we've lived this stuff. We've both been involved with technology for more than 20 years, and over the last 13 years, we've devoted large chunks of time to writing about technologies that fascinate us. We do this because we love explaining complex topics.

Since 1990, Adam has published *TidBITS,* a weekly electronic newsletter that covers topics of interest to Macintosh and Internet users (www.tidbits.com). He has also been a contributing editor at *MacUser, MacWEEK,* and *Macworld.* Along with the best-selling *Internet Starter Kit* series, Adam has written and co-authored a number of other books, including *Internet Explorer Kit for Macintosh* (with Bill Dickson), *Eudora for Windows & Macintosh: Visual QuickStart Guide, The Race for Bandwidth* (ghostwritten with Steve Manes for our late friend Cary Lu), *Crossing Platforms: A Macintosh/Windows Phrasebook* (with David Pogue), and most recently, *iPhoto 2 for Mac OS X: Visual QuickStart Guide.*

During much of that time, Glenn has been a freelance writer. He also founded Point of Presence Company in 1994, one of the first Web site development companies—Peachpit Press was one of his first clients, deploying a market-basket system for buying books in 1995. Then he did a six-month stint as Amazon.com's catalog manager and took some time out to beat Hodgkin's disease. Glenn has co-authored (with *TidBITS* managing editor Jeff Carlson) three editions of *Real World Adobe GoLive* and two editions of *Real World Scanning and Halftones.* Glenn currently writes for publications such as *The*

Seattle Times, InfoWorld, The New York Times, and the O'Reilly Network. He also runs the popular Wi-Fi Networking News Web site (www.wifinetnews.com), is a senior editor at Jiwire (www.jiwire.com), and is widely recognized as one of the leading journalists covering wireless networking.

We met via email in the early 1990s and became close friends when we both lived in Seattle. Since Adam left Seattle to move back to his home town of Ithaca, New York, we see each other mostly at trade shows and other industry events and interact the rest of the time via phone, email, and instant messaging.

What's in this Book

In this second edition of *The Wireless Networking Starter Kit,* we've updated all our discussions from the first edition, added hundreds of pages on new topics, and reorganized the entire book to create smaller chapters that each focus on a specific topic. To that end, we divided the book into six sections and three appendixes.

- **Section I, *Wireless Basics,*** starts from scratch with Chapter 1, *How Wireless Works,* discusses wireless standards in Chapter 2, *Wireless Standards,* and tells you exactly what hardware you'll need in Chapter 3, *Wireless Hardware.* We run through other protocols you might encounter in Chapter 4, *Other Wireless Standards,* and for those wondering what the future holds for wireless networking, check out Chapter 5, *Wireless of the (Near) Future.*

- **Section II, *Connecting Your Computer,*** gets down to the nitty-gritty, with self-explanatory chapter titles including Chapter 6, *Connecting Your Windows PC;* Chapter 7, *Connecting Your Centrino Laptop;* Chapter 8, *Connecting Your Macintosh* (both Mac OS 9 and Mac OS X 10.2 and 10.3); Chapter 9, *Connecting with Linux and FreeBSD;* Chapter 10, *Connecting Your Handheld* (focusing on Palm OS handhelds and PocketPC devices); and Chapter 11, *Connecting via Bluetooth.* These chapters offer step-by-step, illustrated instructions along with background information as necessary. Three additional chapters round out the discussion of connecting computers: Chapter 12, *Creating an Ad Hoc Wireless Network;* Chapter 13, *Sharing Files & Printers;* and one we hope you don't have to read but know you will, Chapter 14, *Troubleshooting Your Connection.*

- **Section III, *Building Your Wireless Network,*** takes the discussion of wireless networking beyond a simple connection to the creation of full-fledged wireless networks. We recommend a thorough approach, starting with Chapter 15, *Planning Your Wireless Network,* followed by Chapter 16,

Buying a Wireless Gateway, and finishing up with Chapter 17, *Setting up a Wireless Gateway.* Then we move on to more esoteric topics, such as all the things you can add to your wireless network in Chapter 18, *Wireless Gadgets.* Chapter 19, *Creating a Software Access Point,* looks at using a computer to do the job of a wireless gateway; Chapter 20, *Bridging Wireless Networks,* helps you figure out how to extend your wireless network; and Chapter 21, *Indoor Antenna Basics,* offers another approach for extending range. Rounding out this section are Chapter 22, *Small Office Wi-Fi Networking,* which looks at security and authentication issues in small offices, and Chapter 23, *Troubleshooting Your Wireless Network,* which offers numerous tests and bits of advice for solving any problems you may encounter across a network.

- **Section IV,** *Wireless Security,* looks at the topic that concerns so many people and businesses: keeping data safe and networks protected. Chapter 24, *Wireless Worries,* offers a way of evaluating the level to which you should be concerned. The following chapters then provide the practical advice you need to keep your data secure: Chapter 25, *Preventing Access to Your Network;* Chapter 26, *Securing Data in Transit;* and Chapter 27, *Protecting Your Systems.*

- **Section V,** *Taking It on the Road,* turns its attention to the needs of the traveler. Chapter 28, *Finding Wi-Fi on the Road,* helps you locate service, Chapter 29, *Configuring WISP Software,* provides guidance on setting up the software provided by the most common wireless ISPs, and Chapter 30, *Using Cellular Data Networks,* helps you make an Internet connection using either your cell phone or a PC Card in your laptop. Lastly, Chapter 31, *Prepping for the Road,* and Chapter 32, *Working on the Road,* offer hard-won advice on using wireless connectivity while traveling.

- **Section VI,** *Going the Distance,* offers a pair of chapters for anyone interested in setting up a long-range wireless network (and by long range, we mean anything between a few hundred feet and 20 miles). Chapter 33, *Long Range Wi-Fi Connections,* provides all the background you need, and Chapter 34, *Long-Range Antenna Basics,* simplifies the complex task of picking the best antenna type and determining signal strength.

- **Appendixes** in this edition of *The Wireless Networking Starter Kit* provide background information that novices may wish to read, but which we believe most of our readers already know. Appendix A, *Networking Basics,* looks at all the details of how wired networks work (useful since almost every wireless network still needs a wired component). Appendix B, *Configuring Your Network Settings*, offers step-by-step instructions for configuring TCP/IP settings for both Windows and Macintosh. Most people shouldn't need this information, since the default settings for most computers are fine, but it's here for those with older machines or computers that others have messed up for you. Finally, Appendix C, *How to Troubleshoot*, gives general troubleshooting advice and a step-by-step process for isolating and eliminating any sort of problem, whether or not it's related to a wireless networking. Chapters 14, *Troubleshooting Your Connection*, and 23, *Troubleshooting Your Wireless Network*, rely on the basics of this appendix.

That's it, so let's dive in!

Wireless Basics

Wireless networking may seem like magic, but like so many other sufficiently advanced technologies, it's actually just extreme cleverness on the part of many bright and dedicated engineers. Much as we both enjoy the magical feeling when setting up a new wireless network or testing some interesting new piece of wireless networking hardware, we also think it's important to understand what is actually going on underneath the virtual hood.

What do you need to know to understand the basics of wireless networking? Chapter 1, *How Wireless Works*, looks at how wireless networking gear manages to transmit radio waves through solid objects and, even more importantly, how it manages to piggyback data onto those radio waves. Chapter 2, *Wireless Standards*, narrows the focus to the three wireless networking standards that comprise Wi-Fi: 802.11b, 802.11a, and 802.11g. Then we get practical in Chapter 3, *Wireless Hardware*, looking at all the different pieces of hardware you need to create a wireless network, with a special focus on what sort of wireless network adapters are available for older Macs.

With the nuts and bolts of Wi-Fi out of the way, Chapter 4, *Other Wireless Standards*, examines a variety of other relevant wireless networking standards in wide use or about to emerge: Bluetooth, cellular data protocols, and a menagerie of 802.11 cousins. Chapter 4 is optional reading if you want to know only about Wi-Fi, as is Chapter 5, *Wireless of the (Near) Future*, which ventures even farther afield to cover mesh networking, Ultra Wideband, and airborne wireless broadband.

How Wireless Works

The wireless telegraph is not difficult to understand. The ordinary telegraph is like a very long cat. You pull the tail in New York, and it meows in Los Angeles. The wireless is the same, only without the cat.

—*Attributed to Albert Einstein*

Although the Albert Einstein Archives in Jerusalem informed us that there's no record of Einstein ever saying this, it's apt: wireless transmission doesn't make intuitive sense; we can only use analogy to understand how information moves from one place to another without physical elements we can see in between. Fortunately for us, wireless just works—look at cordless phones, cell phones, AM and FM radio stations, walkie-talkies, and satellite television dishes. Wireless is all over these days, and unintuitive or not, it is rooted in basic physics.

Wireless networking relies on the same principles that drive cordless phones and all these other wireless devices. A transceiver (a combination of transmitter and receiver) sends signals by vibrating waves of electromagnetic radiation that propagate out from an antenna; the same antenna receives signals by being appropriately vibrated by passing signals at the right frequencies.

In this chapter, we'll explain how wireless transmission works and how wireless networks piggyback data on top of radio waves.

Passing Signals Through Walls

The magical part of wireless networking is how it works not just without cables, but also when you can't even see the access point to which you're connecting. Although we take this obstructed path for granted now, it wasn't always true.

Early wireless networks used frequencies of electromagnetic radiation just below the visible spectrum, namely infrared. Infrared networking had (and still has) a huge limitation: you need perfect line of sight from one infrared transceiver to another. In large offices with numerous cubicles, it is difficult to position the transceivers high enough for the signal to get over partitions and equally hard to ensure that people standing around gabbing don't block the network signal.

Although infrared is still used today with Palm OS-based organizers, PocketPC devices, some cell phones, and many laptop computers, its use is reserved for *ad hoc* (spur-of-the-moment) one-time connections. For instance, you might set up an ad hoc connection to transfer a file or a business card between two

Unlicensed Spectrum

The 900 megahertz (MHz), 2.4 gigahertz (GHz), and large parts of the 5 GHz frequency bands are reserved in the U.S. and in many other countries for unlicensed use. There are two kinds of licenses: those owned by companies operating equipment on various frequencies (such as cell telephone companies), and those using the equipment (like amateur radio operators). These unlicensed bands, as you'd guess from the name, require neither kind of license. However, the equipment that uses these bands must still be certified by the FCC (Federal Communications Commission) and national regulatory bodies.

Because a license isn't necessary, the FCC and similar regulatory bodies in other countries require that unlicensed devices use very little power, which restricts their range. It

also means that these devices must be highly resistant to interference, because there's no guarantee that any user will have exclusive access to any of the unlicensed frequencies. Unfortunately, interference can still happen if a 2.4 GHz cordless phone, wireless camera, or a microwave oven (which can spew 2.4 GHz radiation as it twists water molecules) is used near an access point.

The 2.4 GHz band has a few licensed uses that overlap part of the unlicensed range, including amateur radio in the lower part, and certain public safety, television station remote signal, and commercial microwave transmissions. These licensed users have priority, but, so far, low-power use of wireless networking hasn't caused any major turf disputes.

Palm OS handhelds. Ad hoc infrared connections require very close proximity (we're talking about inches here) and, as with the infrared networks of old, an unobstructed line of sight between the two infrared transceivers.

Wireless networking overcomes the line-of-sight problem by jumping to a different portion of the electromagnetic spectrum. Modern wireless networks typically work at 2.4 GHz or 5 GHz, far below the visible light spectrum (**Figure 1.1**). At those frequencies, the wavelength of each transmission is so small that signals can pass through seemingly solid objects.

Figure 1.1
The electro–
magnetic spectrum.

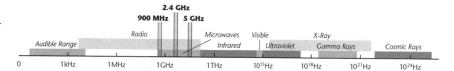

NOTE

Not to get too far into the physics of it all, but solid objects aren't really solid—there's plenty of empty space in between and inside the atoms that make up everything we consider solid. So although radiation like visible light is absorbed by solid objects, lower-frequency radio waves can sneak into those tiny spaces between atoms.

Although modern wireless networks offer the longest range when they have line of sight, they also work perfectly well over short distances in interior spaces (**Figure 1.2**). However, some interior obstacles can reduce signal quality and make it necessary to adjust the network layout. For instance, brick walls can hold a lot of water, and water can block energy from the frequencies at which 2.4 GHz networks work. Some houses and offices have metal in their interiors, such as chicken wire supporting plaster or ductwork, and metal can also interfere with network signals.

NOTE

A Faraday cage is a concept in physics embodied by an enclosure made of a conducting material such as wire mesh. What's unusual about a Faraday cage is that it acts as an electromagnetic shield—that is, electromagnetic radiation like the radio waves used in wireless networking simply can't penetrate the walls of the Faraday cage. Why are we telling you this? If your house has chicken wire supporting the plaster on your walls, many of your rooms may essentially be Faraday cages, which will result in terrible signal strength for your wireless network. Later in this book, you'll learn about a few workarounds that are more appealing than ripping out internal walls.

Figure 1.2
How radio waves travel through space.

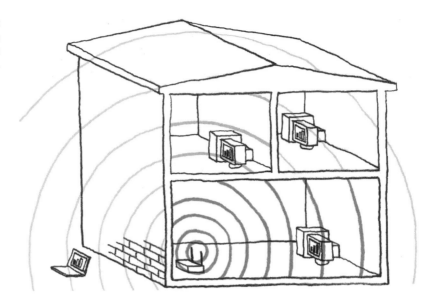

Adding Data to Radio Waves

Using a portion of the spectrum that can penetrate solid objects was an important step toward making wireless networking more popular, but another important aspect of wireless networking needed to be improved as well—how data is actually transmitted via radio waves and sorted out by the receiver.

NOTE

Practically speaking, this is background information—you don't have any choice in what standard any given piece of wireless networking gear uses.

Wireless data transfer can employ one of a few different standards that we talk about in later chapters. But one thing all wireless standards have in common is their ability to sort out overlapping data signals. In especially dense areas, like a café-rich urban street or a busy office, several or even several dozens of competing devices might be transmitting signals at the same time over a set of frequencies. Wireless devices use one of two different approaches to cope with all these overlapping signals: *frequency hopping spread spectrum* (often abbreviated to FHSS or just FH) or *direct sequence spread spectrum* (frequently shortened to DSSS or DS).

With frequency hopping spread spectrum, the frequencies on which data is transmitted change extremely quickly. With one standard, the frequencies change 1600 times per second. In others, the rate of change is slower. But all frequency hopping standards have many hopping patterns so that different networks or groups using the same standard in the same place have a low probability of using the same frequencies at the same time.

In contrast, direct sequence spread spectrum divides a swath of bandwidth into separate channels and never transmits for long on any one frequency in the channel. By using different channels in the same area, many different networks can overlap without spoiling each other's signals. There are several different incompatible methods of encoding data using direct sequence. Newer wireless networking protocols use a faster method, forcing equipment that aims to be backward compatible to support multiple encoding methods, which increases network overhead and reduces overall throughput.

Both forms of spread-spectrum transmission resist interference, because no one frequency is in constant use, and frequency hopping can also resist snooping, because hopping patterns can avoid all but industrial- and military-grade spectrum analyzers.

NOTE

FHSS was co-invented and patented by actress Hedy Lamarr (with composer George Antheil) in 1942 and kept secret (and unused) by the U.S. government during World War II; Lamarr and Antheil never saw a cent from the patent. Lamarr's contribution was rediscovered when spread spectrum became the basis for modern wireless telecommunications. When the Electronic Frontier Foundation gave her a Pioneer Award in 1997, the actress reportedly remarked from her Florida home, "It's about time." She died in January 2000, just before Wi-Fi hit the big time.

Wireless Standards

No matter what the context, successful communication can take place only if all parties are speaking the same language. In the networking world, such a language is called a *specification*, and if it's sufficiently agreed-upon by enough parties or given a stamp of approval by an industry body, it may increase in status to become a *standard*.

That's the theory, anyway, but every industry has a host of so-called standards that fail to work with one another and are a point of competition between manufacturers. However, the wireless networking world has, remarkably, almost entirely evolved beyond this quagmire of competing standards. When you talk about wireless networking, you're talking about a family of standards that work together: equipment that supports one standard is always compatible with other devices that support the same standard. Even better, backward compatibility has been the rule rather than the exception.

From 1999 to 2001, the lead specification was IEEE 802.11b, also known as Wi-Fi, or by Apple's name for the technology, AirPort. 802.11b was wildly successful, and companies have sold tens of millions of devices that support it.

In 2001, the much-faster 802.11a standard finally appeared in shipping equipment, and although it was similar to 802.11b, the two standards couldn't work with each other because they use different parts of the spectrum.

The solution for achieving 802.11a's speed while maintaining compatibility with 802.11b finally came in 2003 with 802.11g. This latest standard runs as fast as 802.11a while working in the same frequencies as 802.11b, thus providing full backward compatibility with all those millions and millions of 802.11b devices.

Realistically, 802.11g will gradually replace 802.11b and will likely consign 802.11a to niche applications. For those who want to hedge their bets, some manufacturers offer "a/b/g" adapters that support all three specifications.

The industry association that controls Wi-Fi has expanded the definition to include all three of these specifications, and anything you buy labeled Wi-Fi will note whether it works in the 2.4 GHz band, the 5 GHz band, or both (**Table 2.1**). All Wi-Fi gear has been certified as working with all other Wi-Fi gear in the same band, which is just another way of saying that all 802.11b and 802.11g equipment will work together, but 802.11a devices will only work with other 802.11a devices.

When we wrote the first edition of this book in mid-2002, there was still a question as to whether Wi-Fi wireless networking would be the ultimate winner, since there were still some competing standards, such as HomeRF.

Table 2.1

Wireless Standards at a Glance

Standard	Frequency	Raw/Real Throughput	Compatible with 802.11b	Year It Became Real	Adoption Trend
802.11b	2.4 GHz	11 Mbps/ 5 Mbps	Yes	1999	Slowing down in computers, ramping up in cheaper electronics
802.11a	5 GHz	54 Mbps/ 25 Mbps	No	2002	Businesses adopting slowly, no consumers
802.11g	2.4 GHz	54 Mbps/ 20 Mbps	Yes	2003	Ramping up everywhere

The IEEE

The IEEE, or the Institute of Electrical and Electronics Engineers, (pronounced "Eye-triple-E") is a non-profit, technical professional association with 380,000 members. The IEEE's mission is to develop consensus-based technical standards for electronics in several industries. Many of the manufacturers of 802.11b equipment are involved with subcommittees of the IEEE.

The IEEE 802 Committee deals with networking: the 802.11 Working Group handles wireless local area networks (WLANs); and the various Task Groups (a, b, e, f, g, h, and i, among others) handle specific types of WLANs or specific problems related to wireless networking, such as multimedia data streaming, inter-access point communication, and security.

Wi-Fi's status is no longer in question: with its competitors dead and with devices in millions of homes and businesses, Wi-Fi is the undisputed king of the wireless networking hill.

Nonetheless, for specialized purposes, other wireless standards have entered the game, such as Bluetooth for short-range, low-power data synchronization, or WiMax, for long-distance, point-to-point network backhaul. We'll talk about all these standards, and ways that Wi-Fi will be extended, in Chapter 4, *Other Wireless Standards*.

Wi-Fi Certification

Wi-Fi is supposed to imply "wireless fidelity" and convey the notion of sending data with high quality. It's actually a trademark of the Wi-Fi Alliance, an industry association that led the charge to ensure compatibility among devices from different manufacturers using the IEEE 802.11b standard, and more recently both 802.11a and 802.11g (www.wifialliance.com). The Wi-Fi Alliance was so successful at spreading the name Wi-Fi that it changed its name from the more clunky but more explanatory Wireless Ethernet Compatibility Alliance. The Wi-Fi Alliance requires substantial membership fees from members who submit their equipment—along with additional fees—to the association's certification lab for testing.

The certification process makes sure that thousands of individual features work correctly using a standard suite of tests. Only if the device passes those tests can a manufacturer legally use the Wi-Fi seal and name (**Figure 2.1**). Although other trade groups have had mixed success in pushing standards, the Wi-Fi Alliance's approach really is a sign of compatibility you can trust. Bluetooth, for instance, is more of a marketing concept, because manufacturers

Figure 2.1
The Wi-Fi logo.

aren't required to undergo a rigorous independent certification process before they can apply the name to their products.

In October 2002, the Wi-Fi Alliance updated the Wi-Fi certification mark to identify whether a piece of equipment could work in the 2.4 GHz band (802.11b at the time, but now also 802.11g), in the 5 GHz band (802.11a), or in both, thanks to equipment that supports multiple specifications. Older Wi-Fi gear just has the mark by itself; with newer gear, you need to check which bands the device supports. The information should be prominently displayed on the box.

More recently, the Wi-Fi Alliance has added additional standards, such as WPA (Wi-Fi Protected Access, a new security specification), to the Wi-Fi certification process to ensure that new, more sophisticated options for wireless networking work together just as well as the basic elements.

802.11b: The Reigning King

802.11b uses direct sequence spread spectrum to transmit and receive data at 11 megabits per second (Mbps). Don't let that number fool you, though. That 11 Mbps includes all the network overhead for the start and end of packets, for synchronizing transmissions, and other fiddly details. The real throughput rate is theoretically about 7 Mbps, close to the real rate of 10Base-T Ethernet (rated at 10 Mbps), but most users see 4 to 5 Mbps at best because of the limitations of inexpensive consumer hardware and signal congestion in most networks.

802.11b supports five speeds, starting at the fastest and backing off to slower speeds if interference or a weak signal prevents data from getting through. The five speeds are 11 Mbps, 5.5 Mbps, 2 Mbps, 1 Mbps, and 512 Kbps (kilobits per second).

 NOTE

The three slowest speeds are actually part of the original 802.11 protocol, which predates 802.11b. Some of the oldest devices can still work with new equipment because of this backward compatibility. The slowest speed, 512 Kbps, doesn't appear to be supported in some of the very newest equipment.

Some wireless cards and access points let you choose the speed you wish to use, but unless you're running a long-distance link that you need to preset to a known level, there's no point in setting a speed manually: the hardware should negotiate the highest possible speed at all times. You can't generally tell what your connection speed is, though it's a safe bet that a full-signal wireless network will run at 11 Mbps, whereas a long-range wireless connection is more likely to run at 1 or 2 Mbps.

TIP

Truly tweaky wireless geeks can sometimes extract slightly better performance by disabling the lowest speeds and forcing all devices to talk at the faster speeds or even just the fastest, 11 Mbps: 802.11b eats up some of its bandwidth with every chunk of data it sends in order to maintain compatibility with slower or more distant systems. Each packet by default starts by speaking very slowly and then speeds up.

Because 802.11b uses direct sequence, each 802.11b access point can be set to one of several channels to avoid conflicts with other wireless devices in the same vicinity. 802.11b uses the unlicensed 2.4 GHz band, which in the U.S. ranges from 2.4000 GHz to 2.4835 GHz. Although that technically provides 14 possible overlapping channels in 802.11b's specification, only 11 are legal for use in the U.S.

TIP

Don't become an international criminal unintentionally. We've heard reports from travelers who turn on their wireless gear using channels that were legal in their home country, but are illegal in the places they're visiting. So far, no one has been tracked down and jailed, but check for local rules. Some cards enable you to choose your current country so as to comply with local regulations. Local residents need to pay attention here too. Because some equipment can't be reset for different countries' rules, you might want to buy Wi-Fi equipment only in your home country, even if it's cheaper outside your borders.

The channels are offset from each other by a few megahertz to allow flexibility in choosing channels in case of interference. For instance, interference could come from portions of the band shared by amateur radio operators, television uplink signals for remote transmission, and limited public safety purposes. Or, interference could occur in an area containing several 802.11b access points—imagine a university library where many students wish to browse the Internet from laptops, all in a small physical space.

Channels 1, 6, and 11 can be used simultaneously right on top of each other without any direct overlap in frequency; side nodes of much less strength don't cause real problems with receiving the signal clearly (**Figure 2.2**). Some experts have argued that channels 1, 4, 7, and 11 could be used with minimal disruption, too, so you might try those if you can't use channel 6 for some reason.

802.11a: Higher Frequencies, Less Interference

Networking equipment adhering to the 802.11a standard started appearing in the middle of 2002, and you may naturally ask why the 802.11b standard came

Figure 2.2
Channels 1, 6, and 11 overlap without direct interference; side nodes overlap without any intensity.

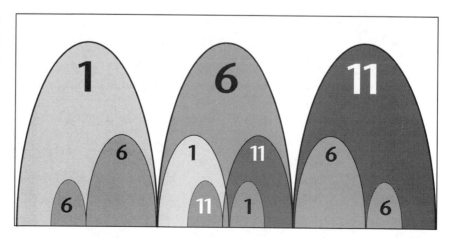

before the 802.11a standard. The IEEE actually approved the mission for the 802.11a task group first and ratified the two protocols simultaneously, but the technology necessary to implement 802.11a and a portion of the spectrum in which it was to operate weren't yet available.

((•)) **NOTE**

The Wi-Fi Alliance originally planned to certify 802.11a devices under the name "Wi-Fi5" but decided instead to modify the Wi-Fi mark to include 802.11a. If a Wi-Fi device supports 802.11a, the text below the Wi-Fi seal notes the 5 GHz band.

802.11a differs in four important ways from its 802.11b sibling. 802.11a

- Uses three parts of the 5 GHz band spanning a few hundred noncontiguous megahertz overall

- Has 12 non-overlapping channels (8 available for indoor use) that enable more access points to cover the same physical location without interfering with one another, with more channels on the way

- Runs at a raw speed of 54 Mbps, or about 25 Mbps of real throughput

- Works only over shorter distances, but has better protocols than 802.11b for sorting out signal reflection indoors

The chief advantages of 802.11a stem from these four differences: the 5 GHz band isn't already used by many other wireless devices, and the 8 distinct indoor channels—which may rise to 11 or more due to additional international frequency allocation—allow a substantially higher number of users at full bandwidth in the same physical space. This makes 802.11a a likely choice for high-density use in offices or server rooms. Other candidates for 802.11a gear include locations with a lot of 2.4 GHz interference, such as commercial manufacturing sites, hospitals, and other institutions that use industrial, scientific, or medical (ISM) devices that occupy the 2.4 GHz band.

Likewise, the four channels reserved in the upper end of the 5 GHz band for 802.11a outdoor, point-to-point use (with external antennas, of course) can employ higher power levels, which may provide a better throughput than 802.11g in the same circumstances. Given the speeds that 802.11a offers, point-to-point transmission is a compelling way to avoid telephone company charges for 45 Mbps T-3 digital lines. T-3 lines can cost several thousand dollars a month for short distances in the same city, and may require expensive equipment on both ends. (The 802.16a standard may replace 802.11a's point-to-point advantage in the same frequencies, since it's designed for long-haul with a single radio on both ends. In contrast, 802.11a is meant to be used by a bunch of clients communicating with a central access point.)

Unfortunately, thanks to its use of the 5 GHz band, 802.11a isn't compatible with the tens of millions of 802.11b devices currently in use. This fact led Apple CEO Steve Jobs to say that 802.11a is doomed to failure as he announced Apple's 802.11g-based AirPort Extreme. It's more appropriate to say that 802.11a is now relegated to niche status for particular purposes. Apple wasn't alone; no other major manufacturer has backed 802.11a as a replacement for either 802.11b or 802.11g. The main area where 802.11a has gained popularity is the home entertainment industry, which appears to have migrated to 802.11a for beaming high-definition digital signals between consumer electronics devices in a house. Microsoft has showed products based on this in which multiple DVD streams fly among multiple devices with nary a glitch in quality.

The cost of 802.11a equipment dropped faster than expected, and many 802.11a devices cost just $50 to $100 more than 802.11b equipment and their cost is on a par with new 802.11g devices. Ultimately, most 802.11a devices will be paired with b and g: manufacturers that initially shipped 802.11a-only cards quickly revamped to offer a/b (dual-mode/dual-band) or a/b/g (tri-mode/dual-band) products. Many access points now can handle a or b/g, or a combination in which all three standards can be used at once. There are some design problems with this approach, since the greater range provided by 802.11b and 802.11g will likely mean that you would need either a more powerful antenna on the 802.11a side or perhaps additional 802.11a access points to provide the same range for both protocols.

Aside from different channel numbers, configuring 802.11a clients and access points is identical to configuring 802.11b devices, which we describe in Section II, *Connecting Your Computer.*

802.11g: Faster and Compatible

In 2002, 802.11b equipment ruled the land. The faster, 54 Mbps, 802.11a devices that shipped starting in late 2001 were compellingly faster, but because they used a different frequency than 802.11b and cost more, only a small number of early adopters and testers bought in. Overall, people liked the idea of the faster 802.11a, but compatibility reigns supreme and 802.11a wasn't compatible with 802.11b, leaving the door wide open for 802.11g.

802.11g operates at 54 Mbps like 802.11a, but it uses the same radio frequencies as 802.11b, while supporting full backward compatibility with that older specification. Because of political and technical conflicts, the 802.11g committee at the IEEE took nearly three years to ratify the protocol, and finally formally adopted it on June 12, 2003.

Technology doesn't wait for engineering groups, though. Against some industry experts' better judgment, but to achieve higher speeds, several companies started to ship equipment using chips based on then-current draft versions of 802.11g in December 2002.

These early devices from Apple, Belkin, Buffalo, D-Link, Linksys, and others worked, but were often flaky in handling mixed networks containing both 802.11b and 802.11g devices. These early 802.11g devices often backed down to 802.11b speeds, thus eliminating 802.11g's advantages. Fortunately, as drafts continued to circulate at the IEEE, manufacturers continually upgraded *firmware* (internal software that runs dedicated hardware devices) to fix these early problems. Shortly after the June ratification, most manufacturers released final 802.11g firmware updates that cemented the 802.11b/g improvements, and even included a throughput boost.

As is the case with most raw network throughputs, 802.11g's net throughput of real data—the content of files or transactions minus networking overhead and conflicts—is lower than its raw speed, closer to 20 Mbps. In contrast, 802.11b's 11 Mbps raw throughput generally translates to about 5 Mbps at best, and it often drops well below that as distance from the access point increases. 802.11g has several intermediate steps for speed, so you don't just drop from 54 Mbps all the way down to 11 Mbps or slower.

In fact, 802.11g may be even a bit slower than an equivalent 802.11a network in the same situation. That's because 802.11g must maintain compatibility with 802.11b devices, which use a different method of encoding data onto radio waves, and the overhead of managing which devices on a mixed 802.11b/802.11g network may send at any given time slows things down.

Some have claimed that 802.11g could be as much as 40 percent slower than 802.11a in such situations, though others believe the slowdown will be only about 10 percent. Realistically, unless performance is your ultimate goal, it probably doesn't make any difference. (And if performance is all-important, wired Ethernet running at 100 Mbps or even 1 Gbps may be the best solution.)

Major wireless chip makers such as Agere, Broadcom, Intersil, and Texas Instruments have plans to improve throughput even with existing equipment. Broadcom and Intersil both offer *frame bursting* technology that works by taking short 802.11g packets and wrapping them into one longer packet. This reduces mandatory pauses or gaps between packets, and Broadcom predicts about 25 percent improvements in throughput with 802.11g alone and 75 percent with mixed b/g networks. This 25 percent improvement brings the 20 Mbps 802.11g throughput up to 802.11a's 25 Mbps.

Depending on the manufacturer, frame bursting may be part of the firmware already, and some of it may interoperate among chips made by different companies. (These changes are part of 802.11e, a specification devoted to improving multimedia streaming and digital voice over wireless.)

802.11g's full backward compatibility with 802.11b isn't optional for manufacturers; it's a mandatory part of the spec. How compatibility will continue to play out with real-world devices is still an open question. Manufacturers may have to continually re-engineer and release updates to improve compatibility.

Ad Hoc Mode

All the flavors of Wi-Fi offer an ad hoc mode, in which two or more computers exchange data directly with no central access point, much like in the old days of using an Ethernet crossover cable or plugging a null modem cable between two computers' serial ports.

In ad hoc mode, one computer creates a network that other computers can see (check out the sidebar, "Connecting with Wi-Fi," in Chapter 3, *Wireless Hardware*). The difference between ad hoc mode and a software or hardware access point, is that ad hoc connections don't have a central point of authority. Ad hoc connections are entirely private among the machines used. (You can set up one computer as a gateway to the Internet, sharing its connection; we discuss how to handle this in Chapter 19, *Creating a Software Access Point.*)

Because ad hoc connections exist only among two or more computers, they're useful primarily for transferring files—if you need to give a colleague a file and have no other way to do it, turning on file sharing and setting up an ad hoc network works well. Next time you have a few extra minutes, we recommend figuring out how to set up an ad hoc network and transfer files, since working through the steps while away from home or the office, possibly with someone you don't know well, can be a bit tricky.

Ad hoc mode is one of the few aspects of Wi-Fi that isn't part of the certification process for devices made before 2002. Older equipment, or equipment that doesn't have the latest firmware updates, won't all necessarily use ad hoc mode in the same way. The Wi-Fi Alliance added an ad hoc standard to its Wi-Fi certification in late 2001, so all new equipment must work together. That said, equipment from the same manufacturer, such as all of Apple's AirPort cards, generally support ad hoc mode when connecting to one another.

An area in which 802.11g had to compromise to maintain backward compatibility is in the number of channels supported. Like 802.11b, it supports 14 channels, only 3 of which don't overlap in the U.S. Contrast that with 802.11a, which has eight indoor non-overlapping channels, making 802.11a more appropriate for dense corporate installations with many users. Of course, anyone setting up such a network might do well to buy network cards that support both 802.11a and 802.11g so traveling users can access more common 802.11b networks in public.

One of 802.11g's big advantages over 802.11b is that it better handles the inevitable signal reflection. Radio signals bounce off different pieces of matter—floors, metal, even the air around you—at different angles and speeds. A receiver must reconcile all the different reflections of the same signal that arrive at slightly different times into a single set of data. 802.11g (like 802.11a) slices up the spectrum in a way that enables receivers to handle these reflections in a simpler but more effective way than 802.11b.

In July 2003, the Wi-Fi Alliance officially added 802.11g to its certification suite, and early in July, companies started to announce that their devices had been tested as compliant. It's expected that all current 802.11g equipment will easily pass the tests given the small number of companies that released chips in the first half of 2003. Clearly, 802.11g is here to stay, and it has almost instantly eclipsed 802.11a. We expect that 802.11g gear, which is already only slightly more expensive than 802.11b equipment, will quickly become the most common choice for consumers and businesses alike.

As with 802.11a, configuring 802.11g clients and access points is exactly the same as configuring 802.11b devices.

NOTE

All public networks currently use 802.11b, but it's possible that as 802.11g gains acceptance, public-space providers will add the higher-speed service. Several providers are already experimenting with the faster speeds. Of course, most public networks provide Internet access at less than 1.5 Mbps, so the difference may not matter much!

NOTE

If you ever see your computer reporting that it has an odd IP address in the 169.254.x.x range, that's a self-assigned address designed in part so ad hoc networks can operate. In an ad hoc network, there's no DHCP server to hand out IP addresses, so both Apple and Microsoft have agreed that in such situations, computers should pick random 169.254.x.x addresses so they can communicate with one another using Internet software over an ad hoc network.

3

Wireless Hardware

At the most basic level, you need only two pieces of hardware for any wireless network: a central access point and a network adapter (**Figure 3.1**). Access points are usually standalone devices that act as the hubs of wireless networks. In contrast, network adapters usually fit inside computers using all the standard methods you might expect—PC Card bay, PCI slots, and custom slots—as well as some methods you might not expect, like CompactFlash and Secure Digital cards. For computers that lack internal slots, you can plug in external adapters that use USB or Ethernet.

Although both access points and network adapters have built-in antennas, more powerful external antennas can increase the signal strength, and thus extend the range of wireless networks. **Table 3.1** gives you a rundown of the basic hardware necessary for a wireless network, and we discuss each item in more detail in this chapter.

Figure 3.1
A typical wireless network with an assortment of devices.

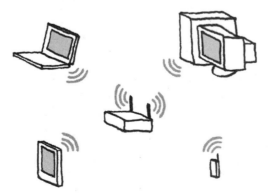

Access Points

An access point is the brains of a wireless network (**Figure 3.2**). It can perform a number of different tasks, some of which are optional, depending on what you need. Unfortunately, you're likely to run across numerous different terms for access point, including "wireless gateway," "wireless router," and "base station." Also, the term is frequently abbreviated to "AP" in technical literature. We stick with *access point* when talking about devices with the features listed below.

Client Association

Most important, the access point contains a wireless transceiver that sends data to and receives data from wireless-equipped computers or other devices. (A

Table 3.1

Wireless Home/Small Office Hardware at a Glance

Device	Connects To	Function	Gotchas	Cost Range
Access Point or Wireless Gateway	Your Internet connection, usually via your Ethernet network	Acts as the hub for your wireless network; shares your Internet connection with other wired and wireless computers; connects wired and wireless networked devices	Typically geared to the Windows world, Apple and Unix/Linux users may face hurdles; non-Windows/IP protocols not necessarily supported	$30 to $250
Wireless Network Adapter	Your computer	Lets a computer or other equipment connect to an access point wirelessly	Less common types require custom drivers	$10 to $150
Antenna	An access point or wireless network adapter	Extends the range of the wireless network; usually built in	Often ungainly	$30 to $600
Wireless Bridge	Your Ethernet network	Can connect wired networks together wirelessly, or bridge a separate wired network to an existing wireless network	Some bridges require one unit per network to hook up	$60 to $120
Wireless Relay	Your wireless network	Extends the range of the wireless network by relaying the wireless signal	Throughput is reduced because a single radio has to both receive and retransmit every packet	$60 to $100

Figure 3.2
Linksys EtherFast
Wireless AP +
Cable/DSL Router
w/4-Port Switch
and Apple
AirPort Extreme
Base Station.

few newer access points have two or more radios.) The connection between an access point and a computer with a wireless network adapter is called a *client association.*

 TIP

Access points don't have to be standalone pieces of hardware, although they usually are. Macintosh and Windows both have built-in options that can turn a regular Mac or PC with a wireless network card into a software access point, without preventing the computer from performing its normal server or desktop tasks. With a software access point, you don't need to buy a separate device, but you must leave the computer on all the time and risk the chance of a crash that disables the network temporarily. We talk about setting up software access points in Chapter 19, Creating a Software Access Point.

Wired/Wireless Bridging

Another common task for an access point is to act as a network bridge that connects the computers on a wireless network with those on a wired network. We explain bridging in Appendix A, *Networking Basics,* but in essence, it's just a matter of plugging an Ethernet cable from a wired network into the access point in order to connect two local area networks (LANs). Wireless gateways often have multiple Ethernet ports for this purpose, one for the WAN to make the Internet connection, and as many as four additional Ethernet ports for wired computers or printers on the LAN.

$((•))$ **NOTE**

Bridging functionality seldom appears in standalone devices that you can use for just the purpose of bridging two isolated networks together. There are a few such dedicated devices, like the Linksys WET11 and WET54G, but they're less common (and often more expensive) than access points that include bridging functionality. The main advantage of a dedicated bridge is that it generally works with access points from any manufacturer, whereas bridging functionality built into an access point may be restricted to devices from the same manufacturer.

Wireless/Wireless Bridging

Newer access points support a technology called WDS (Wireless Distribution System), which is a bridging mode in which the access point can do two things simultaneously: bridge wirelessly to another access point and act as an access point for wireless clients. Some take this capability even farther, acting in essence as a repeater between two other access points. These capabilities are new and still poorly explained by the manufacturers, so turn to Chapter 20, *Bridging Wireless Networks,* for more details.

Internet Sharing

Since sharing an Internet connection among multiple computers is the primary use of most small wireless networks, you can expect most (but not all, so pay attention when purchasing!) access points to offer an Ethernet port, internal modem, or serial port for an external modem to facilitate attaching the wireless network to a high-speed or dial-up Internet connection. A cable modem or DSL Internet connection plugs into the Ethernet port; for a dial-up Internet connection, a telephone line connects to the modem. Either way, when connected to the Internet, the access point now acts as a *gateway,* connecting a LAN with a *wide area network* (WAN) such as the Internet.

When acting as a gateway, an access point often offers a number of network services such as automatically assigning an Internet address via DHCP (Dynamic Host Configuration Protocol), creating private unreachable addresses for local computers with NAT (Network Address Translation), filtering traffic as a firewall, and controlling which clients can associate with it.

((•)) **NOTE**

Flip to Chapter 16, Buying a Wireless Gateway, *for more details on features found in different kinds of access points.*

Security

Access points handle security, too. An access point can restrict access based on an identifier built into a wireless client, or pass along information to other hardware and software on a network to *authenticate* a user in a larger organization. Access points also enable encryption that scrambles the data between the client and access point. In the past, this encryption was made possible with WEP (Wired Equivalent Privacy), a system that can be broken easily in high-traffic networks. The new way of doing encryption is via WPA (Wi-Fi Protected Access), which is believed to be much more secure. See Chapter 25, *Preventing Access to Your Network,* for all the gory details.

Advanced Features

Some access points contain advanced features, like routing (used in network installations to divide networks into smaller pieces), Ethernet address cloning (to alter the access point's unique network identifier, useful when sharing a cable modem connection on some systems), and special support for virtual private networks (VPNs) and other systems. Whether or not you need any of these advanced features depends entirely on your situation.

((•)) **NOTE**

You don't necessarily need an access point for a simple wireless network temporarily linking only a few computers. A network that's created by two wireless network cards talking directly to one another is known as an ad hoc network *because it doesn't require coordination by a fixed access point. See Chapter 12,* Creating an Ad Hoc Wireless Network, *for details.*

Wireless Network Adapters

The second piece of hardware that's necessary for any wireless network is a wireless network adapter. As with access points, you may run into different names for these devices. For instance, Apple calls its wireless network adapter an "AirPort card" or an "AirPort Extreme card." Other manufacturers have other more or less descriptive names, like Dell's TrueMobile adapters which have various flavors of Wi-Fi. Since these adapters install in computers that are clients of the access point, you often see the term "client" added to the name of the software that controls the adapter.

((•)) **NOTE**

A client is part of a pair; a server is the other half. A server handles requests from many different machines or users; clients talk to one server for each task. In wireless networking, the access point is effectively a server, even though it's rarely called that.

Wireless network adapters come in quite a few shapes and sizes, and the variety may seem intimidating. Refer to **Table 3.2** to pick the type that's most appropriate, and then read more details on the following pages.

Internal Wireless Cards

The best option, if it's available for a client computer, is usually an internal wireless network card. They're cheaper and less obtrusive than external adapters. The only downside to internal wireless cards is that they can be more trouble to install and unless they're designed properly, the computer's case can block the network signal somewhat, reducing range.

Table 3.2
Picking the Most Appropriate Wireless Network Adapter

	PC Card	PCI card	Mini PCI card	USB	Ethernet adapter	Compact-Flash	Secure Digital card	AirPort card	AirPort Extreme card	Built-in adapter
Desktop PCs		●[P]		●[1]	●[2]					
Laptop PCs	●[P]		●[P]	●[1]	●[2]					
Pre-AirPort Power Macs		●[P]		●[1]	●[2]					
Post-AirPort, pre-2003 Power Macs		●		●	●			●[P]		
2003 Power Macs		●		●	●				●[P]	
USB-only iMacs				●[P]	●					
FireWire/15" iMacs				●	●			●[P]		
17" iMacs				●	●			●[3]	●[4]	
G3 PowerBooks	●[P]			●[1]	●					
iBooks				●	●			●[P][5]	●[P][6]	
Titanium, FireWire-only PowerBooks	●			●	●			●[P]		
12"/17" PowerBooks	●			●	●				●[P]	
Pocket PC handhelds	●[7]					●[P]	●[8]			●[9]
Palm OS handhelds							●[8]			●[9]

[P] Preferred adapter for simplest or cheapest installation [1] For computers with built-in or add-on USB [2] For computers with built-in or add-on Ethernet [3] For 17" iMacs released before 2003 [4] For 17" iMacs released after 2003 [5] G3 iBook [6] G4 iBook [7] May require an adapter depending on Pocket PC model [8] For Pocket PCs or Palm OS handhelds with SDIO slots [9] Depending on model

PC Card

The familiar PC Card slot is found mostly in laptops. Since laptops are ideal for use with wireless networks, many kinds of wireless network adapters are available initially, and sometimes only, in PC Card form. Most Wi-Fi PC Cards have antennas built in (usually a miniature dipole diversity antenna), and although they're fairly small, they often stick out from the body of the laptop.

It can be hard to choose between Wi-Fi PC Cards from different manufacturers because they're all pretty much the same, thanks in large part to the fact that any card you buy should be Wi-Fi certified. There may be slight differences in performance based on which chip set they use, but since you can't generally find out what chip set a particular card uses, that's not a big help.

Your main decision comes down to transceiver power. Most radios are rated at 30 milliwatts, but you can buy Wi-Fi PC Cards that are rated at 100 or even 200 milliwatts (such as the EnGenius card sold by NetGate at www.netgate.com), and the more power you have, the higher your signal strength and the better your range.

 TIP

Some caveats: Transmit power is actually only half the battle, with receive sensitivity being the other half. Also, doubling transmit power from 100 milliwatts to 200 milliwatts, for instance, is an increase in signal strength of only 3 dB, and according to a white paper from networking vendor Cisco Systems (www.cisco.com/en/US/tech/tk722/tk809/technologies_tech_ note09186a00800e90fe.shtml), a rough rule of thumb says you need a 9 dB increase to double indoor coverage area. So while a higher power card will help increase range, don't expect miracles. See Chapter 34, Long-Range Antenna Basics, *for more on calculating signal strength.*

For the most part, Wi-Fi PC Cards are of interest primarily to PC users— Windows and Unix/Linux—not because of the name, but because many Macintosh users have better choices: all modern PowerBooks from Apple accept an internal AirPort or AirPort Extreme card. However, older PowerBooks still need to use Wi-Fi PC Cards, and Titanium PowerBook G4s often experience improved range when using Wi-Fi PC Cards.

A few original Pocket PCs could use Wi-Fi only via ungainly PC Card adapters. Fortunately, built-in Wi-Fi support and Wi-Fi CompactFlash adapters seem to have taken over from PC Card adapters.

(((•))) **NOTE**

PC Cards used to be called PCMCIA cards. PCMCIA officially stands for Personal Computer Memory Card International Association, despite its waggish expansion to People Can't Memorize Computer Industry Acronyms.

PCI Card

Except for a few particularly compact models, all desktop computers have PCI slots for expansion cards, which is where we recommend you install a Wi-Fi adapter. Some PCI cards have external antennas; others provide jacks for higher-powered antennas. Certain manufacturers, such as Proxim, used a PCI "carrier card" to hold a PC Card-based wireless network adapter; this

Connecting with Wi-Fi

Wi-Fi clients associate with Wi-Fi access points via the following steps:

1. A user activates Wi-Fi on a computer (the client device) by turning the machine on, plugging in an adapter, or selecting a software option to enable Wi-Fi.

2. The client device searches for local networks by scanning all the local legal channels in the 2.4 GHz band for 802.11b/g or 5 GHz for 802.11a.

3. The client offers a display, typically in a pop-up or pull-down menu, of the names of any networks broadcasting their identity (*open* networks).

4. The user selects one of these networks, chooses one from a preset configuration, or types in the name of a network that is *closed* (not broadcasting its name). If only one network is available, or if the client is set to connect to either the network with the strongest signal or to a specific network, the client device can automatically select the appropriate network.

5. The client attempts to associate with the selected network's access point.

6. If successful, the access point and client now have an active network connection over which TCP/IP, AppleTalk, and various Windows and Unix networking protocols can be sent.

7. If the client is configured to accept an IP address automatically and the access point or network is also set to assign an IP address automatically, that dance occurs, and the client ends up with an Internet address—often a private network address that can't be reached from the outside world. (See "Network Protocols" in Appendix A, *Networking Basics*.)

((•)) **NOTE**

When setting up a connection for the first time with a network that's protected by encryption, you must enter a WEP (Wired Equivalent Privacy) or WPA (Wi-Fi Protected Access) key, which is an encryption key used in Wi-Fi to scramble data between a client and access point. Some software forces you to enter the key each time rather than store it in a profile—though, fortunately, we've seen less and less of that over time. For more information about WEP and WPA, see Chapter 25, Preventing Access to Your Network.

((•)) **NOTE**

Wi-Fi may seem a lot like wired Ethernet, and it is: Wi-Fi shares most of its inner workings with wired Ethernet and differs only in the limited part of the specification that covers the physical part of moving bits around using radio signals instead of pushing electrons down a physical wire.

combination can result in strange driver problems as one set of software tries to cope with the carrier card and another with the PC Card itself, and this style of adapter has been phased out as an option.

 TIP

Where possible, if you're not sure whether a built-in card can provide enough signal strength, buy a wireless network adapter with an external antenna or an antenna jack. It's much easier to plug in an antenna than to swap out a card.

Again, with a few exceptions, PC users will be more interested in using PCI card-based wireless network adapters than will Mac users because most modern Power Macs can accept an AirPort or AirPort Extreme card. Older Power Mac G3 owners should read the sidebar, "Outfitting Older and Weirder Macs," later in this chapter.

Mini PCI Card

An increasing number of laptop models, such as the Dell Inspiron 600m and the Gateway 200 series, take an even smaller internal expansion card called a Mini PCI card, in large part because that's what Intel is pushing as part of the Centrino Mobile Technology that many laptop vendors now use.

The beauty of Mini PCI cards is that they're standardized, use little power (important for laptop battery life), and connect to internal antennas to improve range over external Wi-Fi PC Card antennas (and avoid the inelegant bit that sticks out with a PC Card).

Most of the time that you buy a laptop with a Mini PCI card, the card is preinstalled and preconfigured, and often cannot be removed and replaced with a newer model. However, the cost is typically half or less than buying a similar card separately.

Proprietary Internal Support

Since 1999, Apple has built into every Mac an internal connector that accepts a custom wireless network adapter. First Apple used a PC Card-like connector for its 802.11b AirPort cards. In 2003, Apple replaced this connector with a Mini PCI-like slot for the AirPort Extreme card. Note that these slots, despite the fact that the cards use standard form factors, are proprietary and dedicated to wireless networking. You cannot put a PC Card in an AirPort slot, nor a Mini PCI card in an AirPort Extreme slot. And, to be clear, you can't put an AirPort Extreme card into an AirPort slot because it wouldn't fit, and even if such a thing were possible, the bus that the AirPort slot is on can't handle the full speed of the 802.11g-based AirPort Extreme.

Outfitting Older and Weirder Macs

Table 3.2 above outlines the possibilities for older Macs, but the question of how to connect older Macintosh models that can't accept AirPort or AirPort Extreme cards has remained common in email we receive and on discussion forums. We brought together all the information you need in this sidebar. Although many of these options will also work for AirPort- or AirPort Extreme-capable Macs, we always recommend using an AirPort or an AirPort Extreme card in those Macs…with one exception that we discuss below.

Older Power Macs that predate AirPort. These computers can use Ethernet adapters, Wi-Fi PCI cards, and USB adapters, but each comes with various issues.

- A Wi-Fi Ethernet adapter like the Linksys WET11 sidesteps the operating system problem entirely, and might be useful later on as well. (Don't bother with the WET54G since these older Macs have only 10 Mbps onboard Ethernet, which is slower than 802.11g's 54 Mbps throughput.) We'd recommend the WET11 for any older machine, including those that predate the PowerPC G3 processor that have 10 Mbps (10Base-T) Ethernet.

- In Mac OS 8.6/9x, you can use the MacWireless 802.11b PCI card (www.macwireless.com/html/products/80211b/pcicard.html). That's ideal for most of these computers, but since all PowerPC G3-based Power Macs can run Mac OS X (albeit slowly), you might

want a solution for Mac OS X as well. We haven't tested this, but many 802.11g PCI cards using the Broadcom chipset work under Mac OS X 10.2.6 or later if you have version 3.1 or later of the AirPort software installed. This includes cards from Belkin, MacWireless, and others.

- A final option is to add a PCI card that provides USB (and FireWire, while you're at it) ports, and then use a Wi-Fi USB adapter from MacWireless or Belkin. Note that the Belkin unit comes with Mac OS X drivers (see below).

Older USB-only iMacs. These computers lack the PCI slots of Power Macs, so you're down to either a Wi-Fi USB adapter or a Wi-Fi Ethernet adapter (discussed above). As with Wi-Fi PCI cards, finding a USB adapter that will work in Mac OS X with an older Macintosh has been tricky. However, Belkin (www.belkin.com) now offers Mac OS X drivers for its Wi-Fi USB adapter, making it the best choice for putting an older iMac on a wireless network. It's a bit tricky to find the Belkin drivers on the Web site, but this URL — http://web.belkin.com/support/download/download.asp?download=F5D6050 — worked when we were writing the book. If you desperately want to make another vendor's USB adapter work with Mac OS X, and you're not afraid to get your hands virtually dirty, Thomas McQuitty has posted instructions—see www.mcquitty.net/Thomas/

projects/USBWirelessOSX.html—on modifying the Belkin driver to work with a similar USB adapter from Netgear.

Older PowerBook G3s. The situation is different for these laptops, since they all have PC Card slots, and even though Wi-Fi PC Cards stick out a bit, they're more elegant than Wi-Fi Ethernet adapters or mucking about with a USB PC Card adapter and a Wi-Fi USB adapter (an unholy combination that might work, but if not, don't blame us). So stick with a Wi-Fi PC Card for these PowerBooks, and remember that you can buy higher-powered PC Cards that offer greater range than the run-of-the-mill variety. With older Power-Book G3s, though, you run into various issues surrounding software drivers and operating system version.

- If you use Mac OS 9, buy an Orinoco Silver or a WaveLAN Silver (same card, different name), since it uses the same hardware as Apple's AirPort cards and will work with Apple's AirPort drivers.

- In Mac OS X, if you want to use an 802.11b PC Card, you can try the free open source driver (check the Web site for compatibility between the card and the driver before buying, of course) available at http://wirelessdriver.sourceforge.net/. The open source driver works, but hasn't been updated in a long time, so it may have trouble with current versions of Mac OS X by the time you read this. A better-supported option

that handles more cards is the 802.11b wireless driver from the gurus at IOXperts (www.ioxperts.com/80211b_X.html); you can try a demo version for free and if it works for you, buy it for $20. (IOXperts also offers Mac OS 9 drivers for cards other than the Orinoco and WaveLAN Silver.)

- Assuming you're running at least Mac OS X 10.2.6 and have installed the AirPort 3.1 update, Apple's drivers automatically support 802.11g PC Cards that use the Broadcom chip set. Don't worry about trying to identify the internal chip set; most manufacturers say clearly if their 802.11g devices are compatible with Macs.

Titanium PowerBook G4s. Here's that exception we were talking about. Apple's Titanium PowerBook G4 case is so electromagnetically shielded that it halves the computer's wireless network range. To make matters worse, Apple placed the antenna in the base, rather than around the screen, thus giving it suboptimal reception capabilities. To work around these limitations, some users rely on either a Wi-Fi PC Card (some people particularly like the Sony PCWA-C150S because it matches the titanium finish of the PowerBook G4 and doesn't stick out far) or a USB adapter that moves the antenna outside the case; see earlier in this sidebar for details on which Wi-Fi PC Cards and drivers to consider for your operating system version.

Apple isn't the only one building proprietary wireless networking adapters into devices. Although we haven't heard of any PC laptop vendors doing this, it's increasingly common with handheld devices, such as Palm OS handhelds and Pocket PCs. The Palm Tungsten C, for instance, features built-in 802.11b support that enables it to access wireless networks for Internet connectivity and for remote data synchronization.

NOTE

Cards that fit into an AirPort, AirPort Extreme, or Mini PCI connector hook to an antenna built into the case of the laptop or desktop computer itself—often two antennas run up both sides of a built-in LCD display. Because these antennas can typically be both longer and more integrally designed, they offer significantly better range and reception than the tiny antennas jammed into other adapters.

CompactFlash Card

Many handhelds and digital appliances, such as Pocket PC organizers, cameras, and MP3 players, use CompactFlash cards for storage, and some also now support Wi-Fi CompactFlash adapters for connecting to the Internet or synchronizing. Linksys (www.linksys.com), SanDisk (www.sandisk.com), and other manufacturers have CompactFlash wireless adapters that work with Windows CE 2.1 and Windows Mobile 2003 Pocket PCs. We've also heard camera makers talk about using Wi-Fi as a way to stream photos to a nearby computer, instead of storing them on the camera itself (see Chapter 18, *Wireless Gadgets*).

Many devices rely on the CompactFlash card for storage, making a new product from SanDisk that combines a Wi-Fi CompactFlash adapter with 128 MB of RAM the ideal compromise. Many other devices that support CompactFlash for storage can't use a Wi-Fi CompactFlash adapter purely because of the physical form factor. As you might expect, a Wi-Fi CompactFlash adapter still needs a stub for the antenna, eliminating devices that hold CompactFlash cards entirely internally.

NOTE

Not all devices with CompactFlash slots have the built-in software necessary to handle wireless networking; be sure to check for compatibility before assuming your CompactFlash-capable device can use a Wi-Fi CompactFlash adapter.

Secure Digital IO Card

Several handhelds, including some Pocket PC models and some organizers from Palm, accept tiny Secure Digital IO (SDIO) cards. Until very recently, there were no Wi-Fi SDIO adapters, but there's now one from SanDisk (www.sandisk.com), and we expect to see more from other manufacturers as well. Since SDIO slots aren't quite as fast as CompactFlash slots, performance does suffer a bit in comparison. Make sure your device is supported by the Wi-Fi SDIO adapter, since not even all Pocket PCs have the necessary low-level networking software.

External Wireless Adapters

Some computers, such as any iMac or Power Mac that predates the release of Apple's AirPort hardware, must use an external wireless adapter because they lack a slot for an internal wireless card. External wireless adapters can be useful for some modern machines as well, if, for instance, a computer's PC Card slots are full, you're nervous about messing with PCI slots that might be full of adapters, or the computer requires multiple wireless cards. Although locating an external adapter was a major obstacle in the past, they're now commonly available.

 TIP

We have no idea where to categorize this Wi-Fi adapter. The Enfora Wireless LAN Portfolio is a case for Palm handhelds that provides Wi-Fi access by plugging into the Palm Universal Connector. It's not clear if it's shipping yet, but you can learn more at www.enfora.com.

USB Adapter

The USB port, which is often used for plugging in keyboards, mice, and printers, can also accept external wireless adapters. Don't worry about performance degradation with the older 802.11b standard, since standard USB 1.1 runs at 12 Mbps, slightly faster than the 11 Mbps maximum throughput of 802.11b networks. USB 2.0 operates at 480 Mbps which is fast enough to handle either of the 54 Mbps wireless specifications, 802.11a and 802.11g, and Buffalo Technology has just introduced an 802.11g USB 2.0 adapter (www.buffalotech.com/wireless/products/airstation/wliusbg54.php). See Chapter 2, *Wireless Standards*, for details on these specifications.

 TIP

Some USB hubs may not have enough power to handle a Wi-Fi USB adapter. If you run into this, try using a powered USB hub, and failing that, plug the adapter directly into one of the USB ports on your computer.

Ethernet Adapter

Some newer home electronics devices, such as the ReplayTV digital video recorder, Microsoft's XBox, and Sony's Playstation 2, as well as some older computers, have only an Ethernet port or can't accept the software drivers to handle wireless networks. In those cases, you want a wireless network adapter that plugs directly into the device's Ethernet port.

The most popular Wi-Fi Ethernet adapter is the Linksys Wireless Ethernet Bridge (WET11), which costs less than $100 and works well in several odd situations (www.linksys.com/products/product.asp?grid=33&scid=36&prid=432). The popularity of the WET11 has encouraged Linksys to produce a variety of similar devices, such as the walkie-talkie–like Wireless-B Game Adapter (WGA11B), which appears to be essentially a WET11 with a front panel button for selecting the current channel. And if the 11 Mbps of these 802.11b devices isn't sufficient, there are more options from Linksys: the Wireless-G Ethernet Bridge (WET54G) and the Wireless-G Game Adapter (WGA54G)—both of which connect any Ethernet-capable device to a wireless network using 802.11g.

Antennas

All access points and wireless cards have antennas that are built in or that connect to a special antenna jack. However, given the size of these devices, particularly the diminutive wireless cards, there's a limit to the range that these included antennas provide. For better range, you want an external antenna.

In the simplest terms, an antenna increases the power of a transceiver. A transceiver combines a transmitter and a receiver, so by better focusing the electromagnetic energy entering and leaving the radio, the antenna increases both transmission signal strength and reception sensitivity. The power of an antenna is expressed in *decibels*, or *dB*, and every antenna has a power rating in decibels, generally referred to as the *gain*. Decibels increment on a logarithmic scale—a small increase in decibels results in a large change in sensitivity.

(((•))) **NOTE**

It's not necessarily true that the longer or larger the antenna, the better the signal. Instead, shape, composition, and a number of other factors combine to determine gain. Higher-gain antennas, for instance, also focus their energy into narrow beams suitable only for point-to-point interchanges. See Chapter 34, Long-Range Antenna Basics, *for more details.*

Uses for Antennas

By adding an external antenna to a wireless network device, you can extend the device's range from a few hundred feet to thousands of feet or even tens of miles. There are two main reasons you'd want to extend your network's range.

First, and most likely, if you have trouble receiving the wireless network signal in parts of your home or office, a small antenna—either an omnidirectional antenna if your access point is in the middle of your desired area, or a directional antenna if it's on one side—might increase the power enough to punch through the obstacle (see Chapter 21, *Indoor Antenna Basics*). If that doesn't work, you can try other options, which we'll cover in a bit.

Second, if you want to set up a long-range, point-to-point wireless connection, you definitely need an antenna, and it will likely be fairly large. Point-to-point connections generally use parabolic or yagi type antennas, both of which have relatively narrow signals—the farther you want the signal to reach, the more focused it needs to be. We talk in Section VI, *Going the Distance*, about how to create long-distance, point-to-point links.

Connecting an Antenna

Many wireless networking devices have "standard" antenna connections. In these cases, each device offers a plug into which you can hook a *pigtail*

Legal Antennas

All unlicensed wireless networks, such as those using Wi-Fi gear, are subject to strict and enforced power limitations created to prevent unnecessary interference among unlicensed devices and to avoid interfering with the few licensed users of the same band.

Strictly speaking, antennas and transceivers are approved by the FCC and regulatory bodies elsewhere only as complete systems: each antenna and each system are tested and approved together to assure that they don't emit more power than the rules allow, and that they conform to other limits. Some parts of the world are more stringent than others about actually enforcing such regulations.

However, many pieces of wireless gear have plugs or connectors that allow you to connect antennas from a variety of sources, or even homemade ones, such as those developed by community wireless networking groups. These antennas are, unfortunately, illegal to use in most cases, even though enforcement would be likely only if you were broadcasting so much power or in such a way that other people noticed (see Chapter 34, *Long-Range Antenna Basics*).

There's a fine line to skirt here, and while the rules are clear, it's hard for individuals to understand how to act within them without being antenna experts or FCC legal specialists.

Our advice? Most devices you can buy and the antennas that go with them stay collectively within the power output rules and won't violate the spirit of the law. We don't advocate violating the letter of the law either, of course, but if you exercise common sense, you should be okay.

(small cable adapter) that then connects to a coaxial antenna cable. We quote "standard" above because the Federal Communications Commission (FCC), which regulates wireless communication of all types in the U.S., discourages attaching arbitrary antennas to consumer wireless networking gear. That's because the FCC worries about people connecting too-powerful antennas and stepping all over other uses of the spectrum. One way of addressing this concern has been to require that every manufacturer use a different type of antenna connector. So the pigtail that works with your Orinoco Silver PC Card won't work with a Linksys PC Card, and so on. It's annoying, but as long as you're careful when buying (and it's usually easiest to buy from the same manufacturer for that reason), you shouldn't have serious trouble.

Adding an antenna sometimes requires special effort. If you open an original Apple AirPort Base Station and drill a hole in its plastic case, you can add an external antenna, but it's not a modification for the faint of heart. (The Web site www.vonwentzel.net/ABS/ has detailed instructions.) The newer AirPort Extreme Base Station's more expensive model has an external antenna jack and Dr. Bott (www.drbott.com) offers two antennas that are designed and certified to work with it. HyperLink Technologies also supports the AirPort Extreme Base Station (www.hyperlinktech.com/web/apple_antenna_kits.php).

If you haven't yet purchased wireless networking hardware and think you might want an external antenna, make sure to add that feature to your list when comparing different devices.

Other Wireless Standards

Although Wi-Fi has become the standard for moving data at high speeds around a local area network, not all data communications need both high speed and a local network. And even though we have three 802.11 standards already—a, b, and g—more are on the way that supplement these three and improve the way they move data around.

In this chapter, we look at Bluetooth (short range, slow, and low power), cellular data standards (slow but with wide coverage), WiMax/802.16 (long range, fast, and for point-to-point connections), and several members of the 802.11 family that can improve speed, increase international support, and improve the way devices communicate.

Bluetooth

When you realize that you forgot to pack the USB cable necessary for downloading images from your digital camera, try to use infrared to synchronize your Palm, or want to share files without a network in sight, Bluetooth starts to make a lot of sense.

Bluetooth is a short-range, ad hoc networking standard that uses the same 2.4 GHz band as 802.11b and 802.11g. Designed to run at a raw rate of 1 Mbps or a net throughput of about 700 Kbps, Bluetooth omits all the Ethernet-like overhead of Wi-Fi to enable quick connections between computers and other devices, often for short periods or single-item transactions (**Figure 4.1**).

Bluetooth was first envisioned as a cheap and battery sensitive alternative to Wi-Fi. In the years since Bluetooth's introduction, however, Wi-Fi devices have

Figure 4.1
Bluetooth
networking.

*Laptop interacting with
desktop, PDA, and cell
phone over Bluetooth.*

dropped in price and become less power hungry. But Bluetooth's strengths still lie in its energy miserliness and its capability to make fast, simple connections again and again—though only after you've tediously introduced the devices to each other.

Bluetooth Technology

Bluetooth uses frequency hopping instead of direct sequence, and Bluetooth devices change frequencies 1600 times per second. This combination makes Bluetooth highly resistant to interference and obstructions, and allows large numbers of Bluetooth transceivers to work in the same small space without stepping on each other.

Bluetooth's Successors

You might notice that Bluetooth has just a trademarked name and no IEEE number. In 2002, the IEEE 802.15 Wireless Personal Area Network (WPAN) Working Group solved that standards problem by approving 802.15.1-2002. This standard is a large subset of what Bluetooth offers, and is fully approved by the group that controls the Bluetooth standard, the Bluetooth SIG. Expect more devices labeled with 802.15.1 or that quietly support it.

Meanwhile, the WPAN has pushed forward with two new standards that will eventually replace most of Bluetooth's current uses. The 802.15.3a group focused on high-speed, short-distance, simple streaming of media and easy file transfers. Their work is underway in 2003 to offer 110 Mbps at 10 meters and 480 Mbps at 1 meter. The 802.15.3a standard will prob-

ably use ultra wideband, a promising new low-power technology: See Chapter 5, *Wireless of the (Near) Future.*

At the other end of the figurative spectrum, the 802.15.4 committee wanted to extend battery life to months or years while offering just a few Kbps in short-range transfer. This group aims to replace infrared home-entertainment remote controls, alarm wiring, and other low-data but long-use equipment with wireless devices that can easily talk to each other. The trade name for this in-progress standard is Zigbee.

Both 802.15.3a and 802.15.4 have the potential to take over from the two critical sweet spots in Bluetooth's current market, but companies making the equipment expect it won't be until 2006 or 2007.

Bluetooth's range is only about 30 feet, which seems short, except that it was always planned to work at low power to preserve the battery life of handheld devices and cell phones, as well as other kinds of objects that might have embedded Bluetooth chips.

Device discovery is key to Bluetooth's ease of use: instead of having to know anything about a piece of Bluetooth equipment you want to exchange information with, such as a network address or adapter number, you can simply make the device *discoverable*, and the equipment you're connecting from can see it, exchange a short passphrase for authentication, and then pass data back and forth.

Bluetooth and 2.4 GHz Wi-Fi have had a few co-existence problems: makers of both kinds of equipment initially warned against putting transceivers within three feet of each other in order to avoid interference that would reduce the bandwidth of both transceivers. As more devices include or support both Bluetooth and 802.11b or g, such as Apple's 17-inch PowerBook or models of Sony's Palm OS-based Clié handheld, however, manufacturers have worked out compromises to allow both to function with some coordination.

Future versions of both Wi-Fi and Bluetooth—through the efforts of yet another IEEE committee known as 802.15.2—should work side-by-side with fewer conflicts. The 802.15.2 specification requires devices to minimize their use of busy frequencies.

Bluetooth Uses

Originally designed as a "cable replacement" by an industry consortium called the Bluetooth Special Interest Group (www.bluetooth.com), Bluetooth's real utility seems to lie in its role as a universal translator. Bluetooth standards allow radically different hardware devices to connect with minimal configuration and no special drivers.

For instance, with a Bluetooth phone in hand, such as several models of the Sony Ericsson T line, you can use a computer with a Bluetooth adapter to dial the phone, synchronize phone numbers with the phone's built-in address book, and place data calls using the phone's GSM or GPRS interface (**Figure 4.2**).

Apple added full support for Bluetooth to Mac OS X 10.2 Jaguar; Microsoft plans to add Bluetooth support to Windows XP in an update that should be out by the time this book is published (of course, Microsoft said exactly the same thing back when we wrote the first edition of this book).

On the hardware side, a number of devices now offer Bluetooth networking options, including add-on USB adapters and PC Cards made by Belkin, 3Com,

Figure 4.2
Sony Ericsson T608.

D-Link, and others; laptops and desktops with internal cards or built-in support; cell phones, which are starting to include both GSM/GPRS and the more frequently used U.S. standard, CDMA; and plug-in cards for (or hardware included with) Palm OS and PocketPC handhelds. You can even buy a parallel port adapter from 3Com that turns a printer into a Bluetooth device—handy for printing from a computer or handheld in the same room.

One of Bluetooth's promises is that it can turn a cell phone into an accessory that you never touch directly. You could make laptop data connections via your cell phone in your computer bag, dial the cell phone in your pocket from your Palm OS handheld, or talk on a Bluetooth headset that transmits the voice signal to and from your cell phone. See Chapter 11, *Connecting via Bluetooth,* for details.

Although Bluetooth isn't really a competitor for Wi-Fi, it has a real role between robust Ethernet-style networking and the mélange of cables and incompatible standards that are so frustrating when moving bits of information between small devices.

Cellular Data Networks

Cellular phone service is widely available in populated areas, and cell phones have become commonplace in most cities. Imagine if these cell networks could also handle data, not just voice phone calls? Instead of being limited to wireless hot spots, you'd be able to send and receive data practically anywhere.

Of course, cell networks already carry data: the vast majority of the cell networks worldwide now handle digital voice calls, the so-called "second generation" of cell technology (the first generation was analog). With special adapters, a lot of frustration and patience, and a high tolerance for per-minute fees, you can eke maybe a few thousand bits per second out of these digital cell networks. For instance, on Cingular's network, you can make 9600 bps—yes, bits per second—modem calls to an Internet service provider.

((•)) **NOTE**

These interface, speed, and cost problems are still an issue because, remarkably, cell operators weren't thinking about pushing data over their networks when they spent billions in the mid-1990s to buy licenses to operate digital voice networks. The first inkling was AT&T's quickly abandoned Project Angel, which was a never-built trial network that suggested the revolutionary idea that packet data could be sent over cellular networks. Cell telcos' lack of interest is one of the reasons Wi-Fi had a chance to become popular.

Second-generation cell networks are limited, however, by the concept of a connection: the service is available only when you connect to it, and you must maintain a continuous connection to exchange data (or talk to someone else). This connection concept is standard with the telephone network, which is generically referred to as a *circuit-switched network*, because it's like having your very own wire—a circuit—from your telephone to the telephone of the person you're calling.

The Third Generation

A third generation of cell networks, often called 3G for short, aims to turn digital data into the primary application of cell carriers, with voice, multimedia, and Internet access all intermingled through a variety of devices, including phones and computer network adapters, as well as kiosks and new consumer and automotive electronics. In the 3G world, data is available at all times. Because the cell network turns from a circuit-switched network into a *packet-switched network* like the Internet (in which the data to be transferred is broken into packets and sent along any number of paths), the cell phone and cell-enabled devices are always connected to the network.

Cellular data service with the 3G moniker is supposed to offer at least 384 Kbps of bandwidth per user, and many of the systems now in testing have a theoretical peak of 2.4 Mbps, with individual users, in ideal cases, having access to between 400 Kbps and 1.2 Mbps. But 3G's ubiquity means that it could operate more slowly when used by many customers in larger areas, though it would still provide better-than-dial-up speeds. These low speeds could be available in any metropolitan area, on highways, and potentially elsewhere. The highest speeds would conceivably be reached only in the densest parts of cities where cellular companies might install many more "picocells"— tiny areas of high coverage—or even only inside of office buildings that had dedicated interior transmitters.

Because 3G devices are always on the network, even slow speeds aren't a hindrance when, for instance, new maps are being spooled into your car's directional system, or the day's headlines are downloading into your PDA. Services that push information to you take advantage of the network's ubiquity in not tying you down while transferring data.

As of September 2003, only a few U.S. cell operators have been willing to even discuss their plans for deploying 3G. Sprint PCS was still in the lab with the flavor it prefers, 1xEV-DV (Evolution Data/Voice); AT&T Wireless committed to having at least six U.S. cities covered with service by 2005 to meet a loan obligation; and Verizon Wireless was experimenting with 1xEV-DO (Evolution Data Optimized) in San Diego and Washington, D.C. Other carriers' plans are even murkier. Elsewhere in the world, particularly in Asia, cell operators have been deploying earlier versions of 3G more widely. In Europe, carriers spent $100 billion on spectrum licenses—before even knowing whether 3G ideas would work in the real world!

Even more troubling, pricing hasn't been set for any of these services, and few carriers or analysts are even speculating as to what they could cost.

NOTE

The U.S. and the rest of the world didn't agree on which frequencies to use for 3G, which means that a U.S.-based 3G phone won't work in Europe or Asia and vice-versa, unless the phone supports about eight different frequency bands to encompass all the possibilities.

NOTE

As you might expect, where there's 3G, there's 4G. Putative fourth-generation cell data networks will abandon all the proprietary and industry-specific networking protocols in favor of a pure Internet Protocol (IP) network that works, well, just like the Internet. Although many researchers are working on 4G networks, there's no standard yet and no idea when 4G devices will appear. With 4G, it seems likely that Wi-Fi and its ilk will converge with 3G and its cronies.

One Half Step Back

When is 2.5 greater than 3? When you're dealing with a stopgap measure that the cellular operators developed to bridge the digital divide between 2G and 3G service. They call it 2.5G (pronounced "two point five gee"), and it's an amalgam of less-expensive cell tower upgrades and cobbled-together methods of achieving modem-or-better data speeds via digital cellular connections. 2.5G technology is designed to offer something between 10 and 150 Kbps, and tends to be priced at reasonable levels.

Because there are two kinds of cellular networks, there are two kinds of 2.5G data networks, too. In the U.S., CDMA (Code Division Multiple Access) dominates. The rest of the world adopted GSM (Global System for Mobile

Communications), which Cingular, T-Mobile, and AT&T Wireless use or are in transition to use in the U.S.

The 2.5G technology for GSM comes in flavors known as GPRS (General Packet Radio Service) and EDGE (Enhanced Data GSM Environment). GPRS provides from 10 to 50 Kbps; EDGE should top 100 Kbps when it's deployed. Cingular is the first U.S. network to promise an EDGE rollout, and Cingular was testing the service in Indianapolis when we wrote this book. Pricing is still up in the air.

The CDMA half-step comes under a number of names, with 1xRTT (Radio Transmission Technology) being the most common. Some carriers call 1xRTT "3G," but it operates at only a maximum of 144 Kbps in theory (not the 384 Kbps nominally required for 3G), and more like 50 to 70 Kbps in the best cases. Verizon Wireless and Sprint PCS both offer unlimited 1xRTT service for $80 per month via a PC Card, and different deals when you use a cell phone through which you can make voice calls and connect your computer.

$((\cdot))$ **NOTE**

The "1x" in 1xEV-DV, 1xRTT, and other standards refers to the first wave of 3G standards. Eventually, carriers expect to offer 3x, which, you guessed it, has three times the frequency available in 1x—in this case, spectrum per user.

Why Can't We All Get Along?

With 3G not likely to emerge fully until at least 2005 or 2006, and 2.5G offering just tens of kilobits per second, the cell companies faced a dilemma: how to keep customers who might eventually reduce their dependence on cell phones by using, for instance, *voice-over-IP (VoIP)* phones or services that work through any Internet connection?

The solution appears to be to add Wi-Fi to the mix of communications services offered by cell operators. T-Mobile was the first into the act when it purchased the assets of bankrupt hot spot network pioneer MobileStar in early 2002. T-Mobile has since built a U.S. network of Starbucks, Borders, and Kinko's that hit 3000 locations in October 2003. T-Mobile currently doesn't share its network in the U.S. with any other Wi-Fi providers, although it did ink an international roaming agreement in the middle of 2003 with the Wireless Broadband Alliance, which has mostly Asian members and hasn't finalized details as to when it will start allowing roaming.

Meanwhile, Sprint PCS announced in July 2003 that it would resell access to Wayport and Airpath's hot spot networks, while installing at least 1300 of its own hot spots in airports and hotels by the end of 2003. Verizon Wireless said it would start reselling Wayport's service as well during 2003. And AT&T Wireless started with airports, agreeing to run Denver's already-built Wi-Fi network (Denver had searched for an operator for nearly two years) and Newark International Airport. AT&T Wireless now resells Wayport's network, too.

Cingular, which is mostly owned by SBC Communications, will offer some kind of service via SBC, which plans to resell and install 6000 hot spots by 2006, starting, you guessed it, with Wayport's network. Nextel hasn't announced plans as we write this.

In Asia and Europe, cell operators have become even more involved with Wi-Fi, forming partnerships or building out wireless networks. TeliaSonera, the Swedish/Finnish cell giant, operates several hundred hot spots across Scandinavia under the HomeRun brand and offers roaming agreements across Europe. In Japan and South Korea, dominant cell carriers have already installed thousands of hot spots, often in competition with the landline phone companies.

Simultaneous with these rollouts and roaming agreements comes the ongoing development by many wireless networking chip makers of multiple-standard network adapters. These adapters will talk 802.11a/b/g, as well as cellular data flavors including GSM, GPRS, 1xRTT, and even Bluetooth.

Eventually, we expect to see a single PC Card, probably using a tiny, cell phone-style personal authentication card from the GSM world called a SIM (Subscriber Identity Module), that could enable you to roam from cellular network to hot spot to cellular network with uninterrupted access. Or, perhaps your laptop will connect to your cell phone (probably via Bluetooth) to access the Internet.

It's clear that the cell phone companies don't want to leave money on the table, and with tens of millions of laptops already equipped with Wi-Fi adapters, they already have an audience they could serve.

We expect the real breakthrough will be a combination of simplicity and seamlessness: a single bill, a single authentication module, no login or captive portal pages, and transparent service wherever you go.

Meet the Family: 802.11 Relatives

Heaven forbid that we mention even more numbers and letters, but we can't help it. 802.11 is a family of standards, even though we're most familiar now with the letters a, b, and g. Coming down the pipe are several more letters representing task groups that have more specific missions in mind: streaming data, security fixes, higher throughput, international compatibility, and others. Meet the rest of the family in **Table 4.1**.

$((\bullet))$ **NOTE**

Don't make big plans around future release dates. Our research shows that the predicted dates are often a year or more earlier than what actually ends up happening. Building technical consensus in a volunteer organization takes time.

802.11e: Quality of Service

Quality of service, or QoS, is a means of ensuring that network uses that need to take place in real time, such as voice and video, aren't interrupted by other packets containing data that aren't time-sensitive, such as email. With an email message, if it takes a few extra seconds and retransmission attempts for all the packets that comprise the message to arrive at their destination, no one notices. However, if you're talking with someone over a network, even a small number of lost or delayed packets can result in stuttering or garbled speech. That's a bad thing, particularly as more companies start experimenting with voice-over-IP (VoIP) software and hardware that could eventually supplement or replace traditional telephone networks. So, the goal of the 802.11e task group is to develop QoS technology that will help Wi-Fi networks avoid problems when transmitting time-sensitive data like voice and video.

One 802.11e innovation has already started creeping into chips. It's called *frame bursting* or *packet bursting,* and it improves the ratio of data-to-network overhead on a Wi-Fi network by sending larger amounts of data in individual frames, another name for packets. Because 802.11b is relatively slow, Wi-Fi data is sent in small packets with mandatory gaps between them.

As the raw speed of 802.11b quintupled from 11 Mbps to 54 Mbps in 802.11g, the packet size stayed the same, meaning that there were a lot of quickly transmitted packets with those same mandatory spaces between them. Packet bursting can speed up mixed 802.11b/g and 802.11g-only networks.

Packet bursting appears as an optional feature in most of the 802.11g chips on the market today, and it's a subset of the 802.11e draft. Packet bursting from different chip makers might not offer as much improvement initially as having equipment all from the same maker.

We can expect to see a final version of 802.11e by early 2004.

802.11f: Inter-access Point Communication

Right now, Wi-Fi access points aren't very good at communicating among themselves. Depending on the manufacturer, some access points can coordinate certain activities, like allowing a user already logged in to the network to roam to another access point; others don't talk among themselves at all.

With 802.11f, access points will be able to offer *fast handoff*, so authenticated users don't have breaks in service as they roam, which is especially important in logistics operations, like warehouses.

Some of 802.11f's features tie in with the new security standard, 802.11i.

Table 4.1

802.11 Relatives at a Glance

Task Group	What It Does	Expected or Actual Ratification
802.11d	Modifications of earlier 802.11 specifications for compatibility with regulations in other countries	June 2001
802.11e	Adds Quality of Service (QoS) to 802.11a, b, and g for voice and video applications	Early 2004
802.11f	Improves communication between access points for authentication	July 2003
802.11h	Modifications of other 802.11 specifications for compatibility with European regulations in the 5 GHz band	Ongoing
802.11i	Improves security of wireless networks	Early to mid-2004
802.11j	Modifications of other 802.11 specifications for compatibility with Japanese regulations in the 5 GHz band	Ongoing
802.11k	Provides better reporting of signal strength and other physical attributes of radio	Ongoing
802.11l	Doesn't exist because a lowercase L looks too much like the numeral 1	When hell freezes over, if engineers have any say in the matter
802.11m	Minor modifications and fixes to previously published specifications	Ongoing
802.11n	Aims to increase the raw throughput of wireless networks to 100 Mbps or higher and to ensure that more of the raw throughput is actually usable	Ongoing

802.11i: Security

The fact that current Wi-Fi encryption can be broken relatively easily has bothered many people and slowed Wi-Fi's acceptance in the business world, where protecting everything from confidential business documents to credit card databases is paramount. Fortunately, the IEEE has been working on improving security for years, and after a variety of the usual delays—political fights, technical setbacks, and logistical issues over ratification—802.11i is poised both to improve security and to make securing a network easier.

802.11i replaces the broken WEP (Wired Equivalent Privacy) encryption system with TKIP (Temporal Key Integrity Protocol), a backward-compatible method of encrypting data on a wireless network that can work on older equipment. Supplementing TKIP is AES (Advanced Encryption System), the best encryption now available for general-purpose use. AES will be used in newer devices.

802.11i also adds pre-authentication, which enables a user logged in to a corporate-style network—one employing user accounts for wireless access—connected to one access point to move to another access point while maintaining the connection; this feature relies on the inter-access point communication provided by 802.11f, as explained above.

The timetable for 802.11i approval is early to mid-2004.

$((\bullet))$ **NOTE**

You might wonder how 802.11i interacts with WPA (Wi-Fi Protected Access). The Wi-Fi Alliance released WPA in mid-2003, and support gradually appeared in the second half of 2003. In short, WPA is here today, and it offers many of the best features of 802.11i. In fact, WPA is a large and compatible subset of 802.11i, so we can expect to see 802.11i supplementing WPA after ratification. See Chapter 25, Preventing Access to Your Network, *for more details.*

802.11n: Higher Throughput

A consistent complaint about 802.11a and g is that although they have a high raw speed of 54 Mbps, their real throughput—the measure of the actual amount of data transmitted after you subtract networking overhead needed to move data around—is comparatively poor: about 20 to 25 Mbps.

In response, the 802.11n group, which started its work on the heels of 802.11g's completion, will try to increase both the overall speed of future 802.11 protocols—to at least 100 Mbps and maybe over 300 Mbps—and the actual throughput so that more raw bandwidth is used to transfer useful data, rather than just network overhead packets.

802.11d, h, j, and m: Regulatory Compatibility and Maintenance

Just so the lesser relatives don't feel left out, meet a few of the quiet siblings. 802.11d, h, and j were modifications to other 802.11 specs to allow them to work appropriately under the radio regulations of other countries, which often differ significantly from those set down by the FCC in the U.S. 802.11d was ratified in June of 2001, whereas work on 802.11h (Europe) and 802.11j (Japan) continues to achieve regulatory compatibility in the 5 GHz band in those locations.

Finally, 802.11m is a potpourri of minor fixes to clean up and consolidate all the other specifications moving forward.

((•)) **NOTE**

It's possible in the future that you could buy equipment labeled "supports 802.11a, b, d, e, f, g, h, i, j, k, m, and n." Heaven help us all.

WiMax: 802.16 and the Long Haul

Running or leasing wire is an expensive way to create high-speed data networks, whether you're talking about the length of a few city blocks or 100 kilometers in rural parts of India. The notion of using wireless to substitute for wired bandwidth could dramatically reduce the costs of network installations, the time it takes to bring a network live, and the expense in extending the network, all while increasing the speed-to-dollar ratio in your favor.

Thousands of companies around the world are using wireless for *long-haul* and *back-haul* communications already. Long haul carries data over miles or dozens of miles, and used to be possible only over wired links. Back haul brings Internet access to a location, over short or long distances. In both cases, the connections are point-to-point (one transceiver on each end) or, increasingly, point-to-multipoint (one transceiver communicating from a central location to many transceivers scattered about).

Until recently, wireless approaches to both kinds of "hauling" used either adaptations of wireless LAN technologies, like Wi-Fi, which weren't designed for and aren't specifically suited to point-based or long-distance purposes, or proprietary technology sold by a host of companies including Alvarion, Cisco, and Proxim.

Enter the IEEE in its usual role: bringing together many parties to simplify, extend, and standardize. The 802.16 Working Group on Wireless Broadband

Access Standards (www.wirelessman.org) has developed Wireless Metropolitan Area Networking (Wireless MAN) standards that are designed specifically for long haul and backhaul over wireless.

The first iteration of the specification relied on higher frequencies, 10 to 66 GHz, both licensed and unlicensed, but the more significant work happened more recently in 802.16a, which covers use in the 2 to 11 GHz range, encompassing the unlicensed 2.4 GHz and 5 GHz bands currently used by 802.11b/g and 802.11a.

Many companies have already committed to using 802.16 and 802.16a, which should make it almost immediately cheaper and simpler to install long-distance connections because there will be more choices for equipment that all works together. These companies even formed a trade group with a catchy name: The WiMax Forum (www.wimaxforum.org). WiMax, unlike Wi-Fi, really does stand for something: Wireless Interoperability for Microwave Access—think of it as "Axcess."

The upshot of 802.16 and WiMax is that wireless broadband should now expand even more quickly than it has previously. In the home or office, if you see WiMax gear, it will be attached to a window or roof.

Wireless of the (Near) Future

So far, we've talked only about the practical and the available: what you need to know to buy and use today's equipment. In the near future, three new ideas may affect your choices.

Mesh Networking

Mesh networking differs from normal wired and wireless networking in the basic design of the network. In a normal wired or wireless Ethernet network, both of which use a star topology, computers all link to a central point (a wireless gateway or wired switch), and then data transfers among the computers by first passing through the central point.

With mesh networking, each computer can talk directly to any other within range. Mesh networking is especially useful for short-range wireless networking, where a computer can see only one other computer, which in turn can see another, and so on. No machine needs to be within wireless range of a central hub to communicate with other computers or access a central hub's shared Internet connection (**Figure 5.1**). See Appendix A, *Networking Basics*, for more information on different network designs.

$((\cdot))$ **NOTE**

It's not just computers that can form mesh networks, of course: handhelds, cell phones, and other digital devices could be interconnected, too.

Mesh networks can form opportunistic routes, in which each node's router sends data in the most efficient way among many different nodes that it can

Figure 5.1
A mesh network topology.

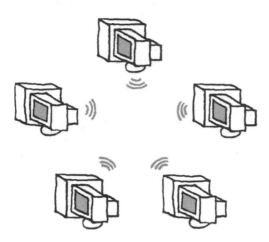

see. This not only reduces choke points but also adds redundancy, ensuring that a single node's outage doesn't bring down a network.

 NOTE

The Internet is supposed to route packets using the most efficient path, and sometimes does, but the number of possible routes on the Internet's high-level, long-haul routes is limited by actual physical connections between networks and machines.

Mesh networking gear thus makes it possible to extend a wireless network or increase its overall bandwidth simply by adding more mesh access points. As long as one of the mesh access points has an Internet connection, every computer connected to the mesh network can use it. With mesh networks, remote communities and dense urban areas alike could enjoy more reliable, more robust, and less expensive Internet connectivity.

The downside of mesh networking is that in order to enable connections, every device must have some limited awareness of every other device. Likewise, because each device must be available to talk and listen, certain nodes on a mesh network can be totally bogged down with opportunistic traffic arriving from other nodes when there are only one or two paths to other systems.

Although there are no consumer devices that use mesh networking yet, the inclusion of Wireless Distribution System (WDS) in an increasing number of inexpensive wireless gateways foreshadows the day when home and small business networks may rely entirely on mesh-like, wireless-only connections rather than a wired connection to the Internet. Although WDS interoperability among equipment from different manufacturers isn't good right now, the protocol shows great promise as a simple way to connect wireless gateways to relay traffic. See Chapter 20, *Bridging Wireless Networks*, for more on WDS.

Here are a few companies that have released actual products, mostly intended for corporate or community networks:

- **MeshNetworks** (www.meshnetworks.com) has the purest and most fulfilled vision of mesh networking currently on the market. The company sells three devices, all of which can use plain Wi-Fi signals to create mesh networks: a PC Card that enables a computer to peer with other computers also using the MeshNetworks PC Card; a fixed wireless router which acts as a repeater and extends the range of a network; and an access point that exchanges data with peers and a larger network or the Internet. The MeshNetworks system can work on its own with just the PC Cards.

- **LocustWorld** (www.locustworld.com) has made its MeshAP software open source and freely available. Consequently, many developers are improving the code, and many community groups are buying either their own or LocustWorld's hardware and building cheap mesh networks. LocustWorld sells most of its gear near cost and consults on larger projects for a fee.

- **Tropos Networks** (www.troposnetworks.com) (formerly known as FHP Wireless) wanted to solve two problems at the same time: creating seamless networks of wireless access and pooling bandwidth without connecting each access point to a separate network connection. The company's products can be used to replace expensive point-to-point links in locations like college and corporate campuses. Tropos Networks' routers find the best paths to each other, and they can automatically reroute if a connection fails. The company typically sells devices with two Wi-Fi adapters: one is used for local service and the other for mesh connections among the nodes.

- **RoamAD** (www.roamad.com), a small company in New Zealand, has found a way to blanket three square kilometers of downtown Auckland with ubiquitous 802.11b access using a combination of cleverly placed access points, wireless mesh-based backhaul (bandwidth from a wired connection distributed to the access points), and some special software that integrates the hardware for seamless roaming. RoamAD guarantees a minimum of 330 Kbps, but Glenn's wireless Web log readers in Auckland report that they usually get much more than 330 Kbps. The company hopes to sell its equipment to cellular operators who could use the equipment to provide cheap, high-bandwidth Wi-Fi access to an entire metropolitan area.

Mesh offers the promise of dramatically expanding wireless network access in communities, since the effort of adding a node to the network is incremental: a single gateway and antenna—no wires, cables, fiber, or other physical connection required. Will a mesh network debut in your neighborhood soon?

Ultra Wideband (UWB)

Modern radios work in much the same way as Marconi's first successful radio, transmitting and receiving in a specific band of frequencies in the spectrum. Because of this technical reality, government agencies around the world have made rules that govern who can use which parts of the spectrum, in what geographic areas they can transmit, how much power they're allowed to use, and for what purposes they can use it. These regulations govern individuals, private organizations, military branches, and government agencies.

Step back from that for a moment. A concept in information science called Shannon's Law defines a so-far immutable set of ideas about the amount of information you can encode into a piece of bandwidth, which is, quite literally, the width of the radio frequency bands used for transmission, measured in Hertz, coupled with the size of the wavelength (higher frequencies offer more room to encode). Shannon's Law says that the more bandwidth you use and/or the higher your broadcast power, the more information you can cram in. However, increasing broadcast power is a problem, because no one wants to be fried by walking in front of an antenna.

Ultra Wideband (UWB) communication uses Shannon's Law to stand the traditional spread-spectrum approach on its head, providing high data bandwidth while ignoring obstructions. (Visit the Ultra Wideband Working Group Web site at www.uwb.org for more information.) Instead of broadcasting continuously on tiny bits of spectrum (a few megahertz for the standards we've discussed) while switching between many frequencies or distributing signals along a continuum, a UWB transmitter broadcasts millions of tiny pulses at trillionth of a second intervals using very low power across enormous swaths of bandwidth: hundreds, or even thousands of megahertz. The receiver extracts the content of the transmission by decoding the rhythm of the pulses. It's a lot like Morse code with millions of dots and dashes being transmitted every second.

UWB advocates claim UWB can coexist with all current uses because existing equipment wouldn't be able to detect the signals—the signals fall well below the threshold of current gear and would seem like noise even within the thresholds. UWB can pass through practically any physical object because some of the frequencies it uses are extremely low, and it can penetrate almost anything (these are the types of frequencies used for communicating with submarines underwater). UWB equipment can coexist with itself, too, as the odds would be very low that two devices would transmit simultaneously.

Since the receiver must determine only the rhythm of the pulses, rather than decode their waves in any way, UWB can use very low power, which is helpful from many different standpoints, not the least of which is laptop battery life. A final advantage is that because the pulses happen so quickly, UWB is highly secure; much of the interest in UWB over the years has come from the military.

An interesting side effect of UWB is that it implicitly transmits location very precisely over short distances. A UWB transmitter several hundred feet from a receiver, even operating at tens of kilobits per second at that distance, could provide an almost exact range and position. This capability may be tied into other standards that need precise location information.

The downside of UWB is that although it's been tested in labs, various regulatory bodies around the world, including the FCC, are dubious about allowing it to be used in the wild without a lot more research. UWB doubters and detractors worry that the transmissions could interfere with a wide variety of existing uses because of UWB's approach of transmitting on wide swaths of spectrum simultaneously.

In 2002, the FCC took a baby step by approving a short-distance, low-power, narrowband version of UWB that can operate up to 30 feet at 100 Mbps using a very narrow slice of bandwidth—several gigahertz, which is small for UWB. Even with those enforced restrictions, UWB could give Bluetooth a run for its money since Bluetooth's current specification operates only at 1 Mbps over similar distances.

The IEEE 802.15 working group, which turned Bluetooth into an IEEE standard, is working on a proposal called 802.15.3a to put a streaming media and file transfer protocol on top of UWB. It runs at speeds of 110 Mbps at 10 meters and 480 Mbps at 1 meter. The intent is that you might be able to use a hard drive next to your computer with the speeds made possible by USB 2.0 or FireWire 400/IEEE 1394a, but without cables. Or, your computer could live in a closet and communicate with multiple monitors without you having to string cables under the door.

Some analysts have already predicted the demise of Wi-Fi within a few years given UWB's awesome, but untested, potential. More likely UWB will become just another letter in the 802.11 family because maintaining speed at a distance will always be constrained in UWB. By the time UWB matures in 2006 or later, hundreds of millions of 802.11a/b/g devices will be in use, and companies don't drop working technologies overnight.

In the more near term, UWB might help home electronics makers as early as December 2004 by carrying high-bandwidth services like video and audio over short distances. Think about putting a solar-powered satellite TV dish on your roof with multiple televisions inside your house receiving the signal from the roof—and no wires whatsoever. However, UWB will have a battle against entrenched technology there too, since companies like Sony and Microsoft have already used 802.11a for early technology demonstrations and a few real products because of the uncrowded spectrum in 5 GHz.

Airborne Wireless Broadband

The most significant problem with transmitting radio waves long distances is dealing with obstacles, such as hills, buildings, and trees. These obstacles prevent wireless ISPs from providing high-speed Internet access via Wi-Fi and thus competing directly with broadband companies that use cable modems or DSL. Finding a clear shot from where you are to an antenna on some tall building or tower is often difficult, and if you're a wireless ISP, figuring out where you can locate your antennas is often frustrating, since you have a strong incentive to maximize the number of customers who can receive your signal.

But what if the signal came from high above you? All you'd need then would be an antenna with an unobstructed view of the sky to receive the wireless signals. We're not talking pie-in-the-sky dreams here—a number of companies have tried to make this a reality, and although their technology is (or was, in some cases) real, the deployments haven't yet happened.

- **Angel Technologies** (www.angeltechnologies.com) planned to operate its HALO Network with special high-altitude planes that would circle the service area at a height of 52,000 feet, well above commercial air traffic. Angel's planes would be piloted, and they would have to take off and land regularly on an overlapping schedule to avoid interruptions in service. (At this writing, Angel's site hadn't been updated since 2000 and all email is bouncing, so the company would seem to be defunct.)

- **AeroVironment** (www.skytowerglobal.com) is working with NASA to develop unmanned solar-electric-powered airplanes that can act as mobile airborne telecommunications stations at 60,000 feet. The hope is that AeroEnvironment's planes will be able to stay aloft for six months or more (and to answer the obvious question, they use rechargeable fuel cells to provide power at night). AeroEnvironment's Helios prototype currently holds the world altitude record for a jet- or propeller-powered plane at

96,500 feet. Unfortunately, in June 2003, the prototype failed and crashed into the sea. The last tests listed on the company's site date to mid-2002, but the company says NASA remains committed to future testing.

- **Sky Station International** (www.skystation.com) planned a somewhat different approach, opting for huge unmanned blimps that would hover above a city at a height of 69,000 feet. It too would rely on solar power to run the networking gear providing connectivity to customers below. We checked several times before this book went to press, and the company's Web site was dead.

- **Advanced Technologies Group** (www.airship.com) is working on a technique along the lines of Sky Station International's blimps. ATG's StratSat blimps are designed to stay in place 60,000 feet up for five years, using a diesel engine for backup power. In 2002, the company won a contract to build a propulsion system for the Japanese government's Stratospheric Airship program, and in August 2003, that program saw the successful launch of a prototype in Japan. Although there hasn't been much other information about the StratSat blimps being used for telecommunications platforms, the company has had some interest from other firms looking for surveillance platforms as part of homeland security programs. Hmm...

- **21st Century Airships and Sanswire Technologies** (www.21stcentury airships.com and www.sanswire.com) fall into the blimp category as well, with their Stratellite balloons, which are slated to live at an altitude of 68,000 feet for a year before needing replacement. They would be powered by regenerative fuel cell technologies and solar-powered hybrid electric motors. Although Sanswire's latest press release about the Stratellite is dated May 2003, and the company has an active Web site, we're not holding our collective breath.

In the previous edition of this book we said that we expected plans for these airborne wireless Internet providers to be delayed, in part because of the loss of venture capital funding in the telecommunications industry, and in part because there appear to be questions that haven't yet been answered (if they've even been asked). For instance, even though the two unmanned services use extremely light materials, both could carry between 500 and 2000 pounds of gear, which is a big load to plummet to earth in case of catastrophic failure (we can just see the headline now, "Router Crashes, Crushing Suburban Home"). Unfortunately, our predictions with regard to the business issues appear to have come true, although at least some of these companies remain in business.

There may be other hitches as well, such as whether Wi-Fi is most appropriate for this use, what sort of equipment will be required at customers' premises, and how reliable the equipment in the blimp or plane will be. But hey, no one ever said innovation was easy.

Nonetheless, the concept of providing permanent wireless network services via high-altitude planes or blimps is innovative, and if it ever proves successful, it could mark a huge change in how many of us connect to the Internet.

Why Not Satellites?

Although the 52,000- to 69,000-foot altitude (about 10–13 miles) above the earth's surface proposed by these companies sounds high, it's nothing compared to the height necessary for a geostationary satellite, which must orbit the earth at an altitude of about 22,300 miles to maintain its geostationary position.

((•)) **NOTE**

Glenn always remembers that 22,300 miles is the height of geostationary orbit because that was the height of the Justice League of America's orbiting satellite. Every issue of DC Comics's Justice League mentioned the distance when introducing scenes in the satellite.

There are two problems with satellite altitudes for wireless communications. The farther a radio signal must travel, the more signal strength is lost, thus forcing you to increase transmit power and receive sensitivity significantly (see Chapter 34, *Long-Range Antenna Basics,* to understand the importance of transmit power and receive sensitivity). Therein lies the attraction of flying at a lower altitude. But satellites that aren't geostationary must orbit above about 200 miles, so you need multiple satellites in lower orbit to provide constant coverage, thus increasing cost and complexity. Also, the long round-trip for packets to travel from your computer up to the satellite, back down to the earth to their destination, up to the satellite with the response, and back down to you can result in long *latency* (the length of time between a packet being sent and the response to it coming back), which can in turn interfere with the quality of interactive services like online games, chatting, and voice communications.

Satellites are also expensive to launch and maintain, which makes it difficult for satellite-based Internet services to offer reasonable rates to individuals at high speed. Services like Direcway (www.direcway.com) and StarBand (www.starband.com) offer speeds between 150 Kbps and 500 Kbps using proprietary hardware and protocols—no Wi-Fi or cheap consumer gear here. That said, we're seeing more and more back-haul, or high-speed connections from the Internet to hot spots or business locations, delivered by satellite feeds. These cost much more than individual connections, but speeds are higher and the service is more reliable. Aloha Networks (www.alohanet.com), founded by a friend of Glenn's, and Hughes Network Systems (www.hns.com) are two of the companies that specialize in delivering high quantities of data from orbit.

Connecting Your Computer

The chapters in this section all focus on connecting to a wireless network, but you should pick and choose which chapters to read depending on which type of computer you use. Chapter 6, *Connecting Your Windows PC*, walks you through simple, intermediate, and advanced connections using Windows XP. Chapter 7, *Configuring Your Centrino Laptop*, offers additional information for laptops using Intel's new Centrino system. Macintosh users won't want to bother with either of those, but Chapter 8, *Connecting Your Macintosh*, offers them the necessary details for both Mac OS 9 and Mac OS X. Chapter 9, *Connecting with Linux and FreeBSD*, provides some tips and background information for Linux and FreeBSD users. Like Alice, Chapter 10, *Connecting Your Handheld*, gets small, providing instructions for connecting both Palm OS handhelds and Pocket PCs to wireless networks.

With Chapter 11, *Connecting via Bluetooth*, we take a breather from Wi-Fi to look at what's necessary to establish Bluetooth connections between Bluetooth-equipped laptops and a variety of Bluetooth-enabled devices. Chapter 12, *Creating an Ad Hoc Wireless Network*, returns to Wi-Fi with instructions on how to set up a wireless network between two computers…no access point necessary.

For most people, the primary goal of a wireless network is to share an Internet connection, but another common use for a wireless network is to enable multiple computers to share files or printers. Chapter 13, *Sharing Files & Printers*, covers that ground. Lastly, Chapter 14, *Troubleshooting Your Connection*, offers different tests and tips that help you track down and fix problems you may have when connecting to a wireless network.

Connecting Your Windows PC

Connecting your Windows computer to a wireless network is a snap—if you're using Windows XP. It's only slightly more complicated for previous versions of the operating system, for which you need to use software developed by companies like Linksys and Proxim.

With Windows XP, Microsoft offers its own well-thought-out connection tool for wireless networks. Or, you can stick with an individual manufacturer's software, if it offers some additional feature that you find helpful. Either way, have no fear: a few selections, or possibly even no selections, and you should be up and running no matter what Wi-Fi connection software you use.

 **NOTE**

Do you have a Centrino laptop computer or a computer with an Intel Pro/Wireless adapter installed? After reading the section in this chapter on "Configuring Windows XP," check out the additional options in Chapter 7, Configuring Your Centrino Laptop.

The first task is to install and configure your network adapter. The next step, however, depends on whether your network has any special requirements. For the vast majority of home and small office Wi-Fi users, you don't need to touch the network settings in your computer. The default settings that Windows offers for a new wireless card are correct.

Installing Hardware

No matter which version of Windows you're using, you must first install your wireless network adapter and configure the network settings appropriately.

NOTE

If your Wi-Fi network adapter is already installed and working, skip to the next section below for configuring your wireless network.

1. Install the drivers for your network card using the CD-ROM or floppy disk that came with it, or using an installer you downloaded from the manufacturer's Web site. Recent versions of Windows include drivers for many adapters, but it's best to install the latest ones.

2. If the installer tells you to, shut the computer down, and connect your network adapter to the computer. Power up again. With PC Cards, you may be asked to insert the card while the installer is running.

TIP

Shutting down isn't essential for PC Card or USB wireless network adapters, but it is for PCI cards or other internal cards, and starting from scratch is never a bad idea.

3. If all goes well, Windows identifies your new wireless network adapter, loads the driver you installed, and creates an entry in the Network (95/98/Me/NT) or Network Connections (XP/2000) control panel corresponding to the hardware (**Figure 6.1**).

 NOTE

If Windows does not automatically detect and configure your new wireless network adapter, refer to Appendix B, Configuring Your Network Settings, *and Chapter 14,* Troubleshooting Your Connection.

Configuring Windows XP

Now that your hardware and network settings are properly set up, it's time to configure the wireless network client software that manages settings specific to the wireless network. This wireless client software is built into Windows XP.

Figure 6.1
Windows recognizes new hardware and configures it.

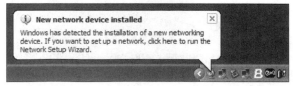

NOTE

If you aren't running Windows XP, or choose not to use its built-in client for some reason, flip forward a few pages for instructions on configuring the Linksys and Broadcom client software, plus some advice on what's necessary for other client software.

We've discovered that most Windows XP systems shipping in 2003 lack the Wi-Fi Protected Access (WPA) upgrade necessary to work with Wi-Fi gateways and ad hoc networks that support this robust new security standard. Microsoft made the update available in March 2003, but it's not a standard XP feature at this writing.

Since we highly recommend using WPA, and upgrades to support it are available for most newer 802.11g equipment, you should download and install the XP patch that provides WPA support. Microsoft doesn't offer a permanent download page, but you can find the patch by visiting Microsoft's Knowledge Base article at http://support.microsoft.com/?kbid=815485, scrolling to the bottom, and following the download link. With the WPA update installed, the configuration for Wireless Network Connections looks slightly different (**Figure 6.8**, later in this chapter).

TIP

If you're using Centrino, make sure to follow the link on the WPA patch download page noted above to update your Centrino driver—if your laptop maker supports it! See Chapter 7, Configuring Your Centrino Laptop, *for more on this issue.*

Let's look at how you enable and configure the Windows XP wireless network client software.

Simple Connection

If you're using a network with no security enabled, you can connect without any fuss. In fact, Windows may have already automatically connected to the network for you.

Hover over the Wireless Network Connection icon in the System Tray. If it shows your network name along with speed and signal strength, you're connected—there's nothing more to do (**Figure 6.2**).

Figure 6.2
Checking to see
if you're already
connected.

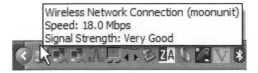

If your network name isn't what shows up or you're not connected, you might still be able to establish a simple connection with only a couple of steps.

1. Right-click the Wireless Network Connection icon in the System Tray and select View Available Wireless Networks (**Figure 6.3**).

Figure 6.3
Selecting networks to connect to.

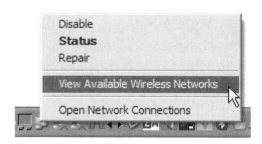

2. In the Wireless Network Connection dialog that appears, select your network (**Figure 6.4**).

Figure 6.4
Selecting your network in the Wireless Network Connection dialog.

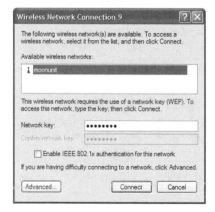

If these steps didn't work for some reason (probably because your network is closed, or requires a password), read "Intermediate Connection," next. Otherwise, you're done.

Intermediate Connection

If you are using networks with WEP or WPA security enabled or connecting regularly to more than one network, you can configure these details in the Wireless Network Connection dialog's Advanced settings.

 TIP

Skip to step 3 if the Wireless Network Connection appears in your System Tray.

1. To enable Windows XP's built-in wireless client software, open My Network Places from the Desktop and click View Network Connections (**Figure 6.5**).

Figure 6.5
Selecting your wireless network in the Network Connections window.

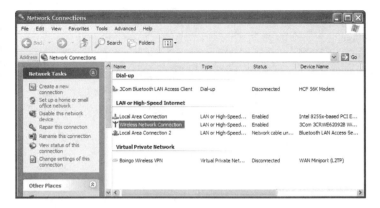

2. Right-click the Wireless Network Connection item under LAN or High-Speed Internet. In the pop-up menu, if you see the option Use Windows to Configure My Wireless Network Settings, make certain that it is selected. (If the option isn't showing, just continue on.)

TIP

Deselecting the Use Windows to Configure My Wireless Network Settings option allows you to use client software provided by the adapter maker, which we discuss later in this chapter.

3. Right-click Wireless Network Connection again, and choose View Available Wireless Networks from the pop-up menu.

4. In the Wireless Network Connection dialog, click the Advanced button (**Figure 6.6**).

Figure 6.6
Windows XP's wireless network client software.

5. In the Wireless Network Connection Properties dialog that appears, click the Add button beneath Preferred Networks to bring up the configuration dialog for a new Wi-Fi network (**Figure 6.7**).

Figure 6.7
Configuring your
new connection.

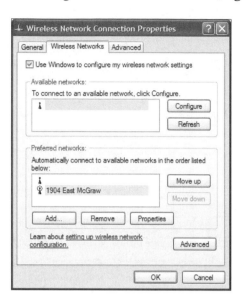

6. Enter the network's name or SSID.

7. If the network is using security, run through the steps for the most appropriate of the following three options:

   - **If you haven't installed the WPA patch (see earlier in this chapter) and are using WEP:** Check Data Encryption and uncheck The Key is Provided for Me Automatically (**Figure 6.8**, upper left). Check the Network Authentication (Shared Mode) box. Enter your WEP key, and then confirm it by entering it a second time.

NOTE

In certain releases of Windows XP, you should also be able to choose your key type (either ASCII or hexadecimal), as well as your key length. If you can't get Windows XP to connect to your access point, you may need to use client software provider by the adapter maker, discussed later in this chapter.

   - **If you have the WPA patch installed and WEP enabled:** Choose Shared from the Network Authentication pop-up menu, choose WEP from the Data Encryption pop-up menu, and uncheck The Key is Provided for Me Automatically (**Figure 6.8**, lower left). Enter the key twice in the format your network uses.

- **If you're using WPA in a normal home network:** Choose WPA-PSK from the Network Authentication pop-up menu, and choose TKIP or AES from the Data Encryption pop-up menu, depending on which kind of key was set in the wireless gateway (**Figure 6.8**, lower right). (AES is national-security grade security, but not available yet in all gateways.) Enter the key in the Network Key field and again in Confirm Network Key.

8. Click Connect.

9. Repeat just steps 4 through 8 as necessary for any other networks to which you want to connect regularly.

Figure 6.8
Configuration with
and without the
WPA patch.

*Without the WPA patch installed (left),
with the patch using an adapter that
doesn't support WPA in its driver
(below left), and with the patch using
a WPA-ready adapter (below right).*

You can change the network to which you're connected in the Wireless Network Connection Properties dialog's Wireless Networks tab (**Figure 6.7**, above). Any networks about which you've entered details (if they're closed) and all networks from which the adapter receives a signal appear in the Available Networks list.

Preferred Networks lists any network connections you've set up as noted earlier. You can change the preference Windows gives to connecting to available networks by selecting a network in the Preferred Networks list and then clicking Move Up or Move Down to reorder its priority.

There is another useful difference between the Available Networks and Preferred Networks lists. Even though it may appear that selecting a network from Available Networks and clicking Configure gives you access to security settings, you cannot make changes from that window. You can modify your security settings and other details about a network only by selecting a network in Preferred Networks and clicking the Properties button to open the Properties dialog for that network.

Advanced Configuration

On networks that require more elaborate security, such as large corporate networks, you may need to enable 802.1X authentication. 802.1X provides a way of securely logging into a server that then provides your computer with a unique encryption key that can be automatically changed without your involvement. If you haven't been given the settings for 802.1X, you don't need to turn on any of these features.

In Windows XP, you enable 802.1X via the Wireless Network Connection dialog box's Advanced mode. Your network administrator must provide you all of the necessary details.

1. Follow steps 1 to 7 in "Intermediate Connection," above, to reach the settings for 802.1X (**Figure 6.8**, above).

2. From the Network Authentication pop-up menu, choose WEP or WPA, depending on your network's encryption type. (Don't choose WPA-PSK: that's a simple password method.)

3. Click the Authentication tab (**Figure 6.9**).

4. For WEP networks, check the Enable IEEE 802.1X Authentication for This Network box. For WPA networks, that box is already checked; it's dimmed since 802.1X is implied with certain WPA options.

Figure 6.9
Authentication tab.

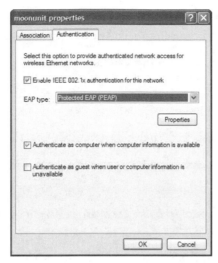

5. From the EAP Type pop-up menu, choose the EAP type based on what your network administrator told you. If you were provided with more details or given a certificate you installed on your computer, click Properties, and configure the additional settings there.

6. Click OK to close the Wireless Network Connection dialog and save your changes.

Configuring Broadcom Software

Broadcom makes the hardware that drives 802.11g and 802.11a/g adapters found in many laptops and in the PC cards and PCI cards made by many major consumer companies. Broadcom's software works almost identically to the Window XP wireless network client software. However, you can troubleshoot connections slightly more effectively with Broadcom's client software than with Microsoft's.

$((\bullet))$ **NOTE**

Although Broadcom's hardware works with WPA, its client software does not. You must use Windows XP's configuration tool with WPA as of this writing.

If Broadcom's client software is available, you see an icon that looks like an "A" in the System Tray (**Figure 6.10**).

Figure 6.10
Identifying the
Broadcom client
software in the
System Tray.

Broadcom's "A" icon in the System Tray.

1. Open Wireless Network Connection by right-clicking its icon in the System Tray and choosing View Available Wireless Networks.

2. Click Advanced to open the Wireless Network Connection Properties dialog.

3. Uncheck Use Windows to Configure My Wireless Network Settings.

4. Click OK to close the Wireless Network Connection Properties dialog.

5. Open the Broadcom client by right-clicking its icon in the System Tray.

 TIP

Most of the tabs pictured above are available even if you let Windows XP manage the wireless network.

The first tab you see is Wireless Networks (**Figure 6.11**). Helpfully, it's identical in almost every way to the built-in Windows XP configuration tool. Consult "Configuring Windows XP" in this chapter for working with its settings.

Figure 6.11
Broadcom client's
Wireless Networks
tab.

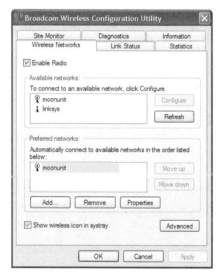

 TIP

Some machines that ship with Broadcom's hardware built in also have a keyboard shortcut for turning the radio off, like Function-F3 on laptops made by eMachines.

The other tabs in the Broadcom client provide useful information for troubleshooting. (See **Figure 6.12** for a panoply of tabs.)

- The Link Status tab shows connection information.

Figure 6.12
Broadcom client's
various tabs.

*The Broadcom client software tabs from upper
left to lower right: Link Status, Statistics,
Diagnostics, Site Monitor, and Information.*

- The Statistics tab offers network traffic statistics, and if the numbers go up over time, you know that data is actually passing over that network connection.

- The controls in the Diagnostics tab let you test the card to discover if it has any fault.

- The Site Monitor tab displays available networks.

- The Information tab offers driver versions, MAC information, and hardware information.

Configuring Linksys Software

Linksys—now owned by Cisco—makes the networking gear that powers much of the consumer world's Wi-Fi networks, according to market research and sales figures. Both Linksys's older 802.11b equipment, like the WPC11, and the company's newer 802.11g adapters, including the WMP54G, can work with Windows XP's built-in drivers. But for older systems or for those people who prefer Linksys's software, you can disable Windows's control.

TIP

If you're using Linksys's 54G equipment, you might prefer to use Linksys's software because it handles configurations for multiple locations whereas Microsoft's does not.

To enable Linksys's software, follow these steps:

1. Open Wireless Network Connection by right-clicking its icon in the System Tray and choosing View Available Wireless Networks.

2. Click Advanced to open the Wireless Network Connection Properties dialog.

3. Uncheck Use Windows to Configure My Wireless Network Settings.

4. Click OK to close the Wireless Network Connection Properties dialog.

TIP

On some systems, when Windows XP is in charge of the network connection, the Linksys software isn't installed at all or disables itself automatically. You may need to reinstall the Linksys software from your original CD-ROM and then download updates from Linksys's Web site. And realistically, that amount of extra work might not be worthwhile.

((•)) **NOTE**

Linksys's connection software doesn't support WPA or 802.1X authentication, although you can set up these features inside the Windows XP connection client and the Linksys software won't disturb them.

Linksys Wireless-B Software

Once you've installed the Linksys software, the Linksys icon should appear in your System Tray. It looks like a little computer with an antenna sticking out the top (**Figure 6.13**). Before you configure a connection, the screen is red; afterward, green or yellow, depending on the link quality. Follow these steps to configure the Linksys client software:

Figure 6.13
Identifying the
Linksys Wireless-B
client software in
the System Tray.

Linksys client software icon

NOTE

If the icon isn't in the System Tray, open your Control Panel directory and look for the iPrism control panel. (Prism is the series name of the set of chips in the wireless adapter.)

1. Open the iPrism control panel or click the Linksys client software's System Tray icon.

2. Click the Configuration tab (**Figure 6.14**).

Figure 6.14
Configuring your connection in the iPrism control panel.

3. Enter the network's name in the SSID field; if the network adapter finds wireless networks in the vicinity, the field turns into a pop-up menu, and you can choose one of the networks to connect to it.

4. If the network uses WEP encryption, click the Encryption tab (**Figure 6.15**). Enter the passphrase, if provided to you, or the hexadecimal WEP key or keys.

5. Click Apply Changes to save your settings.

You should now be connected. The Link Info tab shows signal strength for transmitting and receiving, as well as details about the access point and network you're connected to (**Figure 6.16**). The About tab provides version details for the configuration software itself, the driver, and the firmware on the adapter.

Linksys Wireless-G Software

Linksys radically overhauled its meager software offering between its Wireless-B and Wireless-G releases. The new software offers several excellent features

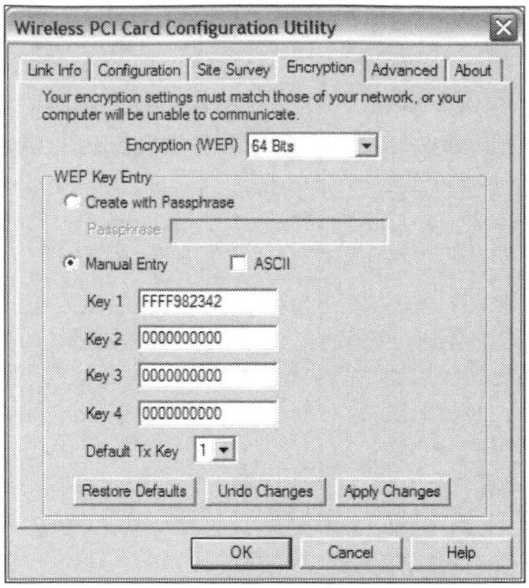

Figure 6.15
Configuring
security settings in
the iPrism control
panel.

Figure 6.16
Viewing connection
information in
the iPrism control
panel.

that might make it a better choice for some users than Windows's built-in wireless network client software. In particular, the Linksys Wireless-G software provides better options for automatically choosing networks, storing multiple configurations, and handling certain connection details. It's also friendlier than Microsoft's software.

Simple Connection

Follow these steps to establish a simple connection using the Linksys Wireless-G software:

1.   Double-click the Linksys icon in your System Tray to open the client software (**Figure 6.17**).

Figure 6.17
Identifying the
Linksys Wireless G
client software in
the System Tray.

Linksys Wireless G client in the System Tray.

2. To connect to a wireless network, click the Site Survey tab, which shows your available networks (**Figure 6.18**).

Figure 6.18
Selecting an
available network.

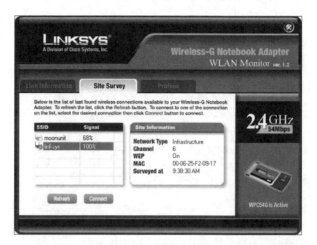

3. Select a network and click Connect, entering a WEP key or passphrase, if necessary. (There's no need to set up a profile.)

The Link Information tab features a somewhat silly graphic that identifies whether your card has connected to a network (**Figure 6.19**). The Signal Strength and Link Quality status bars provide connection feedback, too.

Figure 6.19
Viewing information
about your
connection.

Intermediate Connection

To connect to a closed network, you create a profile that stores your settings. Profiles are also useful for switching among different network configurations, whether or not any of those networks are closed. The Profiles tab lets you use a wizard to configure a storable set of connection parameters.

1. Open the Linksys Wireless-G software, and click the Profiles tab (**Figure 6.20**).

Figure 6.20
Starting a new profile.

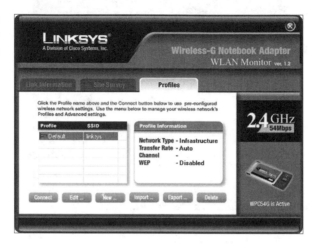

2. Click New, enter the profile's name in the dialog that appears, and click OK (**Figure 6.21**).

Figure 6.21
Naming your new profile.

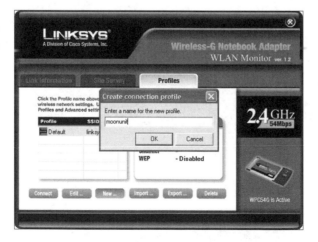

3. The software pre-fills the SSID name with your profile name in the resulting dialog (**Figure 6.22**). Change the SSID if necessary. Usually, you leave the type of network set to infrastructure mode, which is the standard network mode. Click Next.

Figure 6.22
Entering the
appropriate
network name.

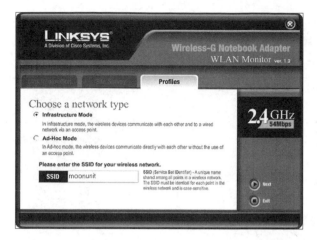

4. Under Network Setting, stick with Obtain an IP Address Automatically (DHCP) unless you have been provided with or need to use a static IP address (**Figure 6.23**). Click Next.

Figure 6.23
Configuring
network settings.

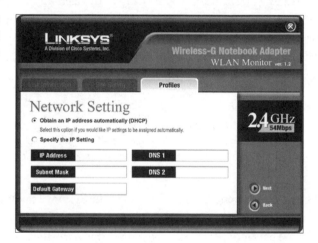

5. If your network uses WEP, select the bit length from the WEP pop-up menu and either enter the hexadecimal key in the Key 1 field at the bottom or type the ASCII passphrase into the Passphrase field (**Figure 6.24**). Click Next.

6. Confirm that your settings are correct and click Yes, or you can go back and revise them.

7. In the final screen, you can choose to switch to the profile now or later.

With one or more profiles created, you can switch networks at any time from the Profiles tab by selecting the appropriate profile and clicking Connect.

Figure 6.24
Entering security
settings.

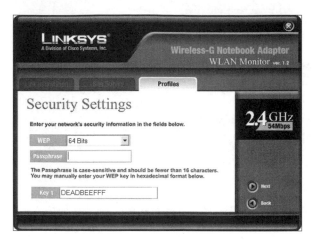

Configuring Orinoco Software

The Orinoco (www.orinocowireless.com) wireless network adapters were once the leading 802.11b PC Cards. Originally released as WaveLAN, Orinoco's maker was purchased by Lucent, and then spun off as part of Agere. Finally, Agere sold the card line to Proxim. Proxim no longer makes cards for the consumer market, but we provide this 802.11b configuration guide, as it's likely you can find inexpensive used Orinoco Silver and Gold cards.

((•)) NOTE

Orinoco 802.11b wireless network adapters can come in Silver and Gold versions: Silver adapters are limited to 40-bit WEP encryption keys, whereas the Gold versions support both 40-bit and 128-bit keys for ostensibly stronger encryption.

The Orinoco client software appears in the System Tray as an iconic set of bars of varying heights (**Figure 6.25**). The number of filled-in bars and the color of those bars indicates signal strength—the more filled-in bars, the better, and the color moves from red to yellow to green as the signal strength improves.

Figure 6.25
Identifying the
Orinoco client
software in the
System Tray.

Orinoco client in the System Tray.

Intermediate Connection

To configure the Orinoco software to connect your computer to a wireless network, follow these steps:

1. Click the bars in the System Tray icon to open the Orinoco client software.

TIP

Right-click the bars to access Add/Edit Configuration Profile directly.

2. Choose Add/Edit Configuration Profile from the Actions menu.

3. In the dialog that appears, name the configuration on the left side and leave Access Point selected at the right (**Figure 6.26**).

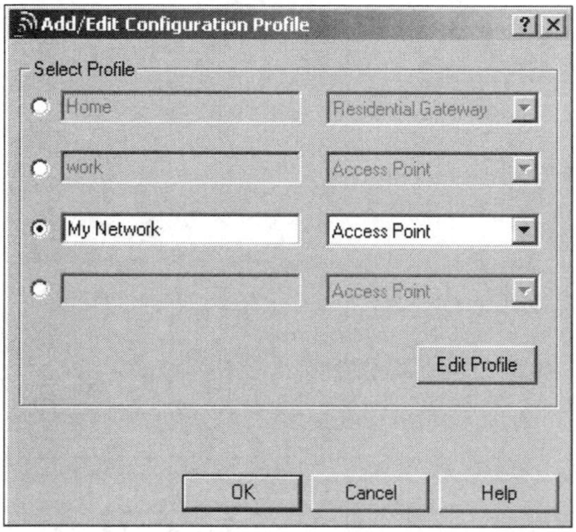

Figure 6.26
Naming your
configuration.

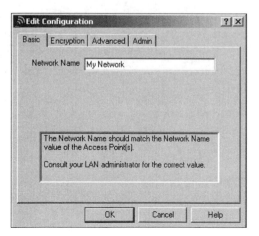

4. Click Edit Profile to bring up the Edit Configuration dialog (**Figure 6.27**).

5. In the Edit Configuration dialog, enter a network name in the Basic tab; if networks are in the vicinity, choose the network from the pop-up menu.

6. If WEP is enabled, enter your WEP key in the Encryption tab.

Figure 6.27
Editing your
configuration.

7. Click OK to close the Edit Configuration dialog, and click OK again to close the Orinoco client.

The Orinoco client has a nifty signal-over-time monitor built in that can help you test access while walking around with a laptop. From the Advanced menu, choose Link Test, and then click the Test History tab (**Figure 6.28**).

Figure 6.28
Monitoring signal strength over time in the Orinoco client software.

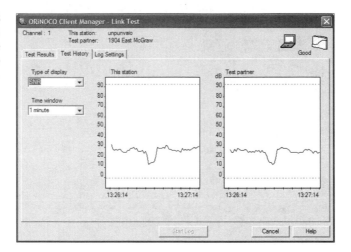

Configuring Other Wireless Client Software

So what if you're not using Windows XP or the Linksys, Broadcom, or Orinoco (802.11b) wireless client software? Don't worry, because as you can tell if you've even skimmed the instructions for these software clients, there's not much to configure. Just make sure you have the information from "Common Settings," next, on hand (particularly network name and WEP or WPA key) when you set up the software.

As with the wireless clients we've looked at, other clients tend to have monitoring tools to show signal strength. Some offer configuration managers to store different settings for different networks, and all offer some way to display the current revision of firmware and driver software, which helps you learn if an upgrade is needed when you're troubleshooting a problem.

 TIP

Windows users may think there's special magic to connecting to an Apple AirPort Base Station, but there isn't: it's just like any other access point—with one exception. If the AirPort Base Station is using WEP encryption, you must extract the non-AirPort-friendly hexadecimal WEP key from the AirPort Base Station. See the sidebar "Connecting to a Base Station without an AirPort Card" in Chapter 17, Setting up a Gateway.

Common Settings

Every wireless client program requires at least one, and sometimes all, of the following settings to be filled in or chosen in order to associate with an access point. Don't worry too much about figuring out all this information right now, but you may want to refer back here when setting things up.

Network Mode

Infrastructure is always the choice for networks; you use ad hoc only for machine-to-machine connections. Network mode is often preset to infrastructure. Sometimes you need a separate program to create ad hoc connections.

Network Name

Technically, the network name is called the ESSID (for larger networks) or SSID (for single access points). In many clients, you can leave the network name empty or enter "any" to connect to any available network. In others, you must select a network name from a list that the adapter has scanned, or enter the name manually.

For closed networks, you may need to bring up a special dialog or create a configuration entry to enter the network name.

WEP and WPA

Many wireless network clients, even for adapters even as recent as mid-2003, support only the WEP encryption standard. Newer hardware and wireless clients can support either WEP or one of several kinds of WPA keys.

- **WEP.** A WEP key is 10 or 26 characters in hexadecimal (hexadecimal numbers are made up of the numbers 0 to 9 and letters A to F). Some networks use a WEP passphrase, in which a short word or phrase is entered; it in turn generates the key.

  Many clients allow up to four WEP keys if the network administrator has defined that many. Confusingly, if only one WEP key has been defined, some of these clients require the entry of the same WEP key in all four slots!

  In most clients, you must select the WEP key size (40/56/64 bits or 104/128 bits) manually, as well as choose whether the key was entered as ASCII or hexadecimal.

- **WPA.** WPA simplifies the entry of keys. In most cases, you select WPA-PSK (pre-shared key) or a similar name, and then enter the text passphrase, which can be between 8 and 63 characters, and use letters, numbers, and a few symbols like underscore and space.

Advanced Authentication

Many corporate networks require certain methods of authentication that rely on a user login, a digital certificate installed by a network administrator, or an external security device like an ID card that generates unique numbers. Software clients provided by adapter makers lack support for required flavors of encrypted tunnel authentication like LEAP (Lightweight EAP), a flavor used by Cisco; EAP-TLS (uses a preinstalled certificate); or PEAP (protected EAP).

Generally, if you need to authenticate with one of these methods, a network administrator will have given you settings or installed an appropriate piece of client software on your computer, which might be settings within Windows XP or software provided by a company specializing in authentication software. If you're setting up this kind of network yourself, see Chapter 22, *Small Office Wi-Fi Networking*.

Radio Settings

Wi-Fi devices are radios at their hearts, and with Wi-Fi networks supporting a variety of speeds and protocols, you might find yourself tweaking these settings more now than you did before the introduction of 802.11g.

Mode

If you have an 802.11g adapter, you can sometimes choose whether to allow the client to connect using 802.11b or 802.11g. This feature is more typically found in an access point, which might restrict itself to allowing only 802.11b or g connections.

Transmit Rate

In clients that let you change this setting, you can lock your system at a specific throughput, such as 11 Mbps, if you're sure you have good enough signal strength everywhere. (Access points can likewise be locked into a faster throughput.) Eliminating the lower speeds increases overall performance, but makes you more likely to lose a connection entirely if you move too far from the access point.

Channel

Channels are selected automatically in client software, because access points can broadcast on only a single channel at a time. You select a channel only when creating an ad hoc network.

Configuring Your Centrino Laptop

Intel's Centrino laptops aren't just about another logo and a pretty name. In fact, when you buy a Centrino laptop, or any PC laptop with one of Intel's newer wireless adapters, you have the option of using a custom configuration tool that stores multiple profiles for all your Internet and network settings and provides detailed, graphical troubleshooting and feedback.

This chapter walks you through the basics of configuring and troubleshooting using Intel's ConfigFree software, which manages wireless connections, as well as settings for wired and infrared networking.

Currently, Centrino and the Intel Pro/Wireless adapters support only 802.11b network connections. As we write this, Intel says it expects to offer 802.11g and dual-band 802.11a/g adapters for Centrino around the beginning of 2004.

NOTE

Intel allows use of the Centrino name only for laptops that include a Pentium-M processor, an Intel Pro/Wireless 2100 mini-PCI adapter (or later similar adapters), and some of Intel's support chips. See www.intel.com/products/ mobiletechnology/ *for more on Centrino, and for more details on the Intel Pro/Wireless 2100 Network Connection card's capabilities, the only currently available Wi-Fi model, see* www.intel.com/products/mobiletechnology/ prowireless.htm?iid=ipp_a2z+p_281_prowire2100.

TIP
You can ignore Intel's software entirely if you want and stick with the Windows XP wireless network connection software. Intel's package is just an option that provides some welcome features.

Managing Connections

Although ConfigFree helps manage, troubleshoot, and display information about a connection, it doesn't actually help you find and connect to networks at all. Instead, you use the built-in tools found in Windows XP, described in Chapter 6, *Connecting Your Windows PC*, in the "Configuring Windows XP" section. We suggest you return there to read the configuration steps for simple, intermediate, and advanced connections, and then come back here for additional information on what ConfigFree can do for you.

((•)) **NOTE**
As we write this in late 2003, WPA may not be available on specific laptop models, such as those made by Toshiba, even though Intel supports WPA for the Pro/Wireless adapter. For WPA support, each manufacturer must include an Intel driver update: IBM and a few others do right now; some others do not. Read more about these WPA issues in Chapter 6, Connecting Your Windows PC.

You can launch ConfigFree by double-clicking its icon in the System Tray or opening it from the Start menu's list of Programs (**Figure 7.1**).

Figure 7.1
Double-click
ConfigFree's icon to
launch.

ConfigFree's icon

ConfigFree does offer some useful features when it comes to managing your connections.

If you check "Enable Wireless When Cable Disconnect Occurs" in ConfigFree's Device Settings tab, your wireless connection automatically kicks in whenever you disconnect your wired link (**Figure 7.2**). Since your wired link is likely to be faster, you probably would prefer to use it when it's available.

ConfigFree also helps you disable your wireless connection quickly, as you might want to do when you're using your laptop on an airplane. Run ConfigFree and click the Disable button in ConfigFree's Device Settings tab (**Figure 7.2**).

Figure 7.2
Configuring
select settings
in ConfigFree.

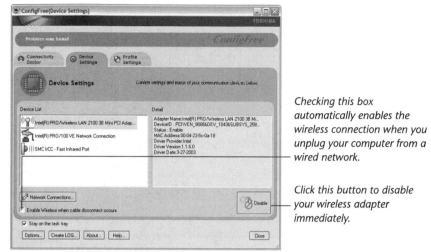

*Checking this box
automatically enables the
wireless connection when you
unplug your computer from a
wired network.*

*Click this button to disable
your wireless adapter
immediately.*

Using Profiles

The most useful part of ConfigFree is its capability to create profiles of settings you've made for individual network connections. Most of the profile systems we're aware of require you to define a profile, activate it, and then edit it if the profile doesn't work. ConfigFree's approach makes much more sense. Follow these steps to create a new profile.

1. Create your various network and Internet settings for both wired and wireless connections.

2. Click the ConfigFree icon in the System Tray, and from the hierarchical Profiles menu, choose Open to display the Profile Settings tab (**Figure 7.3**).

Figure 7.3
ConfigFree's Profile
Settings tab.

3.   Click the Add button to display the Add Profile dialog (**Figure 7.4**).

Figure 7.4
Name and
configure your
profile in the Add
Profile dialog.

4.   Name your profile and select which of your settings (Internet Settings, Devices, and TCP/IP Settings) should be included. You can also have a particular application launch whenever you switch to this profile.

 TIP

*Click Change Icon to select from among some truly horrible icons to identify this profile (**Figure 7.5**).*

Figure 7.5
What second grade
art class drew
these?

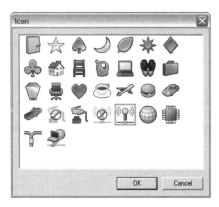

5.   Click OK to dismiss the Add Profile dialog and save your newly created profile so it appears in the ConfigFree pop-up menu and in the Profile Settings tab (**Figure 7.6**).

To see exactly which settings are encapsulated in your profile, click the Details button in the Profile Settings tab (**Figure 7.7**).

To switch to this profile, either choose it from the ConfigFree pop-up menu or select it in the Profile Settings tab and click the Switch button (**Figure 7.8**).

Figure 7.6
Your profile appears
in ConfigFree's
Profile Settings tab.

Figure 7.7
The Details window
reveals the settings
in your profile.

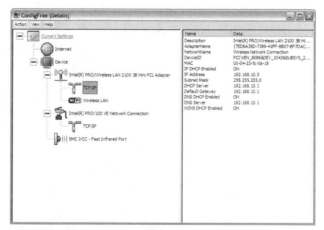

Figure 7.8
Switch among
profiles by choosing
them from the
ConfigFree pop-up
menu.

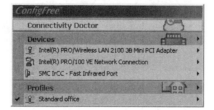

Troubleshooting

The ConfigFree software provides a marvelous, graphical approach to showing connection problems: the Connectivity Doctor, which you access from the ConfigFree pop-up menu (**Figure 7.9**).

Figure 7.9
The ConfigFree
Connectivity
Doctor.

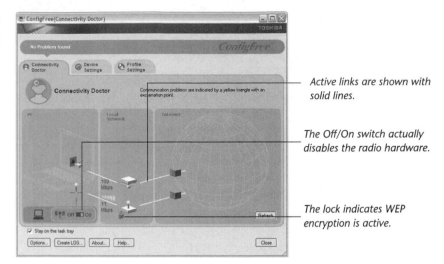

Active links are shown with solid lines.

The Off/On switch actually disables the radio hardware.

The lock indicates WEP encryption is active.

The Connectivity Doctor displays the status of each element of each connection it's managing, enabling you to pinpoint easily the specific location of any failure. The tool also provides specific errors, suggestions, and tests.

In **Figure 7.10**, for instance, the access point failed to provide a valid IP address using DHCP. The connection is fine, as is the WEP key, but the adapter has a yellow warning sign over it, and the troubleshooting guide at the right shows what the Connectivity Doctor thinks is wrong.

Figure 7.10
The Connectivity
Doctor graphically
displays likely
problems and
solutions.

The Connectivity Doctor also provides precise details about any component you hover over with the pointer (**Figure 7.11**).

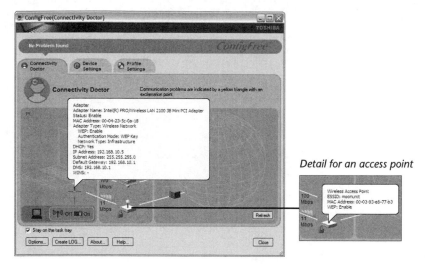

Detail for an access point

We recommend using the Connectivity Doctor whenever possible because it removes so much of the guessing game when troubleshooting a connection.

Connecting Your Macintosh

Because Apple has supported Wi-Fi for so long via its AirPort and AirPort Extreme technology, connecting to an access point has always been a straight-forward process in all recent versions of the Mac OS.

(((•))) **NOTE**

Luckily, most AirPort and AirPort Extreme cards come pre-installed when you buy your Mac; if you install one after the fact, follow the instructions that come with the card, and work carefully inside your Mac.

Simple Connection

If you want to use an open Wi-Fi network that uses either no encryption or AirPort's security system, you can connect without any fuss. In fact, the Mac OS may have already connected to the network automatically. If you can access the Internet, you don't need to follow any additional steps.

Proceed to "Intermediate Connection" if these choices fail or if the network you want to connect to is either closed or relies on a non-Apple access point and WEP or WPA encryption.

Mac OS 8.6 or 9.x

To make a simple connection with Apple's Control Strip, follow these steps:

1. Choose your network from the AirPort menu (**Figure 8.1**).

2. If prompted, enter your AirPort password.

Otherwise, to make a simple connection using the AirPort application:

Figure 8.1
In the Control Strip, choose your network or confirm that the correct network was chosen automatically.

1. Open the AirPort application, typically located in an AirPort folder inside either your Applications folder or the Apple Extras folder.

2. Click the Settings expansion triangle to show additional controls.

3. Choose the desired network from the Choose Network pop-up menu, and enter your AirPort password if one is requested (**Figure 8.2**).

Figure 8.2
In the AirPort application, choose your network or confirm that the correct network was chosen automatically.

 TIP

If you don't use Control Strip currently, but find yourself using the AirPort application regularly, consider turning Control Strip on (make sure it's turned on in Extensions Manager and enabled in the Control Strip control panel), since it makes switching among AirPort networks significantly easier.

Mac OS X

1. From the AirPort menu in the menu bar, choose your network (**Figure 8.3**).

2. If a password is requested, enter your AirPort password and check Add to Keychain to store the password in your secure system keychain so you never have to enter it again (**Figure 8.4**).

Figure 8.3
Choosing your
network in
Mac OS X.

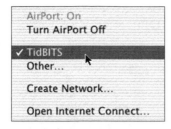

Figure 8.4
Entering your
AirPort password.

 TIP

*If you don't see the AirPort menu, open System Preferences from the Apple menu, click the Network icon, select AirPort from the Show menu, click the AirPort tab, and—finally—check Show AirPort Status in Menu Bar (**Figure 8.5**).*

Figure 8.5
Set AirPort status to
show in the menu
bar.

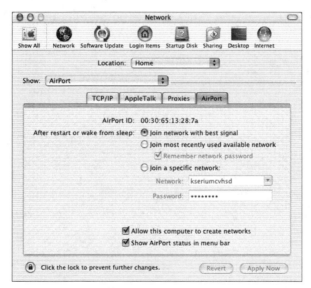

Intermediate Connection

If the network you want to connect to doesn't appear in your Control Strip or AirPort menu, you need to take just a few extra steps to establish your connection.

Also, if the network is run by a non-Apple access point with WEP or WPA encryption turned on, read "Entering WEP and WPA Keys on a Mac" for a few sneaky details.

Mac OS 8.6 or 9.x

If you use Apple's Control Strip utility, follow these steps to connect to a closed network:

Entering WEP and WPA Keys on a Mac

Apple's AirPort software expects that you're using an AirPort or AirPort Extreme Base Station as your access point. When it asks you to enter the network password, you type in a password instead of an encryption key. But if you're using an AirPort- or AirPort-Extreme-equipped Macintosh with any other kind of access point that has WEP encryption enabled, you must instead enter either 10 or 26 hexadecimal characters.

Mac OS X (post-10.2) offers choices for what you're entering in a pop-up menu (**Figure 8.6**). Choosing Password lets you enter an AirPort-style password. The other five choices correspond to the key length (40 or 128 bits) and the encoding (ASCII or hexadecimal), or let you select LEAP, a network login system. Choose the appropriate ASCII option only when your WEP access is via a passphrase. (These WEP passphrases are converted into actual WEP keys, but not in the same way that Apple turns AirPort passwords into WEP keys.)

Entering a hexadecimal WEP key when prompted works fine with recent versions of the AirPort software for Mac OS 9 and Mac OS X. However, with certain earlier versions of the AirPort software in both Mac OS 9 and Mac OS X, and in the password field of

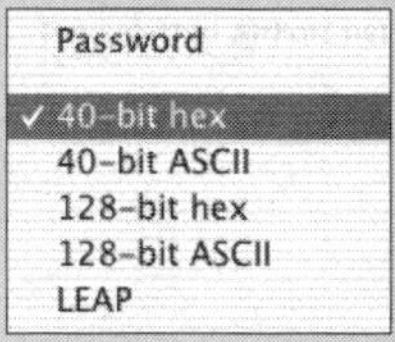

Figure 8.6 Options for passwords in Mac OS X 10.2 and later.

Password
✓ 40–bit hex
40–bit ASCII
128–bit hex
128–bit ASCII
LEAP

the Network preferences pane in Mac OS X, entering the WEP key by itself won't work. The trick with these older systems? Enter a dollar sign ($) before the hexadecimal WEP key, and all will be well. The dollar sign tells the AirPort software to send the exact hexadecimal key to the access point rather than interpreting it as a password to send to the AirPort Base Station.

To enter a WEP-style ASCII key in earlier versions of the AirPort software or in Mac OS X's Network preferences pane (even up to 10.2.6), enclose it in straight double quotation marks. We've found that these WEP ASCII keys aren't always compatible with one another, and we recommend using actual hexadecimal WEP keys instead of their ASCII versions whenever possible when setting up access points other than the AirPort or AirPort Extreme Base Station.

If you're using WPA (Wi-Fi Protected Access), you enter your password exactly as entered on the access point.

1. Choose Other from the AirPort menu to display a dialog asking for the network name.

2. Enter the exact name of the network and the AirPort password or WEP key, if necessary (**Figure 8.7**).

Figure 8.7
In the Control Strip, choose Other.

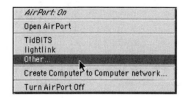

((•)) **NOTE**

Apple has not said if Macs running Mac OS 8.6 or 9.x will be able to connect to WPA-protected networks. We anticipate that such compatibility would require an update to the AirPort software for those versions of the Mac OS.

3. Click OK and you're done! (If for some reason it didn't work, try step 1, next.)

Otherwise, you need to use the AirPort application:

1. Open the AirPort application, typically located in an AirPort folder inside either your Applications folder or the Apple Extras folder.

2. Click the Settings expansion triangle to show additional controls.

3. Check Allow Selection of Closed Networks.

4. Choose Other from the Choose Network pop-up menu (**Figure 8.8**).

Figure 8.8
In the AirPort application, choose Other to open the Closed Network dialog box.

5. In the Closed Network dialog box, enter the exact name of the network and the AirPort password or WEP key (**Figure 8.9**).

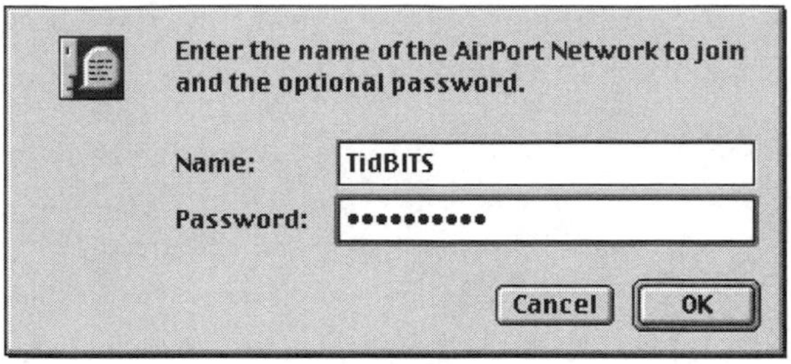

Figure 8.9
In the Closed
Network dialog
box, enter the
desired network
name and
password.

That's all there is to it—if everything has gone correctly, you should be connected to the AirPort Base Station or access point, and if it's sharing an Internet connection, you should be able to access the Internet from a Web browser.

Mac OS X 10.2 (Jaguar)

Mac OS X offers additional options for choosing Wi-Fi networks, so if you want to connect to a closed network that's not advertising its name, or if you want to connect to a network other than the one with the strongest signal, follow these instructions.

Connecting to Closed Networks

1. From the AirPort menu in the menu bar, choose Other to open the Closed Network dialog.

2. Enter the exact name of the network, and if a password is required, choose the password type from the Password pop-up menu and enter the password (**Figure 8.10**).

3. Click OK to establish the connection.

Setting AirPort Network Options

1. Choose System Preferences from the Apple menu, or click its icon on the Dock. Once System Preferences opens, click the Network icon to display the Network preferences pane.

2. Choose AirPort from the Show pop-up menu to display the AirPort preferences. If AirPort doesn't appear in the menu, choose Network Port Configurations, select the On checkbox next to AirPort, and choose AirPort from the Show pop-up menu.

3. Click the AirPort tab.

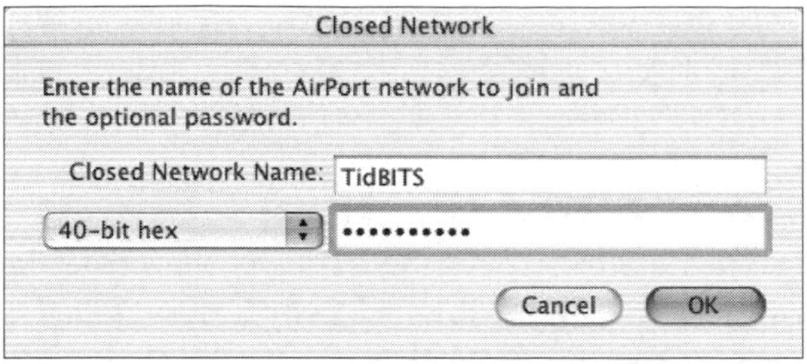

Figure 8.10
In the Closed
Network dialog,
enter the desired
network name
and password, if
necessary.

> **Closed Network**
>
> Enter the name of the AirPort network to join and
> the optional password.
>
> Closed Network Name: | TidBITS
>
> | 40–bit hex ⬍ | ••••••••• |
>
> Cancel   OK

4. On the AirPort tab (**Figure 8.11**), if you plan to use an open network
   without a password most of the time, select Join Network With Best Signal.
   If you want to make sure you always join the network you last used, select
   Join Most Recently Used Available Network and check the Remember
   Network Password checkbox if it has a password. Finally, if you need to join
   a closed network, select Join a Specific Network and enter (or choose) its
   name in the Network field. If the network has WEP encryption enabled,
   enter the password in the Password field that appears.

5. Click the Apply Now button to activate your changes.

 TIP

If you travel regularly and find that you need to change your settings often,
you can create multiple locations using the New Location item in the Location

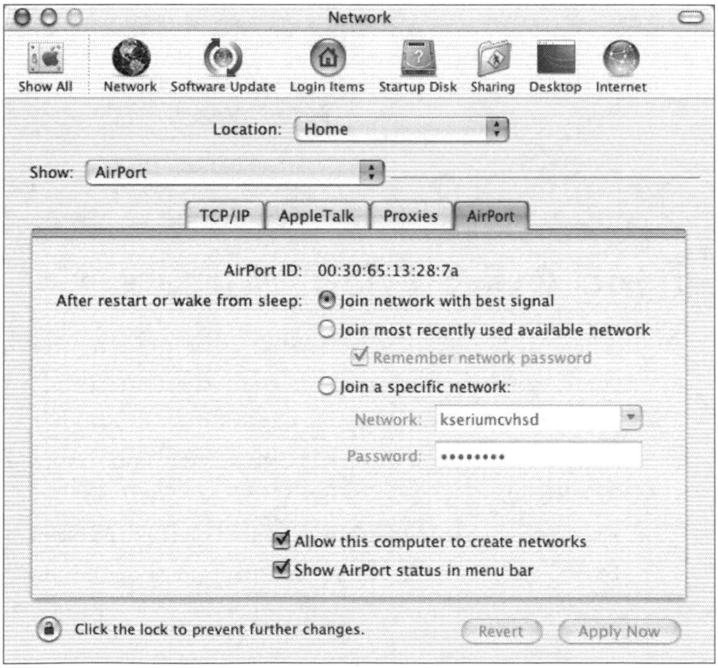

Figure 8.11
Select how you
want the Mac to
connect to wireless
networks.

> ● ● ○   Network
>
> Show All Network Software Update Login Items Startup Disk Sharing Desktop Internet
>
> Location: | Home ⬍ |
>
> Show: | AirPort ⬍ |
>
> TCP/IP AppleTalk Proxies **AirPort**
>
> AirPort ID: 00:30:65:13:28:7a
>
> After restart or wake from sleep: ⦿ Join network with best signal
>
> ○ Join most recently used available network
>
> ☑ Remember network password
>
> ○ Join a specific network:
>
> Network: | kseriumcvhsd ▾ |
>
> Password: | •••••••• |
>
> ☑ Allow this computer to create networks
> ☑ Show AirPort status in menu bar
>
> 🔒 Click the lock to prevent further changes.   (Revert) (Apply Now)

menu at the top of the Network preferences pane. Each location can have its own AirPort configuration, and you can easily switch among them using the Location menu.

Mac OS X 10.3 (Panther)

Mac OS X 10.3 moved around AirPort options without fundamentally changing how they work (**Figure 8.12**). The By Default, Join pop-up menu offers just A Specific Network and Join Network with Best Signal. You should also be able to enter a WPA password as easily as a WEP password.

Figure 8.12
Panther's
slightly different
configuration.

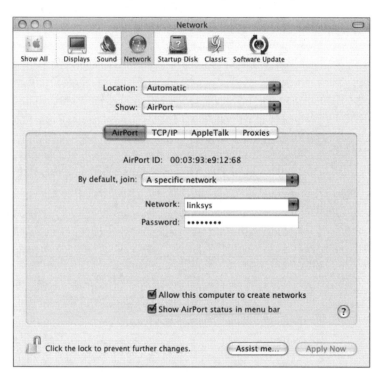

Configuring Other Client Software

The only time you might need to use wireless network client software other than Apple's AirPort software is if you set up a third-party wireless network adapter. For instance, earlier PowerBooks, Power Macs, and iMacs running Mac OS 9 might be wirelessly connected via non-Apple PC Cards, PCI cards, or USB adapters (see Chapter 3, *Wireless Hardware,* for details). Also, 802.11b PC Cards in Mac OS X require third-party drivers, such as the $20 IOXperts 802.11b Driver for OS X (www.ioxperts.com/80211b_X.html) or the open source WirelessDriver (http://wirelessdriver.sourceforge.net).

TIP

The WaveLAN and Orinoco PC Cards work with Apple's AirPort software in Mac OS 9 because AirPort cards are actually custom Orinoco cards.

Luckily, although third-party wireless network client software may look a bit different than Apple's AirPort software, it all requires basically the same settings as Apple's AirPort software, though with slightly different interfaces (**Figure 8.13** and **Figure 8.14**). Just select networks or enter network names and passwords in appropriate places and you'll be fine.

Figure 8.13
The main preferences pane of the IOXperts 802.11b Driver for Mac OS X.

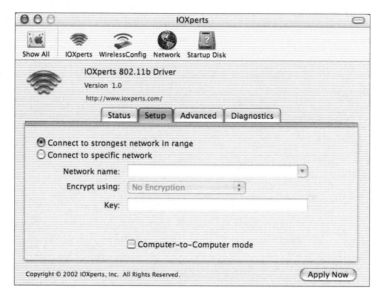

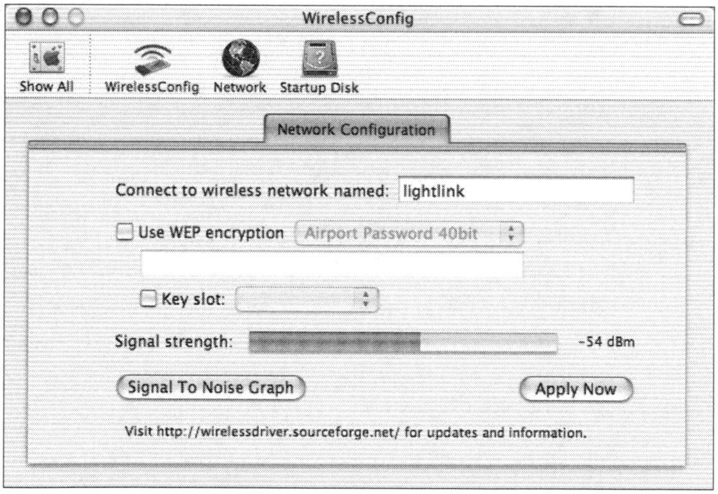

Figure 8.14
The preferences pane for the open source WirelessDriver.

Connecting with Linux and FreeBSD

If you have read even this far in this chapter, you undoubtedly already know that Linux, FreeBSD, NetBSD, and other Unix-like operating systems are varied, mysterious, and complicated, in exchange for being powerful and customizable to a fault. Fortunately, there's a growing and ever-improving body of Wi-Fi support for all of the above, and most notably the variants of Linux and FreeBSD.

Because of the multiplicity of kernel versions you could have installed, we can't provide the step-by-step instructions you would need to configure a specific version of Linux or FreeBSD. However, we can point you to resources that should help.

Linux, FreeBSD, and Wi-Fi

Since Wi-Fi is relatively new (keep in mind that Unix-like operating systems have been around for a lot longer than Windows or the Mac OS), driver support for Wi-Fi hardware wasn't widespread among non-commercial flavors such as Linux and FreeBSD until recently. Fortunately, as with almost everything in the open-source, free-software, and non-commercial software world, demand for Wi-Fi support produced results. Several projects, including one funded by Hewlett-Packard, have resulted in drivers that work under almost all of the last few years' kernel versions and standard distributions.

$(((\bullet)))$ **NOTE**

For the most comprehensive list of support resources related to Wi-Fi and the 802.11 family under all flavors of Linux and FreeBSD, see www.hpl.hp.com/ personal/Jean_Tourrilhes/Linux/Wireless.html, *which is maintained by Jean Tourrilhes, the HP engineer who has led Wi-Fi driver-writing efforts since the late 90s.*

Even better, many Wi-Fi drivers are found in standard distributions, so if you install FreeBSD or certain flavors of Linux, all you need to do to access a wireless network is attach a compatible network adapter and configure your network settings.

Before you purchase new gear or try to repurpose existing hardware, we suggest you read the following sections, which will help you focus on the right combination of equipment for your flavor of Unix/Linux/BSD.

The trick is that specific drivers generally work only with wireless network adapters using chips made by a specific company. That may sound problematic, but there are only three main chip-set manufacturers: Intersil, Orinoco, and Atheros. We also offer a few pointers for people who end up with network adapters that use chips from other companies.

Intersil

Intersil was one of the first companies to make 802.11b chips, and its Prism series powered almost all the early consumer gear from Linksys and others. However, in mid-2003, Intersil left the business, selling its Wi-Fi line to GlobespanVirata (www.globespanvirata.com/prism.html). Since cards containing Intersil chips are still in wide use, they enjoy the broadest support.

You can find extensive information about the Prism line at www.linux-wlan.com/linux-wlan/. Also available at that site are drivers for many of the Linux distributions.

For more information on Prism support in FreeBSD (including a large list of supported wireless network adapters and the specific chip set they use), read www.freebsd.org/cgi/man.cgi?query=wi.

Orinoco

The Orinoco line of wireless networking gear was originally created by WaveLAN, and then purchased by Lucent, spun off with Agere, and bought by Proxim. Whew! The early versions of Orinoco equipment, starting back in 1999, were found in inexpensive professional gear for PCs and in Apple's AirPort

Card and AirPort Base Station. As a result, even though Proxim doesn't focus as much on the consumer market as previous Orinoco owners have, Orinoco gear is extremely widespread.

To learn more about support for Orinoco gear in various Unix-like operating systems, load Jean Tourrilhes's FAQ at www.hpl.hp.com/personal/Jean_ Tourrilhes/Linux/Wireless.html and search for "Orinoco".

Atheros

Atheros was the first company to ship 802.11a-based chip sets and later branched out in other areas. Unfortunately for users who wanted to develop drivers for wireless network adapters using Atheros chipsets, Atheros was also an early developer of software-defined radios, which allow a chip-based radio to work with all kinds of radio frequencies. Before software-defined radios, all radios had to be designed with a baseband that could specifically cope with certain frequencies. Many Wi-Fi radios still use those kinds of basebands.

The unfortunate part is that because Atheros's hardware could handle a huge range of frequencies at different power levels, Atheros couldn't legally release source code for inclusion in various open-source systems, like Linux and FreeBSD. The FCC wouldn't have looked kindly on hackers being able to convert Atheros's hardware to send and receive in licensed parts of the spectrum or at illegal power levels.

Fortunately, Sam Leffler solved the problem by bridging the gap between Atheros's legal and FCC concerns and the Linux/FreeBSD world. He made a binding deal with Atheros that allowed him restricted access to the information he needed to write a bit of software that acts as a hardware abstraction layer (often referred to as a HAL in the documentation). Developers who want to write drivers for Atheros-based gear can write to the specification of Sam's hardware abstraction layer, which limits the driver from accessing the full features of the Atheros chip set. In other words, the hardware abstraction layer ensures that all drivers use Atheros's software-defined radios only in legal ways, effectively keeping Atheros in the clear while making the company's technology available for use outside of drivers it writes.

Sam continues to maintain his hardware abstraction layer and drivers on top of it, which have been integrated into the FreeBSD tree starting with version 5.2, meaning that it has been built in by default (www.freebsd.org/cgi/man.cg i?query=ath&manpath=FreeBSD+5.1-current), and it's also available as a Linux port (http://www.sourceforge.net/projects/madwifi/).

Other Chips

If you want to use wireless network adapters built with other chip sets, you're not entirely out of luck. Your first step is to determine exactly which chip set your equipment has, and for that, you should turn to the Linux-WLAN project, which provides a huge list of which chip sets are used in which wireless network adapters (www.linux-wlan.org/docs/wlan_adapters.html).

Your next step is to look for drivers, and although a Google search is always worthwhile, sometimes you can find what you're looking for more directly. For instance, one group has built drivers for Texas Instruments's ACX100 chip set (http://acx100.sourceforge.net/).

In general, the open source world has spawned numerous projects, as documented in Jean Tourrilhes's FAQ (www.hpl.hp.com/personal/Jean_Tourrilhes/Linux/Wireless.html). Finding the appropriate information may take some searching within that page.

Connecting Your Handheld

It was inevitable that the simple handheld personal digital assistant (PDA) would transform itself from a dedicated calendar and contact manager into a full-scale computer. Today's handhelds have not only the power to run programs typically run on desktop computers five years ago, but also the power to handle some capabilities that were out of reach for many PCs five years ago, such as streaming audio and video.

In 2003, as handhelds gained multimedia and communications capabilities that outstripped USB synchronization or even Bluetooth's 1 Mbps speed, moving data—especially audio and video—to and from a handheld became necessary. The concept of using a portable handheld while connected to a wired Ethernet was (and is) a slightly bizarre idea—wireless is the right counterpart to a handheld. Adding Wi-Fi to handhelds makes perfect sense: the devices are small but need speedy wireless connections.

As we write this chapter, two handheld systems control the vast majority of the marketplace: the Palm OS found in PDAs made by Palm, Sony, and a few other companies; and the Pocket PC platform, running what Microsoft has dubbed Windows Mobile 2003, that runs on equipment from many companies, including HP (formerly Compaq), Dell, and Toshiba.

In this chapter, we walk you through the basics of using Wi-Fi with the latest versions of the Palm OS and Windows Mobile 2003, and show you how easy it is to connect wirelessly. For each platform, we provide three sets of instructions:

- **Simple Connection,** which should be all most people need most of the time.

- **Intermediate Connection,** which covers slightly more complicated topics like WEP and closed networks.

- **Advanced Connection,** which adds instructions on dealing with authentication methods, VPNs, and other more esoteric topics.

Palm OS

The Tungsten C from Palm was the first of its kind to have integrated Wi-Fi capabilities: no add-on cards, no slot-loading connections, just the necessary wireless networking hardware and antenna built into the handheld. Also, Palm added wireless connection software to Palm OS 5.1, which comes on the Tungsten C. Unfortunately, in Palm OS 5.1, you must run through a setup wizard each time you want to connect to a new network, even if the network has no encryption or other login requirements.

 TIP

Although we're using the Tungsten C for our examples, any Palm OS-based handheld running Palm OS 5.1 will work similarly. If you're using an older Palm OS-based handheld, you may have to use proprietary wireless client software, which will look different from what we show here.

Simple Connection

If the Wi-Fi network isn't using encryption or other security features, follow these steps to connect:

1. Press the Home button and tap Wi-Fi Setup.

2. Tap Next (**Figure 10.1**).

3. The Palm searches for networks and lists those it found under Select a Network. If a listed network is selected, the Palm displays signal strength bars next to the selection (**Figure 10.2**).

4. Select your network and tap Next (**Figure 10.3**).

 TIP

If your network doesn't appear, tap Other and enter the network name (SSID). That should be all that's needed.

5. The final screen shows the current signal strength (**Figure 10.4**). Tap Done to exit Wi-Fi Setup.

Figure 10.1
Getting started.

Figure 10.2
Searching for networks.

Figure 10.3
Choosing a network.

Figure 10.4
Finalizing setup.

Intermediate Connection

If the Wi-Fi network uses WEP encryption, follow these steps to connect:

1. Press the Home button and tap Wi-Fi Setup.

2. Tap Next (**Figure 10.1**, above).

3. The Palm searches for networks and lists those it found under Select a Network. If a listed network is selected, the Palm displays signal strength bars next to the selection (**Figure 10.3**, above).

4. If your network is listed, select it and tap Next. Or, if your network doesn't appear in the list:

   a. Tap Other (**Figure 10.3**).

   b. Enter your Network Name or SSID (**Figure 10.5**).

   c. Check WEP Encryption.

   d. Tap the field next to WEP Keys.

Figure 10.5
Setting up
advanced options.

Figure 10.6
Entering the WEP
key.

5. If you have a WEP key, you can enter it now (**Figure 10.6**).

    a. Choose the type of key from the pop-up menu.

    b. Enter the key and tap OK.

    c. If you chose a listed network in step 4, tap Next. Otherwise, tap OK
        and then tap Next.

6. The final screen shows the current signal strength (**Figure 10.4**, above).
    Tap Done to exit Wi-Fi Setup.

Advanced Connection

If you need to control more detailed network settings or are using the wireless
network to connect to a VPN, these steps provide additional details beyond those
offered in "Intermediate Connection." Make these changes or enter these settings
only if you received the details you need from a network administrator.

Networking Settings

The Palm OS lets you choose whether you can connect only to wireless
infrastructure networks or also to wireless ad hoc networks, and you can also
modify your TCP/IP settings if necessary. You perform these modifications
in a nested dialog available by tapping the Details button that appears in step
4a in "Intermediate Connection" previously. Follow these steps to work with
an ad hoc network or modify TCP/IP settings while connecting.

1. Tap Details in the Other screen reached through Select a Network
    screen.

2. By default, a new network configuration looks only for access points on
    a network, not other computers running ad hoc networks. Choose Peer-
    to-Peer (Ad-Hoc) from the Connect to pop-up menu to connect to an ad
    hoc network, or to create one (**Figure 10.7**).

3. Tap Advanced.

4. You can modify three TCP/IP settings here (**Figure 10.8**). You can enter a specific IP address and a specific set of DNS servers. Finally, you can check whether or not to use a short preamble, which disables slower Wi-Fi speeds but improves network throughput.

5. Tap OK to save your changes and continue at step 4b.

Figure 10.7
Specifying a different kind of network architecture.

Figure 10.8
Setting the IP address and DNS servers.

VPN Settings

After you connect to a network, the final Wi-Fi Setup screen has a VPN Setup button at the bottom (**Figure 10.9**), which provides access to the Palm OS's VPN capabilities. Follow these steps to create a VPN connection:

 TIP

The Palm OS supports only the Microsoft-style PPTP (Point-to-Point Tunneling Protocol) form of VPNs, not the more advanced IPsec-over-L2TP.

1. Tap VPN Setup in the final Wi-Fi Setup screen.

2. Tap Next (**Figure 10.9**).

3. Enter your account, user name, password, and server details.

4. If you need to set more specific parameters, tap Details (**Figure 10.10**).

   • If Required is checked next to Encryption, the connection will work only if the VPN server enables encryption.

   • Unchecking To VPN (next to Send All) will cause the Palm to use the VPN only for DNS requests and specific programs that request a VPN connection.

   • You can set the DNS server numbers or the IP address by unchecking Query DNS and/or Automatic next to IP Address. Tap OK.

Figure 10.9
Starting VPN
configuration.

Figure 10.10
Setting VPN details.

5. Tap Done in the final screen, and your VPN should be enabled.

Modifying an Existing Network

The Palm OS doesn't let you change the settings of an existing Wi-Fi network via Wi-Fi Setup. That would be too obvious and simple. Instead, you must follow an alternate path that leads to identical dialogs.

1. Press the Home button.

2. Tap the Prefs icon.

3. In the Communication set of options, tap Wi-Fi.

4. Tap Info.

5. Tap Edit Network.

Now you have access to all the settings noted for intermediate and advanced connections previously.

Once you set up a network connection, you can't delete it, though you can modify the settings.

Windows Mobile 2003

For many Windows Mobile 2003 users, connecting to a local Wi-Fi network involves almost no configuration. For a public hot spot network or a home or office network with no password protection, you can follow the "Simple Connection" instructions below. For networks protected with encryption, or if the simple instructions fail, try "Intermediate Connection." If you're using corporate encryption, including VPNs or special methods of network login, see "Advanced Connection."

Simple Connection

In most cases, the following steps will be all you need to connect to an open, unencrypted Wi-Fi network.

1. Tap the Connectivity icon in the menu bar.

2. If the Pocket PC (**Figure 10.11**) lists the network and shows the signal strength at right, then you're done!

Figure 10.11
Simple connection.

Intermediate Connection

If you need to access a closed Wi-Fi network, enter a WEP key, or restrict the list of accessible networks to those provided by access points (and to avoid ad hoc networks), follow these steps to connect.

1. Tap the Connectivity icon in the menu bar.

2. Tap the Settings link (**Figure 10.11**, above).

3. Tap the Advanced tab at the bottom of the Settings window (**Figure 10.12**).

4. Tap the Network Card button (**Figure 10.13**).

5. If your network is set up as an open network, even with encryption enabled, it shows up in the Wireless Networks list (**Figure 10.14**). If it's there, and a green halo is around the antenna at the left and "Connected" appears to the right of the network name, then you're done.

6. If your network doesn't appear, from Networks to Access, choose All Available. If it still doesn't appear, follow the "Adding a New Network" instructions, next.

Figure 10.12
Advanced settings.

Figure 10.13
Network Card
settings.

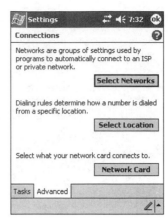

Figure 10.14
Wireless Networks
list.

 TIP

If you're in an area with many networks and you think some of them are ad hoc networks, choose Only Access Points from the Networks to Access menu. We wish Microsoft would add this option to Windows XP!

7. Select the network name, which opens the Configure Wireless Networks dialog.

8. If WEP encryption is enabled on the network you want to access:

    a. Tap the Authentication tab at the bottom of the dialog (**Figure 10.15**) to open the Configure Network Authentication dialog.

    b. Uncheck The Key is Provided for Me Automatically. (If that's not true, see "Advanced Connection," next.)

    c. Enter your hexadecimal WEP key.

9. Tap Ok to connect to your Wi-Fi network.

Figure 10.15
Authentication tab.

Adding a New Network

1. Follow steps 1 through 6 of "Intermediate Connection," above.

2. Tap Add New Settings.

3. Enter the network name in the Network Name field (**Figure 10.16**).

Figure 10.16
Entering the
Network Name.

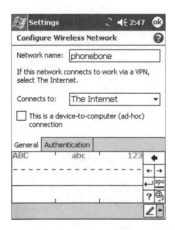

4. Choose Work from the Connects To pop-up menu unless you're using a VPN. If you are using a VPN, see "Advanced Connection" next.

5. Continue with step 7 in "Intermediate Connection" previously.

Removing a Network

1. Follow steps 1 through 4 of "Intermediate Connection."

2. Tap and hold the stylus over the network you want to delete until a menu appears.

3. Tap Remove Settings in that menu (**Figure 10.17**).

Figure 10.17
Removing a
network setting.

Advanced Connection

Corporations may require advanced security for employees using wireless networks, and Windows Mobile 2003 offers two unrelated options in this field. The first supports special kinds of logins over Wi-Fi, the second is a VPN of either the Microsoft-style PPTP or the more standard IPsec-over-L2TP. You should make these changes or enter these settings only if you received the details you need from a network administrator.

Network Authentication

To log in to your network using 802.1X, follow these steps:

1. Follow steps 1 through 8 under "Intermediate Connection," above.

2. In the Configure Network Authentication dialog, check Enable Network Access using IEEE 802.1X (**Figure 10.18**).

3. Select the appropriate EAP (Extensible Authentication Protocol) option. In both cases, you must already have installed a certificate. If you don't have a certificate, consult your network administrator (**Figure 10.19**).

4. Tap Properties.

5. Enter your user name and password.

6. Tap Ok.

VPN

To create a VPN tunnel to your network, follow these steps:

1. Follow steps 1 through 3 in "Intermediate Connection," above.

2. Tap Select Networks.

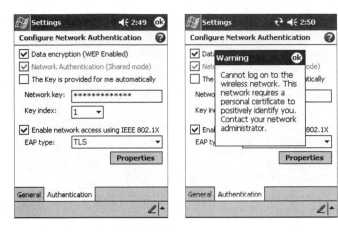

Figure 10.18
Enabling 802.1X.

Figure 10.19
Editing 802.1X
properties.

3. From the second pop-up menu—"Programs that automatically connect to a private network should connect using"—tap Edit (**Figure 10.20**).

4. Tap the VPN tab at the bottom of the window (**Figure 10.21**).

Figure 10.20
Getting to the VPN
settings.

Figure 10.21
The VPN start
screen.

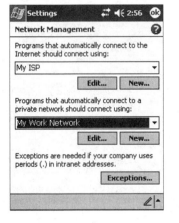

5. Tap New.

6. Enter the name of your VPN and its host name or IP address, and then select the VPN protocol type (**Figure 10.22**).

7. Tap Next.

8. Choose whether to use a certificate already installed on the Pocket PC or a preshared key (**Figure 10.23**).

9. Tap Next.

10. Enter your user name, password, and domain (**Figure 10.24**).

11. If you need to set your IP address or DNS servers manually, tap Advanced (**Figure 10.25**).

  a. Set the IP address, if needed.

  b. Tap the Servers tab at the bottom of the window.

  c. Set your DNS server addresses, if needed.

  d. Tap Ok.

12. Tap Finish.

13. In the My Work Network dialog, tap and hold the stylus over the name of the VPN until a menu appears.

14. Tap Connect from that menu.

Figure 10.22
Naming the
VPN connection.

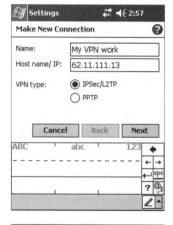

Figure 10.23
Entering a key
or choosing a
certificate.

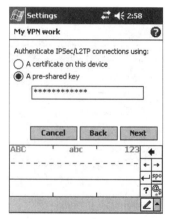

Figure 10.24
Entering a
user name and
password.

Figure 10.25
Configuring
IP settings, if
necessary.

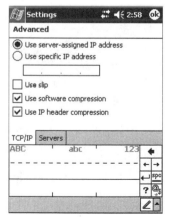

Connecting via Bluetooth

As a short-range wireless cable replacement technology, Bluetooth holds great promise in creating small wireless networks of small battery-powered devices like cell phones, handheld personal digital assistants, and input peripherals (keyboards, mice, joysticks, and touchpads, for instance).

With Bluetooth, you first associate devices with one another in a process known as *pairing*. Once paired, multiple devices can form networks, often with a Bluetooth-capable computer as the coordinating hub. For instance, the computer can dial numbers for you on a Bluetooth-enabled cell phone or act as a modem in order to connect to an ISP via its modem banks; the handheld PDA can synchronize data with your computer via Bluetooth instead of USB; or the computer can stream audio to a set of Bluetooth headphones.

In this chapter, we walk through the basics of pairing and then show you how to set up Bluetooth connections on the major operating systems. We also examine how some common Bluetooth devices work together.

Pairing

When you pair a set of Bluetooth devices, you perform two tasks:

- Pairing enables the devices to prove their identity to each other, which is an important security step, because otherwise any Bluetooth-enabled computer within range of your Bluetooth cell phone could cause it to dial out. You can think of pairing as introducing two devices; after they've been introduced, they can communicate with each other.

- Pairing makes available a set of common services, like printing, file transfer, or dial-up networking. In essence, through the pairing step, the devices agree on what they can do with each other.

You can set up pairing to work both ways (if appropriate) or in only one direction. As an example of bidirectional pairing, you could set your PDA and your computer to synchronize contact and calendar information in both directions. You'd use one-way pairing for your computer to use Bluetooth to access the Internet via your cell phone, since the cell phone doesn't access the Internet via your computer.

((•)) **NOTE**

In some cases, you may be allowed to set up pairing in only one direction; in other cases, even though it may not make sense, you might be required to set up pairing both ways. Read the documentation that comes with any Bluetooth device for the specifics.

Pairing Basics

Here's how pairing works in general—we talk about specific platforms next (**Figure 11.1**).

1. **Turn on discovery on one device**. Bluetooth uses *discovery*, or scanning for available devices, to find other equipment. With discovery, you don't have to enter any identifying information (such as an IP number) about your devices. Different equipment turns discovery on in different ways. For instance, to make a Jabra Bluetooth headset discoverable, you hold down its power button for at least 10 seconds. A cell phone might hide discoverability deep in a nested menu, while most computer operating systems offer discovery as a top-level menu item.

2. **Have the other device select the discoverable device**. A device that needs access to resources on another piece of Bluetooth gear selects it through some option that scans for available Bluetooth adapters and presents them in a list.

3. **Enter a passphrase**. The passphrase is a small piece of text. You enter the passphrase on the device that's discoverable, and then the device requesting the pairing prompts you to enter the same passphrase.

 TIP

Often, you duplicate these steps, running them once in each direction so that each device discovers the other.

The devices are now paired and can communicate with each other.

Figure 11.1
Bluetooth pairing.

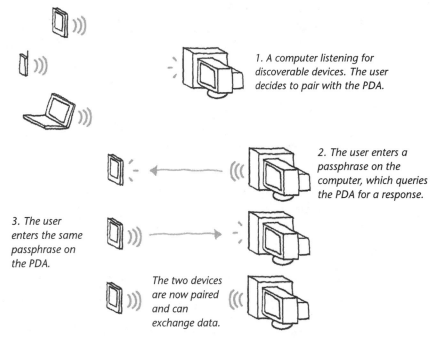

1. A computer listening for discoverable devices. The user decides to pair with the PDA.

2. The user enters a passphrase on the computer, which queries the PDA for a response.

3. The user enters the same passphrase on the PDA.

The two devices are now paired and can exchange data.

NOTE

Simpler Bluetooth devices usually have passphrases preset by the manufacturer, like 0000 for the Jabra headsets. This isn't a security risk because you turn on discovery only once through a special mechanism, after which the pairing is complete. Pairing is unique based on a Bluetooth's adapter network identification number.

NOTE

There's an ease of use in Bluetooth that we'd like to see in Wi-Fi, and there's some hope it could happen. The Zeroconf protocol, designed by a working group of the Internet Engineering Task Force (IETF), provides discovery to devices using TCP/IP, much as AppleTalk did for early Macs and NETBIOS did for Windows-based PCs. Apple calls its implementation of the Zeroconf protocol Rendezvous, but since it's an open standard, any company can develop Zeroconf-compatible devices for wired, Wi-Fi, or other TCP/IP systems. In fact, Apple uses Rendezvous to help its AirPort Admin Utility find AirPort Extreme Base Stations.

Pairing Under Windows XP

Microsoft doesn't offer a uniform built-in Bluetooth configuration tool as it does for Wi-Fi. Instead, it gave hardware makers a package that enables them to use a standard interface. Few that we've seen have chosen Microsoft's software.

In practical terms, this means that every Bluetooth adapter you purchase could have its own drivers that you must install, and its own set of steps to pair with other devices. Even worse, if you were to switch to a different adapter from another company, you would have to redo all your pairings before you could use your Bluetooth devices again.

 NOTE

We've also found that some Bluetooth software can't co-exist with other Bluetooth software, requiring a full uninstall of the older drivers before working with the newer ones.

For the steps below, we used the Actiontec BTM200 USB Bluetooth adapter, which relies on the Widcomm Bluetooth client software. It closely mimics how Windows XP handles files and network devices.

TIP

Your mileage may vary with other Bluetooth adapters and clients, although we've found them all to be quite similar.

Setting a Windows XP PC to Be Discovered

The Widcomm software places a Bluetooth icon in the System Tray (**Figure 11.2**). To set your computer to be discovered, install the Bluetooth adapter and then follow these steps:

Figure 11.2
Bluetooth icon in
the System Tray.

Bluetooth icon

1. Right-click the Bluetooth icon and select Advanced Configuration to open the Bluetooth Configuration dialog.

2. In the General tab, enter a name for the computer and choose the Computer Type from the pop-up menu (**Figure 11.3**).

3. Click the Accessibility tab, and confirm that Let Other Bluetooth Devices Discover This Computer is selected (**Figure 11.4**).

4. Click Apply or OK to apply the settings.

The Windows machine remains discoverable as long as the Let Other Bluetooth Devices Discover This Computer checkbox in the Accessibility tab is selected.

Figure 11.3
Setting the
computer's name
and type.

Figure 11.4
Turning
discoverability on.

Discovering Other Devices

Once you've made the device or computer you want to pair with discoverable, the next step is to discover other devices. Follow these steps:

1. Double-click the System Tray Bluetooth icon to open the My Bluetooth Places window (**Figure 11.5**).

2. Click the Bluetooth Setup Wizard link under Bluetooth Tasks.

3. In the Bluetooth Setup Wizard, select the second item in the list—"I want to find a specific Bluetooth device..."—and click Next to make the Bluetooth adapter search for available devices (**Figure 11.6**).

Figure 11.5
The Bluetooth
Setup Wizard's link.

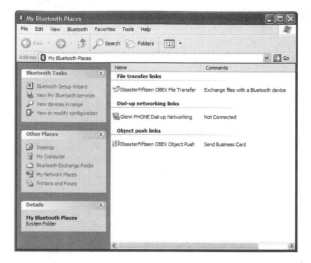

Figure 11.6
Choosing the
Bluetooth
configuration task.

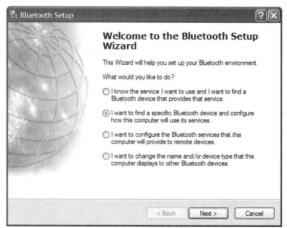

4. Wait for the software to complete its search for Bluetooth devices. The flashlight will stop waving. Choose the device you want to configure from the list and click Next (**Figure 11.7**).

5. Check the services you want to attach to the device (**Figure 11.8**). You can select dial-up networking (for cellular data), OBEX File Transfer (to exchange files), and Bluetooth-PDA-Sync (for Palm OS/Pocket PC synchronization). For each service, click the Configure button to configure its settings (**Figure 11.9**).

6. Click Finish.

You can change settings by running through these steps again, making the desired changes as you go.

Figure 11.7
Selecting available
Bluetooth devices.

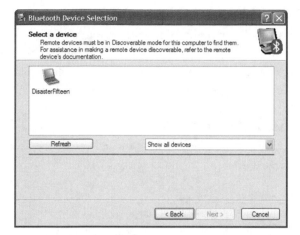

Figure 11.8
Choosing Bluetooth
services.

Figure 11.9
Configuring
services.

((•)) **NOTE**

For concrete examples, read "Practical Bluetooth," later in this chapter.

Pairing Under Mac OS X

Apple now offers built-in Bluetooth adapters with many of its new desktop Macs and PowerBooks, or you can buy an inexpensive Bluetooth adapter. Once you have the necessary hardware, you configure Bluetooth in Mac OS X in the Bluetooth preferences pane available in System Preferences.

Setting a Mac to Be Discovered

If you have the Bluetooth menu turned on in the menu bar, just choose Discoverable from that menu (**Figure 11.10**).

Figure 11.10
Choosing Discoverable from the Bluetooth menu.

TIP

*To turn on the Bluetooth menu, select System Preferences from the Apple menu and click the Bluetooth icon to open the Bluetooth preferences pane. Click the Settings tab, and then check Show Bluetooth Status in the Menu Bar (**Figure 11.11**).*

If you don't want to devote menu bar space to the Bluetooth menu, you can turn on discoverability by opening System Preferences, clicking the Bluetooth icon to open the Bluetooth preferences pane, and selecting Discoverable in the Settings tab (**Figure 11.11**).

NOTE

If Bluetooth is turned off, as it can be on some PowerBooks and Power Macs, click the Turn Bluetooth On button in the Bluetooth preferences pane to turn it on.

The Mac remains discoverable for as long as Discoverable is selected on the Bluetooth menu or the Discoverable box is checked in the Bluetooth preferences pane. Its Bluetooth name is the same as the name of your computer in the Sharing preferences pane.

Discovering Other Devices

After making the device you want to pair with a Mac discoverable, you can use the Bluetooth Setup Assistant to help you connect to it.

Figure 11.11
Enabling the
Bluetooth menu.

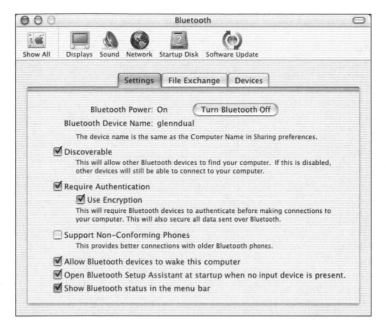

1. Open System Preferences and click the Bluetooth icon to open the Bluetooth preferences pane.

2. Select the Devices tab (**Figure 11.12**).

3. Click Set Up New Device and follow the Bluetooth Setup Assistant's prompts (**Figure 11.13**).

Figure 11.12
The Devices tab.

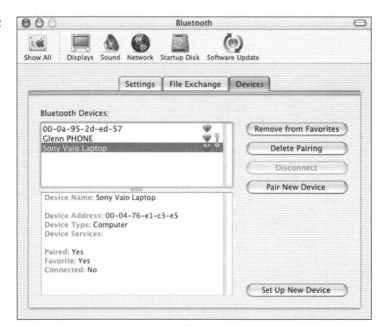

If you're more inclined to handle the details yourself, or if the device requires manual configuration for some reason, follow these steps:

1. Open the Bluetooth preferences pane.

2. Select the Devices tab.

3. Click the Pair New Device button.

4. Select the device you want to pair with from the Device list (**Figure 11.14**). (If it doesn't appear, try resetting the other device and clicking Search Again.)

5. Click Pair.

6. The Mac prompts you for a passphrase (which Apple calls a "passkey"), if needed (**Figure 11.15**).

Figure 11.15
Entering the passphrase on a Mac.

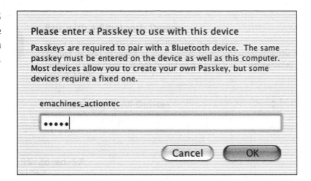

7. If the other device requires a passphrase, enter the same passphrase when prompted (**Figure 11.16**).

Figure 11.16
Entering the passphrase on another device (a Windows PC in this case).

Practical Bluetooth

Pairing devices is like introducing yourself to someone at a dance: a necessary first step, but not exactly the goal. We offer three practical scenarios for how you might use Bluetooth: synchronizing a Palm, exchanging files, and adding a wireless mouse.

 TIP

Cell phones are increasingly sold with Bluetooth support built in, and more applications are taking advantage of this support. So why aren't we giving a cell phone example here? Because we talk about using a cell phone for cellular data in Chapter 30, Using Cellular Data Networks, *where we show how to set up an Internet connection.*

TIP

We also recommend that you look at the extensive Bluetooth coverage in Rob Flickenger's book Wireless Hacks, *which demonstrates using a variety of interesting applications, including Salling Clicker (*http://homepage.mac.com/ jonassalling/Shareware/Clicker/*), a Mac OS X program that lets you control your Mac via a cell phone!*

Palm Synchronization

There are, of course, two sides to a Palm synchronization: you must first pair your computer to the Palm, after which the Palm will accept connections from the computer. Make your computer discoverable as described earlier in this chapter. Then follow these instructions for Palm OS 5.2.

Pairing with the Computer

1. Tap the Prefs icon in Applications Launcher.

2. Tap Communication; then tap Connection (**Figure 11.17**).

3. In the Available Connections dialog, tap the New button (**Figure 11.18**).

4. Enter a name for the connection in the Name field (**Figure 11.19**).

5. Tap the arrow next to Connect To and choose PC.

6. Tap the arrow next to "Via:" and choose Bluetooth.

7. Next to the Device label, tap the box marked "Tap to Find." The Discovery Results dialog appears, listing all the available devices (**Figure 11.20**).

8. Select your computer from the list.

TIP

If you don't see your computer in the Discovery Results list, make sure you've made it discoverable.

9. Choose No when the Palm prompts you to add the PC to the Trusted Device List. (Palm says to choose No; we're not sure why it matters.)

10. Back in the Edit Connection screen, tap OK, and then tap Done.

Windows XP Setup

With the Palm Desktop and HotSync software installed, follow these steps:

1. Right-click the HotSync Manager icon in the System Tray and choose Local Serial if it doesn't already have a checkmark next to it (**Figure 11.21**).

Figure 11.17
The Palm's
Communication
preferences.

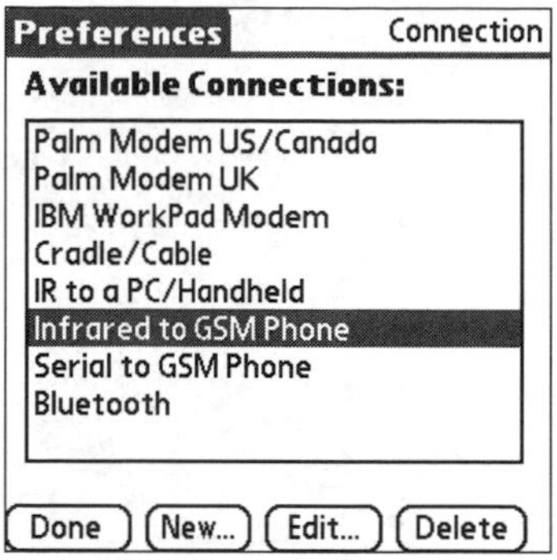

Figure 11.18
Starting a new
connection.

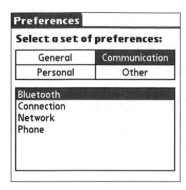

Figure 11.19
Setting up your
new connection's
details.

Figure 11
.20
Choosing a
computer to
sync to.

Figure 11.21
Making sure Local
Serial is checked.

2. Right-click the HotSync Manager icon again and choose Setup to open the Setup dialog.

3. Click the Local tab.

4. Choose the COM port that's been assigned by the Bluetooth software to the serial port (**Figure 11.22**).

5. Click OK to finish the setup and close the Setup dialog.

Figure 11.22
Selecting the
assigned COM port.

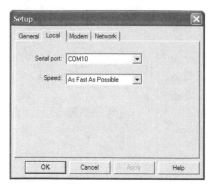

Mac OS X Setup

With Palm Desktop and the Palm's HotSync Manager software installed,
follow these steps:

1. Open HotSync Manager (likely in the Palm folder in your Applications
   folder).

2. Select the Enabled radio button (**Figure 11.23**).

3. Click the Connection Settings tab.

4. Check the box next to "blueto…nc-port", which is short for "bluetooth-
   pda-sync-port" (**Figure 11.24**).

5. Quit HotSync Manager.

Palm HotSync

You're finally ready to synchronize data after all those steps—remember that
you must set Bluetooth synchronization up only once, and then it should work
until you switch to a new computer or Palm handheld.

Figure 11.23
Enabling HotSync.

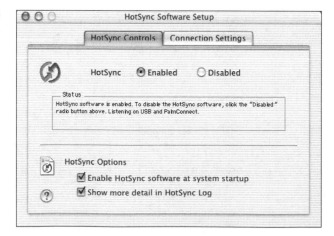

Figure 11.24
Enabling the
Bluetooth PDA
synchronization
port.

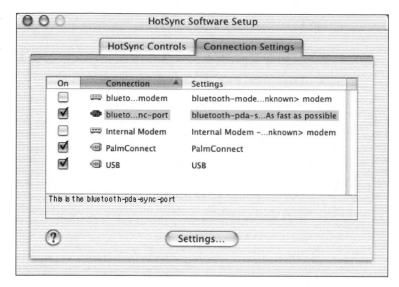

1. From the Applications Launcher, tap HotSync.

2. Tap the Menu icon in the Graffiti area. If the Options menu does not drop down, tap Options.

3. Choose LANSync Prefs from the Options menu to open the LANSync Preferences dialog (**Figure 11.25**).

4. Tap LANSync.

5. Tap OK to return to the HotSync screen.

6. Tap Local.

7. Tap the box below the HotSync icon and choose the Bluetooth connection you created in the "Pairing with the Computer" steps (**Figure 11.26**).

8. Tap the HotSync icon to start synchronization.

Figure 11.25
Setting LANSync.

Figure 11.26
Selecting the
Bluetooth
connection.

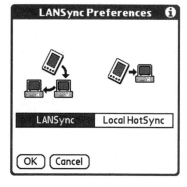

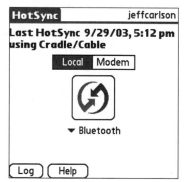

Exchanging Files

Bluetooth isn't ideal for transferring files, because of its low speed: after subtracting network overhead, it shoots data at well under 1 Mbps. But there are many cases in which you want to move smaller files around without the overhead of enabling Wi-Fi, setting up ad hoc networking, and connecting to a network. Once you've paired two computers or a handheld and a computer, transferring files is a breeze.

First, follow the instructions earlier in this chapter under "Pairing" to connect two devices. You may have to pair in both directions for a file exchange. Then run the file exchange utility appropriate to the platform you're using.

Windows XP

In Windows, you should open your Bluetooth software. Using the Widcomm software we discussed earlier, follow these steps to exchange files:

1. Right-click the Bluetooth icon in the System Tray and choose My Bluetooth Places to open the My Bluetooth Places window (**Figure 11.27**).

Figure 11.27
Opening a paired device for file transfer.

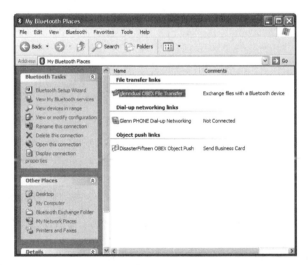

2. Under File Transfer Links, double-click the icon for the device you want to transfer files with to open a normal directory window displaying the files on the other device (**Figure 11.28**).

3. Drag files in or out—just as you would when moving or copying files normally—to transfer them between the two devices.

Figure 11.28
Viewing shared files.

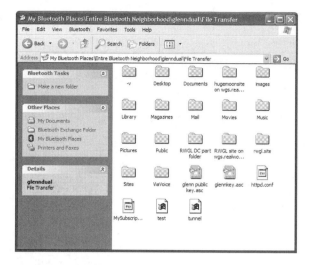

Mac OS X

Follow these steps to exchange files between a Mac running Mac OS X and another Bluetooth device.

1. Launch Bluetooth File Exchange in the Applications folder's Utilities folder.

2. The program immediately presents you with a standard file browsing dialog. Select a file to transfer and click Send (**Figure 11.29**). This doesn't send the file, but queues the file up for the next step.

Figure 11.29
Choosing a file to send.

3. Select the paired device to receive the file (**Figure 11.30**).

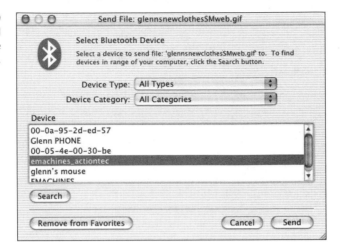

Figure 11.30
Selecting the paired
device to receive
the file.

4. Click Send.

NOTE

*If you choose a file that the receiving device won't understand, you should see an error message like the one in **Figure 11.31**.*

Figure 11.31
An error message
appears when
you try to send an
unsupported file
type.

 TIP

*You can also browse and copy the files in a shared directory on the other device by choosing Browse from the File menu in Bluetooth File Exchange, and then choosing a device (**Figure 11.32**).*

Adding a Bluetooth Mouse

There are several Bluetooth mice on the market now, including models offered by Apple and Microsoft. We thought we'd show you the ease with which you could add the Apple Wireless Mouse to a Mac.

NOTE

We failed to make the Apple Wireless Mouse work with a Windows machine. Apple said the mouse wasn't designed to be entirely compatible with Windows,

Figure 11.32
Browsing files in
a chosen paired
device's shared
directory.

and the company's engineers hadn't tweaked it to work with the many different Bluetooth adapters and drivers available for Windows as of this writing.

1. If necessary, install the Bluetooth software that comes with the mouse.

2. Turn the mouse on using its power switch.

3. Run the Bluetooth Setup Assistant program found in the Applications folder's Utilities folder, and at the first screen, click Continue.

4. In the Select Device Type screen, choose Mouse and click Continue (**Figure 11.33**).

Figure 11.33
Selecting the mouse
as the device type.

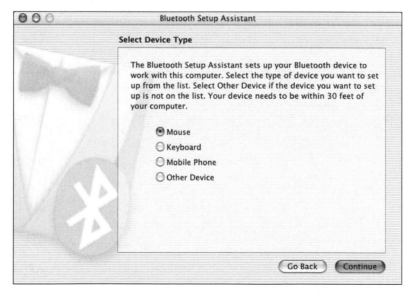

5. From the Bluetooth Mouse Set Up screen, select your mouse from the Mice list and click Continue (**Figure 11.34**).

6. Mac OS X automatically pairs with your mouse (**Figure 11.35**). Click Continue to display the final screen, and then click Quit.

7. Open the Keyboard & Mouse preferences pane, and then click the Bluetooth tab. From this tab, you can name the mouse (or an Apple Wireless Keyboard), and keep track of the life left in its batteries (**Figure 11.36**).

Figure 11.34 Selecting your wireless mouse.

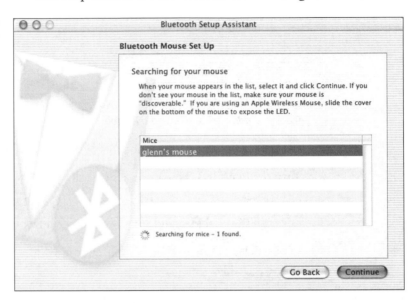

Figure 11.35 Automatic device pairing.

Figure 11.36
Adjusting Wireless
Mouse settings.

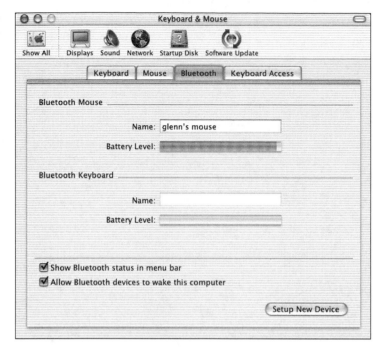

Creating an Ad Hoc Wireless Network

Wi-Fi devices support two networking modes: the *infrastructure* mode in which clients associate with access points acting as central routing points, and a more informal mode called *ad hoc*, which means, in this context, "for a particular purpose at hand." Ad hoc networks are created among two or more machines that then act as if they're on the same tiny network.

 TIP

> *Windows ad hoc networks can be routed to another network, such as an Internet-connected dial-up or Ethernet network. We discuss this in Chapter 19,* Creating a Software Access Point. *If you're connecting Macs, you don't need to create an ad hoc network before turning on Software Base Station (Mac OS 9) or Internet Sharing (Mac OS X).*

No one machine maintains the network, but it remains in effect as long as any machine is in ad hoc mode. A network of one is pretty lonely, though.

 TIP

> *Ad hoc networking may not work correctly among wireless network adapters sold by different companies before 2002. See Chapter 2,* Wireless Standards, *for more on this topic.*

How you enable ad hoc mode on your computer varies depending on the operating system and software. Typically, you enable a setting in the client software that turns on "computer-to-computer networking" or "ad hoc mode" (different manufacturers use different names). You must also pick a channel over which the two computers will connect, but once you set a channel, other computers will find it automatically. You can almost always enable WEP encryption over an ad hoc connection, although it's probably not worth the effort unless you believe there are other people nearby who can connect to your ad hoc network, you believe they have ill intent, and you will be transferring sensitive data over your ad hoc network.

 NOTE

Luckily, you don't have to configure your network settings when all you're doing is connecting a pair of computers to each other in ad hoc mode. That's because both Windows XP and Mac OS 8.6 and later support a standard method of choosing IP addresses in the 169.254.x.x range that don't conflict.

Creating an Ad Hoc Network in Windows XP

The process of creating an ad hoc network in Windows XP requires a number of steps, but they're not difficult to carry out.

TIP

If you're using another version of Windows, the process of setting up an ad hoc network is usually performed inside the connection utility bundled with your Wi-Fi adapter.

1. From the Control Panel, choose Network Connections, and then open the Wireless Network Connection dialog.

2. Click Properties.

3. Click the Wireless Networks tab.

4. Click Advanced at the bottom of the window.

5. Select Computer-to-Computer (Ad Hoc) Networks Only, and deselect Automatically Connect to Non-Preferred Networks (**Figure 12.1**).

6. Click Close.

Figure 12.1
Creating a computer-to-computer network in Windows XP.

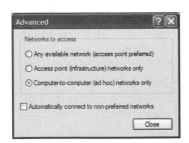

7. Click the Add button under Preferred Networks.

8. Enter a network name for your ad hoc network (**Figure 12.2**). (Note that Windows identifies the connection as ad hoc in the bottom of the window using a strange method of a checkbox option that's selected but dimmed and disabled.)

Figure 12.2
Configuring a computer-to-computer network in Windows XP.

9. Set any WEP options you want.

10. Click OK.

In the Preferred Networks list, you now see your network with a PC Card icon next to it to indicate it's an ad hoc network. A red X brand on the icon indicates no other computers are yet connected.

Other Windows XP clients see this network in their list of Available Networks with the same PC Card icon, and computers running other operating systems see it as they would any other wireless network.

Creating an Ad Hoc Network in Mac OS 8.6/9.x

Under Mac OS 8.6 and 9.x creating an ad hoc network is a simple operation.

1. If you use Apple's Control Strip utility, choose Create Network from the AirPort menu on the Control Strip and then jump to step 5.

2. Otherwise, open the AirPort application, typically located in an AirPort folder inside either your Applications folder or the Apple Extras folder.

3. Click the Settings expansion triangle to show the extra settings.

4. In the AirPort Network section, from the Choose Network pop-up menu, choose Create Computer to Computer Network (**Figure 12.3**).

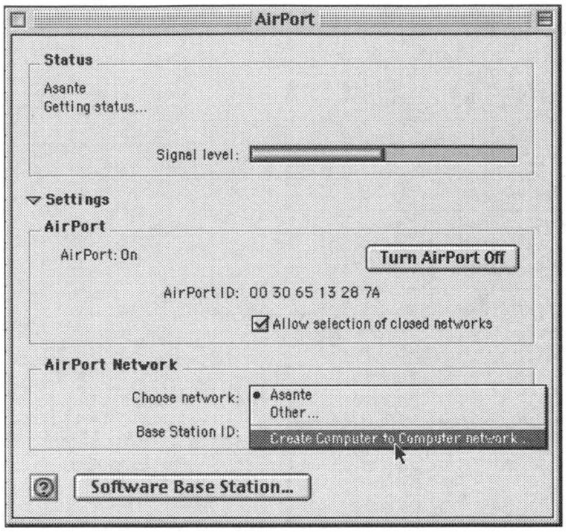

Figure 12.3
Creating a computer-to-computer network in the Mac OS 9 AirPort application.

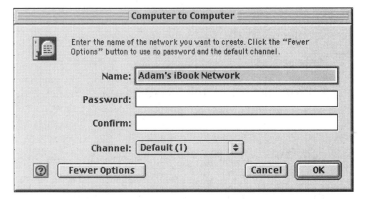

5. In the Computer to Computer dialog box that appears, name your network (**Figure 12.4**).

Figure 12.4
Naming your computer-to-computer network.

6. If you want to assign a password or change the default channel, click More Options and set the desired information. (**Figure 12.4** shows a Fewer Options button because we've already displayed the extra options!)

7. Click OK when you're done.

Once you've created an ad hoc network, other people connect to it just as they would to any other wireless network, whether they're using Macs or PCs.

Creating an Ad Hoc Network in Mac OS X

Creating an ad hoc network in Mac OS X is even easier than either of the other operating systems.

1. Choose Create Network from the AirPort menu in the menu bar.

 TIP

You can also open the Internet Connect application and choose Create Network from the Network pop-up menu, but that's more effort and doesn't give you the option of enabling WEP.

2. Either way, in the Computer to Computer dialog that appears, enter a name for your network and pick a channel (**Figure 12.5**).

Figure 12.5
Creating a computer-to-computer network in Mac OS X.

> **Computer to Computer**
>
> Please enter the following information to create a Computer to Computer Network:
>
> Name: Adam Engst's iBook
>
> Channel: Automatic (11)
>
> ☐ Enable encryption (using WEP)
>
> Password:
>
> Confirm:
>
> WEP key: 40-bit (more compatible)
>
> (Hide Options)   (Cancel)   (OK)

3. If you want to password-protect your ad hoc network, check the Enable Encryption (Using WEP) checkbox and enter your password.

4. Click OK when you're done.

Once you've created an ad hoc network, other people connect to it just as they would to any other wireless network, whether they're using Macs or PCs.

Sharing Files and Printers

For most people, the primary goal in setting up a wireless network is to share an Internet connection. Second only to that is sharing files locally, or over the Internet using local file servers on your end or remotely. You can set up file sharing on both Windows and the Macintosh with relative ease, and you can even share files between operating systems, as **Table 13.1** shows below. You need a program called Dave from Thursby Software Systems (www.thursby.com/products/dave.html) to share files between Mac OS 9 and Windows.

 NOTE

*We include Unix in **Table 13.1** (and we use the term loosely to mean Unix, Linux, BSD, and other variants) for completeness, since Unix is remarkably adept at talking to old and new Mac and Windows systems. In fact, with Samba or Netatalk running (see table footnote), mounting a Unix volume is identical to mounting a Windows or Mac volume.*

Let's look at how you set up basic file sharing.

TIP

Both Windows and the Mac OS offer instructions for setting up file sharing in their help systems, in case you need help beyond what we provide here.

Windows XP

The specific instructions for sharing files varies among different versions of Windows, although the basics are the same. We concentrate on Windows XP as the simplest and newest version.

Table 13.1

File Sharing Compatibility at a Glance

Connecting Platform	Connects to Windows XP File Server	Connects to Mac OS 9 File Server	Connects to Mac OS X File Server	Connects to Unix File Server*
Windows XP	Yes	Requires Dave in Mac OS 9	Yes, if Windows File Sharing is turned on in Mac OS X	Yes, if the SMB (Samba) service is running on the Unix machine
Mac OS 9	Requires Dave in Mac OS 9	Yes	Yes	Yes, if Netatalk or similar package is installed on the Unix machine
Mac OS X	Yes	Yes	Yes	Yes, if Samba or Netatalk is installed on the Unix machine
Linux	Yes	Yes	Yes	Yes

Most Unix variants shipped in the last several years either include or can easily have installed Windows-style Samba servers (www.samba.org), Netatalk for AppleTalk and AppleShare (http://netatalk.sourceforge.net/), and other packages for Windows and Mac compatibility.

(((•))) **NOTE**

If you're using Windows 2000 Server or Windows Server 2003 (other than the Web Edition), you can also turn on AppleTalk and Services for Macintosh, which enable Macs (even those running Mac OS 9 or earlier) to connect to shared folders. Check Microsoft's help system for additional instructions.

Sharing Files

Follow these instructions to share a folder in Windows XP.

1. From Control Panel, open Network Connections, open Wireless Network Connection, and click the Properties button to open the Properties dialog.

2. Check both Client for Microsoft Networks and File and Printer Sharing for Microsoft Networks, and then click OK (**Figure 13.1**).

3. Locate the folder you want to share, right-click it, and choose Sharing and Security.

4. In the Network Sharing and Security part of the Shared Document Properties dialog, check Share This Folder on the Network, enter a name for the shared folder, and if you want people to be able to add and modify files in the shared folder, check Allow Network Users to Change My Files (**Figure 13.2**).

Figure 13.1
Enabling file
sharing.

Figure 13.2
Sharing a folder.

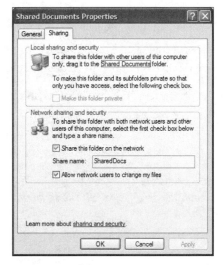

5.   Click OK.

That's all there is to it; the files in the shared folder should now be accessible to any other computer on your network that can access a Windows shared folder.

Accessing Shared Files

Follow these instructions on a computer running Windows XP to access shared network folders.

1.   From the Start menu, choose My Network Places.

2. Click View Workgroup Computers. By default, Windows shows you just the machines in your own workgroup (**Figure 13.3**). To reach computers in other workgroups, use the location bar at the top of the window to navigate up a level.

Figure 13.3
Accessing a shared folder.

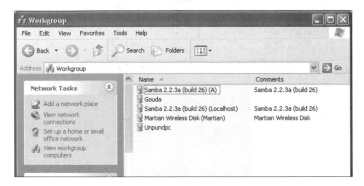

3. Double-click the name of the computer to which you want to connect.

4. Typically, Windows prompts you to enter the user name and password for access; it's not wise to have unprotected folders, but some people still do.

The shared folder is now mounted, and shows up in lists of available volumes in My Computer and other views. You can open and browse it just as you would any other volume.

 TIP

You can use the Map Network Drive option in the Tools menu to set a remote volume to mount automatically with the same drive letter each time you restart.

Mac OS 9

Sharing and accessing files in Mac OS 9 is relatively easy, but remember that you need Dave to integrate Mac OS 9 with Windows.

 NOTE

Dave provides its own control panel for setting up file sharing, although it integrates into the Chooser for accessing shared folders.

Sharing Files

In Mac OS 9, if you're the only person using file sharing among your computers, you can skip some of the configuration steps. Otherwise, you must work through all the steps below.

1. From the hierarchical Control Panels menu in the Apple menu, choose File Sharing to open the File Sharing control panel.

2. In the Start/Stop tab, make sure you have an owner name and computer name entered. If there's any chance someone else could access your Mac over the network, enter an owner password (**Figure 13.4**). Always enter a password if you enable TCP/IP file sharing in the next step.

Figure 13.4
Configuring the File Sharing control panel.

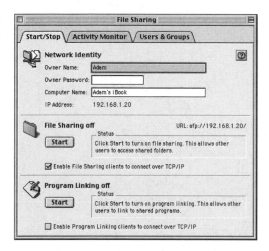

3. Click the Start button in the File Sharing section of the control panel, and if you want File Sharing to be available over TCP/IP as well as AppleTalk, check Enable File Sharing Clients to Connect over TCP/IP. If you are the only person who connects to your computer from other machines, you're done, because you need only your owner name and password to connect.

TIP

Enabling file sharing over TCP/IP is necessary if you want to share files over the Internet. It also simplifies connections with Mac OS X machines, since they must otherwise have AppleTalk turned on for the active network adapter.

4. Click the Users & Groups tab. You can create users and groups if you want fine-grained control over who can access which folders, but for this situation, just double-click the default Guest user, select Sharing from the Show menu, and check Allow Guests to Connect to This Computer (**Figure 13.5**). Close the File Sharing control panel.

5. Select a disk or folder to share, Control-click it, and from the hierarchical Get Info menu, choose Sharing to open the Get Info window's Sharing view (**Figure 13.6**).

Figure 13.5
Enabling a guest
user to connect.

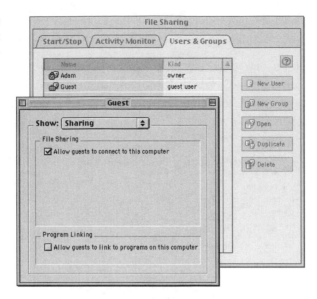

Figure 13.6
Sharing a disk.

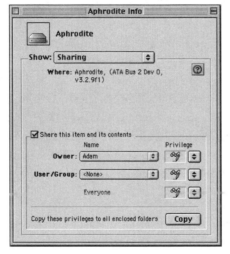

6. Check Share This Item and Its Contents, and from the pop-up menu next to the Everyone line, choose the privileges you want to give to people who connect.

(((•))) **NOTE**

Read & Write privileges let users see, copy, add, change, and delete files. Read Only privileges let them see and copy files. Write Only (Drop Box) lets people copy files to the folder without being able to see anything else that's there. And, of course, None prevents them from seeing or touching any files.

7. Close the Get Info window.

You're done!

Accessing Shared Files

Once you've shared a disk or folder on one Mac, you can access them from other Macs, though not Windows. Follow these steps on a Macintosh running OS 9.

1. From the Apple menu, choose Chooser.

2. In the Chooser, click the AppleShare icon.

    If any of your Macs use AppleTalk to share files, they appear in the list under Select a File Server (**Figure 13.7**).

Figure 13.7
Browsing for
shared Macs in the
Chooser.

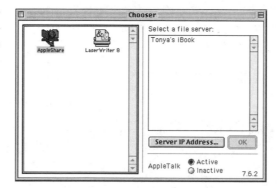

3. Either double-click a Mac in the list or click the Server IP Address button and, in the dialog box that appears, enter the IP address of the server to which you want to connect, and click the Connect button (**Figure 13.8**).

Figure 13.8
Entering the IP
address of a
shared Mac.

4. In the dialog box that appears, enter your user name and password for the Mac that's sharing the files you want to access, and then click Connect (**Figure 13.9**).

 TIP

Check Add to Keychain in the Connect dialog box if you don't want to type your password each time you access this Mac.

A dialog box appears with a list of accessible volumes (**Figure 13.10**).

5. Select the volume you want to access and click OK.

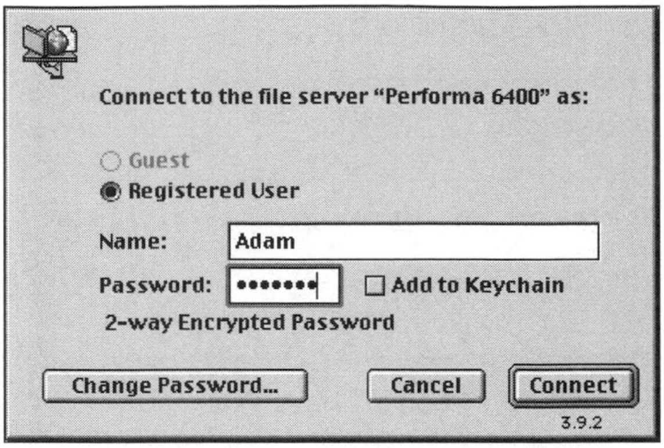

Figure 13.9
Entering your
user name and
password.

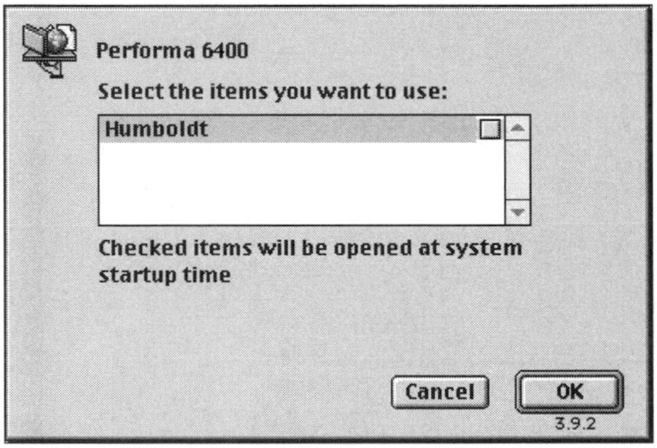

Connect to the file server "Performa 6400" as:

○ Guest
● Registered User

Name: Adam

Password: •••••••   ☐ Add to Keychain

2-way Encrypted Password

[Change Password...]   [Cancel] [Connect]
                                          3.9.2

Figure 13.10
Selecting a volume
to access.

Performa 6400

Select the items you want to use:

Humboldt   ☐

Checked items will be opened at system
startup time

[Cancel] [OK]
              3.9.2

The shared disk or folder to which you're connecting appears on your Desktop like any other disk icon, and you're done.

TIP

You can make an alias to any file or folder on the shared volume and double-click it to mount the volume automatically in the future. If you want a particular network volume available all the time, put an alias to the server in the Servers folder in the System Folder.

Mac OS X

Apple simplified the process of sharing files and connecting to shared folders in Mac OS X, and added the capability to share files with Windows computers and to access Windows shared folders. Dave works with Mac OS X, but it may be needed only to replace Mac OS X's built-in capabilities in specific situations, such as on certain large networks.

Sharing Files

To share files with Macs and Windows-based computers, follow these steps:

1. Open System Preferences, and click the Sharing icon to display the Sharing preferences pane.

2. In the Services tab, select the On checkbox next to Personal File Sharing. If you want to share files with Windows users or via FTP, select the On checkboxes next to those services as well (**Figure 13.11**).

Figure 13.11
Configuring the
Sharing preferences
pane.

3. To share files, put them in the Public folder in your Home folder, at which point anyone can access them without needing a special user name or password.

 TIP

Once file sharing is turned on, anyone who has an account on your Mac OS X machine can access it remotely using their normal user name and password, but they'll be limited to seeing the files that they can see when logged into the machine normally.

 TIP

If you want to share files outside of your Public folder with specific users, check out HornWare's SharePoints, which makes Mac OS X work a bit more like Mac OS 9 in terms of sharing files and working with users and groups. You can find it at www.hornware.com/sharepoints/.

Accessing Shared Files

In Mac OS X 10.2, follow these steps to access folders shared via standard Macintosh file sharing (AppleTalk File Protocol, or AFP), Windows file sharing (SMB), FTP, or WebDAV.

TIP

Apple provides additional hints about this process at http://docs.info. apple.com/article.html?artnum=106471.

1. From the Finder's Go menu, choose Connect to Server to bring up the Connect to Server dialog (**Figure 13.12**).

Figure 13.12
Accessing shared folders in the Connect to Server dialog.

2. If the shared folder (or the workgroup that contains it, for Windows machines) you want to access appears in the list of servers, double-click it to mount it. If it doesn't appear, type the server's URL in the Address field at the bottom of the dialog and click Connect.

TIP

You don't have to type afp:// *at the start of the address if you're connecting to another Mac sharing files via personal file sharing (AFP); however, to connect to Windows, FTP, and WebDAV servers, you must prefix the IP address or domain name with* smb://, ftp://, *or* http://, *respectively.*

TIP

In Mac OS X 10.3 Panther, Apple simplified this process significantly. Just open a new Finder window and click the Network icon to see available servers.

A Connect To dialog appears, asking for your name and password (**Figure 13.13**).

3. Enter your name and password, and click Connect.

TIP

Click Options and check Add Password to Keychain if you don't want to type your password each time you access this particular shared folder.

Figure 13.13
Entering your
user name and
password.

A dialog that lists accessible volumes appears (**Figure 13.14**). If you're connecting to a Mac OS X machine with an administrator account, you see at least two volumes: one for the hard disk and another for your Home directory.

Figure 13.14
Selecting a volume
to access.

4. Select the volume you want to access and click OK.

   The shared folder or disk to which you're connecting appears on your Desktop like any other disk icon, and you're done!

 TIP

As with Mac OS 9, you can make an alias to any item on a shared volume and then double-click it to mount the volume automatically and open the item. To connect to a server at startup, just drag its icon into your Login Items preferences pane.

Sharing Printers

Sharing files between computers running different operating systems is relatively straightforward. Sharing printers, particularly those that are directly connected to a computer, is another story entirely, which is why we offer these notes rather than step-by-step instructions.

- Your best hope for sharing printers between Macs and PCs is to use a PostScript laser printer that connects directly to your wired Ethernet network or plugs into the Ethernet port of a wireless gateway. Every operating system version should be able to print to such a printer.

- If you want to print from Classic applications in Mac OS X, you must configure the printer setup from within Classic as well.

- If you share a USB-based inkjet printer from a Mac running Mac OS X, other Macs running Mac OS X will have no trouble printing to it. However, if you want to share the same printer with Macs running Mac OS 9, you must launch the Classic environment, with the USB Printer Sharing Extension enabled.

- To make a USB printer connected to a Mac—either Mac OS 9 or Mac OS X—available to Windows-based computers, you need Dave from Thursby Software Systems.

- Similarly, to make a USB printer connected to a PC running Windows accessible to Macs, you need Dave. Sensing the theme here?

- You can connect a printer to the parallel port of a wireless gateway that also offers a print server, but Macs won't see the printer unless it's a PostScript printer. It should be readily available to PCs.

- Sharing a USB printer by connecting it to the USB port on an AirPort Extreme Base Station works only for Macs running Mac OS X 10.2.3 or later. Also, not all printers are compatible; see a list of compatible models at www.apple.com/airport/printcompatibility.html.

- If all else fails, you might be able to work around not being able to share a printer by printing to PDF files, transferring them to the computer that can print, and printing from there. You can, of course, create PDFs with Adobe's full Acrobat package, but that's often overkill. For fast and easy (and cheap) PDF creation in Windows, try pdfFactory (www.pdffactory.com) or activePDF Composer (www.activepdf.com). In Mac OS 9, check out James Walker's PrintToPDF utility (www.jwwalker.com/pages/pdf.html), and in Mac OS X, just click the Save As PDF button in any Print dialog.

Troubleshooting Your Connection

For the most part, connecting to a wireless network is fairly easy and trouble-free. However, that's not to say that you'll never run into trouble, particularly when you set up a new wireless network adapter, move to a new wireless network, or change a setup that was previously functional.

In this chapter, we've broken down common problems you may experience while making a connection to a wireless network into broad categories. In each case, we offer suggestions for tests you can run or questions you can ask to shed light on your problem. The result of one of these tests or the answer to one of the questions should point to your solution.

((•)) **NOTE**

*We **strongly** recommend that you read Appendix C, How to Troubleshoot, before you read farther. That appendix has basic advice and steps for working through any problem, not just those you might encounter when troubleshooting a recalcitrant wireless networking connection.*

((•)) **NOTE**

This chapter addresses problems from the standpoint of making a connection work in a situation where you may or may not have control over the access point or wireless network. For suggestions on how to troubleshoot problems related to setting up and running a wireless network, read Chapter 23, Troubleshooting Your Wireless Network.

TIP

Even if you don't use a Mac, it's worth reading Apple's detailed troubleshooting guide for AirPort wireless networking technology—AirPort is just 802.11b so the guide covers more than just Mac-related information. Find it at http:// docs.info.apple.com/article.html?artnum=106858. *Also try the Wireless Network Troubleshooting page at* www.practicallynetworked.com/support/ troubleshoot_wireless.htm.

TIP

*In the Windows XP help system, you'll find an interactive, network troubleshooting guide that includes some wireless advice (**Figure 14.1**). It can walk you step-by-step through common problems and advise you on configuring or reconfiguring your settings.*

Figure 14.1
The Windows XP Network Troubleshooter offers advice about wireless network problems.

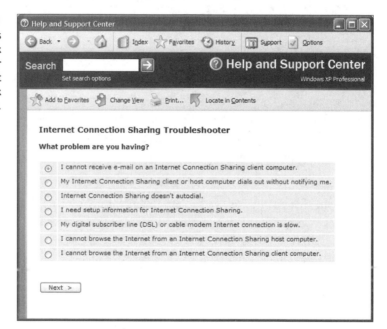

Problem: Can't See Wireless Network

Q: **My wireless network client software can't see a wireless network that I know exists. What can I do to convince it to connect?**

A: This is, unfortunately, a broad problem, with many different types of tests to run:

- This may seem obvious, but make sure your wireless network adapter is turned on. PC Cards and Apple's AirPort and AirPort Extreme cards can be turned off through a software setting to save power in laptops.

- Does the activity LED flash or come on at all? If not, the card, or perhaps the slot or port into which you're plugging the card, could be dead. It's also possible that external power is required in the case of a USB or an Ethernet adapter.

- Disconnect and reconnect your wireless network adapter and any cables that connect to it. You'd be amazed how many problems are solved by re-establishing physical connections. And, yes, we realize how annoying this can be to do with an internal card.

 TIP

If your adapter is a PC Card, you may have to tell the system to halt the card so it can be removed. However, if your system won't even recognize the card, you must remove it while it's technically still active. Triple-check before removing an active card, or, better yet, shut down the computer entirely first. In Windows, you typically halt a card by right-clicking its System Tray icon and choosing the appropriate menu item; on the Mac, you may need to Control-click the card's Desktop icon and choose Eject.

- If possible, plug the network adapter into another computer and see if it works there. If it doesn't, it may be dead, and you should check the warranty. (Try it in a third machine, if you can, just to be on the safe side.)

- Ask to have the access point reset or power cycled (turn it off, wait about 30 seconds, turn it back on). It's quite common for inexpensive wireless gateways to become wedged and need to be reset. Pressing a reset button may not be as effective as cycling the power.

 NOTE

Make sure other users aren't in the middle of something important before you cycle the power. Power cycling an access point disables everyone's access, and it can shuffle out new DHCP-assigned addresses.

- Make sure you have the latest wireless network client software (which resides on your computer) and firmware (which resides on the adapter itself). If you don't have the latest appropriate versions, update them as necessary. Sometimes an inability to update drivers or firmware indicates deeper, non-wireless problems with the system. Visit the manufacturer's Web site for downloads.

TIP

Most wireless adapters and access points had one or more major firmware updates in 2003 to support a variety of security and other changes. If you've never updated the firmware, you should.

- If you're using third-party wireless network client software, reinstall it from the original CD-ROM or installer.

- Under Windows, try uninstalling all wireless adapter drivers, and then reinstalling just the one you need.

- Under Windows, you can try to boot in "Safe Mode with Networking," which can help by disabling other services and subsystems. Restart the computer, and then—once the text "Starting Windows" appears in the text part of the startup process—hold down the F8 key. If the problem goes away, you can conclude that the problem most likely relates to something that didn't load under "Safe Mode with Networking." Your next step might be to reinstall the operating system or to test other networking software to see if it is causing the problem.

- In Windows XP, make sure your Wireless Zero Configuration service is started. Even if it's running, try restarting it by clicking the Stop button and then the Start button (see the sidebar "Windows XP Wireless Network Connections Dimmed," later in this chapter).

- In Mac OS 9 or earlier, reboot using the "Mac OS All" set of extensions to rule out a conflict with a third-party extension (**Figure 14.2**). If the network adapter works under the "Mac OS All" set of extensions, you must figure out which third-party extension is conflicting. Once you identify the conflict, you can turn off the offending extension or find out if an update to the extension solves the problem.

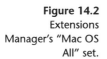

Figure 14.2
Extensions Manager's "Mac OS All" set.

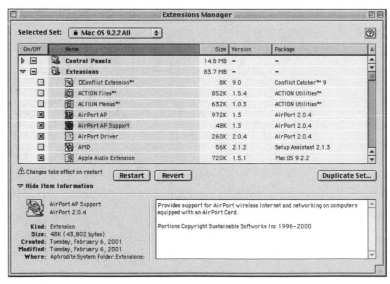

- If you have both Mac OS 9 and Mac OS X installed, test in both operating systems to determine if the wireless network adapter works in one but not the other.

- In Mac OS X's Network preferences pane, use the Location pop-up menu either to switch to another location or to create a new location and switch to it. Then switch back. This process sometimes lets you choose Turn AirPort On from the AirPort menu, convinces a previously unresponsive network to appear in the AirPort menu, and forces AirPort to display in the Show pop-up menu if it wasn't appearing before.

- Also in the Mac OS X Network preferences pane, choose Network Port Configurations from the Show pop-up menu and drag the AirPort entry to the top of the list. That tells Mac OS X to use it in favor of any other ports that might be available.

- On a Mac, if you have an external hard disk that can boot the computer, try booting from the external hard disk to see if the problem relates to something on your normal boot disk or if it happens no matter which disk you boot from.

- If possible, verify that the port or slot into which you're plugging the wireless network adapter works. You can do this by trying another network adapter in that port or slot.

- If you're positive that all the hardware is functional, consider reinstalling your operating system. Be careful that you don't erase any of your data in the process, and always make sure you have a recent backup before proceeding with such a major step.

Problem: No Wireless Connectivity

Q: **My wireless network adapter seems to see the access point, but won't let me connect. Any ideas?**

A: In this situation, the problem is often related to over-enthusiastic security settings, although there can be other problems too:

- If possible, see if other computers can connect. If so, the problem is specific to your computer. Knowing that the problem relates only to your computer should narrow the field of future tests and solutions.

- It's possible that you're too far away to connect reliably despite your adapter's software reporting that it can see the access point. Many signal-strength

Windows XP Wireless Network Connections Dimmed

Glenn once had an annoying problem in which his Windows XP laptop, a Sony Vaio, stopped working with his wireless cards from Linksys and Proxim (Orinoco).

After working through standard troubleshooting, Glenn contacted tech support at every company involved: Sony, Linksys, Proxim, and even Boingo, whose software he was running and which couldn't recognize either card. He didn't call Microsoft, which may have been a mistake, but he used its online help, as well as the extensive step-by-step Network Troubleshooter in Windows XP. None were able to help initially.

Eventually he discovered that uninstalling all the Linksys and Orinoco drivers allowed him to insert his Orinoco card and have it come up on a network.

But the Linksys card still wouldn't work. Then, he received a final email from Proxim that hinted at the root of the problem. There's a piece of software, a "service" in Windows parlance, that handles setting up wireless connections when a card is installed or an adapter added. That service needed to be started; why it was stopped, Glenn still has no idea, but it still happens frequently on that machine.

Should you run into a similar situation, follow these steps:

1. On the Desktop, right-click My Computer and select Manage.

2. In the list of items that appears in the Computer Management window, expand Services and Applications at the left, and then select Services (**Figure 14.3**).

3. In the right-hand pane, scroll down to Wireless Zero Configuration and double-click its icon.

4. In the General tab of the dialog that appears, make sure that Startup Type is set to Automatic, and Service Status is set to Started.

5. If Service Status is not set to Started, click the Start button (**Figure 14.4**). (You can also click Stop, and then click Start to restart the service.)

Glenn has to start the Windows Zero Configuration service regularly on this system now, although he didn't before installing multiple wireless drivers. His colleague Jeff had the same problem with a new PC: certain cards require this intervention; others don't.

indicators in software don't correspond proportionately to signal quality. Try moving closer and check if the problem goes away, or download NetStumbler (www.netstumbler.com) or MacStumbler (www.macstumbler.com) to gather more data on signal strength.

- Recheck that you've entered your WEP or WPA key correctly. Especially when you type a long WEP key of 26 characters, it's easy to make a mistake,

Figure 14.3
Computer
Management
window.

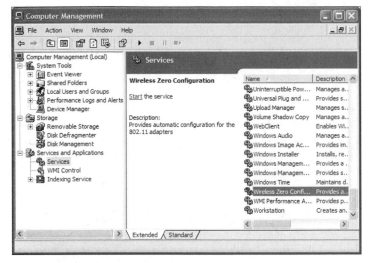

Figure 14.4
Wireless Zero
Configuration
dialog.

and a single error negates the entire key. Some software doesn't alert you that
the WEP or WPA key is incorrect, making data-entry-related problems
harder to troubleshoot.

- See if the person in charge of the network can turn off WEP/WPA and MAC
  address filtering in the access point temporarily to find out if these settings
  are preventing you from connecting.

- Make sure the network name is short and has no spaces or special characters
  in it.

- Ask to have the access point reset or power cycled (turn it off, wait about 30 seconds, turn it back on). It's quite common for inexpensive wireless gateways to become wedged and need to be reset. Note that pressing a reset button may not be as effective as cycling the power.

- If computers running Windows XP can connect, but those running other operating systems cannot, the problem may relate to an administrator enabling 802.1X authentication. 802.1X authentication, though a good tool for large organizations, is supported only with software installed on each wirelessly connected computer.

Problem: Signal Strength Is Poor

Q: I have trouble receiving wireless connections in a variety of locations. Is there anything I can do to increase the signal strength?

A: Yes, there are quite a few ways you can improve signal strength:

- Turn your computer 90 degrees. Seriously, sometimes that's all you need to do to improve signal strength enough to keep working. It's like the old days when people would get up on their roofs and fiddle with their TV antennas to improve television reception for the big football game.

- Try other angles in other planes. Even well-designed access point antennas send some signal in all directions. To quote the wise Mr. Spock on Ricardo Montalban's character in *Star Trek II: The Wrath of Khan*, "He is intelligent, but not experienced. His pattern indicates two-dimensional thinking."

- If your computer has an internal antenna, make sure the antenna is plugged into the wireless network card.

- This is painfully obvious, but we have to say it. Try moving closer to the access point. As a solution, it's cheap, it's easy, and yes, we know you should be able to work anywhere you want. If you don't want to let the evil radio demons win, move on to the next suggestions.

- Consider buying a new wireless network adapter with a higher signal strength, rated in milliwatts (mW). Most cards are about 30 mW, but you can find cards that push out 100 mW and even 200 mW (such as the EnGenius card sold by NetGate at www.netgate.com).

- We realize it's an awkward solution, but consider adding an external antenna that will boost your signal strength. This solution isn't just for desktop machines; many PC Cards have tiny antenna jacks (usually protected by little plastic plugs), and there are even antennas for internal AirPort cards in Apple's Titanium PowerBook G4 from QuickerTek (www.quickertek.com).

- Speaking of Titanium PowerBook G4s, which have notably poor wireless network reception, there are a few ways to help them. First, see if you can massage the little rubber plugs on either side of the PowerBook's base such that they're flush with the surface rather than pushed in. They're the radio "windows" for the antenna, which Apple foolishly ran around the base of that particular model. If that's not sufficient, you can try either a QuickerTek antenna or an external PC Card.

Problem: No Roaming Network/Internet Access

Q: **When I'm traveling, I can connect to access points and am assigned an IP address by the DHCP server, but I can't actually see the network or reach the Internet. Which setting is askew?**

A: If these are access points that you don't have a direct connection to, there are only a few probable explanations:

- If you're visiting a college campus or a business, it may not offer visitor access. Your wireless adapter might associate, but lacking credentials, it can't send or receive traffic. Some of these networks may have visitor access codes, but you might need to ask for access or have special software installed.

- If you're at a free or paid hot spot, you may have failed to click through an acceptable use policy or pay for access. Quit and relaunch your browser, and then try to visit any Web page to see if a captive portal page appears advising you on how to get access.

- The access point's connection to the rest of the network or the network's connection to the Internet might be down, and there's nothing you can do, except call tech support (if such a thing exists at the network you're trying to use).

- If you're gamboling about, dowsing for access, stop it! You're not getting real access for a good reason, darn it!

Building Your Wireless Network

Building your own wireless network is pretty easy, with the effort necessary to set up a simple wireless network limited to unpacking a wireless gateway, plugging it in, and turning it on. But it can get more complicated—after all, how do you know if a given wireless gateway will meet your needs? That's where the chapters in this section come to the rescue.

Chapter 15, *Planning Your Wireless Network*, is a must-read: it offers a crash course in how to plan your wireless network before you even buy the hardware. Chapter 16, *Buying a Wireless Gateway*, addresses the issue of exactly what to buy, not with instantly obsolete product recommendations, but by offering a feature checklist you can use to make sure a gateway meets your needs. Once you've bought your gateway, it's time to read Chapter 17, *Setting up a Wireless Gateway*, for specific instructions on three popular wireless gateways, plus generic help on others.

Then we take a sharp left turn in Chapter 18, *Wireless Gadgets*, and look at a variety of unusual wireless devices you can add to your network. Chapter 19, *Creating a Software Access Point*, explains how you can turn your computer into a wireless gateway. Another advanced network topic follows in Chapter 20, *Bridging Wireless Networks*, which discusses how to extend the range of your network with a wireless bridge. Chapter 21, *Indoor Antenna Basics*, provides background information on how an antenna can extend the range of your wireless network, and Chapter 22, *Small Office Wi-Fi Networking*, examines topics of interest to those setting up somewhat larger and more complex wireless networks (including authentication and additional security).

Planning Your
Wireless Network

It's tempting when you're setting up a network to skip the planning step and just buy the pieces you think you need and plug them all together. Resist that temptation!

The first task you should perform when contemplating creating a new network or making a major change to an existing network is to draw a *network diagram*, which is a picture of how you expect all the pieces of your network to fit together. Putting a little effort up front into a network diagram clarifies exactly what you need to buy, reveals mistakes you might be about to make, ensures you won't forget some essential piece, and smoothes the entire process.

Don't think network diagrams are just for novices. We have friends who install networks for a living, and they always make a network diagram first. The main difference is that their network diagrams are gorgeous, whereas ours (well, at least Adam's) look like they were made for preschool art class (the diagrams in this chapter come courtesy of professional illustrator Jeff Tolbert). Luckily, no one will grade you on the aesthetics of your network diagram—it's simply a reference tool.

One final word before we dive into the steps of creating a network diagram: if you have a drawing program on your computer, it's best to use it, not so much because your diagram will look better, but because having the diagram as a file on your hard disk makes it easy to keep around. If you draw by hand on paper, make an effort to file that piece of paper where you can find it. Having your network diagram around later reduces your work if you want to make a major change to the network, and more important, it can help in troubleshooting should something go wrong.

 TIP

Try Microsoft Visio for Windows (www.microsoft.com/office/visio/), or for Mac OS X try ConceptDraw (www.conceptdraw.com) or OmniGraffle (www.omnigroup.com/applications/omnigraffle/) if you want to create professional drawings that have some smarts: as you move objects around in a network diagram, the connections between them move automatically.

Drawing a Network Diagram

Consider the following situation, which, although invented, is by no means exaggerated. Amanda and Bob Quiggle both work at home, she as a freelance bookkeeper and he as a programmer. Amanda's accounting programs run on a desktop PC, while Bob writes and tests code on a Power Mac G4, a desktop PC, and an Apple iBook. They have three children, Sam, Chloe, and Nick, each of whom has a computer. Although Sam is a freshman at college, he lives at home and has a PC laptop that he uses constantly, whereas Chloe and Nick are still in grade school and use an older Macintosh Quadra and a Power Mac handed down from their father to do homework and play games.

The Quiggles have just moved into a new house, and they want to network all their computers to share a cable-modem Internet connection and their two printers, a color USB printer attached to Bob's desktop PC and an elderly, LocalTalk-based LaserWriter. They want their laptops to connect to a wireless network, and both Bob's iBook and Sam's laptop PC have wireless network adapters. The family's desktop computers will need to connect to one another via Ethernet, although Chloe's and Nick's Macs aren't anywhere near Bob's Power Mac and desktop PC, so an additional hub will be necessary.

The major oddity is Amanda's PC, which, because of being in her otherwise inaccessible basement office, will connect to the rest of the network via HomePlug bridges. She thought about installing a HomePlug network adapter in her PC, but she wanted to leave open the possibility of connecting additional computers without being forced to buy additional HomePlug hardware.

The Quiggles decided to be modern and use 802.11g, the faster compatible flavor of Wi-Fi, because all their desktops and laptops also have 100 Mbps wired Ethernet built-in, and they play games, stream audio, and transfer files over their home network.

((•)) **NOTE**

Inaccessible rooms are common in houses. Glenn helped a friend set up a network in his three-story house, and they found an impenetrable barrier at the ground-floor kitchen. Signal strength was fine to that point, even with the access point on the top floor (where the cable modem was located). Step through the kitchen's entrance, however, and the signal disappeared.

Does that seem like a lot to keep in your head? Good, because it's exactly how networking in the real world works. Fortunately, a network diagram makes it easy to see at a glance how everything should go together.

Your network will undoubtedly look different than the Quiggles' network, but their network diagram should give you an idea of what's involved. Don't feel the need to draw anything fancier than labeled boxes, though, and that's what we'll assume you're drawing in the instructions.

If you're sketching the network on paper, we recommend reading through these instructions before starting so you have an idea of where to leave the appropriate amount of free space before you start. We provide the finished diagram first, so you can see how it all comes together (**Figure 15.1**).

((•)) **NOTE**

We're not attempting to overlay this network on a picture of their house—that level of detail is simply unnecessary and can, in fact, cause confusion because the physical position of the computers may have no relationship to where they fit into the network.

1. For each hub or wireless gateway (which, as we note in Appendix A, *Networking Basics,* is essentially a hub), draw a small rectangular box (**Figure 15.2**). Leave plenty of room around each box. The Quiggles' network will need four hub-like devices—two wired hubs and a wireless access point with a wired hub built in—but since their wireless gateway combines both an access point and a normal hub, we draw only three devices.

2. Near each of the hub boxes, draw squares that represent each computer, and next to each square, write the name of the computer so you can tell which square goes with which computer (**Figure 15.3**). If you have a device like a wireless gateway that combines a wired and wireless hub, draw the computers that will connect via wires on one side of the access point and the computers that will connect wirelessly on the other side. Draw them on different sides to organize them separately on the diagram.

3. If you have a printer that you want to share via the network, draw an oval (**Figure 15.4**). Where to position the printer depends on the printer type.

Figure 15.1
The completed
diagram.

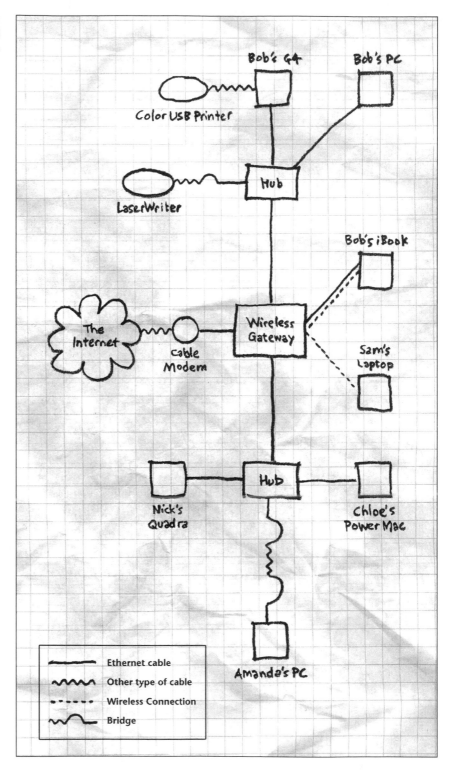

Figure 15.2
Start by drawing the network hubs.

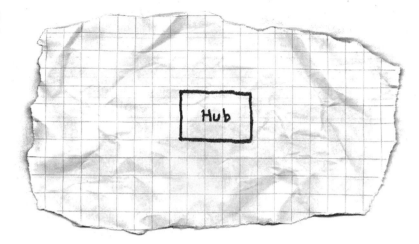

Figure 15.3
Add in the computers on the network.

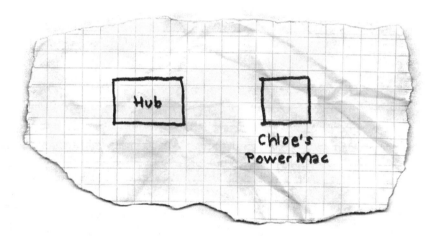

If it's a USB printer connected to a computer that shares it on the network, draw the printer near that computer's square and connect it with a squiggly line to indicate that they're connected in some way other than Ethernet. If it's a network device in its own right that will plug into a hub, draw it near the hub in question. If the printer uses a networking technology like LocalTalk that requires a bridge to connect to your network, draw the printer at the side of the hub it will eventually connect to, and between the printer and the hub, draw a small arch to represent the bridge. The Quiggles have a USB printer and an old, LocalTalk-based LaserWriter, so we draw them in **Figure 15.4**, connecting the LaserWriter to its bridge with a squiggly line.

4. Off to the side of the page, roughly near the device you plan to use as your gateway, draw a cloud shape to represent the Internet. Then draw a small

Figure 15.4
Next, draw the printers and their connecting cables.

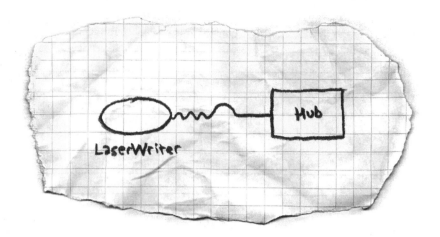

circle to represent the cable modem, DSL modem, or whatever device connects your network to the Internet. Label it appropriately, as we've done with the Quiggles' cable modem (**Figure 15.5**).

Figure 15.5
Expand the diagram by adding the Internet and the device that you use to connect to it.

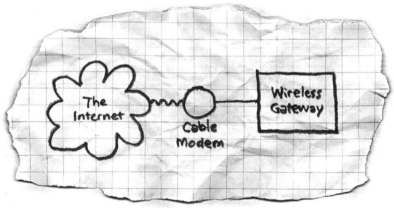

 TIP

Some cable or DSL modems can connect directly to any Ethernet hub, but others, most notably those from the large, cable ISP Road Runner, must connect directly to a gateway device or a computer, as shown here.

5. If, like Amanda, you need to connect a computer to the rest of the network using HomePlug bridges, draw a small arch for each bridge, and draw a squiggly line between the bridges to show the connection (**Figure 15.6**).

6. Lastly, connect all the wired computers to their hubs with solid lines that represent Ethernet cables, and connect all the wireless computers to their access points with dashed lines (**Figure 15.1**, earlier in this chapter).

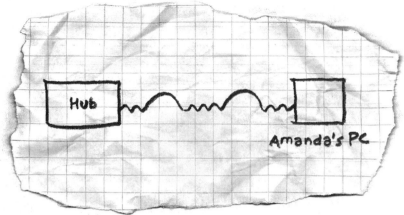

Figure 15.6
Show any necessary
bridges.

 NOTE

It's entirely possible for a computer to have two network adapters, one for wired Ethernet and one for wireless Ethernet, and to switch between them depending on the situation. If that's the case, draw the computer between the appropriate hubs, and connect it with both a solid and a dashed line. Bob's iBook falls into this category in our sample network.

That's it! The beauty of a network diagram is that you can use it to determine the next two steps in actually creating your network: compiling your shopping list and configuring your network.

Shopping and Configuring

To create your shopping list, first look at your network diagram and determine what network devices you'll need to buy. For instance, the Quiggles will need a wireless 802.11g gateway, a LocalTalk-to-Ethernet bridge for their Laser-Writer, a pair of 10/100 Mbps Ethernet hubs, and a pair of HomePlug Ethernet bridges. Then look at each computer and determine if you need to buy a network adapter for it, and if it will be connecting via wired Ethernet, if you'll need a cable. You may have some of the hardware and cables already, but make sure any existing cables are long enough to reach between the desired locations. It's faster, easier, and cheaper if you can order everything you need at the same time, rather than piecing the network together slowly as you figure out what comes next.

TIP

Take our word on the utility of planning before you buy and configure equipment—because of wanting to share two Internet connections among all his computers, Adam set up a particularly complicated network when he moved into his current house. Since the diagram for his network was so complex, and because he was swapping different devices in and out, he went for the evolutionary process. Although it worked out fine, it took months to finish.

Once you have all the pieces, it's time to connect the wires and configure your computers and devices. Go through each item on the diagram again, and connect them to one another according to the diagram. Then configure your wireless gateway, without which the rest of the network is unlikely to work properly. (Instructions and advice for configuring your gateway come in Chapter 17, *Setting up a Gateway*.)

Locating Access Points

We said earlier that there's no point in overlaying a network diagram on top of a picture of your house or office because it makes the diagram unnecessarily complicated. That's true, but you do need to translate it to your house or office at some point. This process requires few resources, but gear borrowed from a friend can help you make smart purchasing decisions.

For networks in which all devices are within line of sight of an access point, you might not need to give the structure of the network any thought at all: just plug everything in and it works. But for more complicated situations in which, for instance, your network might cross several walls and floors, or run several hundred feet, planning is critical.

Start with a walking tour of the location.

- If your location is a house, be realistic about where you might want to work. Will you really work in a hammock in the backyard? Are you using only desktop PCs? If you're a ReplayTV user, would you want to add a wireless Ethernet adapter to avoid drilling holes and running a long wire through several walls to your Ethernet switch?

- If your location is an office building, think about the interior walls and the density of users. How much distance, with and without walls, will the network need to cover? Can you add an access point to the network with existing wired connections, or will you need to pull wire or set up bridges?

- Also think about multiple sites. Might you want to connect your network to others, perhaps in different office suites or buildings, or even in your neighbor's house?

Most smaller sites need only a single access point, but once you introduce distance or walls—especially brick walls, which can absorb water and thus absorb Wi-Fi signals—you must consider the possibility of needing multiple access points across your network.

Here's how borrowed equipment can help: plug an access point into a likely location, and then walk around with a wireless-enabled laptop while watching the signal strength indicator in your wireless network client software. With stumbling tools, you can also see an indication of signal strength as you walk around (see "Stumbling onto Wi-Fi," Chapter 25, *Preventing Access to Your Network*, for more on these tools). If the initial access point location doesn't provide the coverage you want, move it and repeat the process of mapping signal strength until you find the ideal location for the access point.

After you have your gateway working, configure each computer to access the Internet through your gateway. For that, refer back to the appropriate chapter in Section II, *Connecting Your Computer*. Setting up file sharing is next, followed by ensuring that each of the other computers can connect to the file sharing machines. If you have printers that you want to share, make sure they're set up to be shared, and configure all the computers so they can print to the shared printers. If you have trouble, refer to Chapter 14, *Troubleshooting Your Connection*, and Chapter 23, *Troubleshooting Your Wireless Network*, for troubleshooting advice.

 TIP

In our experience, connecting to the Internet is easy, whereas getting shared printers working requires more trial and error involving driver installation and other unpleasant tasks. Luckily, even if it takes some time to share the printers properly, you can usually print from a computer directly connected to the printer in question.

Multiple Access Points

If your network needs multiple access points to reach more locations or users, some additional planning and configuration is in order:

- Don't assume you can mix and match access points. It might work, but the only safe approach is to verify that a specific access point supports roaming and buy multiple units of that access point. For instance, we know Apple's original AirPort Base Station supports roaming with no trouble, but the Asanté FR1004AL does not (particularly when paired with a Linksys BEFW11S4).

- Make sure you have electrical power to each location where you want to add an access point. You can also use *Power over Ethernet* (PoE), a way of putting DC power into a modified Ethernet cable. You could make these cables yourself with advice found online or in Rob Flickenger's book *Wire-*

less Hacks, but it's much easier to purchase prefabricated cables and adapters from on-line sources like HyperLink Technologies (www.hyperlinktech.com) or MacWireless (www.macwireless.com). PoE allows you to avoid running electricity to rooftops or hard-to-reach places. (Solar power can also be an option for outside installations!)

- Connect all the access points to a common network using Ethernet cables or wireless bridges. All the access points need this interconnection to allow access to the Internet from any client anywhere on the network. (We talk about wireless bridging in Chapter 20, *Bridging Wireless Networks.*)

- Name each access point using the same SSID or network name. The SSID is the identifier that clients use to associate with an access point; a group of access points with

(continued on next page)

Multiple Access Points (continued)

the same SSID are said to have an ESSID or Extended Service Set Identifier. In networks with two or more access points, as long as all the access points share the same name, a client typically connects to whichever unit has the most signal strength.

- Choose non-overlapping channels for adjacent access points. Channels 1, 6, and 11 have no overlapping frequencies for 802.11b and 802.11g: you could stack three access points with those channels on top of each other, and they would work just fine. Which of the three channels you choose for each point is irrelevant, as long as they're different (**Figure 15.7**). Two side notes: first, outside the U.S., channels 1, 6, and 11 may not all be available for legal use, or you might have channels 1 through 14 available; second, if you're working with 802.11a, you have eight indoor non-overlapping channels.

- Enable DHCP service on just one of the access points. Most DHCP servers can (as an option) bridge DHCP service onto the wired network to which they connect as well as provide addresses to wireless clients. There's no advantage to running DHCP servers on every access point, and having multiple DHCP servers can cause confusion. Using a single DHCP server with NAT enabled creates a single, local private network.

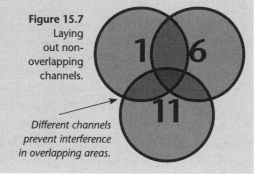

Figure 15.7 Laying out non-overlapping channels.

Different channels prevent interference in overlapping areas.

Buying a Wireless Gateway

In Wi-Fi terms, an *access point* is just the hardware and built-in software that enables wireless adapters to connect and exchange data. But an access point isn't very useful unless you're using it on a network that already has resources installed that share connections, restrict access, and handle a myriad of tiny details.

Whereas institutional networks often have servers for each of these tasks and more, home users and small offices can rely instead on a *wireless gateway*, sometimes called a *home gateway* or *wireless router*, which doesn't do justice to most of these devices' hidden power.

A wireless gateway is a single piece of equipment that provides all the features of a full Wi-Fi access point as well as assigns IP addresses; protects local machines; prevents access by outsiders; and bridges traffic across wired, wireless, and broadband connections. Many wireless gateways offer features sufficient for networks of up to 50 users.

Let's examine the common features found in wireless gateways and what you need to consider before buying one.

((•)) **NOTE**

> *We usually don't recommend specific models when talking about each of these features because equipment and its internal software is updated so frequently that our suggestions would be out of date by the time this book appears in print.*

((•)) **NOTE**

> *All the network protocols and services mentioned here, like DHCP, NAT, PPPoE, and AppleTalk, are covered in more detail in Appendix A,* Networking Basics.

NOTE

Inexpensive access points, such as the Linksys WAP54G, lack any gateway features. They're designed to extend a network's range and rely on the networking features in a gateway (they can also be useful for providing just wireless connectivity in a larger, existing wired network). If you try to use two wireless gateways on the same network, you must usually turn off all the gateway features in one device to avoid conflicting services.

Hardware Options

Because Wi-Fi is so uniformly compatible among devices sporting a Wi-Fi label, your hardware options tend to be few, but critical: what type of Wi-Fi do you want, what do you want to plug into your gateway, and how will you extend your network? These choices are important because inexpensive networking hardware can almost always be upgraded only by swapping in new equipment.

 TIP

On the plus side, most of this hardware is sufficiently cheap these days, so switching to a new wireless gateway doesn't involve a major financial investment.

Speed and Compatibility

The old standby is 802.11b, the original Wi-Fi flavor. Gateways that work with just this standard have become cheaper since the introduction of 802.11g. If you're using only older equipment that already has 802.11b built-in, if you have no need to move a lot of data around your network, and if you have a broadband connection slower than 3 Mbps, buying a wireless gateway that supports a faster standard like 802.11g won't provide any benefits.

If you plan to move large amounts of data around your network (network backups are a common example), or if you already have an 802.11g adapter, then you should spend a small amount more and buy an 802.11g-based gateway. Remember that because 802.11g is backward compatible with 802.11b, you can still use older equipment with it. If you wind up using only 802.11g gear, many gateways let you turn off backward compatibility in the interest of speed.

While 802.11a operates as fast as 802.11g, only corporations and a few universities seem to have deployed it. It's not a terrible choice for a standalone network that has no visitors, as it's resistant to the kind of interference you might find in the home or workplace, including microwave ovens and cordless phones. However, 802.11a equipment tends to be more expensive and more oriented towards information technology professionals.

If you think you might have a mix of visitors or local users who could come bearing 802.11a- or 802.11b/g-compatible laptops, a combination gateway might be an ideal solution. Many manufacturers offer gateways that can work with a and b or b/g at the same time. However, these often cost twice as much as a gateway that supports only one of the Wi-Fi flavors.

 NOTE

If you want to use 802.11a at home or in the office while being able to connect with 802.11b/g networks on the road, an alternate choice would be to deploy just 802.11a gateways, but purchase a combination 802.11a/b or even 802.11a/b/g network adapter, which costs only slightly more than a single-mode adapter.

Points to consider when buying: Buy the fastest access point you can afford that supports the standards you need. The amount of data you'll send around a network will only increase over time.

Antenna Jack

Many, but by no means all, wireless gateways offer either an antenna jack or removable dipole antennas that can be replaced by a higher gain antenna. You might want to add a small antenna to increase signal strength and coverage area within your home or office, or, if you want to network between separate buildings, an antenna will likely be necessary to distribute the signal to other remote access points.

TIP

Just because a wireless gateway has a visible antenna doesn't mean that you can necessarily remove it and replace it with one that has higher gain. Make sure you can buy a compatible antenna or pigtail *(a converter cable) before buying a given gateway.*

The FCC requires every wireless manufacturer to use a different connector type to reduce the chance that novices will combine an access point with a powerful antenna in such a way as to exceed legal signal strength limits. As a result, it's often easiest to buy antennas from the maker of your wireless gateway, although some companies, like HyperLink Technologies (www.hyperlinktech.com), offer products with a variety of connector types.

For more information about antenna types, necessary cables, and adding an antenna to a wireless gateway, see Chapter 21, *Indoor Antenna Basics,* and Chapter 34, *Long-Range Antenna Basics.*

(((•))) **NOTE**

Most long-range wireless Internet connections connect to a wireless client (like a wireless Ethernet bridge) on your end, and most wireless gateways can't operate in client mode. So you wouldn't add an antenna to a wireless gateway to establish a long-range wireless Internet connection, though you would to extend the range of your own network.

Points to consider when buying: If you believe you might need to increase the coverage area of your wireless gateway or if you plan to set up multiple access points in far-flung buildings, make sure to buy a gateway to which you can add an external antenna.

Ethernet

A gateway must have at least two Ethernet ports: one for the WAN connection to a broadband modem, and one or more for the LAN connection, either to connect computers directly or to connect to a hub.

Most newer gateways offer a full 100 Mbps connection on the WAN port, even though there are few ways to bring more bandwidth than 10 Mbps into the home or office, because you might connect your gateway to a switch and not directly to a DSL or cable modem.

The LAN Ethernet ports can act either as a hub or as a switch, and most are switches. A hub is a pool of shared bandwidth, whereas a switch separates traffic, allowing each port to have the full available bandwidth. This distinction is important if your local network often has a lot of traffic, as is the case with an active file server or even just a network backup program that transfers gigabytes of data when performing full backups.

The LAN Ethernet ports are normally 10/100 Mbps auto-switching ports. (Auto-switching lets the port determine if the connected device supports 10 Mbps 10Base-T or 100 Mbps Fast Ethernet.) Most gateways with multiple LAN ports also offer at least one port that can work as an uplink connection, which is a way to connect to another hub or switch without a special cable. Some even automatically sense the cable type, avoiding the need for an uplink port or toggle switch.

Gateways also make their network services—DHCP, NAT, and firewall features—available to computers connected to the LAN ports, just like any computers connected wirelessly. Some gateways offer an option that lets you turn off these features on the LAN side. Look for a checkbox labeled "Bridging DHCP" or something similar.

Points to consider when buying: Even the most wire-free wireless network will likely wind up with one or two wired devices, and even the cheapest gateways include one or more LAN Ethernet ports. If performance on the wired side is important, make sure the gateway offers a switch rather than just a passive hub.

Modem

Not everyone is so fortunate as to have broadband Internet access, and for those of you relying on dial-up access to reach the rest of the world, a gateway with a built-in modem is a godsend. A few access points sport either a built-in "56K" modem or an RS-232C serial port into which you can plug an external modem or ISDN modem.

We don't know of any modem-equipped gateways that support the newer V.92 modem standard, which has options for faster connections, sensing incoming voice calls, and suspending calls. Still, keep your eyes peeled, as it's likely that V.92 will become more commonly supported in time.

 TIP

Because you can share a dial-up connection through an access point, Glenn intends to carry an access point to his in-laws' house this holiday season to avoid having to plug and unplug telephone cables frequently, and so he can work on the (warmer) ground floor of the house!

(((•))) **NOTE**

As with all other modems, the "56K" modems in wireless gateways can receive data only at up to just above 50 Kbps, and that level of performance is unlikely in real-world conditions where phone lines aren't perfect. Plus, "56K" modems send data at only 33.6 Kbps.

Points to consider when buying: If you ever need to access the Internet via a dial-up connection, find a gateway with a modem or serial port. If it has a serial port, verify with the manufacturer which modems work with it; there's usually a long list on the maker's Web site.

Configuration Interfaces

Most gateways offer a Web-based interface for configuring settings, rebooting the device, and installing *firmware* updates. (Firmware is the gateway's built-in software.) A few gateways require proprietary Macintosh or Windows software to manage them, limiting their markets but making them easier to configure from those platforms.

Linksys, for one, requires a Windows-only program that hunts down the default shipping IP address of a gateway in order to connect to it, after which you can configure it entirely via a Web-based interface. We provide instructions in Chapter 17, *Setting up a Gateway,* on how to bypass this program in favor of Linksys's Web interface.

Some Web-based gateways use Windows tools for firmware upgrades or have limitations that unnecessarily prevent Web-based tools from performing upgrades under Linux or Mac OS.

Points to consider when buying: Mac and Linux users must either make sure the gateway they're considering can be entirely configured from those platforms, or make sure they have access to a Windows machine for at least initial configuration.

Network Services

Network services are features that the wireless gateway offers for individual computers or the network as a whole. Gateways always offer a variety of these services, which include sharing a connection among multiple machines, routing special protocols, and more.

DHCP Server

All gateways, practically by definition, include a DHCP (Dynamic Host Configuration Protocol) server that provides IP addresses to computers and other devices on the local area network. These DHCP servers almost always work in bridge mode as well, which enables them to provide DHCP service to both wired and wireless clients.

Some gateways limit how you can configure a DHCP server. For instance, the Linksys WRT54G, a popular model, can be configured to provide up to a certain number of addresses beginning at a specific IP address on the local network. If you have three computers on the network 192.168.1.0, you can have your DHCP server hand out up to five DHCP addresses (which might be necessary, for instance, if you have three computers in use, and then two guests with their own laptops visit and wish to connect to the Internet) from 192.168.1.10 through 192.168.1.14.

Unfortunately, none of the DHCP servers in the modestly priced gateways we've seen offer a useful option: linking a particular IP address to a network adapter's MAC (Media Access Control, not Macintosh) address, which is unique for every Ethernet and Wi-Fi adapter. This option can prove helpful when you want to connect to a specific computer via file sharing. With linked IP and MAC addresses, you can know, for instance, that your iBook is always 192.168.1.10 and your Windows 2000 box is 192.168.1.11 without having to check what IP address they've most recently received from the DHCP server.

Having the DHCP server assign the same IP address to a particular computer is also useful in combination with port forwarding or trigger services (see later in this chapter). We hope this option will appear in more gateways in the future.

TIP

You can work around the problem of IP addresses changing by setting the DHCP lease time to the longest possible period in some cases and to zero in others. The lease time is the length of time before which a computer must obtain another IP address from the DHCP server or renew the existing address. A long or infinite lease time can often ensure that a machine keeps the same IP address.

TIP

Those with the technical chops and interest can run their own DHCP servers under Mac OS X, Linux, Unix, and many flavors of Windows (remember to turn off the DHCP server in your wireless gateway if you do this). When you run your own DHCP server, you can set options that allow directly connecting a MAC address with an IP address.

Points to consider when buying: If the gateway doesn't have a DHCP server, don't buy it: it's not a gateway, but rather an access point that lacks network services you need.

NAT

Gateways also by their nature support NAT (Network Address Translation), a network service that makes it possible to share a single IP address with many computers. NAT and DHCP work hand in hand: DHCP assigns private addresses that can't be reached from the Internet to local computers, and NAT then reroutes incoming and outgoing traffic to the correct machines. Since only the IP address of the gateway is visible to the outside world, NAT provides an extra level of security.

NAT servers can be configured in several ways, but most gateways lack sophistication in this area. At best, you can specify only the maximum number of addresses that a DHCP server can offer.

NAT is particularly helpful for home users because most broadband ISPs offer just a single IP address at their lowest monthly rate. Ironically, many consumer

DSL and cable ISPs use NAT themselves: the single address they assign to you is itself a private address inside the ISP's network. Nested NAT can cause problems with some software, but increasingly companies are learning to cope with multiple levels of NAT. It's just how the Internet works these days.

Points to consider when buying: If you need to share a single IP address, you need a NAT server. Even if your ISP provides you with a number of addresses, you may want a gateway with NAT for additional security.

Special Protocols

Different operating systems have different proprietary protocols for communicating among file servers and printers. Whereas TCP/IP is a universal language, these other protocols require some repackaging. Every gateway supports TCP/IP, but not all of them work with proprietary protocols like Microsoft's NetBEUI.

Even less common is complete support for Apple's AppleTalk, which can still be useful when communicating with older Macs or Apple printers. Even though most gateways pass AppleTalk properly among wired computers or among wireless computers, most gateways don't bridge AppleTalk *between* wired and wireless computers. When buying a gateway, lack of support for the protocols you need is a showstopper.

Points to consider when buying: Check the networking protocols you use—and it's likely that you use only TCP/IP—and then confirm that the gateway supports all of them. AppleTalk, in particular, is supported by only a very few gateways from Mac-savvy companies like Asanté and Proxim (and Apple, of course), but unless you have older Macs or Apple printers to which you want to connect, AppleTalk support isn't important.

Dynamic DNS

Normal DNS (Domain Name Service) maps domain names to the permanent IP addresses of computers that act as Internet servers. This mapping allows people to connect to servers using just the domain names, without even knowing the cryptic IP addresses. But if your ISP provides only a dynamic IP address and you still want to run a server that people on the Internet can find, you need *dynamic DNS*. Dynamic DNS allows computers that have IP addresses that change to be found through an unchanging domain name. Each time your computer's IP address changes—when it connects to the Internet, for example, or its DHCP lease time runs out—a small program triggers a DNS server to reset the domain name to point to your computer's new IP address. (You can also trigger this change manually through a Web site.) For more information about dynamic DNS, visit www.technopagan.org/dynamic/.

A few gateway manufacturers have recently incorporated this feature directly into their firmware, eliminating the need for additional software. For instance, several models of D-Link gateways have a configuration option to enter a dynamic DNS provider (`http://support.dlink.com/faq/view.asp?prod_id=1280`).

If you couple dynamic DNS with port forwarding (discussed later in this chapter), you can maintain a permanent Web site even with an ISP-assigned dynamic IP address and network address translation!

Points to consider when buying: If you want a permanent host address (like www-adam.dyndns.org), you'll find it easier to use a gateway that supports dynamic DNS internally than to use separate dynamic DNS software.

Security and Filters

You can secure your network to prevent malefactors from stealing passwords, snooping through your traffic, or even taking over your computers. For significantly more detailed discussions of security, read Section IV, *Wireless Security.*

Firewall

Firewalls are designed to block malevolent traffic that might endanger the computers on your network. They work by examining inbound traffic to see whether it meets certain patterns or is aimed at vulnerable resources. Traffic that matches the preset patterns is dropped so it doesn't reach its destination, and some firewalls keep a running log of what they detect so you can tell if the firewall is working properly.

Most gateways offer firewall features that let you filter specified kinds of traffic, like that aimed for a given Internet service. A few can filter in both directions. Most of these firewalls are simple, enabling you only to limit either all unsolicited incoming traffic that's not in response to an outgoing request you made or specific Internet services, like FTP.

Because many gateways also include multiple Ethernet ports, you can create a firewall not just between your broadband Internet connection—connected to the WAN port—and your wireless computers and devices, but also between the wireless network and any machines connected to the LAN Ethernet ports on the gateway.

Generally, putting your computers behind NAT, turning off unused services, and enabling the built-in firewall capabilities on each computer running recent versions of common operating systems can protect you as well as a gateway firewall. (See Chapter 27, *Protecting Your Systems,* for more on firewalls.)

Points to consider when buying: A firewall in a gateway can help protect your network, while still allowing full access for legitimate users.

Port Forwarding and Triggers

If you're using NAT or a firewall, it can be tricky for computers outside your local network to connect to your computers when you actively want them to. Many gateways offer an option—called *port forwarding, port mapping, pass-through,* or *punch-through*—to alleviate this problem.

Port forwarding works by associating traffic destined for a specific port to a computer on the internal network that isn't otherwise accessible from the outside. For example, if you want to run a public Web site on one of your machines, you can set your gateway to forward traffic arriving at port 80 (the port reserved by default for Web servers) on the static IP address assigned to the gateway to port 80 on one of the private IP addresses on the local network.

TIP

Keep in mind that gateways allow only a one-port-to-one-machine mapping: that is, you can't run Web servers on multiple local machines all at port 80. You can work around this limitation by configuring software on a dedicated computer behind the gateway, but you might be better off using a dedicated Web hosting service instead of jury-rigging a solution.

 NOTE

If you want to forward all incoming traffic to a specific machine, you can use a broader version of port forwarding, called DMZ (a wildly inappropriate use of the term "demilitarized zone") or virtual server. DMZ lets you expose a single machine to the outside world; it's reachable just as if it were on the Internet, even though NAT is translating all traffic to and from it.

Game players often run into a related problem, which is that some network games require incoming traffic on a range of ports. The solution is a feature called *triggers.* When a local machine tries to connect out on a trigger port, the gateway notices the outbound request and reconfigures itself to allow inbound traffic to a range of ports back to that local machine. Triggers thus allow full interactivity with multi-player Internet or networked games. If you're a gamer, search on Google (www.google.com) for setup instructions for different gateways and different games. We've also noticed that more and more gateways have special gamer settings for use with the Xbox and other consoles that can be turned on with a single checkbox.

Points to consider when buying: If you want to expose certain services on certain machines or want to play Internet-based games, you need a gateway that supports port forwarding and triggers or has special gaming support.

WEP and WPA

Because any machine that's in the range of a Wi-Fi network can view all the traffic passing over the network, wireless gateways feature encryption options that prevent passersby from easily sniffing and extracting your data. Unfortunately, the first standard built into all gateways was deeply flawed; a newer standard fixes its flaws and reduces the effort to turn this encryption on in the first place. (We talk about the flaws and fixes in Chapter 25, *Preventing Access to Your Network*.)

WEP (Wired Equivalent Privacy) is the original standard, and we devote space throughout the book to coping with its obscure settings and hexadecimal keys. All older adapters and gateways support WEP, even though some, like Apple's AirPort and AirPort Extreme systems, mask the complexity with a friendlier face.

When using WEP, you can enter one to four keys in your gateway that are used to encrypt traffic. On each wireless client that wants to connect to the gateway, you must likewise enter at least one of these WEP keys. (Some adapters support up to four keys, too.)

WEP comes in two forms: a shorter key form known as 40, 56, or 64 bits (all of which are actually the same) and a longer form called 128 bits; the difference is in the length of the encryption key. All devices on a network must use the same key length.

Fortunately, starting in mid-2003, WEP was gradually replaced with WPA (Wi-Fi Protected Access). WPA not only addresses WEP's numerous problems, but it also supports a simple password interface: you can enter just one plain text password into the gateway and use the same password on all your adapters. We highly recommend buying only new equipment that supports WPA or promises a WPA update in the near future. Although older equipment is supposed to be upgradeable to WPA, we haven't yet seen a single upgrade for any device that came out before 2003.

All WPA-capable gateways can handle WEP just fine. However, if even a single WEP device is used on a WPA network, the entire network reverts back to WEP's inadequacies.

Points to consider when buying: WEP's time has come and gone; buy only gateways that handle WPA out of the box or that promise simple firmware upgrades.

VPN

VPNs (virtual private networks) use end-to-end encryption to make sure that traffic can't be sniffed or intercepted in legible form between a user's machine and the end point—a VPN server—inside a company network. There are two protocols for VPN in wide use: PPTP (Point-to-Point Tunneling Protocol) and IPsec (IP security) over L2TP (Layer 2 Tunneling Protocol), commonly called just IPsec.

If you need to use a VPN via your gateway, make sure the gateway can pass the protocol your company uses. Support varies widely and changes constantly. Many consumer-level wireless gateways didn't offer pass-through IPsec support just a year ago, but most now do because of its increasing use.

A related problem is that if you're using NAT to translate between the gateway's public IP address and the private addresses of machines on your local network, you may have trouble using a VPN. Check with your organization's Help Desk to see if it has suggested configurations that work around the problem.

Points to consider when buying: If you're using a VPN to connect to your company's internal network, make sure that the gateway you buy can handle the necessary protocol and ask your organization's Help Desk for recommendations.

Network Authentication

For small office and institutional networks, the security options offered in consumer-level wireless gateways generally aren't robust and flexible enough to restrict access to a wireless network to only those people that a network administrator wants to have access. For an additional level of security, gateways must support one of several methods of requiring that users log in to a wireless network using standards like LEAP from Cisco (Lightweight Extensible Authentication Protocol), RADIUS (the acronym no longer means anything), or 802.1X/EAP.

For all these protocols, the gateway provides a configuration area that enables you to enter the information about the server that has user accounts stored on it. For instance, the AirPort Extreme Base Station has a tab in its advanced configuration that allows you to punch in the requisite details.

We talk more about these features and how to build a simple network employing them in Chapter 22, *Small Office Wi-Fi Networking*.

ISP Interaction

Many broadband ISPs require some kind of login or authentication check to make sure you're using only a single computer or only a computer that you registered with the ISP. In response to this annoying and unnecessary limitation many gateway makers have added features that enable you to share your connection by simulating aspects of a single computer's connection to the broadband provider.

DHCP Client

Almost all gateways feature a DHCP client that can request an IP address from a broadband provider's DHCP server. That's good, because without support for picking up an IP address via DHCP, gateways wouldn't work with ISPs that hand out dynamic IP addresses. Once your gateway has an IP address, it can use NAT to provide Internet access to the rest of your network.

 TIP

Adam once had trouble convincing an Asanté FR1004AL wireless gateway to hold on to a DHCP-assigned IP address from his cable ISP. After much hair pulling, a firmware upgrade solved the problem.

Some ISPs use the DHCP Client ID, a proprietary field added to DHCP by Microsoft years ago, and now supported by everyone for parity. The Client ID is an extra bit of text sent as part of a request for an address by a DHCP client. ISPs that use the Client ID field often require some specific text to be entered, which helps them confirm your identity.

Points to consider when buying: If your ISP assigns you a single dynamic address, you must have a DHCP client in your gateway, and if your ISP requires the use of a DHCP Client ID, make sure the gateway supports it.

PPPoE

Many broadband ISPs rely on a technology called PPPoE (PPP over Ethernet) as a security measure and to control session length. In essence, PPPoE treats an always-on Ethernet connection as though it were traveling over a modem. With Internet accounts that use PPPoE, your gateway must log in with a user name and password before the ISP's DHCP server will provide an IP address and start passing traffic.

ISPs like PPPoE because it enables them to track which of their customers are connected at any given time and the length of time any given customer has been connected. PPPoE also integrates with the authentication servers many

ISPs already run for their dial-up customers. Internet purists hate PPPoE because it's a subversion of the concept that broadband connections should be available at all times.

Points to consider when buying: Not all gateways support PPPoE, so determine whether you need it to connect to your ISP before buying a gateway.

Cloning MAC Addresses

A few broadband providers use MAC addresses (the unique Ethernet Media Access Control address assigned at manufacture to every network adapter) to limit access to a single machine. Some cable modems, for instance, lock on to the first MAC address they see when they're turned on, and work only with that one unless they're powered down and started up again. More problematic are the ISPs that actually record the MAC address of a single computer and refuse to work with any other MAC address ever again unless you ask the ISP to change the allowed MAC address.

The solution to this problem is to *clone,* or replicate, the MAC address of the acceptable machine in the gateway, after which the ISP's equipment thinks the gateway is the acceptable computer.

Points to consider when buying: It's rare that you'll need cloning, but if your ISP works this way, support for MAC address cloning is invaluable.

Firmware and Firm Problems

Beware one problem Glenn faced when helping his friend Patrick solve a network problem. Patrick's ISP had told him that he needed to both set a static IP address for his gateway, a Linksys gateway, and use PPPoE to connect to the ISP's network. After an hour or more of messing with settings on the router's main configuration page, Glenn was flummoxed. He could convince a single machine to connect directly, but not the gateway.

Finally, he did what he should have done first: visited Linksys's Web site and downloaded the latest firmware, or internal software, for the gateway. A short install and reboot of the router later, Glenn had a new main configuration screen that correctly separated static IP selection from PPPoE. You can't do both, and the ISP had misled Glenn's friend. He needed to use just PPPoE which, in turn, assigned an address to the gateway.

The things we learn in hindsight always seem so obvious, even though at the time we were pounding our heads repeatedly against the table.

Miscellaneous

There are some additional variables that don't fit into any existing category, but which might play a role in which gateway you choose.

Wireless Distribution System (WDS)

In 2003, wireless gateways started offering a new feature called WDS, or Wireless Distribution System, which lets you extend a wireless network by adding additional wireless access points that act as go-betweens between wireless clients and a master wireless gateway. Although relatively few wireless gateways support WDS right now, we expect it to become increasingly common.

Those manufacturers that do support WDS explicitly, such as Apple and Buffalo, aren't testing their equipment with one another, so it's always safest to buy gear from a single manufacturer. That said, our testing has shown that Apple's AirPort Extreme Base Station and Buffalo's WLA-G54 access point (it's not a gateway, just an access point) are in fact compatible. For more information about WDS, see Chapter 20, *Bridging Wireless Networks*.

Points to consider when buying: If you think you may want to extend your network wirelessly in the future, make sure to buy a wireless gateway that supports WDS.

Printer Sharing

A few gateways include print servers, which let you connect a printer directly to a parallel port on the gateway. You then send print jobs to the gateway's print server, which passes the print jobs to the printer. Having the print server hidden inside your gateway lets you avoid having the printer permanently connected to a computer that must be turned on whenever you want to print. Apple's AirPort Extreme Base Station allows you to plug in and share a USB printer, currently a unique option, but offers connections only via Rendezvous, Apple's implementation of Zeroconf (www.zeroconf.org), making it currently incompatible with other operating systems.

NOTE

Printer sharing is different from print spooling. With printer sharing, the printer must be connected to the print server, and both devices must be turned on and accessible. With print spooling, if the printer itself isn't on or accessible, the print spooler holds the job until the printer is turned on. We're not aware of any wireless gateways that offer print spooling, in part because a print spooler requires a fair amount of storage space to store print jobs when the printer is turned off.

Most of these print servers work only with Windows-style printing. They won't work with Macs unless you use extra software like Thursby Software System's Dave (www.thursby.com/products/dave.html) or the open source Gimp-Print (http://gimp-print.sourceforge.net/MacOSX.php3). A few also handle Unix LPR-style printing, which is accessible to both Macs and PCs (and any Unix or Linux box). See Chapter 13, *Sharing Files & Printers,* for more information.

Points to consider when buying: If you have a printer that must be connected to a computer through which print jobs are sent, you can offload the task to a gateway, but make sure you know which platforms you need support for.

Simultaneous Users

The number of computers supported by each gateway varies, and you can't necessarily believe manufacturers' recommendations. There's a sharp distinction between the maximum number of IP addresses a unit can feed out via DHCP (usually 253 at most) and the number of users it can actually cope with simultaneously.

Many companies claim that their gateways can support the number of addresses the DHCP server can dole out, not the actual number of users that can use the wireless gateway simultaneously. If you see a number like 35 to 50, it's more likely to be a true count of users, whereas a limit of 100 or 250 is unrealistic for consumer equipment.

Enterprise-grade access points used in large organizations can sometimes cope with several hundred simultaneous users, but they also cost $400 to $800.

Points to consider when buying: Count the number of machines that need to be connected, and if you're near the edge of the user limit, consider adding extra access points rather than overloading a single $100 device.

America Online

Tens of millions of people connect to America Online (AOL) every week, but there's only one wireless gateway that can connect to the Internet via AOL and make that connection available wirelessly: Apple's AirPort Extreme Base Station. You can also use the previous 802.11b-based AirPort Base Station with version 2.0 or later of the AirPort software for those models. Also necessary is version 5.0 of the AOL software for Macintosh. Keep in mind that sharing your AOL connection among multiple computers requires multiple AOL accounts.

Points to consider when buying: If you're a Macintosh AOL user, your decision is easy, since only the AirPort Base Station will help. Unfortunately, Windows

AOL users are out of luck because the AOL Windows client software doesn't support the Apple AirPort Base Station appropriately.

Cost

The price band for gateways dropped quite a bit during 2003, with the cheapest gateways available for $50 to $75 after rebates, and the most full-featured units costing no more than $250 to $300, even for devices that handle 802.11a, b, and g at the same time.

It's difficult to draw conclusions based on price, since most wireless gateways are quite similar. However, there are two times when you should be suspicious of a too-cheap gateway:

- Some inexpensive gateways cut corners in ways that may not be obvious initially. For instance, a particularly cheap gateway might come with an external dipole antenna, but one that can't be replaced with a higher gain antenna.

- Sometimes you may find inexpensive devices that are just plain wireless access points, not full-fledged wireless gateways. If you're looking for a wireless gateway, make sure the device comes with NAT and DHCP support, Ethernet ports, and the other features discussed in this chapter.

Points to consider when buying: Cheap gateways aren't necessarily bad, but make sure the very cheapest ones have the features you need.

Setting up a Gateway

Most wireless gateways have a lot in common despite minor cosmetic and organizational differences in their interfaces. In this chapter, we look at three popular gateways: the Linksys EtherFast Wireless AP + Cable/DSL Router w/4-Port Switch (model number BEFW11S4), the Linksys WRT54G Wireless-G Broadband Router, and Apple's AirPort Extreme Base Station. For each one, we'll provide two sets of instructions, one for a simple, open wireless network and another for a more secure wireless network.

((•)) **NOTE**

Linksys makes several EtherFast models, but when we say EtherFast in this chapter, we mean specifically the BEFW11S4. The Web-based interfaces of the other models look much the same. A newer version, the WRT54G, supports 802.11g networking, and we also cover its differences in this chapter.

If you use a gateway from another manufacturer, the instructions should be relatively similar; also see **Table 17.1** at the end of this chapter for a comprehensive listing of standard settings.

Linksys BEFW11S4

The Linksys EtherFast Wireless AP + Cable/DSL Router w/4-Port Switch (BEFW11S4) was one of the most popular 802.11b gateways sold for many months, making it a good example of access points that use a Web-based interface. Web-based interfaces used by other gateways all rely on the same set of information.

(((•))) **NOTE**

The newer 802.11g-based Linksys WRT54G has an almost identical configuration. We cover its differences in the next section.

To connect via the EtherFast's Web-based interface, your computer must be on the private 192.168.1.0 network; see the sidebar, "Configuring Your Computer to Perform Initial Setup," to set your computer up properly. The EtherFast is set to be at the IP address 192.168.1.1 out of the box, and its default password is admin (no user name is necessary).

Configuring Your Computer to Perform Initial Setup

To configure an access point with a built-in Web server that has its default IP address on a private network (usually the 192.168.1.0 network), you must set your computer's networking options so it's on the same network. You typically make this initial connection over an Ethernet cable connecting the computer and the gateway, not wirelessly, though you can perform all subsequent configuration via the wireless connection.

To configure Windows XP:

1. Open Control Panel, open Network Connections, and open the Local Area Connection device corresponding to your Ethernet adapter.

2. Click Properties in the General tab.

3. Select Internet Protocol (TCP/IP) and click Properties.

4. To avoid disturbing an existing connection, select the Alternate Configuration tab.

5. Select the User Configuration radio button.

6. Set the IP address to 192.168.1.49, subnet mask to 255.255.255.0, and gateway to 192.168.1.1. You may leave the other fields blank (**Figure 17.1**).

7. Click OK.

To configure Mac OS X:

1. Open the Network preferences pane, and choose Network Port Configurations from the Show pop-up menu.

2. Click the New button, select Built-In Ethernet, and enter Private Configuration as the name.

3. Make sure the box next to Private Configuration is checked, and select Private Configuration from the Show menu.

4. In the TCP/IP tab, set the IP address to 192.168.1.49, subnet mask to 255.255.255.0, and gateway to 192.168.1.1 (**Figure 17.2**). You may leave the other fields blank.

5. Click Apply Now.

You can later disable or delete these network configurations if you desire.

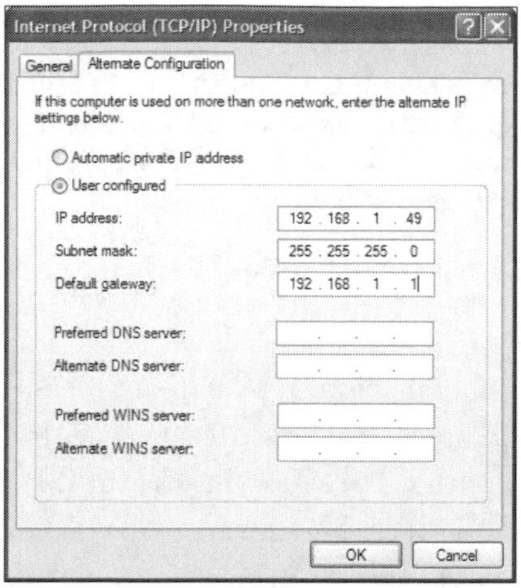

Figure 17.1
Configuring
Windows XP to
connect to a
gateway for the first
time.

Figure 17.2
Configuring Mac
OS X to connect to
a gateway for the
first time.

Simple Setup

Follow these instructions to set up a simple wireless network that shares your cable- or DSL-based Internet connection.

1. Once you've configured your computer appropriately, open a Web browser and in the Address field, type 192.168.1.1, and then press Enter.

    Your browser connects to the EtherFast's built-in Web server and presents you with a password dialog.

2. Enter admin as the password (you can leave the user name field blank), and press Enter again to convince the EtherFast that you are indeed allowed to configure the gateway.

    The EtherFast presents the Setup tab.

TIP

If you have the same model of EtherFast that we're configuring here, but its interface looks quite different, visit Linksys's Web site and see if there's a newer version of the firmware. As you can see, we're using version 1.42.7, from April 23, 2002, but earlier versions looked different.

3. Change the SSID field from "linksys" to whatever you want to name your network.

4. From the WAN Connection Type pop-up menu at the bottom of the screen, choose the appropriate connection type. In most cases, it will be Obtain an IP Automatically (which means your ISP assigns you a dynamic IP address) or Static IP (which means your ISP has given you a set IP address that never changes). Other options include PPPoE, RAS, and PPTP (**Figure 17.3**).

Figure 17.3
Configuring basic settings in the EtherFast's Setup tab.

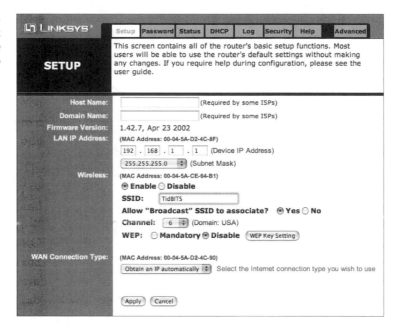

5. Click the Apply button, and when the EtherFast reports "Settings are successful" click the Continue button.

6. Click the Password link at the top of the screen to switch to the Password tab (**Figure 17.4**).

7. Enter your desired password in both Router Password text fields.

8. Click the Apply button, and when the EtherFast reports "Settings are successful" click the Continue button.

Figure 17.4
Changing the
EtherFast's default
password.

 TIP

*Although the EtherFast defaults to not allowing anyone outside of your local
private network to manage the gateway, even if they have the password,
you should still change the default password in the Password tab to prevent
someone from connecting via a wireless connection and messing with your
settings. If this were to happen, your only recourse would be to reset the
EtherFast to its factory defaults and reconfigure it.*

9.   Verify that you can connect to the wireless network and out to the Internet.
      You may wish to reset your computer to use DHCP to do this.

That's it—you should have a working wireless network that shares your Internet
connection and assigns IP addresses via DHCP.

Secure Network Setup

If you want your wireless network to be more secure, you must configure some
additional settings:

1.   Perform the instructions in "Simple Setup," and make sure everything
      works properly before enabling security settings.

2.   In the Setup tab, change Allow Broadcast SSID to Associate to No. That
      closes your network so passersby won't automatically see it listed with
      available networks.

3.   Set WEP to Mandatory, and click Continue next to the WEP options.

      The EtherFast displays the WEP Key Setting window.

4.   Choose either 64Bit or 128Bit from the first pop-up menu. 128Bit is slightly
      more secure, assuming all your equipment supports it, but requires that
      you enter a much longer WEP key each time you want to connect.

5. Either enter a passphrase and click the Generate button, or enter WEP keys manually. The advantage of the passphrase is that the keys are more random; the disadvantage of the passphrase is that random keys are much harder to remember and type (**Figure 17.5**).

Figure 17.5
Configuring basic settings in the EtherFast's Setup tab.

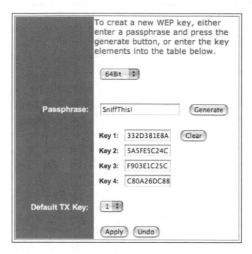

6. Click Apply to save your WEP key settings, and click Continue when the EtherFast reports "Settings are successful."

7. Back in the Setup tab, click the Apply button, and when the EtherFast reports "Settings are successful" click the Continue button.

8. Verify that you can still connect to your network, which requires that you enter the network name manually, along with the WEP key that you entered.

 TIP

If you screw something up and can't connect, remember that you can always reset the EtherFast to its factory defaults by pressing the reset switch on the back for 3 to 5 seconds. You should then close the network and verify that you can connect, and then enable WEP and verify that you can connect again.

Other Interesting Controls

The EtherFast's manual is good and rich with detail, but let's discuss a few of the more interesting things you can do with the EtherFast that may not be obvious initially.

*   In the Password tab, you can reset the EtherFast to its factory defaults, which may be easier than holding down the reset button for a few seconds, depending on where you've positioned the EtherFast.

- In the Status tab, you can check on the EtherFast's IP setup, which is useful if you're troubleshooting a connection problem with your ISP.

- In the DHCP tab, you can not only enable, disable, and configure DHCP settings, you can also check to see what computers the EtherFast has assigned IP addresses to by clicking the DHCP Clients Table button. This could help you determine if outsiders are using your network. Remember that the number of addresses you set here doesn't affect how many client computers the EtherFast can actually handle at the same time.

$((\bullet))$ **NOTE**

Because the EtherFast routes the whole local network out to the Internet whether or not addresses are assigned by DHCP, you can also set static IP addresses on the local network below the starting address you define. For instance, if you start DHCP at address 192.168.1.100, you could assign static addresses to machines that use port forwarding or other features requiring a fixed address to 192.168.1.2 through 192.168.1.99. Adam always does this so he can easily connect to all the computers on his local network by IP address.

- Click the orange Advanced button to switch to a different set of tabs where you can configure more advanced settings.

- Most people aren't likely to want to use the EtherFast's filters to prevent computers on a network from getting out via certain points, but it might be useful for preventing an addicted teenager from playing games for too many hours each day.

- If you want to make Internet services on a local machine available to computers on the Internet, you have two choices. You can enter that computer's IP address in the DMZ Host tab, which exposes all ports on that computer to the Internet, or you can make specific ports available in the Forwarding tab (**Figure 17.6**). Here we've forwarded traffic for port 80 (which is the Web) to the computer at 192.168.1.11, which is running a Web server. The Port Triggering button lets you set triggers for gaming.

- If your ISP allows only one specific MAC address to connect, you can have the EtherFast use that MAC address in the MAC Addr. Clone tab.

Linksys WRT54G

The Linksys WRT54G, as we noted at the start of this chapter, is nearly identical in configuration to its earlier cousin, the BEFW11S4. We wanted to highlight a few differences, though, which relate to its more advanced features.

Figure 17.6
Configuring port forwarding for the EtherFast.

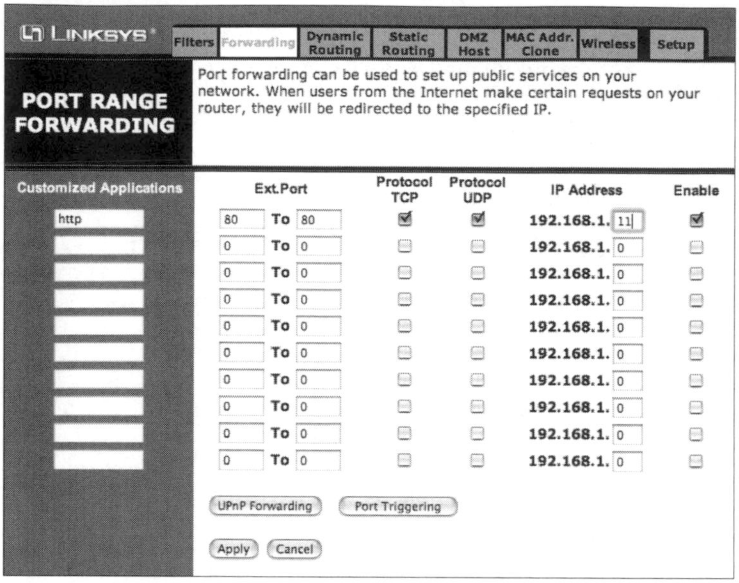

Security Options

In the Setup tab, selecting the Enable radio button next to Wireless Security and then clicking Edit Security Settings lets you choose more modern encryption options (**Figure 17.7**).

Figure 17.7
Security settings.

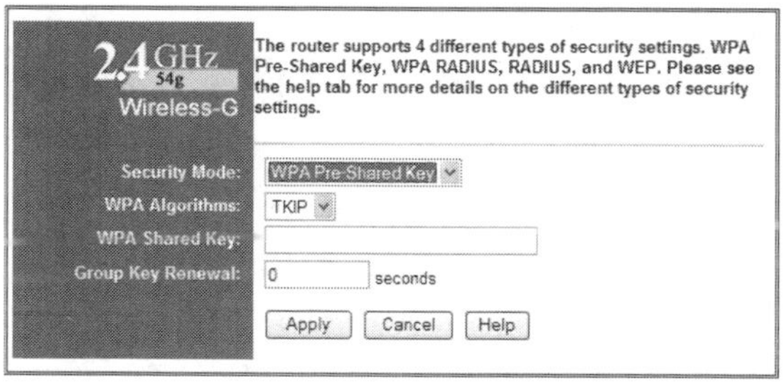

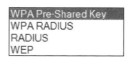

The encryption and authentication options (above) for the WRT54G.

The encryption options available from the Security Mode pop-up menu now extend way beyond WEP. They include:

• **WPA Pre-Shared Key.** The most likely option you would choose is WPA Pre-Shared Key, which lets you employ the strongest and simplest form of encryption available. (We discuss it in depth in Chapter 26, *Securing Data in Transit*.) When using WPA Pre-Shared Key, choose TKIP from the WPA, the most compatible key used with WPA, and enter a key of 8 to 26 characters, including punctuation, spaces, and numbers. The group key renewal feature isn't well explained: it's unclear whether it improves security at all.

- **WPA RADIUS.** This option enables you to use WPA with a back-end authentication server (see Chapter 22, *Small Office Wi-Fi Networking*).

- **RADIUS.** You can select RADIUS for WEP encryption with an authentication server (again, see Chapter 22, *Small Office Wi-Fi Networking*).

- **WEP.** Use old, broken WEP with this option.

Advanced Wireless

Click the Advanced tab at the upper right of the WRT54G's Web configuration screen, and then click the Advanced Wireless tab to set options that tune your high-speed performance (**Figure 17.8**).

Figure 17.8
Advanced Wireless
options.

The options that are most important when running an 802.11g-based network include:

- **Transmission Rate.** Use this pop-up menu to lock a speed on your network. Choosing a value other than Auto prevents some remote devices from connecting at all. For instance, if you set a value of 12 Mbps or higher, 802.11b adapters can't connect.

- **Frame Burst.** Enabling this option can improve throughput enormously on 802.11b/g and 802.11g networks. (See "802.11e: Quality of Service" in Chapter 4, *Other Wireless Standards*, for more details on frame or packet bursting.) Frame bursting is entirely compatible with other adapters: even those that don't offer frame bursting as a feature can still interpret frames that have been rewritten (or burst).

Dynamic DNS

The Linksys WRT54G supports dynamic DNS, so you can map a human-readable domain name to the dynamic IP address assigned to your computer by your ISP (see Chapter 16, *Buying a Wireless Gateway*). Click the Advanced tab at the upper right and then select the DDNS tab to access the dynamic DNS features (**Figure 17.9**). You can choose one of two providers, DynDNS.org or TZO.com.

Figure 17.9
Dynamic DNS
options.

AirPort Extreme Base Station

Apple's AirPort Extreme Base Station is a joy to configure—its settings are clearly labeled and have distinct purposes, and it provides a dedicated piece of Macintosh software, the AirPort Admin Utility, instead of a Web interface. (If you don't have a Mac, you have several other options; see the sidebar.)

Configuring without an AirPort Card or Macintosh

If you lack a Macintosh, a Mac with an AirPort card, or a Mac running a new enough Mac OS to run the Airport Admin Utility, you can still use one of two tools to configure an AirPort or AirPort Extreme Base Station:

- A Java-based configuration program that runs on several platforms. Download it from http://edge.mcs.drexel.edu/GICL/people/sevy/airport/.

- Apple's unsupported AirPort Extreme Admin Utility for Windows. Download it from http://docs.info.apple.com/article

.html?artnum=120226. This utility supports only the AirPort Extreme Base Station and the newer snow AirPort Base Station, not the original graphite AirPort Base Station. At this writing, it's not just unsupported, it's also a beta version.

Of course, you can always do what Windows users did before these utilities appeared: invite a friend with an iBook or PowerBook over to dinner. Once you've configured a base station, you usually don't need to use Apple's Admin Utility again.

NOTE

You cannot configure an AirPort Extreme Base Station if your Mac runs Mac OS 9 or earlier.

NOTE

Many of the settings discussed in this section—except for WDS and the 802.11g choices—are identical for the older graphite and snow AirPort Base Stations that support only 802.11b.

NOTE

Often after installing an AirPort software update, the next time you connect to your AirPort Base Station, the AirPort Admin Utility will prompt you to update the unit's firmware. Before updating firmware, it's a good idea to save the unit's configuration just in case the upgrade erases any of your settings.

Simple Setup

AirPort Admin Utility hides most settings from you on your first connection, presenting you with just the critical settings you need to set up a straightforward Wi-Fi network.

1. Open AirPort Admin Utility (likely located in the Utilities folder inside your Applications folder).

2. In the Select Base Station window you see any AirPort or AirPort Extreme Base Stations on the local network; selecting one displays additional details about it (**Figure 17.10**). To connect to a base station, double-click it. You must also enter its password if it's not already stored in the system Keychain.

Figure 17.10
Connecting to local
base stations.

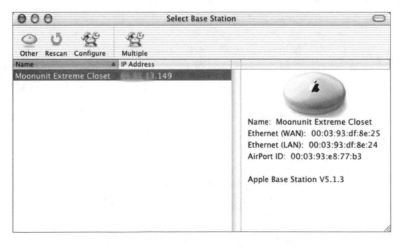

TIP

If your base station doesn't appear in the list but has a static IP address, you can connect to it by clicking Other and entering the IP address and password in the connection dialog that appears. You can also configure base stations over the Internet this way.

TIP

The default password for a new base station is public *(all lowercase).*

3. AirPort Admin Utility shows the Show Summary tab by default (**Figure 17.11**). Click the Name and Password button.

Figure 17.11
Summary tab's
display.

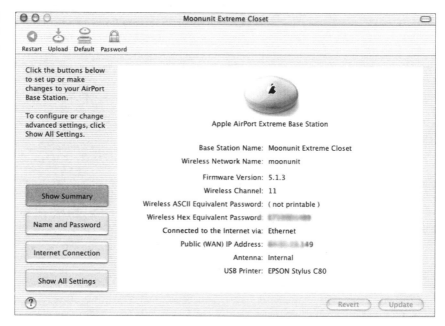

4. In the Name and Password screen, enter a name in the Base Station Name field that identifies this base station uniquely, and then click Change Password and set the password necessary to access the base station (**Figure 17.12**).

5. Rename the network by entering a new name in the Wireless Network Name field, which is the SSID for this device.

TIP

If you have multiple base stations connected to your Ethernet network and want to enable roaming among them, make sure to use the same network name for all of them.

6. Click the Internet Connection button.

Figure 17.12
Setting the base station's name and password.

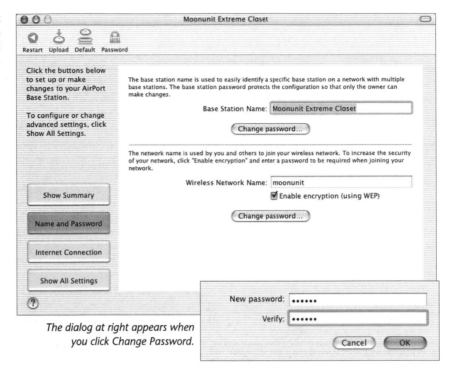

The dialog at right appears when you click Change Password.

7. In the Internet Connection screen, enter the settings necessary to connect your base station to the Internet as outlined in the list below (**Figure 17.13**).

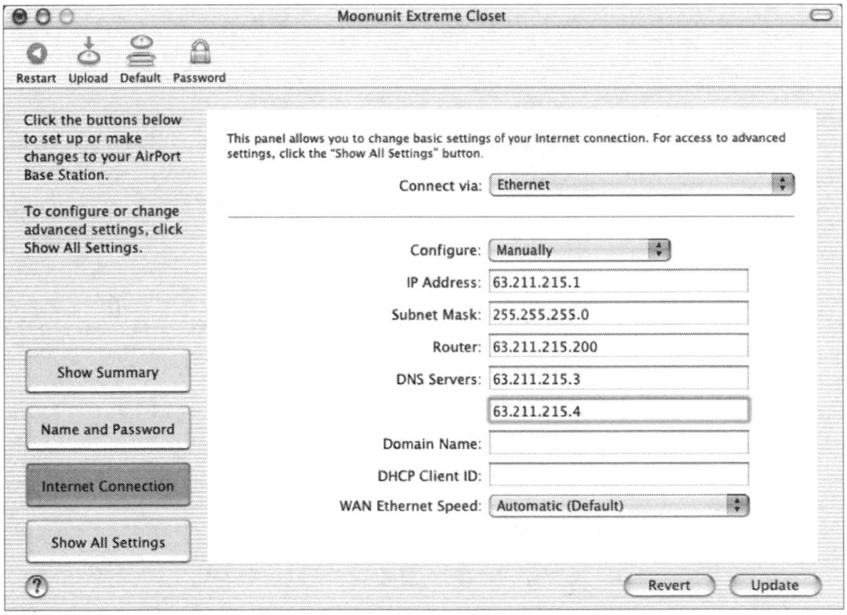

Figure 17.13
Configuring your Internet connection.

- For DSL and cable modem Internet connections, choose Ethernet from the Connect Via pop-up menu, and choose DHCP from the Configure pop-up menu. If your ISP requires that you use a DHCP Client ID, enter it in the DHCP Client ID field (this setting is often essential to making a connection work).

- Some broadband services require that you log in using PPP over Ethernet. If that's true of your ISP, choose PPP over Ethernet (PPPoE) from the Connect Via pop-up menu, and enter your account name and password (**Figure 17.14**).

- For dial-up Internet connections, choose the Modem setting that's available, and enter your ISP's dial-in information.

Figure 17.14
Setting up PPP over Ethernet.

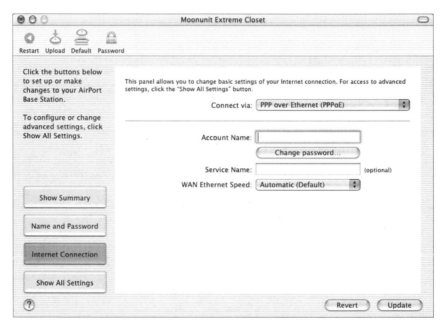

8. Click Update.

The base station should reboot and connect to the Internet.

Secure Network Setup

If you want to turn on WEP encryption, which we recommend, follow steps 1 to 5 in the previous section, and in the Name and Password tab perform the following steps:

1. Check Enable Encryption (Using WEP), and click the Change Password button.

2. Enter the WEP password as text and from the WEP Key Length pop-up menu, choose 40-bit or 128-bit (**Figure 17.15**). Stick with 128-bit WEP unless you have older devices that can handle only 40-bit WEP.

Figure 17.15
Entering the
WEP password
and choosing
encryption depth.

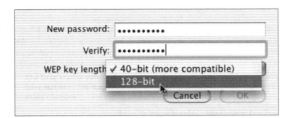

3. Continue by following steps 6, 7, and 8 in the previous section.

NOTE

According to a statement that Apple made in June 2003, Apple will add WPA (Wi-Fi Protected Access) as an option by the end of 2003. Check our site for updates.

Advanced Controls

The basic controls to set up a network are just the tip of the iceberg with Apple's AirPort Admin Utility. After you've connected to a base station, click the Show All Settings button in the main screen, and the full set of tabs and details appear in their full glory. Some of these are repeated from our instructions above, but they appear typically with more detail here.

NOTE

After making any changes, click the Update button at the bottom of the window to save your changes and reboot the base station with the new settings. Click Revert to abandon changes and go back to the previously loaded configuration.

AirPort Tab

The AirPort tab contains basic information about the AirPort Base Station, including details such as the name of the unit (used to identify it in the AirPort Admin Utility's Select Base Station window), and optional details such as the contact person and location (**Figure 17.16**). You can set the administrative password by clicking Change Password.

Click the WAN Privacy button to set a few obscure items that affect how visible the base station is on the Internet and local network (**Figure 17.17**).

- SNMP (Simple Network Management Protocol) allows network management software to monitor the base station's performance.

Figure 17.16
Naming and
locating the base
station.

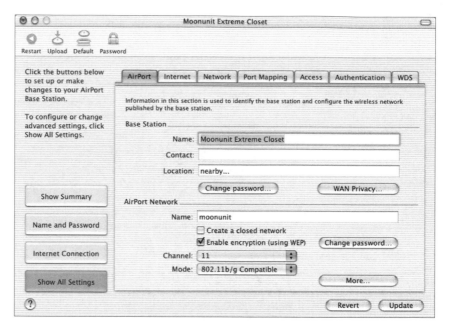

Figure 17.17
Setting WAN
privacy options.

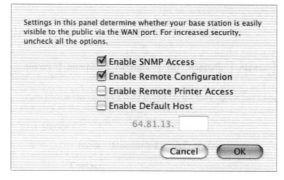

- Remote Configuration is dangerous: when enabled, anyone on the Internet can try to connect to your base station (otherwise, it's possible to connect to the base station only from your local network).

- Enabling remote printer access allows people outside your local network to print to a USB printer connected to the base station.

- We were unable to find documentation on Enable Default Host at Apple's site or elsewhere!

 TIP

If you select Enable Remote Configuration, make sure to change the default password!

The AirPort tab lets you set the basic access point settings (**Figure 17.16**, above). The Name is your network name (as opposed to the base station's name). Checking Create a Closed Network prevents the base station from broadcasting its name, and thus hides the network from casual users.

Check Enable Encryption (Using WEP) to turn on WEP encryption, and click the Change Password button to configure your WEP key. See step 2 under "Secure Network Setup," earlier.

TIP

If you want PCs or non-AirPort-equipped Macs to connect after you set a WEP password, choose Equivalent Network Password from the Base Station menu to retrieve your WEP key in hexadecimal, suitable for entering into other wireless client software.

Choose a channel from the Channel pop-up menu. Make sure that if there are multiple base stations within range, you choose non-overlapping channels. (See Chapter 2, *Wireless Standards*, for details on selecting a channel.)

The Mode pop-up menu lets you exclude either 802.11b or 802.11g clients from your network, although most of the time you want to allow mixed 802.11b/g networking by choosing 802.11b/g Compatible.

Click the More button to set a few radio settings that may seem esoteric but can be surprisingly helpful in many situations (**Figure 17.18**).

Figure 17.18
Setting radio options.

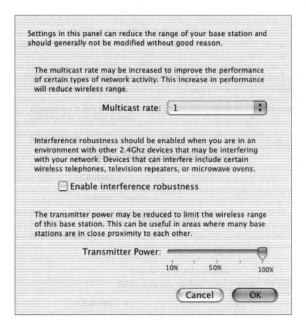

- Multicast sets the lowest threshold for connection, which can prevent more-distant computers with weak signal strength from associating with the AirPort Base Station. You can speed up a network but reduce the effective network range by raising the threshold above 1 Mbps.

- Check Enable Interference Robustness if your network appears to have problems with competing networks or other sources of interference like a 2.4 GHz cordless phone or nearby microwave oven.

- Reducing Transmitter Power from 100 percent reduces the range of the base station, but also decreases the likelihood of interference with adjacent Wi-Fi access points.

Internet Tab

In the Internet tab, you set the options for connecting your base station to an ISP (**Figure 17.19**). The Connect Using menu allows you to choose the network method, such as Ethernet, PPPoE, Modem, or AOL. If you use a cable or DSL modem without PPPoE, choose Ethernet.

Figure 17.19
Configuring your
base station to
connect to your ISP
with Connect Using
options inset.

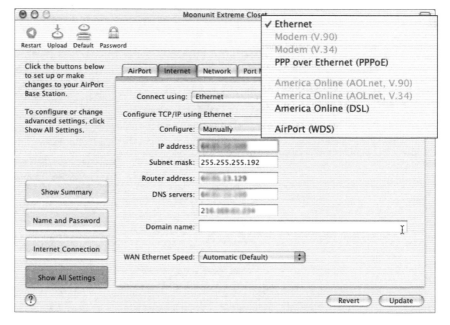

The settings you enter here are identical to what you would use when connecting to your ISP from a single computer, so refer to the information provided by your ISP for the details.

The AirPort (WDS) item in the Connect Using pop-up menu enables you to bridge multiple base stations to extend a network wirelessly. See Chapter 20, *Bridging Wireless Networks*, for detailed instructions on using WDS (Wireless Distribution System).

Network Tab

The Network tab offers a variety of interrelated options that together provide network services like DHCP and NAT. Contextual help at the bottom of the window explains each setting as you select it.

Checking Distribute IP Addresses turns DHCP service on, which tells the AirPort Base Station's DHCP server to offer IP addresses to all the computers that connect to it. You have two choices for how addresses are shared: using DHCP and NAT or using a range of IP addresses with just DHCP.

If your ISP provides you with multiple static IP addresses to use for computers connected to your AirPort Extreme Base Station, you can choose Share a Range of IP Addresses (Using Only DHCP) and enter your IP address range (**Figure 17.20**).

You should select Share a Single IP Address (Using DHCP and NAT) if your Internet connection provides you with only a single IP address, which is probably the most common situation (**Figure 17.21**). Apple suggests, in its pop-up menu ranges, three well-known, non-routable, private address ranges. However, you can also choose your own from the Other menu.

Figure 17.20
Configuring your base station to share a single IP address.

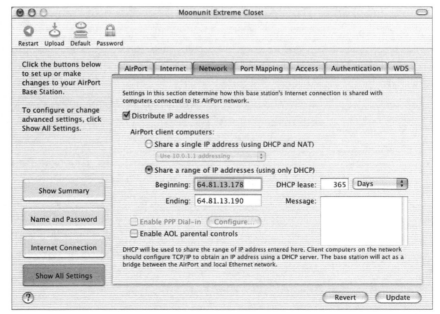

Figure 17.21
Configuring your
base station to
share a range of IP
addresses.

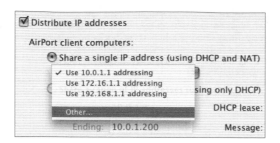

You can set the length of time a DHCP number can be used by one of your client computers. If you have more computers that might want to connect than available IP addresses, set the DHCP lease time low to avoid tying them all up. If you have more than enough IP addresses to share out to your regular users, then you can set the DHCP lease time high so each individual user is likely to keep the same IP address for a while.

Checking Enable PPP Dial-in lets you turn an AirPort Extreme Base Station into an Internet modem bridge, so you can connect to your local network while you're traveling. Click Configure and a dialog lets you set access parameters (**Figure 17.22**).

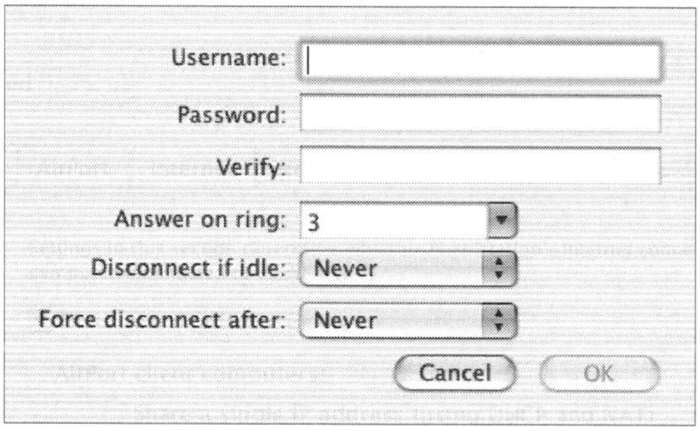

Figure 17.22
Enabling dial-in
access for an AirPort
Extreme Base
Station.

Username:	
Password:	
Verify:	
Answer on ring:	3
Disconnect if idle:	Never
Force disconnect after:	Never

Cancel　　OK

Lastly, the Enable AOL Parental Controls checkbox works in conjunction with dialing into AOL or using AOL Broadband, and it lets parents enforce policies within the base station.

Port Mapping and Access Tabs

The options in the Port Mapping tab let you map outside ports to computers on your wireless network that you want to be accessible from the Internet. We talk about port mapping in Chapter 16, *Buying a Wireless Gateway*. The Access tab offers options for controlling which unique wireless devices can connect to the base station; for more about controlling access by MAC address, see Chapter 25, *Preventing Access to Your Network*.

Authentication

The Authentication tab provides settings for configuring your base station to communicate with an authentication server to handle user logins. Users must have client software on their computers that enables them to enter their credentials when prompted; the base station hands these credentials off to a RADIUS or other authentication server, and then allows users to connect only if the authentication server confirms their identity.

Unless you're in an office or corporate environment, you can ignore this tab. (See Chapter 22, *Small Office Wi-Fi Networking*, for details on authentication servers.)

WDS Tab

We explain WDS and the WDS tab in Chapter 20, *Bridging Wireless Networks*.

Common Gateway Settings

To configure any access point, you must enter a few pieces of information. Although this may seem intimidating, most gateways ship with a default configuration or pick up some settings appropriately once you've made the necessary connections. Other settings you determine when planning your network, by referring to the documentation from your ISP, or talking to a network-savvy friend or colleague. **Table 17.1** outlines common settings, alternate names, and the type of information you'd enter for each.

Connecting to a Base Station without an AirPort Card

PC users and Mac users with older equipment may face the task of trying to connect to an AirPort or AirPort Extreme Base Station without having access to Apple's AirPort client software. That's usually not a problem, since connecting to one of these base stations is much like connecting to any other access point. The one difference is in determining the WEP key used to encrypt communications.

If WEP is enabled on the base station, you must use Apple's AirPort Admin Utility to obtain the non-AirPort WEP key.

1. Launch AirPort Admin Utility.

2. Connect to your base station.

3. In the list of icons at the top of the window, click Password, or choose Equivalent Network Password from the Base Station menu.

If you don't have a Mac that can run the AirPort Admin Utility, try the two tools noted in the sidebar, "Configuring without an AirPort Card or Macintosh." WPA might complicate this option; visit our Web site for updates.

Table 17.1

Common Configuration Settings for Gateways

Setting	What It Might Also Be Called	Explanation	Example Settings and Values
SSID (Service Set Identifier)	Network name, ESSID (Extended SSID for networks with two or more access points)	Clients connect to Wi-Fi networks by name. For networks with multiple access points, all should be named identically.	moonunit
Access point name	Base station name, unit name	Some configuration software uses this name to distinguish among available access points.	Bobmarley
IP address	WAN IP address	The gateway's external IP address. With most ISPs, your gateway picks this address up via DHCP, although you can also enter it manually. (You won't see this or the next three settings with PPPoE.)	24.6.5.130
Gateway		The IP address of the Internet router to which your gateway connects. Again, DHCP usually provides this automatically.	24.6.5.1
Subnet mask		The subnet mask defines the size of the local network. DHCP provides this in most cases; otherwise ask your ISP.	255.255.255.0
DNS servers	Name servers	DNS servers are necessary mainly if the gateway acts as a DHCP server, so the DNS addresses can be passed on to the client computers. Your ISP's DHCP usually provides DNS server information.	24.6.15.100 24.6.15.22
Local IP address	LAN IP address	The gateway's address on your internal network.	192.168.1.1
Channel		802.11b has 14 channels, only certain of which are allowed for use depending on the country you're in; to avoid signal overlap, choose among channels 1, 6, or 11 for adjacent access points in dense networks.	6
Closed network	Hidden network, turn off beaconing	Hides the network name from casual browsers.	

PPPoE	PPP over Ethernet	Used to login to an Internet account, most often with cable modems.	Username: tristane Password: 98fink1e!
DHCP client		Turn on the DHCP client if your gateway needs to identify itself to acquire its IP address from a DHCP server.	DHCP Client ID: SWBELL001
DHCP server		A DHCP server provides IP addresses to client computers on your network. Some gateways let you pick the range of addresses to use and the length of time a DHCP lease lasts.	192.168.1.1–192.168.1.150 Lease time: 1 day
NAT	Network Address Translation, private address server	NAT is often built into the DHCP server option rather than broken out separately.	
Firewall	Filtering	Restricts traffic from or to specific services or IP addresses.	Ban all traffic from network 36.44.0.0.
Port forwarding	Port mapping, punch-through	Redirects incoming requests to a specific service to a port on a specific machine.	Inbound port 80 on the gateway connects to port 8127 on machine 192.168.1.53.
DMZ	Virtual server	Allows a single machine to appear as though it, instead of the gateway, is directly accessible from the Internet.	
Trigger		Enables compatibility with games that need to accept incoming traffic on ranges of ports.	When a local computer connects out via port 3307, open inbound ports 4000–5000 to that machine.
WEP	Encryption, security, network password	Allows up to four keys to be used to encrypt all traffic passing between adapters and the access point.	F71A82FF0D
WPA	WPA-PSK, WPA passphrase	Uses a new encryption method that relies on a passphrase to generate robust keys automatically.	Inky, dinky, foo.
Antenna diversity		Units with more than one antenna can have one antenna set to receive and the other to transmit, or both to overlap these functions.	

Setting	What It Might Also Be Called	Explanation	Example Settings and Values
Transmit speed	Tx speed, compatibility	For full compatibility with 802.11b, gateways must handle lower speeds; turning this off in smaller, close-range networks can improve overall network performance.	
802.11b/g		Newer gateways with 802.11g support may work in a g-only mode, mixed mode, and/or b-only mode.	g only
Admin password		All gateways let you secure the configuration by setting a password.	ish234#kab
Clone MAC address	Rewrite MAC address	Lets you change the unique Ethernet address on the access point to match, for instance, a registered address of another machine that an ISP allows onto its network.	08:23:1c:55:F4:0D
Firmware	Upgrade software	Not a setting, but a control that typically lets you select a firmware upgrade file to upload to the gateway, after which the gateway reboots.	
Modem settings		Enter the ISP's phone number, and often an alternate, along with user name and password information.	Number: 123-4567 Username: tristane Password: 98fink1e!
Dynamic DNS	DDNS	Choose a service, like DynDNS.org, from a pop-up menu and enter your account details to have your gateway's IP number matched to a host name, even when the IP number changes.	User name: stinkelfuss Password: 98finkle! Host Name: shoe.leather.com
WDS	Wireless Distribution System	Choose other access points with which this gateway exchanges data wirelessly, and other settings to make a gateway a master in a WDS network.	MAC address: 03:08:3F:AC:EE:66

Wireless Gadgets

Since 802.11b's introduction, we've been waiting for Wi-Fi technology to migrate from pure network devices for computers into digital appliances and consumer electronics, like cameras, media players, and even clothing. The future is finally here.

The utility of having Wi-Fi in consumer electronics and other digital devices is ubiquitous communication with your computer, with the Internet, and with other Wi-Fi devices. The advantages enjoyed by the business traveler accessing the Internet via a Wi-Fi network in an airport may be even more exciting for the photographer who can use a Wi-Fi–enabled digital camera to transfer photos automatically to a shared server as they're taken or for the digital media buff who can now play MP3s streamed wirelessly from a computer to a media player attached to a stereo.

All work and no play makes a wireless network dull, so read on for brief descriptions of gadgets that use Wi-Fi to liven up your network and your life.

((•)) **NOTE**
> *The consumer electronics world changes quickly, so it's almost certain that details you read here will have changed since we wrote about them. Think of these product descriptions as launch pads from which you can find out more about what's possible and what's available.*

Cameras

What could you possibly use wireless for in a digital camera? Storage, actually. High-resolution, digital still cameras store photos that can take up 6 MB or even much more space on an internal device. CompactFlash and SD (Secure Digital) cards continue to grow in size, with CompactFlash now available in sizes up to 1 GB. But since you almost always transfer photos to a computer for culling and processing, why not take advantage of the massive hard disks in today's computers and use Wi-Fi to send photos directly to the computer?

Even if you don't replace the internal storage on the camera with wireless connectivity, being able to transfer photos from the camera's internal memory card to a computer via Wi-Fi is a welcome improvement over fussing with USB cables or memory card readers.

((•)) **NOTE**

You can also find cameras that support Bluetooth for transferring photos. The problem with them is speed—Bluetooth doesn't have the bandwidth to transmit a high-resolution picture quickly. We've seen transmission times from 20 seconds to 145 seconds...per photo! Ouch.

Lastly, digital cameras can take advantage of wireless communications to send photos to compatible printers (though we've never understood why people want to print directly from the camera without at least seeing the photo at full size on a computer monitor first), or to a computer to send by email.

It's even easier to see wanting Wi-Fi connectivity to stream video from a video camera to a computer. Today's cameras might be able to stream only lower-quality video, but with the combination of the latest video compression standards, like MPEG-4, and the latest Wi-Fi standards, like 802.11g (54 Mbps) and 802.11e (streaming media), we might see digital-video-quality streams in the near future.

Digital Still Cameras

Wi-Fi is just starting to appear in digital cameras as we write, with Nikon's D2H Pro being the first one that goes beyond the prototype stage, though it's not yet available for sale (**Figure 18.1**). The D2H is a 4.1-megapixel camera that can capture up to eight frames per second. It's clearly aimed at the professional photographer, particularly photojournalists and sports photographers. What makes it interesting to us, though, is the optional WT-1A Wireless Transmitter accessory, which screws on the bottom of the camera, draws its power from the camera's battery, and connects to the camera's USB 2.0 port via a short cable. A supplied antenna provides connectivity within 100 feet (30 meters); an optional antenna increases that range to 490 feet (150 meters). Internally, the Nikon D2H uses an FTP client to transmit photos from its memory card to a remote FTP server. It always buffers the images on the card, but can transmit

Figure 18.1
Nikon D2H Pro
camera.

while writing to the card. You can read more at www.nikonusa.com/templates/ main.jsp?content=/fileuploads/slr_0703/slr_0703.html.

Similarly enticing is the 3.24-megapixel Caplio Pro G3 from Ricoh, which can reportedly accept optional cards for Wi-Fi, Bluetooth, or GPS (Global Positioning System, for marking the exact coordinates of where photos were taken). We were unable to find additional details about this camera in English, but if you can read Japanese (or want to try the Babel Fish translation service at http://babelfish.altavista.com/), take a look at www.ricoh.co.jp/dc/product/ pro_g3/. It's apparently for sale in Japan for 99,800 yen, or about $850.

Nikon and Ricoh may be the first to ship Wi-Fi–capable cameras, but in July 2003, Sanyo Electric showed the DSC-SX560 prototype, a 1.5-megapixel camera that supports a Wi-Fi CompactFlash adapter for transferring images via Wi-Fi rather than storing them on an internal memory card. The information is available only in Japanese, and we were unable to find details about when the camera might ship or what it might cost.

Shortly after Sanyo showed its prototype, Fuji Photo Film showed a prototype of a 3-megapixel camera that could use wireless networking to send photos either to remote computers or to wireless-capable printers. Company representatives noted that the camera would also be able to receive photos sent from computers and said that transmission time would take only seconds. Price and release date for the camera haven't been set yet.

Video Cameras

Wireless networking vendor D-Link offers a pair of Wi-Fi video cameras for webcam or surveillance use (**Figure 18.2**). Both cameras have motion

Figure 18.2
D-Link wireless
video cameras.

detection capabilities. The D-Link DCS-1000W (www.dlink.com/products/ ?model=DCS-1000W) costs about $275 and provides a picture up to 640 by 480 dpi in size, with frame rates between 1 and 20 frames per second. It uses 802.11b or 10/100 Mbps Ethernet to connect to your network and provides a built-in Web server for serving the video stream. Then there's the DCS-2100+ (www.dlink.com/products/?pid=17), which costs about $330 and adds frame rates up to 30 frames per second and audio.

Never one to be left behind, in September 2003, Linksys released the Linksys Wireless-B Internet Video Camera, which is a standalone webcam with its own IP address for attaching to any wired or wireless network (**Figure 18.3**). It uses MPEG-4 video compression to provide a 320 by 240 dpi video image, and it can detect motion, record images with date and time stamps, and send email with a short video clip attached when motion is detected. True to form,

Figure 18.3
Linksys Wireless-
B Internet Video
Camera.

Linksys sells the camera below the cost of competitors, for about $230. For more information, see www.linksys.com/products/product.asp?grid=33&scid =38&prid=566.

TIP

Avoid video cameras from X10. Even ignoring the fact that X10 had one of the slimiest advertising campaigns on the face of the Internet, the company uses a proprietary method of transferring video in the 2.4 GHz band and these cameras will interfere horribly with 802.11b and 802.11g networks. Just before this book went to press, they had filed for bankruptcy, too!

Moving up in cost, we next come to the Toshiba IK-WB11a, an $800 Wi-Fi camera that offers video streams at a much higher resolution (1280 by 960 dpi) than the D-Link cameras. It too is designed for monitoring, with indoor/ outdoor mounts, a Secure Digital card slot that records to the card should the network go down, an email alarm feature, motion detection, and remote pan and tilt. Toshiba will even rent you 500 GB of storage on a Web site so you can archive what Toshiba estimates as 30 days of continuous footage. Like pretty much all these devices, you configure and control it via a Web browser, and it offers both 802.11b and 10/100 Mbps Ethernet connections. You can find full specifications at www.toshiba.com/taisisd/netcam/.

Lastly, we find the IQinvision IQeye3, which initially seems comparable to the Toshiba camera (**Figure 18.4**). It offers 1288 by 968 dpi resolution and digital pan, tilt, and zoom, but then it goes beyond the Toshiba camera with bandwidth throttling, privacy zones, day/night mode, and support for power over Ethernet. You can program it to transfer the video it collects via FTP or email. The IQeye3 is designed for standard industrial mountings and accepts standard lenses, along with an optional Wi-Fi card if you don't want to use the built-in 10/100 Mbps Ethernet port. It's not cheap, though, at about $1300. Learn more at www.iqinvision.com/prd/IQe3.htm.

Figure 18.4
IQinvision IQeye3
video camera.

Printers and Adapters

It's easy to take printers for granted, at least until you realize you want to locate one in a place that isn't easily reached by cables—either USB cables from your computer or Ethernet cables from your wired network. Luckily, there are Wi-Fi and Bluetooth solutions for just this problem.

Printer Adapters

If you already own an Ethernet-capable printer, the easiest way to make it wireless is with a simple wireless Ethernet adapter, like the Linksys WET11 or Linksys WET54G (www.linksys.com). There's nothing printer-specific about these products: all they do is stand in for a chunk of Ethernet cable. In most cases, there's probably little advantage to using a faster 802.11g wireless Ethernet adapter.

That's not to say that you can't buy devices aimed specifically at printers. The IBM 802.11b Wireless Print Adapter costs $215 and converts any IBM Infoprint 1000 family printer from Ethernet to wireless. It's unclear if there's anything special about either the IBM Wireless Print Adapter or the Infoprint 1000 printers such that you must use one with the other. See www.printers.ibm.com/internet/wwsites.nsf/vwWebPublished/wgwirelessadapter_ww for more information.

Changing technology gears, what if you have a USB printer and a Bluetooth-capable handheld or laptop? Epson's $130 Bluetooth Print Adapter works with a small set of Epson USB inkjet printers to enable wireless Bluetooth printing within 30 feet from Palms, Pocket PCs, and PC laptops (no Macintosh compatibility that we could find, unfortunately). Learn more at www.epson.com/cgi-bin/Store/ProductQuickSpec.jsp?oid=16489220.

More generic is the Axis 5810 Print Plug (www.axis.com/products/axis_5810/), which plugs into the parallel port of any printer and enables a small number of Bluetooth-enabled devices (though not Macs) to print to it. The catch? It's available only in Japan and Europe. A similar device, the Troy WindConnect Bluetooth Wireless Printer Adapter (www.troygroup.com/wireless/products/wireless/windconnect.asp), may be available, though one retailer claimed it had been discontinued.

Print Servers

For USB-based printers, and those with only parallel ports, you can't often get away with just a wireless adapter, because the printer doesn't have the internal software necessary for it to act as a network printer. For such situations, you need a Wi-Fi print server, which combines wireless capabilities with the necessary code to manage print jobs submitted from computers on the wireless network. All these devices cost around $100.

For instance, you might check out the D-Link DP311U, which connects a USB-based printer to your wireless network, or the D-Link DP311P, which does the same for printers with parallel ports. Linksys offers a pair of similar products: the $85 EtherFast PPS1UW Wireless-Ready USB PrintServer (which requires that you add a wireless card) and the $125 WPS11 Wireless PrintServer (**Figure 18.5**).

Figure 18.5
Linksys wireless
print servers.

A number of wireless gateways, such as the Asanté FR1004AL (www.asante.com/ products/routers/FR1004AL/), also include print server capabilities, so you can plug your parallel port printer into them and access it from any computer on your network. More unusual is Apple's AirPort Extreme Base Station (www.apple.com/airport/), which includes a USB port for sharing USB printers with Macs, an uncommon feature.

 TIP

Macintosh users beware. Other than the AirPort Extreme Base Station, print servers that work with USB and parallel port printers make those printers available to Macs only if the printer supports PostScript, a high-end printing language.

Axis has a Bluetooth print server as well, the 5800+ Mobile that works much like the 5810 Print Plug, but it too is available only in Japan and Europe. You can learn more about it at www.axis.com/products/axis_5800p/.

You might not bother with a wireless print server at all if location isn't that important, since both Windows and the Mac OS offer printer sharing capabilities: you can plug a printer into a Mac or a PC and share it with all the other computers on your network, wired and wireless. The main caveat here is that sharing printers between operating systems can be quite tricky. Dave from Thursby Software Systems (www.thursby.com/products/dave.html) helps smooth out problems between Windows and the Mac.

TIP

These products are print servers, *not* print spoolers, *and that's an important distinction. For a print server to work, the printer must be turned on, and when you send it a print job, the printout appears right away. With a print spooler, the device acting as the print spooler holds onto the print job if the printer isn't turned on and prints it only when the printer comes online. That's great if, for instance, your printer is in another room and you forget to turn it on before printing. Adam loves print spooling because much of what he prints isn't time sensitive, so he likes being able to send the print job one day and turn on the printer hours or even days later to get it out.*

Printers

Of course, if you're buying a new printer and know that wireless access is a must, you can always look for a printer that has Wi-Fi built in. Samsung offers the ML2152W, a 21 page-per-minute, monochrome laser printer with access via 802.11b. It uses PostScript 3, prints at 1200 by 1200 dpi, and costs about $550. See www.samsung.com/Products/Printer/Laser/Printer_Laser_ML_2152W.htm for more information.

If Samsung's beefy laser printer isn't geeky enough for you, there's always the Nomad printer from Mobile Command Systems (**Figure 18.6**). It's a 4-inch thermal roll printer you can wear on your belt and communicate with via optional Wi-Fi or Bluetooth cards. It's not cheap at $800, but let's face it, it's designed for vertical market applications like printing on-site receipts for delivery folks. See www.mobilecommand.net/files/nomad.html for details.

Figure 18.6
Mobile Command
Systems Nomad
printer.

Wi-Fi Detectors

Don't want to fire up NetStumbler or KisMAC on your laptop to see if any Wi-Fi networks are in your vicinity? A couple of cool gadgets aim to give you an alternative.

 TIP

A PocketPC handheld with MiniStumbler is way more expensive than either of these devices, but it might be the best option. You can download MiniStumbler from www.netstumbler.com. *Make sure you have a supported Wi-Fi card.*

Kensington's Wi-Fi Finder is a slim, handheld device that detects nearby wireless networks with the press of a button, indicating signal strength with three lights. Unfortunately, it's not all it's cracked up to be. It has trouble detecting all but the strongest 802.11b access points, and early users reported that it didn't see 802.11g networks at all (though that may, of course, change by the time you read this). It also reportedly can't see WEP-encrypted networks, and its LEDs are too dim to see easily in the sun. On the positive side, it costs only about $30. Visit www.kensington.com/html/3720.html to learn more, or search the Web to see reports about it.

For a competing product, check out the Smart ID WFS-1 Wi-Fi detector (**Figure 18.7**). It's roughly the same size and price as the Kensington Wi-Fi Finder. It also checks only when you press a button, but has four LEDs to indicate signal strength, and online reports such as www.securityfocus.com/infocus/1727 indicate that it works better than Kensington's product. Read more about it at www.smartid.com.sg/prod01.htm.

Figure 18.7
Smart ID WFS-1 Wi-Fi detector.

Lastly, there's the WiFisense, which isn't so much a product you can buy (you can't) as a wearable art project (**Figure 18.8**). It's a shiny silver handbag studded with 64 red LEDs that light up to indicate the availability, quality, and accessibility of nearby wireless networks. Whenever the WiFisense detects a wireless network, it uses patterns of light and sound to provide details about the network's signal strength and status. It's extremely cool as a demonstration of technology that could be built into other products, though a little bright for us. See the WiFisense Web site at www.wifisense.com.

Figure 18.8
WiFisense handbag
detector.

 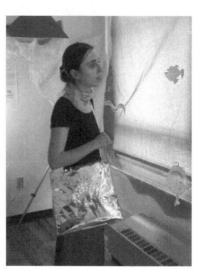

File Servers

You may think that file servers are only for businesses, but two firms are trying to change that impression with small, silent file servers that connect to your other computers via Wi-Fi.

The slim NetDrive Wireless from Martian Technology is essentially a low-power x86-compatible computer running a Linux kernel and dedicated to file and printer sharing tasks. It comes standard with either a 120 GB ($480) or a 40 GB ($400) hard drive, or you can buy a $380 kit that comes with a CD-ROM player for installing the operating system on any drive you choose to add. You connect the NetDrive to your network via an 802.11b (with 802.11g available by the time you read this) or a standard 10/100 Mbps Ethernet cable. Once installed and turned on, you can store files on it or plug a USB printer into it for printer sharing with Windows and Linux machines (or Macs using Gimp-Print). The NetDrive uses SMB for file sharing, which means it's compatible with Windows, Mac OS X, and Linux, and it has beta support for AppleShare, which will enable it to work with Mac OS 9. Mac users aren't limited to storing normal files on it as a network volume; it also supports iTunes Music Sharing, so you can store all your MP3s on it and have them automatically appear in iTunes everywhere on your network. It even works with the SLIMP3 music player (discussed later). See www.martian.com for full details and ordering information.

((•)) **NOTE**

We're so distraught! In the final checks before going to press, we learned that Martian Technology is no longer selling directly to the public. Sorry!

The Martian NetDrive is extremely cool, but for an even smaller and geekier Wi-Fi file server, check out the Sony FSV-PGX1, which is also a Linux-based file server with support for 802.11b. While the Martian NetDrive Wireless is about the size of a ream of paper or a thick reference book, the Sony product is more the size of a paperback book. It has only a 20 GB hard drive, and it supports SMB, NFS, and FTP for sharing files. It's actually meant as a portable device (for moving data between home and work, for instance), so although it must be in its dock for power, it does have an internal battery that acts as a backup for orderly shut down when you remove it from the dock. The dock also provides a 10/100 Ethernet port, should you want faster connections than are available via 802.11b. The Sony FSV-PGX1 is available only in Japan right now, for about $600. You can see more about it, in Japanese (or via Babel Fish) at www.sony.jp/products/Consumer/PGX/.

Music and Photo Players

We're both devotees of converting our audio CDs to MP3 format and storing the MP3s on a server so we can access them from any of our computers. It works extremely well for us, but we have older computers we can dedicate to the job of playing MP3s through our stereos. What do you do if you want to play MP3s through your stereo without hooking a computer to it directly? And if you're sending MP3s to your stereo, what about showing your digital photos on your television?

The SLIMP3 is probably the best-known device designed for playing MP3s from your network on your stereo. It costs $240, and for that you get a box that sits on top of your stereo, shows you what's playing via a fluorescent green display, and works with Windows, Mac OS X, Linux, and other Unix variants. You connect it to your Ethernet network and use an RCA patch cord to connect it to your stereo. Once it's set up, you control it either using an included remote control or through its built-in Web interface. If you want it to be wireless (lots of people do), Slim Devices recommends using a standard wireless Ethernet adapter like the Linksys WET11, the SMC2670W EZ Connect Wireless Ethernet Adapter from SMC Networks, or the Orinoco/EC from Proxim. It's a neat device, and you can learn more about it at www.slimp3.com or by reading the *TidBITS* review at http://db.tidbits.com/getbits.acgi?tbart=07150.

For a device with built-in Wi-Fi, look to the HomePod, from Gloo Labs. Although it wasn't shipping at press time, it should be available soon for $200. It claims to offer basically the same feature set as the SLIMP3, so the comparison may come down to price and interface, and since the pictures on the Gloo Labs Web site look different from the devices Adam was shown at Macworld Expo in January 2003, there's no telling exactly what the HomePod will look like when it ships. Visit www.gloolabs.com for more information.

Linksys beats both on price with the Wireless-B Media Adapter, which plays MP3s on your stereo and displays photos on your television for about $175 (**Figure 18.9**). It also has a 10/100 Mbps Ethernet jack, if you have Ethernet wiring nearby. Linksys includes a remote control and provides an interface on your television screen, although it lacks a display on the device itself, unlike both the SLIMP3 and the HomePod. It's also Windows-specific. Read more about it at www.linksys.com/products/product.asp?prid=554.

Very similar to the others, though more expensive, is the $300 Digital Media Receiver ew5000 from Hewlett-Packard, which acts as a wireless MP3 player and displays photos stored on your computer on your television. Although

Figure 18.9
Linksys Wireless-B
Media Adapter.

the product information isn't entirely clear about this, we strongly suspect that it works only with Windows-based computers, so Macintosh and Linux users should probably stick with another option. You can find some additional information at http://h30027.www3.hp.com/mediaReceiver/.

The c200 and c300 models from cd3o have the peculiar, unique notion that it's all about audio: there's no LCD display. Instead, the device speaks its menus and options to you over the stereo. The two models, which cost $180 and $200, respectively, handle either 802.11b or 10/100 Mbps Ethernet connections, but require a Windows machine to run the jukebox software. The Windows machine must have an audio card installed in order to run the voice synthesis software to create the spoken names of songs, artists, and albums that are transmitted to the player. You can read about model details at www.cd3o.com/products/models.html.

 TIP

Just before press time, Creative Technology released the Sound Blaster Wireless Music, yet another wireless device for playing MP3s from your computer on your stereo. It's $250 and you can learn more at www.americas.creative.com/products/product.asp?product=2092.

Lastly, we found the Go-Video D2730 Networked DVD player which, along with being a standard DVD player, connects to your computer via a wired or wireless network for playing MP3 audio files on your stereo, showing JPEG photos on your television, and even playing MPEG-1 and MPEG-2 video files. Like Hewlett-Packard's Digital Media Receiver, it works only with Windows. Nonetheless, it's neat to see such features showing up in consumer electronics, and you can read the full details at www.govideo.com/?ID=D2730.

TVs, Monitors, and Projectors

For the most part, you can't really stream full-quality video via 802.11b, and it can be iffy even with 802.11a or 802.11g unless you have good signal strength and the latest video compression software. That said, a number of products do mix Wi-Fi and video display.

Television Transmitters

Continuing in the theme of cool products that haven't been seen outside Japan, we come to the Sony AirBoard, which Sony describes as a "wireless Web pad." It's a good description, since the AirBoard is basically a portable flat-panel television that receives digital video streamed from a base station over a Wi-Fi link and lets you read email or browse the Web. The base station contains a television tuner, an Ethernet jack, a modem port, and connections for other devices such as DVD players. You interact with the base station via a touch screen interface mounted on the main 12.1-inch color LCD screen; the latest incarnation also comes with a remote control. It also accepts Sony Memory Stick cards and can display photos from them. Unfortunately, the battery lasts only 1–2 hours, depending on the brightness of the screen. Even more unfortunate, it costs about $1100, making it more expensive than many low-end laptops, which have higher resolution screens (the AirBoard runs at 800 by 600 dpi), and may even weigh less (it checks in at 4.9 pounds). Overall, it sounds like Sony is experimenting with the AirBoard to see how people interact with portable display devices. You can watch a Flash video about it at www.sony.jp/airboard/indexpc.html.

For a less ambitious product that's also available only in Japan, consider the Casio XF-800, a Wi-Fi color television. Like the Sony AirBoard, the Casio XF-800 communicates with a base station that provides the television tuner and transmits the video via Wi-Fi. Casio makes a big deal about it (and its remote control) being waterproof, apparently because they anticipate people watching a lot of television in the bathroom. It seems that waterproofing the XF-800 costs a lot; it reportedly sells for 160,000 yen, or about $1300. Take a look at www.casio.co.jp/tv/xfer/.

Monitors

Want to use your desktop PC without sacrificing the portability of a laptop? Check out ViewSonic's Airpanel V110p and V150p Smart Displays (**Figure 18.10**). They're wireless monitors for your desktop PC, displaying exactly what you'd see if you were sitting at your desk, but doing so anywhere within range of your Wi-Fi network. The Airpanel V110p (www.viewsonic.com/products/airpanel_airpanelv110p.htm) is a 10-inch LCD monitor that weighs about 3 pounds, and the 6-pound V150p (www.viewsonic.com/products/airpanel_airpanelv150p.htm) offers the same functionality with a 15-inch display. Battery life is about 4 hours. Unfortunately, they're not cheap, with the V110p at $800 and the V150p at $1000—you might be better off getting an inexpensive laptop and using Timbuktu Pro or PC Anywhere remote control software.

Projection

Switching to a more corporate use for wireless networking, many different models of LCD projectors support Wi-Fi in order to help multiple people display presentation slides through the projector without plugging and unplugging VGA cables. This could be particularly useful in a business conference room,

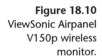

Figure 18.10
ViewSonic Airpanel
V150p wireless
monitor.

for instance, where multiple people may need to present in quick succession, and being able to connect wirelessly would reduce setup and switching time, particularly if there was only one seat for the presenter. You do have to be careful, since 802.11b doesn't provide enough bandwidth for movies or video, so stick with static slides. For an old article about this topic that links to information about many projector models that support Wi-Fi, visit www.projectorcentral.com/wi-fi.htm. Costs vary widely, of course.

If you already have a projector that doesn't support Wi-Fi, check out the Linksys WPG-11 Wireless Presentation Gateway and the WPG-12 Wireless Presentation Player. The Wireless Presentation Gateway connects to your projector via VGA and to remote computers via Wi-Fi. It includes client software that makes the computer send a copy of the screen image to the Wireless Presentation Gateway for display on the projector. The Wireless Presentation Player offers similar functionality, but adds 32 MB of internal RAM so you can essentially upload your presentation to it, and then present it using an included remote control—no computer necessary. The client software works only with Windows. Both cost about $300, and you can read more about them at www.linksys.com.

Wi-Fi Phones

Let's talk convergence. The phone company uses only the equivalent of 64 Kbps of bandwidth per call on its voice network: 56 Kbps of content and 8 Kbps of overhead. With more compression, voice quality can still be retained down to 20 Kbps.

Many businesses and individuals have high-speed Internet connections that have more than enough bandwidth to support calls in both directions. And many people with broadband also have Wi-Fi networks. Mix the two together, add an up-and-coming technology called Voice-over-IP (VoIP), and you arrive at the Wi-Fi telephone, occasionally called Voice-over-Wireless IP (VoWIP). Put simply, the Wi-Fi phone uses Wi-Fi to communicate with your access point, sending VoIP packets out to other VoIP phones or a device that connects VoIP traffic with the PSTN (Public Switched Telephone Network). The PSTN is the skein of wires and central offices that forms the backbone of the regular voice telephone network.

Standard wired IP phones from Cisco Systems (www.cisco.com) are gaining popularity, particularly in organizations where it's easier to add phones to an Ethernet network than it is to run separate wiring. Right now, IP phones are quite expensive and difficult to set up, which limits their appeal to consumers. However, that may change soon, with inexpensive IP phones appearing from Grandstream Networks (www.grandstream.com), services that connect IP phone users like Free World Dialup (www.freeworldialup.com) and SIPphone (www.sipphone.com), and even companies like Vonage (www.vonage.com) that offer seamless connections between normal phones, your Internet connection, and the PSTN.

Both Cisco and another business firm, SpectraLink, offer VoIP in corporate networks with the addition of gateway servers that handle finding and tracking users across internal wireless networks and routing calls to and from the PSTN. Cisco's 7920 wireless VoIP phone, for instance, looks like a bulky cell phone and works with Cisco's access points and CallManager software. SpectraLink guarantees that its Wi-Fi phones work with a variety of access points, but its products may not work perfectly with untested equipment. (SpectraLink's preferred Wi-Fi hubs use a form of in-progress 802.11e that assures voice packets have priority over plain data.) Visit www.cisco.com/en/US/products/hw/phones/ps379/products_data_sheet09186a00801739bb.html to read more about the 7920, or visit SpectraLink's Web site at www.spectralink.com.

 TIP

Right before we went to press, Pulver Innovations announced a $250 Wi-Fi phone that works with the Free World Dialup Voice-over-IP service. Find out more at www.pulverinnovations.com/wisip.html.

Although we aren't aware of any other Wi-Fi phones right now, Nextel Communications, a major cellular carrier, has announced plans to offer a Motorola mobile phone that can make calls over a standard Wi-Fi network, as well as over Nextel's normal cellular network when away from the Wi-Fi network. The tricky part of such a dual-protocol phone is the handoff—transferring the call from Wi-Fi to the cellular network and back again as necessary. Apparently Nextel's current prototypes can transfer from Wi-Fi to the cellular network, but not back.

Lastly, we find the Vocera Communications System, which is more akin to Star Trek communicators than today's clunky telephones. The Vocera Communications Badge is a two-ounce, voice-controlled communicator that uses Wi-Fi to communicate with a central server running the Windows 2000-based Vocera Server Software (**Figure 18.11**). The badge contains a speaker, a microphone, the wireless radio, and a small LCD screen for caller ID information or text messages. The system is designed for hands-free communications within a wireless-enabled building or campus, but an optional add-on connects it with the PSTN so you can use it as a telephone as well. Thanks to a steep list price ($30,000 for an entry-level system with 75 user licenses and 25 badges), Vocera's early customers have mostly been hospitals and warehouse stores, both places where key workers (like nurses and managers) are rarely near a fixed phone, lack cell service as a good option, and often have their hands full. One interesting capability of the system: a manager could say to the communicator, "find me all cashiers on the second floor," and proximity information about access point locations could be used to connect the manager by voice to those cashiers. Learn more at www.vocera.com.

Figure 18.11
Vocera
Communications
Badge.

Miscellaneous

These devices defy easy categorization, but deserve mention. Linksys markets a pair of special wireless network adapters dedicated to connecting Ethernet-capable game consoles. The Linksys Wireless-B Game Adapter (802.11b; see www.linksys.com/products/product.asp?grid=33&scid=38&prid=550) and Wireless-G Game Adapter (802.11g; see www.linksys.com/products/pr

oduct.asp?grid=33&scid=38&prid=558) let you connect a game console like a Sony PlayStation 2, Microsoft Xbox, or Nintendo GameCube to your wireless network for Internet access to online games. If you have multiple game consoles in the house, you can also use Linksys's game adapters to connect the consoles together for multi-player games. The Wireless-B Game Adapter sells for about $65 now; the Wireless-G Game Adapter costs about $115.

Creating a Software Access Point

Although we've been talking entirely about hardware so far, there's no reason an access point can't exist entirely in software on a regular PC or Macintosh. In fact, years ago, Apple embraced the notion that with an AirPort card, you should be able to turn a computer into the equivalent of an access point even while it carries out other tasks.

NOTE
Despite Apple's early Software Base Station support in Mac OS 8.6 and then Mac OS 9, Mac OS X lacked the feature for nearly its first year and a half, until Mac OS X 10.2 Jaguar came out in August 2002.

NOTE
Thanks to an exclusive agreement with chip-set makers for its AirPort and AirPort Extreme cards, only Apple can enable a special software mode that makes a software access point act identically to a hardware access point.

Although Microsoft hasn't built a true software access point feature into Windows, you can simulate it using ad hoc networking. Microsoft is unlikely to add this feature because it has recently started selling hardware wireless gateways; other equipment makers are equally unlikely to offer it for the same reason.

The main advantage of a software access point is clearly cost: Mac users, for instance, can get virtually all the features of an AirPort Extreme Base Station, including DHCP, NAT, and even a firewall, using Mac OS X's built-in Internet Sharing feature, all without ponying up the $200 or more for an AirPort Extreme Base Station. Secondary advantages are the possibility of more precise control and a better interface than the often-clumsy Web-based interfaces.

However, there are limitations to running a software access point in favor of a hardware model:

- **Range.** Wireless network adapters for computers may not have the range of the more advanced or higher-gain antennas found in hardware access points and gateways.

- **Availability.** Making a computer into a software access point turns it into something you must monitor and maintain. Standalone equipment tends to be more robust than most desktop operating systems, and although even hardware access points can become confused, they require less maintenance and fiddling than the computers that run software access points.

- **Electrical power.** If you're the sort of person who likes to turn off the lights when you leave a room, the extra wattage used by a computer turned on all the time may irritate you. A hardware access point burns maybe a dozen watts, while a computer could run at 150 watts with its monitor turned on. The cost savings is probably minimal, but the principle of not wasting power unnecessarily is what matters.

- **Intermittent connectivity.** We don't recommend using a software access point in conjunction with an intermittent dial-up Internet connection, particularly if you want your computers to communicate with one another when you're not connected to the Internet. The reason is that when you're connected to the Internet, your software access point will hand out IP addresses via DHCP, perhaps in the 192.168.1.x range. But when you're not connected to the Internet, your computers will revert to self-assigned IP addresses in the 169.254.x.x range. This switching of IP addresses is likely to cause irritating problems that go away if you rely on a hardware access point to connect to the Internet and dole out a single set of IP addresses.

Configuring Software Base Station in Mac OS 8.6/9.x

You configure the Software Base Station feature in Mac OS 8.6 and 9.x via the AirPort application, typically found in the Apple Extras folder inside your Applications folder. To share an Internet connection among the wireless computers that connect to your Software Base Station, you must also have a working Internet connection via Ethernet from a cable or DSL modem, or via standard dial-up.

(((•))) NOTE

If you want to share files between two wireless computers, you can create an ad hoc wireless network without using Software Base Station. For more on ad hoc networking and file sharing, see Chapter 12, Creating an Ad Hoc Wireless Network, *and Chapter 13,* Sharing Files & Printers.

1. Open the AirPort application and click the Software Base Station button in the main screen's lower-left corner.

2. In the Start/Stop tab, enter a name for your network (SSID) in the Network Name field and choose the channel from the Channel Frequency pop-up menu (**Figure 19.1**).

Figure 19.1
Configuring the
Software Base
Station in the Start/
Stop tab.

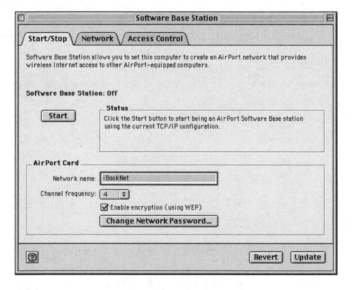

3. If you want to enable WEP encryption, check Enable Encryption (Using WEP) and click the Change Network Password button to enter the WEP key.

4. Click Start to begin sharing the Internet connection.

Apple's Software Base Station always provides IP addresses to client computers via DHCP; in the Network tab, you can select if you also want to provide IP addresses to wired computers connected via Ethernet. Finally, use the Access Control tab to restrict access to specific network adapters by entering their MAC addresses.

TIP

If you're using a third-party wireless network adapter or want more control than Apple's Software Base Station feature provides, check out Sustainable Softworks' IPNetRouter (www.sustworks.com/site/prod_ipr_overview.html). It can do everything Software Base Station can do and much more, in part because Sustainable Softworks wrote much of Software Base Station for Apple.

Configuring Internet Sharing in Mac OS X

In Mac OS X 10.2 Jaguar, Apple renamed the Software Base Station feature to Internet Sharing and relocated it from the AirPort utility to the Sharing preferences pane in System Preferences.

(((•))) **NOTE**

To share files between two wireless computers, you need only an ad hoc network; it's not necessary to turn on Internet Sharing. You can learn more about ad hoc networking and file sharing, in Chapter 12, Creating an Ad Hoc Wireless Network, *and Chapter 13,* Sharing Files & Printers.

Before starting, make sure you have either an Ethernet or an Internal Modem connection set up in the Network preferences pane, as you can't create a software access point without one or the other active. Unlike the Software Base Station in Mac OS 9, Jaguar's Internet Sharing feature works whether you receive your Internet connection via Ethernet, Internal Modem, or even AirPort. For this example, we assume your Internet connection comes via Ethernet from a cable modem.

1. Open System Preferences, click Sharing, and click the Internet tab (**Figure 19.2**).

2. In Mac OS X, check Share Your Internet Connection with AirPort-Equipped Computers. In Mac OS X 10.3, choose either Built-in Ethernet or Internal Modem (whichever matches how you access the Internet) from the Share Your Connection Using pop-up menu, and then select AirPort in the To Computers Using list.

3. In Mac OS X, if you want to enable DHCP service across both your wireless and your connected wired network, check Share the Connection with Other Computers on Built-in Ethernet.

4. Click AirPort Options to set the network name, channel, and WEP key.

5. Click Start.

Figure 19.2
Configuring
Internet Sharing
in the Internet
tab of the Sharing
preferences pane.

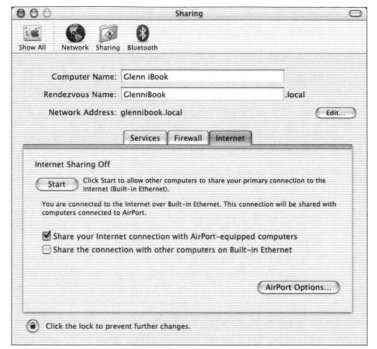

 TIP

If you turn on WEP in Mac OS X 10.2 and anticipate PCs or Macs without AirPort cards ever wanting to access your network, we recommend you set the WEP key using a dollar sign, followed by the 10-digit or 26-digit hexadecimal key. Why? If you set the key using a normal passphrase, there's no way for you to extract a hexadecimal password for use with non-AirPort wireless network adapters. Mac OS X 10.3 tells you to choose either a 5 character password for 40-bit WEP or a 13 character password for 128-bit WEP for compatibility with non-Apple hardware.

Windows XP and Routing Software

Although it isn't possible to enable a true software access point under any version of Windows, you can simulate one with ad hoc networking. Although ad hoc networking doesn't rely on a single machine to route traffic among machines on a network, you can still have one of the computers on an ad hoc wireless network also connected to an Ethernet-based Internet connection. That Internet-connected machine can then act as the gateway that enables the other machines on the ad hoc network to reach the Internet. This approach isn't as robust as a true software access point, but it can work fine in small networks of only a few machines.

Under Windows XP, you accomplish this sleight of hand by combining ad hoc networking with Windows XP's feature for sharing a network connection with other computers. As an added bonus, this feature turns on DHCP service.

First, follow the instructions in "Creating an Ad Hoc Network in Windows XP" in Chapter 12, *Creating an Ad Hoc Wireless Network*, to set up ad hoc networking. Next, make sure you have an Internet connection active through another interface, either Ethernet or a dial-up connection. Now follow these steps:

 TIP

Windows 2000 can also share a network connection; in Network and Dial-up Connections, open the connection associated with your wireless network adapter, click the Properties button, click the Sharing tab, and check "Enable Internet Connection Sharing for This Connection."

1. From the Control Panel, select Network Connections, and then select the Wireless Network Connection item.

2. From the left vertical task list, click Change Settings of This Connection under Network Tasks to open the Wireless Network Connection Properties dialog (**Figure 19.3**).

Figure 19.3
The Wireless
Network
Connection
Properties dialog.

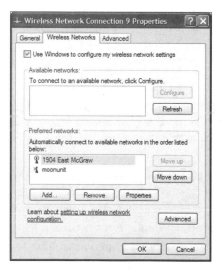

3. Click the Advanced tab.

4. Check Allow Other Network Users to Connect through This Computer's Internet Connection (**Figure 19.4**).

Figure 19.4
Configuring
Internet sharing in
Windows XP.

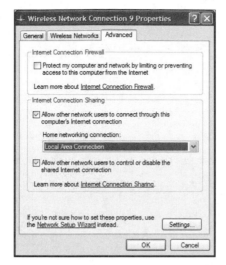

5. From the Home Networking Connection pop-up menu, choose your wireless network adapter to share the wired or dial-up connection with other devices on the wireless network.

6. Click OK.

TIP

To make more complex Internet sharing setups in Windows XP, you can use its bridging option to connect multiple networks via your computer. Use Windows XP's built-in help to read more about this feature.

You've now turned your Windows XP system into something approaching a software access point, complete with sharing an Internet connection and serving IP addresses to other computers on the ad hoc network via DHCP.

Bridging Wireless Networks

Once you've been bitten by the wireless networking bug, it's all too easy to keep adding machines and expanding your network until suddenly you come up against a brick wall, perhaps literally. Your next expansion is stymied because some client computers cannot reach your single access point.

It's common for a larger house and almost every small office to lack an ideal place where a single access point can serve all the client computers. As we note in Chapter 15, *Planning Your Wireless Network*, in the "Multiple Access Points" sidebar, adding another access point via Ethernet to create a roaming network can solve the problem. But a roaming network requires a wired Ethernet connection running among all the access points to connect them into a seamless network.

Cheap though it is, cable may not be your best option because of distance or physical barriers. How many holes do you want to drill in your home? How badly do you want to persuade a building owner to let you pull wire through her walls? Instead, you can use a variety of inexpensive bridges and access points to connect individual access points wirelessly, retaining (and indeed enhancing) the advantage of wireless networking without requiring additional wires. It usually saves you money, too.

Bridging Basics

The concept behind wireless bridging is that you connect a single access point to an Internet connection, which almost always involves an Ethernet or telephone cable. Even if your Internet connection arrives wirelessly, as Adam's does, you still run an Ethernet cable from the incoming feed to at least one gateway.

Then you install one or more access points to add coverage to an area unreachable by the first. The second access point must be located at a point where it can still connect wirelessly to the first access point (**Figure 20.1**). You may be able to daisy-chain additional access points from that second one to extend the network in a straight line. Alternatively, if you want to increase the radius of your wireless coverage, you may be able to add additional access points that all spread out from the central hub of the first access point (**Figure 20.2**).

Figure 20.1
A typical two-access point bridge in which client computers connect to access points which connect to each other.

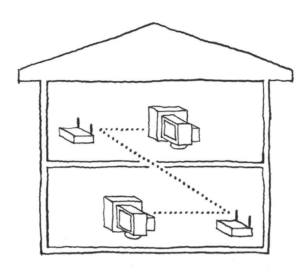

Figure 20.2
A more complex arrangement radiating from a central, Internet-connected gateway.

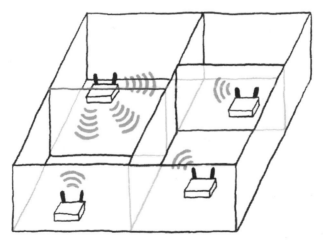

The magic comes in configuring the access points (or wireless bridges connected to the access points) to move traffic from the second access point's wireless client computers, through the second access point, across a wireless connection to the first access point, and out to the Internet.

Bridges are a great solution for a few common situations, such as expanding an office network into multiple rooms, floors, or buildings; hooking up a larger network across a home; or bypassing an obstacle that blocks the wireless signal between two areas.

In effect, a bridge allows you to bypass even more of the physical limitations of the world, and send your wireless network into larger and more far-flung connections.

Kinds of Bridges

There are four ways to bridge wireless networks over Wi-Fi without involving other protocols or expensive, corporate-grade equipment:

- Via the Wireless Distribution System (WDS), a technology built into an increasing number of wireless gateways that enables them to function simultaneously as a bridge and an access point, both serving local clients and bridging traffic.

- Using a special Wi-Fi–to–Ethernet bridge that plugs into a wired connection on one side and carries all the traffic from its wired connection over Wi-Fi to a single access point; these can connect to any standard access point.

- Using two or more Wi-Fi access points that can be set to act in a bridge-only mode but can connect only to similar or identical devices for point-to-point or point-to-multipoint connections.

- With a computer that has two or more Wi-Fi cards installed, which bridges traffic on one of them and acts as a software base station on the other.

Deciding which of these four alternatives makes the most sense for your situation depends on the distance the bridge must traverse, your current set of equipment, and the nature of your network.

Bridging with WDS

The Wireless Distribution System is one of the most useful additions to Wi-Fi technology because it enables you to create an all-wireless network that's much larger than would be possible with a single access point. It creates a cloud of coverage by giving access points the capability to pass data among themselves wirelessly.

 TIP

If you don't need a cloud of wireless coverage around each access point in a WDS network that connects areas together, look at the next two solutions.

((•)) **NOTE**

Some wireless gateways, including the Linksys WAP54G, use WDS in a specialized way: when in bridging mode, they can't act as an access point and vice versa. In this section, we talk only about WDS-capable gateways that can work simultaneously as bridges and access points.

That said, there are some limits to WDS:

- No manufacturer we spoke to is testing whether its version of WDS works with any other version. Since many companies selling consumer equipment use the same set of silicon chips and underlying firmware—notably Linksys, Buffalo, Apple, and a few other—you might be able to make WDS work among varied equipment (and in fact, we've verified that WDS gear from Apple and Buffalo works together). But no guarantees!

- You need some patience to gather all the information you need and to enter it in several places manually when you first configure the system.

How WDS Works

WDS is a clever part of the original 802.11b specification from 1999, but it wasn't until 2003 that it started appearing in standard, inexpensive equipment. WDS connects access points wirelessly as if they were ports on an Ethernet switch.

On an Ethernet switch, each port keeps a list of all the machines connected to it and broadcasts that list to each other's port. Every computer on the switch's network receives these broadcasts and uses them to discover the MAC addresses of all the other accessible machines. Whether a computer wants to send data to another computer that's on the same or a different port, it makes no difference: the originating computer still puts the same destination address on the packet. The switch, however, recognizes the destination address of each packet and routes it to the correct port and on to the destination computer.

Each access point in a WDS-connected network works in just the same way as a port, tracking the MAC addresses of all the connected computers and broadcasting lists of addresses to other access points. When a computer connected to one access point wants to send a packet to a computer connected to another, WDS ensures that the first access point delivers the packet to the appropriate access point, even through intermediate access points.

In the end, WDS appears seamless to you, and no special magic is involved. It's just a clever way of keeping track of which computers are connected to which access points and making sure data can flow from any computer on the network to any other computer.

- Because each remote access point must receive packets and retransmit them using a single radio, overall throughput drops significantly on each segment. That may not be a problem if your primary goal is to share an Internet connection (which is comparatively slow). If it's a concern, look into one of the other bridging methods or set up multiple access points connected via Ethernet to form a roaming network.

Planning for WDS

To begin, set up a single wireless gateway near your Internet connection. This station will be your *master* in the WDS configuration, and other access points will connect to it.

Next, use a laptop or handheld device to determine the area that your master gateway covers. Your goal is to figure out precisely where you want to locate each *remote* or *relay* access point, such that it can receive the signal from the master and retransmit it in such a way to extend wireless coverage beyond where the master can reach.

What's the difference between a remote and a relay? At least for Apple, a remote access point communicates with both the master and any wireless clients, whereas a relay not only connects with the master and serves local clients, but also allows remote access points to connect to it in order to reach the master.

((•)) **NOTE**
You need at least two gateways to use WDS, but you can link up as many as six depending on the device. At this writing, we know that Buffalo's WLA-54G can handle a total of six remote access points, and both models of Apple's AirPort Extreme Base Station can handle take up to four relays, each of which could conceivably take four remote access points.

Some systems allow four or five remote devices to connect to the master; others may allow relay devices that connect to the master and which can support connections from remote gateways (**Figure 20.3**).

Configuring WDS

After diagramming your network, buying the number of access points that you need, putting them all near each other, and firing them up, you need to configure them by connecting to each one in turn. You should connect directly via Ethernet to a LAN port on each access point: with several wireless access points all set to the same default channel and turned on at the same time, you're unlikely to be able to connect reliably over Wi-Fi. Follow these steps to configure WDS:

Figure 20.3
Three scenarios for
WDS.

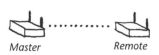

In the simplest WDS configuration, two access points connect with each other.

Master   Remote

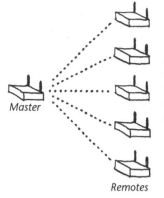

But WDS also allows a much more complex setup in which a master access point acts as a hub for several remote access points in a point-to-multi-point network.

Master

Remotes

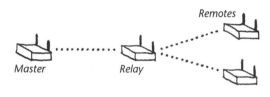

Remotes

For more far-flung networks, a relay access point uses WDS to connect back to a main unit while also having multiple downstream access points connect to it.

Master   Relay

1. For each access point, obtain and write down its MAC (Media Access Control) address, which is a unique number for every network adapter.

2. Label each access point with a name or number that corresponds to its MAC address so you can keep track of which unit will go in which location. Of course, with remotes, it doesn't really matter which unit goes where: they're interchangeable.

 TIP

Apple places a label showing the MAC address on the bottom of each AirPort Extreme Base Station, but other manufacturers may require that you connect to the unit to get its MAC address.

3. Connect to the unit that will be the master access point in the network. Configure it to connect to your Internet connection just as if it were a standalone access point. (See Chapter 17, *Setting up a Gateway.*)

4. Enable WDS on the master unit, which likely involves a separate tab in the access point's configuration interface (**Figure 20.4**).

Figure 20.4
Configuring WDS
for the Apple
Extreme Base
Station.

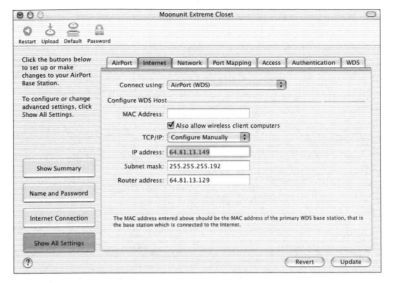

5. Still on the master unit, enter the MAC address of each remote access point and each relay access point that will connect directly to the master unit.

6. Save your configuration, and restart the master access point.

7. Turn off local client access on your master access point so you can test the relays and remotes as you configure them (**Figure 20.5**).

8. For each relay or remote access point:

   a. Set it to act as a WDS relay or remote, depending on your network.

Figure 20.5
Setting local client
access in WDS.

Uncheck this box to disable local client access.

b. Enter the MAC address of the master access point.

c. Save and restart.

d. With the remote or relay right next to the master access point, try to connect to the Internet through the remote or relay. With the master's access point features off, you should be able to connect only via the currently active remote or relay. (If you can't, check your settings.)

e. Turn off the relay or remote, and move it to its permanent position.

f. Fire up the relay or remote, and, once again, make sure you can connect to the Internet.

Clients don't need any special configuration to use a WDS-bridged network. Wi-Fi adapters connect to the network just as they would to a single gateway.

Bridging to Any Access Point

WDS is a great solution for creating a cloud of wireless access using equipment from a single manufacturer, but what if you already own some gear and still want to add a bridge, especially if you don't need a cloud of access around the bridge itself? That desire brings us to our second bridging option, which is a good alternative to WDS. In this scenario, you use a specialized wireless bridge that can carry any kind of traffic between a wired network and any access point. You don't need any additional hardware for your existing access point, nor do you need to change any settings on the access point.

How It Works

This approach requires a special wireless bridge, such as the 802.11g-based Linksys WET54G or the 802.11b-based Linksys WET11. You plug the bridge into an Ethernet switch or attach it to a single computer via an Ethernet cable, and then configure it to communicate with your access point. On many networks, you don't need to change any of the defaults.

Once configured, the bridge acts like a plain Wi-Fi adapter on a regular computer. The only difference is that if you've plugged the bridge into an Ethernet switch that also connects other wired computers, it makes the wireless connection available to all of them at once and vice versa. How many will it support? Depending on the bridge, you can connect from four to dozens of wired computers (**Figure 20.6**).

You can even plug an access point into the wired side of the bridge, enabling you to bridge traffic using equipment from different manufacturers. This technique

Figure 20.6
Wireless bridge
connecting wired
machines to a
wireless gateway.

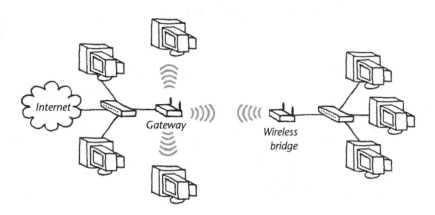

gives you the effect of WDS without buying identical or new hardware and—more critically—without suffering the performance degradation inherent to WDS. The bridged access point can operate on a different channel.

 TIP

Of course, the problem with using a special bridge along with a secondary access point is that you may end up buying a bridge and another access point, which may not be any cheaper than simply buying two new access points that support WDS and selling your old one.

The MAC Attack

Although this approach to bridging may sound ideal, there are a few minor problems with the way that most of these bridges work. Most notably, they translate all the unique Ethernet addresses for devices connected to them to a single MAC address, that of the bridge itself. It's a bit like the way NAT translates all the private IP addresses of computers on a local network so traffic from them appears to come from the single, public IP address of the gateway.

Although such a limitation may sound esoteric, this particular kind of MAC address translation can cause weird problems because some software and hardware relies on the MAC address to authenticate a computer or other piece of networking equipment. All network identities are tied to MAC addresses, so having multiple IP addresses that all look like they're coming simultaneously from the same MAC address can confuse network servers, making them unavailable or flaky.

On the other hand, because this kind of bridge can pass any kind of protocol that runs over Ethernet, and because it works with any access point, a little discomfort and fiddling with settings might save you the cost of hundreds of dollars of new equipment.

Bridging in Pairs or Multiples

Bridging in pairs or multiples is the most expensive bridging option, as it requires at least two bridge devices that do nothing but talk to each other. So why would you bother? It's the optimal approach for creating longer links between two or more locations because you can connect high-gain directional antennas to each of the bridges. With the two previous approaches, the access points can use either their built-in antennas or perhaps omnidirectional antennas. However, using directional antennas on the master and the remotes in a WDS setup, or on the access point and the bridge in a standard bridged network, won't work, because wireless coverage for any access point with a directional antenna would be too directional. Walk around the back of the access point, and you might not be able to pick up a signal.

((•)) **NOTE**

We talk about long-range connections and antennas in Chapter 21, Indoor Antenna Basics, *and Section VI,* Going the Distance.

You can use a pair of identical bridges, like the 802.11b-based Linksys WAP11 or the 802.11g-based WAP54G to create a point-to-point bridged network, with one pod of connected computers on either end; this is probably the most common approach (**Figure 20.7**). However, if you have more than two pods of computers that you want to connect, you can create a point-to-multipoint network in which one of the bridges acts as a master and several other identical bridges connect to it.

Figure 20.7
A pair of identical bridges connects more easily over long distances than WDS access point/ bridges or bridge-to-any connections.

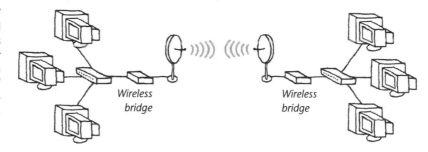

Wireless bridge

Wireless bridge

((•)) **NOTE**

The early 802.11b versions of these bridges tended to act just as protocol bridges: that is, they could carry any traffic that used one of several protocols they supported. The Linksys WAP11, for instance, handles TCP/IP, IPX, and NetBEUI, but ignores AppleTalk. Later 802.11g bridges tend to use WDS in a dedicated mode where they can't also act as an access point, but can seemingly bridge any kind of Ethernet protocol.

Indoor Antenna Basics

Perhaps the main frustration when you build your wireless network is discovering areas in your home or office where you can't receive a strong signal, or any signal at all. Perhaps the distance is simply too great, or perhaps a concrete wall is blocking the signal. If your computer can receive some signal in the desired location, or can at least receive it nearby, one solution is to boost your access point's signal strength with a higher gain antenna.

((•)) **NOTE**

To be clear, antennas don't actually amplify the signal (that's what amplifiers are for!), they merely concentrate it in specific directions. If you've ever used a flashlight like Mag Instrument's Maglite, which provides a focusing ring for the beam, you can visualize what an antenna does with radio waves. The narrower the beam, the brighter the light in the covered area, even though the flashlight bulb isn't actually producing more light.

That's not to imply that antennas are the best solution for all situations. The designers of the Wi-Fi protocols intended for Wi-Fi networks to be expanded primarily through the addition of multiple access points, not by adding powerful antennas. As such, an external antenna will probably give the best results when you want to boost signal strength a little bit for your entire network (pushing the boundaries out somewhat in the process) or when you want to set up a long-range point-to-point network (see Chapter 34, *Long-Range Antenna Basics,* for details and for more about antennas in general).

Unfortunately, whereas you can calculate how powerful an antenna you'll need for a long-range connection, the variables of how radio waves interact with walls, furniture, and other internal obstacles of potentially unknown construction ensure that picking an antenna to expand the range of an indoor network comes down to trial and error.

That said, here's a guide to adding an antenna to your wireless access point to extend the range of your network. This advice also applies to adding antennas to wireless bridges, though if you're bridging networks between buildings or over longer distances, be sure to read Chapter 20, *Bridging Wireless Networks*, as well.

((•)) **NOTE**

Don't worry about health concerns when adding a more powerful antenna to an indoor wireless network (within reason, and exercising common sense, of course!). See the sidebar "Health Concerns" in Chapter 34, Long-Range Antenna Basics, *for more details.*

Confirming Compatibility

Before you do anything else, you must make sure it's possible to add an antenna to your access point. In many cases it is, although some manufacturers don't make it easy. For instance, the graphite and snow AirPort Base Stations from Apple didn't provide any way of getting to the antenna jack on their internal Wi-Fi PC Card, so although adding an antenna is possible, it requires surgery with a Dremel tool. (Apple solved this by adding an external jack to one of the two models of the AirPort Extreme Base Station.)

((•)) **NOTE**

Visit www.vonwentzel.net/ABS/ for instructions on adding an antenna to an AirPort Base Station.

When purchasing an antenna or when purchasing an access point that can accept one, usually the easiest option is to buy them both from the same manufacturer. Next easiest is to purchase your antenna from a company that lists compatibility with specific access point models. Why are we bothering to tell you this?

The Federal Communications Commission (FCC) in the U.S. mandates that every manufacturer of wireless networking gear that works in unlicensed bands, such as 2.4 GHz and 5 GHz, use a different connector from every other manufacturer. (In practice, a few seem to double up, perhaps since there aren't enough connector types to go around.) The method behind this seeming madness is that the FCC wants to discourage users from hooking up antennas that might bring the total power of the system above legal limits. (See "Staying Legal" in Chapter 34, *Long-Range Antenna Basics.*)

Realistically, the FCC's concern applies mostly to long-range installations where you want to boost signal strength significantly and where exceeding legal limits could cause problems for other users of the same unlicensed band. Indoors, you're much less likely to want as much antenna gain, but since the same networking equipment can be used for both indoor and outdoor installations, the FCC's mandate affects both uses.

In summary:

- If you already own an access point to which you want to add an antenna, first check with the manufacturer to see if it sells an appropriate antenna that can connect to your access point.

- If the manufacturer doesn't make an appropriate antenna, check out one of the independent antenna manufacturers like HyperLink Technologies (www.hyperlinktech.com/web/antennas_2400_in.php) or YDI Wireless (www.ydi.com/products/24ghz-antennas.php).

Indoor Antenna Types

All wireless network adapters and access points have antennas built in, but for the most part they're designed for small size rather than for maximum signal strength boost (**Figure 21.1**). Most PC Card wireless network adapters cram the entire antenna into the 1-inch by 2-inch part that juts out from the laptop when the card is plugged in.

Figure 21.1
Normal built-in antennas.

There's no requirement that antennas be so small and offer such minimal improvement to signal strength, and when it comes to boosting signal strength, you can add three types of antennas to your access point: omnidirectional, panel, and dipole.

TIP

You could also add an antenna to your computer, assuming your wireless network adapter would accept one, but with laptops in particular, external antennas are unwieldy at best. See QuickerTek for more Macintosh antenna options (www.quickertek.com).

Omnidirectional Antennas

As you can imagine from the name, an omnidirectional antenna—also called a vertical whip antenna—is primarily useful in a location where you want the signal to radiate from the antenna in all directions. That's not quite accurate, because an omnidirectional antenna is usually shaped like a vertical stick, so the signal radiates to the sides in a circle, but doesn't go up or down much (**Figure 21.2**).

Figure 21.2
An omnidirectional antenna.

Indoor omnidirectional antennas don't offer much extra gain, usually between 3 dBi and 8 dBi, and they're generally available either in desktop models that sit next to your access point or in ceiling-mount models that hang from the ceiling. Because of the way they radiate in all directions, you should locate an omnidirectional antenna roughly in the center of the space you want to cover.

Panel Antennas

Panel antennas, sometimes called patch antennas, are solid flat panels with a directional beam. Panel antennas are inexpensive, feature good gain of up to 14 dBi for internal use, and blend in well with their surroundings. They don't look like much—just small flat boxes (**Figure 21.3**).

Figure 21.3
A panel antenna.

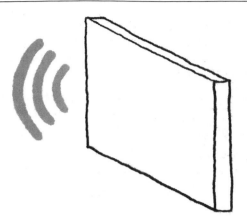

When considering a panel antenna, it's important to pay attention to the horizontal and vertical beam width, because wireless clients outside the beam won't receive much signal at all. Most of the time, you'll want to mount a panel antenna on a wall, pointing into the interior space you want to cover. It doesn't have to mount flat against the wall if, for instance, you want to direct the beam up or down to cover a higher or lower floor as well.

Dipole Antennas

Dipole antennas are commonplace on access points, and they often come in pairs. Some access points let you choose whether you want both antennas to send and receive and combine their results (like stereo vision; a process called *signal diversity*), or to put the antennas into a mode in which one antenna sends and the other receives (**Figure 21.4**).

NOTE
Dipole antennas are essentially the same as the rabbit ear antennas used for television reception years ago, except dipole antennas used on wireless networking gear are much smaller. They are smaller because 802.11b uses

Figure 21.4
An access point with a pair of dipole antennas.

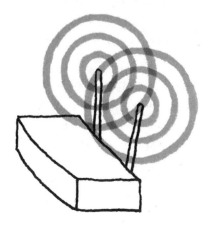

frequencies in the 2.4 GHz (or 2400 MHz) part of the radio spectrum, whereas television uses frequencies in the 100 MHz part of the spectrum. As the frequency increases, the size of the wavelength decreases, and thus the antenna size can also decrease.

Most dipole antennas have a limited gain between 2 and 3 dBi, and although you can purchase replacement dipole antennas, you should consider them only replacements, not range extenders. In fact, the main utility of an access point with removable (not all are) dipole antennas is that it's much easier to add a more powerful external antenna. Life is easier if you don't have to drill holes in your access point or solder connections between your access point and external antenna.

Antenna Installation Tips

Although every indoor installation is different, we can offer a few tips that should apply in most situations.

- Don't assume that the higher the gain, the better the antenna. Antennas increase gain by concentrating the radio waves, so usually the higher gain antennas are highly directional. If you need broad coverage, a lower gain omnidirectional antenna will probably work better.

- Before you install your antenna, spend some time with a signal strength monitoring tool to determine where signal strength is the weakest. See "Stumbling onto Wi-Fi" in Chapter 25, *Preventing Access to Your Network*.

- If possible, position a laptop (in ad hoc mode) roughly where you anticipate installing the antenna to evaluate whether or not the position is likely to work.

- Before finishing the installation of your antenna, check signal strength in all the areas you had trouble before. Remember that all antennas have specific radiation patterns, so you may need to reorient the antenna in some direction to achieve the desired signal strength.

- The longer the cable connecting the antenna to your access point, the more signal strength you lose, which is why most antennas sold for use indoors have short cables. Keep that in mind when planning how you'll use an antenna, since you may need to run more Ethernet cable to position your access point near where you want the antenna.

Small Office Wi-Fi Networking

If your organization is large enough to have an IT (information technology) or IS (information services) department, you might already have all the resources you need to set up and run a Wi-Fi network securely and efficiently both in your office and for your traveling users. But in this chapter, we're aiming to help those millions of businesses that use computer networks but don't have extensive—or any—dedicated in-house technical resources.

Small offices typically face two problems in building and using Wi-Fi networks in their facilities and in making it possible for employees to access network resources from the road:

- Creating an encrypted tunnel to protect data passing over a local network or data being sent back and forth to a wireless worker on the road who is likely on an open Wi-Fi or wired network

- Permitting only authorized users to access network resources, and, the flip side, allowing safe guest access

In this chapter, we offer some simple and cost-effective suggestions that won't send you scuttling to the classifieds to hire an expensive staffer. Instead, you might be able to set up a secure, small-office wireless network by yourself, or at least spend only a few hours with a consultant.

Safe Passage

A small office's biggest concern with wireless networking is usually that when employees transmit information they're broadcasting the organization's secrets, even if those are mundane secrets. As we explained earlier in the book, the most widespread simple encryption system, WEP, isn't particularly secure, and offices—even small ones—are potential targets because of the volume of traffic and the probability that snooped traffic could produce a financial return.

Worse, when workers labor outside the office—on the road, at home, or at client locations—they might be accessing company resources, including file servers, mail accounts, and Web-based resources, on open wireless and wired networks that could harbor snoops.

A small organization has several choices for securing its traffic in its local office, and a somewhat different set of options for employees when they hit the road.

Local Traffic Protection

In a local office, because you can usually control what software is installed on which machines, you have a single reasonable choice for locking down a network: Wi-Fi Protected Access (WPA), using the TKIP (Temporal Key Integrity Protocol) encryption key.

There are many provisos, but WPA is the best option with the fewest additional pieces to manage. As we describe in Chapter 26, *Securing Data in Transit*, TKIP under WPA fixes all the encryption and related problems in WEP while simultaneously reducing complexity.

The only downside with TKIP under WPA is that, as we write this, only certain newer PC Cards, PCI cards, and wireless access points support WPA. Although upgrades to WPA for equipment already on the market were initially promised, we haven't seen them come to fruition. You may need to replace older equipment to have the WPA advantage. Fortunately, the newest and most sophisticated gear is inexpensive, making the upgrade or initial buying decision easier.

((•)) **NOTE**

If you need the extra security and audit trail afforded by network logins that we describe in "Authorized Access," later, make sure and read this section first as WPA and TKIP are also applicable to authenticated access.

TIP

A cheaper but more complicated way to protect a small local network with only local users without upgrading to WPA is to use VPN connections via the Linksys WRV54G wireless gateway we describe below. All your users must use newer versions of Windows or Mac OS X 10.3 which include free VPN client software. The Linksys box also requires a lengthy one-time setup for each client that wants to connect.

When you use WPA on a local network, your primary risk is that the TKIP passphrase you use to protect the network—often called the *pre-shared key* (PSK) or *pre-shared secret*—is leaked or misused. To reduce the chances of this happening, we recommend that you change your TKIP key regularly, such as on the first of every month, or every eight weeks. Set a reminder for yourself. This reduces the chances that social engineering or other faults will break your encryption. We also strongly suggest that you change your TKIP key immediately after an employee leaves your company for any reason (voluntary or as the result of a firing or layoff).

((•)) **NOTE**

The major effort related to changing your TKIP key is that users must enter it to access the wireless network again, so think about how you'll disseminate the new key to employees in such a way that it will cause minimal disruption.

Most wireless client software hides the pre-shared key as it is entered. For instance, when you enter your TKIP key in Windows XP's Wireless Network Connection software, it's hidden as you type and you cannot retrieve it in plain text. (See Chapter 6, *Connecting Your Windows PC.*)

Roving Traffic Protection

Once users leave the security of your local network and the simplicity of relying on WPA's encryption, options can become slightly trickier. Our primary recommendation for securing a long-distance connection over any network—not just from hot spots, but also from a hotel's wired broadband or from guest connections on other companies' networks—is using a virtual private network (VPN).

We describe the nature and utility of VPNs in Chapter 26, *Securing Data in Transit*: they securely encrypt all the data entering and leaving your network. Until recently, a small business would have had to spend many thousands of dollars and pay for real IT expertise to purchase, configure, and maintain a VPN server or service.

Fortunately, recent changes have revolutionized the VPN world: you can now find "free" (or built-in, at least) VPN software in Windows XP and Mac OS X 10.3 for the two major VPN styles, and you can purchase a variety of VPN solutions without spending much on equipment or monthly service charges.

 TIP

VPNs can also be used to lock down local office Wi-Fi connections if upgrading to WPA is too expensive for you. A VPN-based security system is often more complicated than WPA, and places increased load on a server because of the high volume of local bandwidth. WPA is a lightweight protocol which distributes its cost across all the clients and access points on a network. If you use a local VPN server to secure your network, place your Wi-Fi gateways outside a firewall that restricts access except to the VPN server. Local users create a VPN connection through the firewall to the VPN server. Anyone gaining access to the Wi-Fi connection can't get into your network, and all data sent and received by local users is strongly encrypted. For more on firewalls, see Chapter 27, Protecting Your Systems.

Let's survey your options for creating a VPN.

Software Servers

Most large organizations use dedicated hardware to support hundreds or even thousands of VPN connections; these hardware devices rely on special chips to handle the massive computation necessary to encrypt and decrypt all network traffic.

But you can install VPN server software even if you just support only dozens of simultaneous users, and it will work even on machines that already act as Web or email servers. That said, monitor performance carefully to ensure that you're not being penny-wise and pound-foolish and destroying your Web performance to run your VPN.

It's not inconceivable that you might have the time, money, and know-how to run your own software-based VPN server, but make sure you consider the ongoing support time and effort.

- **Windows Server 2003.** This high-end Microsoft product, which costs thousands of dollars, might already be installed on your network if you're running a Windows shop and need the kinds of services it provides. Windows Server 2003 includes full support for the two popular flavors of VPN (PPTP and IPsec-over-L2TP). Its advantage is that there are piles of Microsoft certified technicians who can consult on configuring and maintaining it for you. The downside, of course, is cost: a 25-user version with all the trimmings costs $4000. Read more about its VPN

services at www.microsoft.com/technet/prodtechnol/windowsserver2003/
deploy/confeat/rmotevpn.asp.

- **Mac OS X Server 10.3 (Panther).** Apple revised its server software in
  version 10.3 to include both PPTP and IPsec-over-L2TP VPN servers
  (www.apple.com/server/macosx). The software runs only on Macintosh
  hardware, and includes a host of other network services, just like Windows
  Server 2003. The difference? Apple's server allows unlimited users and
  costs just $999; a 10-user version is $499. If you purchase Apple's Xserve
  rack-mounted system intended for server closets, an unlimited version of
  Mac OS X Server is included in the price.

- **FreeS/WAN.** You can have VPN software for free, but the tradeoff is that
  the configuration might drive you mad. The open-source project FreeS/
  WAN (www.freeswan.org), short for Free Secure Wide Area Network, is
  an impressive, well-supported endeavor to allow encrypted machine-to-
  machine communications using IPsec and related protocols. The main part
  of the work was initially focused on server-to-server encryption, and thus
  much of the documentation tells you how to configure two machines to talk
  to each other, and not how to set up a roaming machine with a graphical
  VPN client to talk to a FreeS/WAN server. FreeS/WAN is designed
  for Linux, and works best with Red Hat Linux, a platform for which the
  developers have prepared totally prefabricated installations, customized
  for each micro-release of the kernel.

((•)) **NOTE**

*Glenn spent many hours poking at FreeS/WAN and was able to get a fully
functioning version running on his Red Hat Linux 7.3 system. However, the
nomenclature that describes its configuration is so esoteric and different from
the client software that one uses to connect to a VPN server that he finally gave
up. The problem is that FreeS/WAN's documentation is organized around digital
certificates, not user accounts, which are what the client programs use.*

Subscribing to a VPN Service

If the VPN options listed above made your pocketbook ache or your eyes glaze
over, you might consider another alternative for roaming users: subscribing to
a service that offers VPN connections from wherever the user is out to a secure
network operations center (NOC) somewhere else on the Internet.

Typically, the least secure link in any connection is the local network: the sniffed
or penetrated Wi-Fi or wired network over which traffic proceeds unencrypted
out to the Internet connection. Once traffic is on the broader Internet, it's much
less likely that any snoop would be able to intercept it—in essence, your traffic

becomes more secure once it leaves the local network you're connected to. By creating a secure client-to-NOC connection, you eliminate nearly all of the places that people could sniff or intercept network traffic.

We currently know of two companies offering VPN services for hire that are specifically designed for hot spot users:

- **WiFiConsulting** (www.hotspotvpn.com) offers an $8.88 per month VPN service wherein you can use WiFiConsulting's HotSpotVPN service and create a secure PPTP-based connection from a single client to WiFiConsulting's NOC. It's straightforward and designed for the hot-spot user. HotSpotVPN's VPN connection doesn't require any special software, just an ordinary PPTP client, found in Mac OS X 10.2 and 10.3 and many versions of Windows (for details, see Chapter 26, *Securing Data in Transit*).

- **Boingo Wireless** (www.boingo.com) offers a built-in VPN client in its wireless connection software. (The software works only in Windows at the moment.) To use the service, you need to set up an account with Boingo and download Boingo's software, but the VPN service is currently free: you can have a pay-as-you-go account that has no extra VPN charges attached. Keep in mind that Boingo has always indicated that it might charge users who don't have a paid subscription to use its outbound authenticated email service and VPN tunnel.

Businesses with more resources or specific needs might want to hire a corporate VPN service provider. Prices are all over the place, and some providers may require installing purchased or leased hardware on your network. Check out http://findvpn.com/providers/ for a lengthy list of VPN service providers.

The Linksys WRV54G

We've left an inexpensive, although slightly baffling, option for last. Just as we were finishing this book, Linksys shipped a much-awaited product: the WRV54G Wireless-G VPN Broadband Router (www.linksys.com/products/ product.asp?grid=33&scid=35&prid=565). This all-in-one device, which costs about $230, can support up to 50 simultaneous VPN connections using the robust IPsec-over-L2TP protocol.

The WRV54G relies internally on a variety of open-source software packages, including the above-mentioned FreeS/WAN. However, Linksys packaged the often inscrutable open-source software nicely, hiding many of the ugly bits that would frighten children and sterilize farm animals. Instead, Linksys offers a somewhat complex, but not overwhelming, interface for configuring the various VPN tools, and a good configuration guide that walks you through the necessary steps. It's still daunting, if only because Linksys expects that you'll set up a separate tunnel connection for each connection that might be initiated. This works for home workers with static IP addresses on their home networks, but not for Wi-Fi road warriors.

(((•))) **NOTE**

The WRV54G, by the way, isn't just a VPN device: it has four auto-sensing 10/100 Mbps Ethernet ports, a full wireless gateway, and a DHCP and NAT server system, just like its basic WRT54G cousin.

Authorized Access

Enabling WPA or putting access points outside a firewall and using a VPN can effectively eliminate the potential of unauthorized people gaining access to your network resources, even if they can associate with your access point or passively sniff data. Those methods are broadly effective.

But if you want to have more granular tracking of users with access to your network, and if you're not ready for the expense of a VPN or a WPA upgrade, you do have another option: using authenticated logins with a system known as 802.1X that combines accountability with security.

(((•))) **NOTE**

The 802.1 task group is one of the overarching networking groups in the IEEE, and the capital X indicates that this is the full standard.

We first give you some background in the underlying principles of this kind of authentication, and then we provide practical advice on implementing it without great expense.

What is 802.1X?

The 802.1X protocol is essentially a way of putting a gatekeeper in front of a network. The gatekeeper's job is to prevent access to the network until a client who wants to connect proves itself worthy by providing credentials which can range from a simple user name and password up to biometric control systems confirming fingerprint or hand geometry.

802.1X defines three roles: a client, which is called a *supplicant*; an access point, which acts as an *authenticator* or gatekeeper; and a user database server or *authentication server*, which confirms a user's identity (**Figure 22.1**).

Figure 22.1
The 802.1X roles.

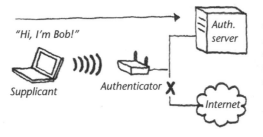

"Hi, I'm Bob!"

1. *First, a supplicant, having associated with an access point, sends its login credentials (like a username and password) to the authenticator, which passes them along to the authentication server. The access point doesn't give the supplicant Internet access at all.*

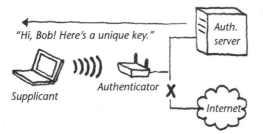

"Hi, Bob! Here's a unique key."

2. *Next, the authentication server confirms the supplicant's identity and then responds, again via the authenticator, providing the supplicant with a unique encryption key for using the local network.*

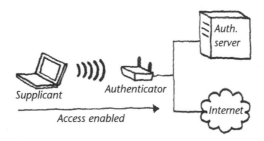

Access enabled

3. *Finally, with the encryption key in hand and its credentials confirmed, the supplicant can pass traffic through the authenticator out to the Internet (or local network, as the case may be).*

NOTE

802.1X works over both wired and wireless networks; in wired networks, the authenticator is an Ethernet switch.

When a user (supplicant) wants to join the network, she uses an 802.1X client to log in (**Figure 22.2**). The authenticator (access point) receives a request for a login from the supplicant. The supplicant can't access any network resources at all except a single network port devoted to handling 802.1X logins.

The authenticator sends the user's credentials to the authentication server, often the same one used for regular network logins to access file servers and other network resources (step 2 in **Figure 22.1**). The authentication server tells the authenticator that the login is valid, and the authenticator opens up network access to the supplicant (step 3 in **Figure 22.1**).

NOTE

Microsoft's Wireless Network Connection tool includes 802.1X support as does the Internet Connect application in Apple's Mac OS X 10.3 Panther, while

Figure 22.2
An 802.1X login
here shown in
Mac OS X 10.3.

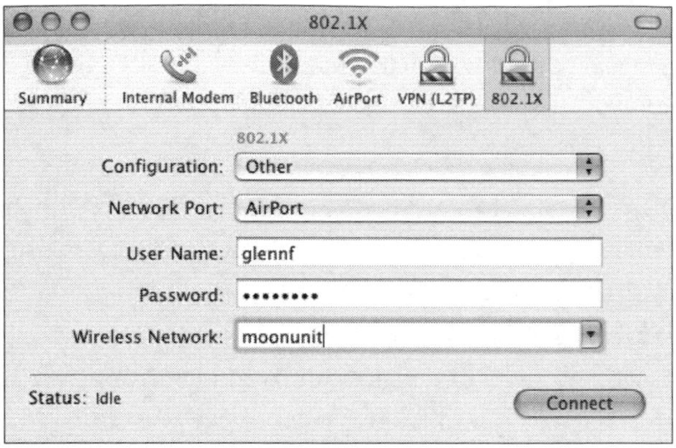

companies like Funk and Meetinghouse provide commercial software that works on a whole range of platforms, including many versions of Windows, Unix, Linux, and Mac OS.

The 802.1X transaction has already kept the network safe from those who don't have passwords. But it gets better. Once the user has been verified, the authentication server can provide a unique WEP or WPA encryption key to that specific client. This way, each client on the network can have its own key, making it possible to maintain link security even with WEP.

To overcome WEP's weaknesses, the authenticator can automatically rotate the WEP key on any terms allowed by the software that manages the keys: after a certain number of packets or period of time. On WPA networks, the interval between key rotations could be quite long without compromising security.

The only known flaw in 802.1X is that the transaction that results in the network connection isn't encrypted. The user name is typically sent in the clear, and the password, while scrambled, can be extracted in exactly that form and potentially replayed later.

Various companies have proposed ways of taking the authentication messages, which use EAP (Extensible Authentication Protocol), a relative of PPP, and encrypting them inside an SSL-like tunnel (see Chapter 26, *Securing Data in Transit*). The leading proposal as we write this is Protected EAP (PEAP), which is supported by Microsoft and Cisco.

$(((\bullet)))$ **NOTE**

Cisco has long had its own flavor of protected EAP (Lightweight EAP or LEAP), which isn't sufficiently robust, so the company has encouraged its customers to move away from LEAP.

Unfortunately, Microsoft supports PEAP in only Windows XP and 2000. You need to purchase a commercial 802.1X client from Meetinghouse, Funk, or one of a few other companies to use PEAP on any other Windows release or other platforms.

Still, using 802.1X could be a good investment for network protection, and it's a one-time expense to provide strict network access control.

Using 802.1X

The complexities of 802.1X can be hidden from view entirely because many wireless gateways, including inexpensive ones from Linksys and others, can work as an 802.1X authenticator.

Your big expense or complicating factor really happens on the back-end with the authentication server. If your network already has some kind of authentication server, such as a RADIUS (formerly an acronym, but no longer) server, for handling user logins via dial-up or other methods, you might simply be able to enable 802.1X as a mode on that server.

But if you're starting from scratch you have a few options.

- **Wireless Security Corporation** (www.wirelesssecuritycorp.com) appeared on our radar in late 2003, and it has an interesting option for small offices that want the power of 802.1X without the hassle of a server. You can use any of a variety of access points on your local network and point to Wireless Security's authentication servers over the Internet. The company even offers software that you can run on a local computer as a backup to prevent loss of network access in case your Internet connection drops.

- **Meetinghouse Aegis Server** (www.mtghouse.com) comes from Meetinghouse, one of the most ecumenical software makers. Meetinghouse offers clients for all platforms, and server software that runs under Linux, Solaris, and Windows XP and 2000. Its server isn't cheap, starting at $2500 for 50 clients. But it's probably the right standalone software solution for those who don't want the complexity of…

- **Windows Server 2003**—once again, Microsoft's server product has the full solution embedded in it. It's not a cheap offering—see earlier in this chapter—but if you're already using it or need the resources it provides, you can combine it with standard access points for 802.1X-protected login.

Troubleshooting Your Wireless Network

Most of the time, setting up a basic wireless network is almost surprisingly simple. Usually, you just plug in your access point and connect it to the device that handles your Internet connection, like a cable or DSL modem. But that's not to say that you won't ever run into trouble, either in the setup phase or in using a wireless network that was previously functional.

In almost all cases with a wired network, you either have a connection or you don't. Wired networks are binary—either on or off—and that makes sense to those of us who have become accustomed to computers. Wireless networks are different. They're fuzzy. Sometimes you can receive a strong signal while sitting on the couch; other times you won't be able to pick up anything in the same location. Frankly, this drives us nuts, and to judge from the problems we've helped people solve, it drives almost everyone else nuts too.

Luckily, the fuzziness of wireless network reception goes away when you look at the edges of the network: any problems you may have with your wireless network adapter or with reaching local network services or the Internet obey the more understandable rules of computer troubleshooting.

(((•))) NOTE

This chapter addresses problems from the standpoint of setting up or maintaining a wireless network. For suggestions on how to troubleshoot problems related to connecting to a wireless network, many of which are likely to be relevant here, read Chapter 14, Troubleshooting Your Connection.

In this chapter, we've broken down the common problems you may experience while setting up or running a wireless network into a number of broad categories. In each case, we offer suggestions for tests you can run or questions you can ask to shed additional light on your problem. In almost all cases, the result of one of these tests or the answer to one of the questions will point to your solution. For the most part, our solutions are generalized, although if we know of a specific solution for a particular device or operating system, we give that as well.

 NOTE

We strongly recommend that you read Appendix C, How to Troubleshoot, before you read farther. That appendix has basic advice and steps for working through any problem, not just those you might encounter when troubleshooting a recalcitrant wireless networking connection.

 TIP

Even if you don't use a Mac, it's worth reading Apple's detailed troubleshooting guide for AirPort wireless networking technology—AirPort is just 802.11b so the guide covers more than just Mac-related information. Find it at http:// docs.info.apple.com/article.html?artnum=106858. *Also try the Wireless Network Troubleshooting page at* www.practicallynetworked.com/support/ troubleshoot_wireless.htm.

 TIP

*In the Windows XP help system, you'll find an interactive, network troubleshooting guide that includes some wireless advice (**Figure 23.1**). It can walk you step-by-step through common problems and advise you on configuring or reconfiguring your settings.*

Problem: Signal Strength Is Poor

Q: **I have trouble receiving the wireless connection in parts of my house. Is there anything I can do to increase the signal strength of my network?**

A: Yes, there are quite a few ways you can improve signal strength for your entire network:

 TIP

Use a program like NetStumbler (www.netstumbler.com) or MacStumbler (www.macstumbler.com) to test signal strength in different locations.

- First, test with multiple computers, if possible, to determine if the problem is with a particular computer or with your access point.

- Reorient your access point or its antennas. Seriously, sometimes that's all you need to do to improve signal strength enough to keep working. It's like

Figure 23.1
The Windows
XP Network
Troubleshooter
offers advice about
troubleshooting a
wireless network.

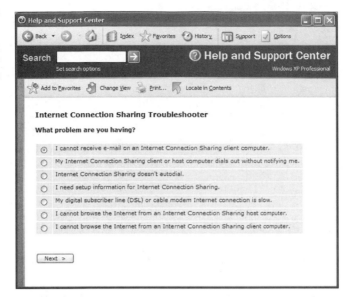

the old days when people would get up on their roofs and fiddle with their
TV antennas to improve television reception for the big football game.

- Try orienting your access point in other planes. To quote the wise Mr.
Spock on Ricardo Montalban's character in *Star Trek II: The Wrath of Khan*,
"He is intelligent, but not experienced. His pattern indicates two-
dimensional thinking."

- If there's a lot of metal (such as junction boxes in an electrical wiring closet)
near your access point, the metal may be blocking the signal—see if you
can move the access point to a spot where it's less obstructed.

- Verify that antennas, either external or internal, are properly connected
for both the access point and any wireless clients.

- This is painfully obvious, but we have to say it. Try moving your computer
closer to your access point. As a solution, it's cheap, it's easy, and yes, we
know you should be able to work anywhere you want. If you don't want to
let the evil radio demons win, move on to the next suggestions.

- Consider moving your access point to a more central location. This may
not be feasible without running a long Ethernet cable somewhere, and
although we know that the entire point of a wireless network is that you
don't have to run cables, sometimes there's no way around running one.

- Add an antenna to your access point. You can buy small indoor antennas
that increase the signal strength somewhat, although some access points may
not allow you to connect an external antenna (check with the manufacturer

of your access point first, since many actually sell stronger antennas or "signal boosters" that are really just higher-gain antennas).

- Think about buying a new access point that has a jack for an external antenna or that includes a more powerful antenna. Many access points, including the original AirPort Base Station, rely solely on the tiny antenna on a PC Card inside.

- Consider buying one or more new access points and setting them up either for roaming (where they're all connected to the same wired Ethernet network) or in a WDS-connected network (where the connection between access points is wireless). Either way should help you extend the range of your network. See Chapter 20, *Bridging Wireless Networks*, for more information.

Problem: Signal Is Intermittent

Q: **Most of the time I have no trouble maintaining a connection with my access point, but sometimes it drops and comes back up later. What could be going on?**

A: When you see this kind of intermittent problem, think interference:

- Do you have a microwave oven that's frequently in use? Microwave ovens create interfering signals in the 2.4 GHz radio band. Test by watching the signal strength indicator on your computer while running the microwave. You may be able to solve the problem by moving the microwave farther from your wireless network devices. Some industries use microwaves for sealing plastic, among other purposes, and if you're in an industrial building or neighborhood, that could be a problem as well.

- Do you or, worse, your neighbors in an apartment building, have a 2.4 GHz cordless phone? These phones are common, but because they operate on the same frequency as 802.11b/g wireless networks, the two can interfere. You probably wouldn't hear anything more than some crackling on the phone, but the phone can cause the network to drop out entirely. Try separating the phone's base station from your access point or computer. If you're buying new cordless phones, 900 MHz phones offer voice quality and range similar to that offered by the 2.4 GHz models, despite what the manufacturers claim. You can also buy a 5 GHz cordless phone.

- Look out for any other 2.4 GHz devices, such as X10 spy cameras or devices for transmitting audio or video to a stereo or television. Adam once tested a device that transmitted audio played from his computer to his stereo—as soon as he turned the device on, his wireless network came to a screeching halt.

Problem: Reception Is Impossible

Q: **At my workplace, a concrete-block wall prevents my wireless network from covering the entire office. How can I extend the wireless network to the currently dead areas?**

A: We're assuming that you've already tried the advice about increasing signal strength. Repositioning the access point, adding another access point using WDS, or adding an antenna (particularly if you can borrow one to test) is an easy fix. If those approaches don't work, you have a couple of options:

- Do you really need wireless access on the other side of that wall? If not, it's probably easier to drill a hole through and run an Ethernet cable. Just because wireless networks are incredibly cool doesn't mean there's anything wrong with using wires occasionally.

- If you must have wireless on the other side of the wall, and you can run wire through the wall, drill a hole, run an Ethernet cable through, and connect another access point.

Buying a New Access Point

When he moved into his current house, Adam realized that the cable modem had to be installed in the downstairs northeast corner of the house because of where the cable connection came in. Unfortunately, that meant his access point, which had to plug into the cable modem, also had to be installed in that location. Initially, using a graphite AirPort Base Station, he could provide wireless network access to every room in the house except his wife's office, which is located in the southwest corner of the second floor.

Using an iBook (which has a better antenna than an AirPort Base Station) running Software Base Station as the access point solved the problem, except for tying up a perfectly useful iBook. Next Adam decided to run an Ethernet cable through the ceiling up to the second floor, where he had verified that an access point could reach his wife's office. Like many cable-pulling jobs, it was tiresome and difficult, but solved the basic problem.

Reception still wasn't as good throughout the house as he would have liked, so after he cannibalized his AirPort Base Station's Lucent WaveLAN PC Card for use with his long-range wireless connection, Adam bought a Linksys EtherFast gateway with a pair of small dipole antennas that provide noticeably better signal strength. The gateway still lives in Adam's closet in the bedroom.

- Drilling holes isn't always feasible or advisable. If that's your situation, consider a pair of HomePlug or HomePNA Ethernet bridges, one on each side of the wall, with a second access point plugged into the bridge on the far side of the wall. Obviously, HomePlug is ideal if all you have is electrical connections; give HomePNA some thought if there are telephone wires you can use.

- Knock down the damn wall. (Assuming it's not load bearing—it's a bad idea to take a sledgehammer to a load-bearing wall unless you want to drop the ceiling on your head.)

Problem: No Wireless Connectivity

Q: **Wireless clients seem to see my access point, but can't connect. Any ideas?**

A: In this sort of a situation, the problem is often related to over-enthusiastic security settings, although there can be other problems too:

- If you're testing with only one computer, see if other computers can connect. If so, the problem is likely specific to that first computer. Knowing that the problem relates to one particular computer should narrow the field of future tests and solutions.

- It's possible that the clients are too far away to connect reliably despite claiming that they can see the access point. Many signal-strength indicators in software don't correspond proportionately to signal quality. Try moving closer and check if the problem goes away, or download NetStumbler (www.netstumbler.com) or MacStumbler (www.macstumbler.com) to gather more data on signal strength.

- Recheck that users are entering your WEP or WPA key correctly. Especially when typing a long WEP key of 26 characters, it's easy to make a mistake, and a single error negates the entire key. Some software doesn't alert users that the WEP or WPA key is incorrect, making data entry-related problems harder to troubleshoot.

- Turn off WEP, WPA, and MAC address filtering in your access point to find out if they are preventing clients from connecting.

- Make sure your network name is short and has no spaces or special characters in it.

- Reset or power cycle (turn off, wait 30 seconds, turn back on) your access point.

- Check to see if you need to upgrade your firmware.

- Don't try this without asking the vendor's tech support engineers first, but you may need to downgrade your firmware instead of upgrading. Newer versions are not always better.

- If computers running Windows XP can connect, but those running other operating systems cannot, the problem may be related to an administrator enabling 802.1X authentication, which we describe in Chapter 25, *Preventing Access to Your Network*. 802.1X authentication, though a good tool for large organizations, is supported only with software installed on each wirelessly connected computer.

NOTE
Before you power cycle, make sure network users aren't in the middle of something important. Power cycling an access point disables everyone's access, and it can shuffle out new DHCP-assigned addresses.

Problem: Frequent Need to Reset Access Point

Q: **Every few days to few weeks, my access point seems to freeze up: I can't connect to it, and it needs rebooting. What's wrong with the gateway?**

A: Some gateways and access points appear to require regular rebooting:

- If you own a first-generation Linksys WAP11, be aware that many reports and our experience show that it required regular power cycling, after which it seemed to work just fine. Later firmware releases helped—1.4i being the latest for that model—and an updated WAP11v2 is immune to the problem. Early versions of the Linksys EtherFast gateway had this problem as well.

- The graphite version of the first-generation Apple AirPort Base Station has a reputation for requiring regular but infrequent reboots. Later graphite units and the newer snow AirPort Base Stations do not have this problem.

- If you experience this sort of problem regularly, consider upgrading the firmware in your access point.

Performing a Ping Test

One of the most basic ways to test connectivity between computers is with a ping test, which is essentially sonar for computers. One computer sends a ping to another computer or device and waits for an answer back. If an answer comes back, the remote computer is working and connected; if not, the problem is related either to the connection or to low-level network software. To run a ping test, all you need to know is the IP address of the computer you want to test.

To determine a computer's IP address in Windows 98/Me, click the Start menu and choose MS DOS Prompt from the hierarchical Programs menu. (Microsoft has moved this command around over time; look in Accessories in Windows XP.) Then, type ipconfig to find the IP address. Under Windows XP, click the connection icon in the System Tray that corresponds to the network adapter you're using, and then click the Support tab. On the Mac, look for the IP address in the TCP/IP control panel (Mac OS 9) or the Network preferences pane (Mac OS X).

Once you've found the IP address, you can perform a simple ping test in Windows by choosing Run from the Start menu and typing ping 192.168.1.1 (replace that IP address with the address of the machine you want to test). In Mac OS X, open Terminal and type the same command. In Mac OS 9, you need a utility such as Sustainable Softworks IPNetMonitor (www.sustworks.com/site/prod_ipmonitor.html) or Stairways Software's Interarchy (www.interarchy.com). Both of those products are also available for Mac OS X, where they provide graphical interfaces on ping and other network utilities.

The ping test is successful if you see a series of lines of sequential numbers, each with a time at the end. If you see lots of gaps in the sequential numbers, then there could be something wrong with your link to the local network, your network's link to the Internet, or the Internet connection between your ISP and higher-level networks.

You may have to press Control-C under Windows and Mac OS X to halt a ping test in progress; in some operating systems, ping continues indefinitely until stopped. If a ping test works, move on to other troubleshooting tests. If it doesn't work, look for bad cables and check to make sure the basic network settings are configured properly. Some DSL modems that allow telnet connections also have ping utilities built in, and can help eliminate the local network as a problem.

One caveat: some firewall software has an option to ban IP addresses from which ping tests originate to prevent certain kinds of denial-of-service attacks! You can turn this off, but it can be awfully mysterious if you forget, since you could have inadvertently banned your own machines. Other firewall software can disable ping responses altogether (so it's a good idea to perform some ping tests when everything is working right, just to gather some baseline data).

- Think about the usual solutions: add a surge protector to deal with electrical problems; try using an uninterruptible power supply (UPS) to prevent problems resulting from brief power outages that aren't long enough to entirely reset the gateway; and consider sending the gateway in for repair if it's under warranty.

Problem: No Link between Wireless and Wired Networks

Q: **My wired and wireless computers can't see each other. What's wrong?**

A: In most cases, these sorts of problems are caused by improper settings for wired-to-wireless bridging or bad cables:

- Check your access point to make sure that bridging between wired and wireless networks is set up correctly and turned on.

- If you're using a software access point, make sure the computer's network settings are still correct and that a reboot or other change didn't disable bridging.

- Verify that the cables to your wired computers are plugged in properly. Don't ignore the possibility that a cable has been damaged by someone stepping on it or a mouse eating through it.

- If you have more than one wired computer, make sure they can see each other.

- If your wireless gateway has a reset switch, push it to clear errors. (See the note earlier in "No Wireless Connectivity" about notifying other users.)

- Unplug your wireless gateway, wait 30 seconds, and plug it back in. Sometimes this clears errors not fixed by pushing a reset switch.

- If the problem relates to a specific service, like file or printer sharing, make sure the software is installed and configured properly on all the computers in question.

Problem: No Internet Connection

Q: My wireless network basically works, but I can't see out to the Internet through my modem/DSL/cable/broadband Internet connection. What could be wrong?

A: Unfortunately, there are many different problems that could cause an Internet connection to disappear, and some of them are out of your control:

- If you're using dynamic addressing, verify that your computer has been assigned a DHCP address. If not, the problem may be with your gateway or network's DHCP server.

- DHCP might not be broadcasting across all access points: most DHCP servers in access points need to have an option enabled to bridge DHCP onto the wired network.

- A rogue access point might be offering IP addresses that aren't routed to the rest of the network. We've seen this on our own networks and at a recent conference.

Linksys EtherFast Gateway Gets Confused

Adam's main wireless access point is a Linksys EtherFast Wireless AP + Cable/DSL Router w/4-Port Switch, and for the most part, it's served him well. After he bought it, about once a month, his cable-modem Internet connection became unreachable even though the wireless connection to the gateway remained solid. There turned out to be two slightly different problems. One was solved by pressing the reset switch; the other required cycling the power to the gateway. After suffering through those irritations for a few months, Adam updated the gateway's firmware to the most recent version, and those problems disappeared almost entirely.

Then, while researching WEP for this book and turning WEP on and off and changing keys, he somehow managed to put the Linksys gateway into a state where everything seemed fine (and nothing had changed with the Internet connection), but none of the computers could access the Internet. To solve the problem, Adam first verified that the Internet connection was still working by connecting an iBook directly to the cable modem. Then he wrote down all his custom settings in the Linksys gateway and reset it to factory defaults. After re-entering his settings, everything worked perfectly again.

- Worse than a rogue, someone may have turned on an ad hoc network with the same name as the network you're trying to connect to. We've also seen this at conferences. Find that person and stop him, or make sure you're selecting only from infrastructure networks. (In Windows XP, select Wireless Network Connection, click Advanced, and click Advanced again. In Mac OS X, choose only from the infrastructure list at the top of the AirPort menu, not the computer-to-computer network list at the bottom of the menu.)

- Check your firewall settings. To associate with most access points, your computer or other device must accept DHCP broadcasts, and an overly tight firewall can restrict DHCP broadcasts, even from a local network. (Glenn experienced this mystery for several months when he traveled until he discovered his own overzealousness.)

- If your wireless gateway has a reset switch, push it to clear errors, but only after alerting any other users on the network (see "No Wireless Connectivity," earlier). Failing that, unplug your wireless gateway, wait 30 seconds, and plug it back in. Sometimes this clears errors not fixed by pushing a reset switch.

- Verify that the cable to your Internet connection (whether modem or router) is plugged in properly. Don't ignore the possibility that the cable was damaged by someone stepping on it or a rodent chewing it.

- Reset your modem, router, DSL modem, or cable modem, or if it has no reset switch, unplug it, wait 30 seconds, and plug it back in. (And we repeat again: warn other users on your network, first!)

- Reset or power cycle your modem or router again, but take care to turn off your gateway first, turning it back on only after the modem has come back up.

- If possible, test the connection by connecting a single computer directly to your modem or router. If the problem persists, contact your ISP's tech support and ask for help.

- Write down any custom settings in your wireless gateway or access point, and then reset it to the factory defaults. Enter your settings again.

- Upgrade the firmware in your access point. Adam recently saw an Asanté access point that couldn't hold onto its DHCP-assigned IP number from the cable ISP until he installed new firmware.

- Try a different wireless gateway or access point.

Problem: WDS Doesn't Work

Q: I'm trying to use Wireless Distribution System (WDS) to link several access points together wirelessly, but I can't get the units to talk to each other. What gives?

A: WDS isn't standard across equipment from different manufacturers and can require numerous manual settings to be entered. Consider the following:

- Are you sure you entered each MAC address correctly? MAC addresses are six sets of two characters, and a single error dooms the connection.

- Did you follow our instructions in Chapter 20, *Bridging Wireless Networks*, to test that each remote access point in a WDS network could see the master when they're in close proximity? You might need to move access points around to get enough signal strength for it to work.

- Are you experimenting with access points made by different companies? Although we know that the Buffalo WLA-G54 and the Apple AirPort Extreme Base Station (firmware release 5.1.1) worked with each other in late 2003, later firmware releases could render this undocumented, unpromised support inoperable.

- Apple's AirPort Admin Utility can tell you whether or not a given access point is connected via WDS. Connect to the master AirPort Extreme Base Station, click Show All Settings, click the WDS tab, and examine the entries. If the software reports "no connection" next to an access point, check the access point itself and the MAC address you entered.

Wireless Security

We all like to think we have privacy, even when often we don't. Some people move into the Alaskan outback, 50 miles from the nearest truckstop, to ensure that they have no chance of running into another human being. Others maintain psychological limits while living in dense environments: though Glenn can see neighbors through his kitchen window, through mutual unspoken consent, he and his neighbors never acknowledge each other's presence in their respective food preparation areas.

These anecdotes illustrate the extremes of wireless networking as well. As long as our wireless networks are isolated, we don't have to worry about others. The minute someone comes within range, our privacy can be compromised. Transmissions over wireless networks, because they go through walls, ceilings, floors, and other obstructions, are easily intercepted by consumer-level equipment just like the gear you use to connect your computers and access point.

So what do you need to know to stay secure? Chapter 24, *Wireless Worries,* looks at just who should worry about security, and what aspects of security should concern a reasonable person (paranoids can skip to the nuts and bolts chapters that follow). Chapter 25, *Preventing Access to Your Network,* presents a number of methods you can use to keep unwanted visitors from connecting to your network and sharing your Internet connection. Even if you don't mind sharing your connection, you should still read Chapter 26, *Securing Data in Transit,* for advice about how to protect your valuable data from other legitimate users of your wireless network. And lastly, it's worth checking out the recommendations in Chapter 27, *Protecting Your Systems,* for basic suggestions on how to keep miscreants out of your computers.

Wireless Worries

Security is something we as a society tolerate, not embrace. Any given person's comfort level with security may vary enormously depending on their background and location. For instance, growing up in rural New York State in the early 1980s, Adam left his car keys in his elderly Dodge Colt when it was parked at home. No one lived within a mile; cars driving by were infrequent, easily seen, and usually announced by the family dog; and hey, it wasn't like a rusty Dodge Colt that needed bits of a mouse nest cleaned out of its fuel filter on a regular basis was worth much. Living in a populous suburb of Seattle a decade later, Adam not only didn't leave his keys in the car (then a shiny red Honda Civic) when it was parked in the driveway, he also locked the doors.

It's often easier to understand wireless security after thinking about a real-world example like Adam's behavior toward his car keys. In rural New York with an old car, the likelihood of someone stealing the car was low, and the potential liability for the worst case was also low. In suburban Seattle with a new car, the likelihood of theft had increased significantly, as had the value of the car, causing Adam's site-appropriate behavior—more paranoid or more realistic, you take your pick. Now translate the two concepts of likelihood and liability to wireless networking. You can easily determine your own balance of fear and realism by answering two simple questions:

- How likely is it that someone will break into your wireless network or sniff (listen in on) the traffic going across your wireless connection?

- What is the potential liability if they do?

Currently, Adam lives far enough from the population center in Ithaca that he and his wife Tonya aren't worried about the potential of a snooper: it would be difficult for someone to share their connection without parking in their driveway. In contrast, Glenn and his wife Lynn reside in a moderately dense part of Seattle. One day, soon after younger neighbors started renting the house next door, Glenn flipped open his laptop and spotted their wireless network. So, for Adam the likelihood of a security breach is low, whereas for Glenn it's moderately high. If your company is in an office building that holds other companies, the likelihood of someone accessing your network is probably very high.

On the potential liability side, a business might be concerned about whether someone in its parking lot could access its confidential data, such as invoices as they pass between employees and a database, email containing information that might interest competitors, or even customer credit card numbers that might be encrypted over a link between a company Web server and a customer's browser, but totally unprotected on a local network. Home users have fewer worries, of course, but should still protect passwords that an attacker could use for logging in to an online banking account or bill-paying system, for instance.

Unlike privacy fanatics, we don't want to turn you into a tic-ridden paranoiac. Instead, we want to present a fair discussion of the risks and potential outcomes when you rely on wireless networks.

(((•))) **NOTE**

Adam wrote an article for his newsletter TidBITS *that talks about a theory of privacy and why most people don't give it much attention. Read it at* http://db.tidbits.com/getbits.acgi?tbart=05951.

Let's look first at how your location plays into security considerations, then at the kind of data that might travel across your network, and finally at how to evaluate your individual risk factors so you can see which of the remaining chapters in this section you need to read.

Likelihood of Attack

Before you think about what you're sending or receiving over your wireless network, you should first consider where you use wireless networks, because location affects the likelihood that someone would try to connect to your network and snoop. It's likely that you use wireless networks in one or more of the locations in **Table 24.1**. And when we say "use wireless networks," we're talking about either your own network or networks run by others, because when you access someone else's wireless network, you're still at some level of risk.

Table 24.1
Likelihood of Snooping in Different Locations

Location	Details	Likelihood of Snooping
Rural/far away	In your home and far from other houses	Extremely low
Long-range	Over a long-range, point-to-point link with a wireless ISP or neighbor	Low, due to the directional nature of most point-to-point links
Dense urban or suburban	In your home in a dense urban area or with at least several other houses close by	Moderately high, particularly if you have high-tech neighbors, but actual attacks are unlikely
Mixed-use	In a mixed-use residential and commercial neighborhood	Moderately high, since businesses are more attractive targets and are more likely to use wireless networks
Public-space neighborhood	In a neighborhood near a public park or where people can park on the street	High, since community networks receive high use by a diverse, anonymous population
Office building	In an office building having multiple businesses or a nearby parking lot within line of sight	Very high, due to proximity and the attractiveness of targets
Roaming	While on the road in airports, cafés, hotels, and other locations	Moderately high, due to the ease of monitoring, but relatively low risk because no one knows to watch for your particular data

For most people (given that point-to-point long-range connections are still relatively uncommon), unless you fall only into the rural/far away category, there's a non-trivial likelihood that someone could access your wireless network or watch your traffic without your knowledge.

Pay special attention to the roaming category. Even if you protect your own network, using your computer while connected to untrusted networks can still put your data at risk. Whether the network is free or for-fee, you have no control over the network-based security precautions, and everyone else using the same network may have the ability to see your data in transit on a wired or wireless link.

Determining Liability

Now that you have a sense of how transparent your network is, you need to consider what your liability would be if someone else were to access your network. Different people have different concerns, but they basically break down into three categories:

- **Access Liability.** What happens if someone uses my wireless network to share my Internet connection?

- **Network Traffic Liability.** What happens if someone is able to eavesdrop on my wireless network traffic?

- **Computer Intrusion Liability.** What happens if someone on my wireless network breaks into my computer?

Let's look at each of these briefly, and then you can turn to the next three chapters to learn how to protect yourself.

Access Liability

Do you want to allow unknown people access to your wireless network? This sort of thing doesn't come up with wired networks, since no one installs Ethernet jacks on the outside of a house or office. Since many people believe strongly in the sharing ethic, asking this question isn't unreasonable. Although intentionally allowing people to connect to your network does increase your security risk, the fact that you're aware of the presence of outsiders on your network means that you're probably also more aware of the security considerations their presence engenders.

No matter how you answer that question, a few problems can arise whenever someone accesses your wireless network for friendly, or at least benign, purposes.

- If you have a modem-based Internet connection that you share via a wireless gateway, someone connecting to your wireless network could (and likely would) cause your modem to dial out. That may or may not be a problem in itself, depending on how many phone lines you have, but if you're trying to use the connection at the same time, your performance would suffer.

- If you use a cable- or DSL-based Internet connection, performance isn't likely to be a concern most of the time, assuming the unknown visitor isn't uploading or downloading vast quantities of data. However, you may be in unintentional violation of your ISP's terms of service or acceptable use policy by sharing your connection at all. In the worst-case scenario, your Internet connection could be shut off for that violation.

- If you pay for traffic on your Internet connection, which is quite common outside of the U.S., letting unknown people share your Internet connection could result in a nasty and unexpected bill.

- Although we'd like to assume that anyone happening on an open wireless network would use it responsibly, the possibility for abuse does exist. It's possible that an unknown visitor could use your wireless network to send spam or launch an Internet worm attack, for instance, and while neither would likely hurt you all that badly, your ISP might shut you down for being the source of the abuse.

- Lastly, consider the slavering legal hounds of the Recording Industry Association of America (RIAA), those moralistic guardians of a corrupt and abusive industry. If someone were to use your wireless network to share copyrighted songs, it's not inconceivable that the RIAA could come after you as the putative source of the copyright infringement. They've sued universities for their students' behavior; how far away are you as a *de facto* ISP, even if your service is free?

((•)) **NOTE**

We certainly don't encourage anyone to violate copyright, ludicrous as current copyright law may be thanks to Disney's well-funded lobbying, but we also find the RIAA's tactics utterly offensive.

Your mission, then, is to determine how concerned you are about each of these access-related possible scenarios, after which, of course, you can read the next few chapters to address your concerns.

Network Traffic Liability

You likely believe that most of your private data sits on your computer, that you transmit and receive only limited amounts of sensitive information, and that someone would have to listen at a specific time to capture those bits. The reality of the situation is that we all transmit and receive quite a lot of sensitive data that people with common equipment and widely available software can extract easily.

All data sent or received over a wired or wireless network is transmitted *in the clear* to anyone else able to join or plug into the network. "In the clear" simply means that the data is sent in a form that a human being can intercept and then either read directly or convert easily into a usable program or image data.

Here's a list of what you might be sending or receiving in the clear:

- Your email account password

- The text of all email messages sent and received

- The contents of any documents sent or received as attachments

- The location and contents of any Web pages viewed

- Your user name and password for any non-secure Web sites (sites that don't use SSL)

- Your FTP user name and password

- Any files you transmit via FTP

- The text of any instant messages you send or receive

- The contents of any music or other files you send or receive using LimeWire, Kazaa, or other peer-to-peer file sharing programs

- The IP addresses and port numbers of any connections you make

- Timbuktu session control or file transfer sessions

These items are *not* sent in the clear:

- The contents of encrypted sessions using SSH, SSL, or a VPN (described in Chapter 26, *Securing Data in Transit*)

- Your email password if your ISP uses authenticated SMTP (outbound) or APOP (inbound)

- Timbuktu Pro or pcAnywhere passwords

- AppleShare passwords (if both client and server have encryption enabled)

- Any secure SSL Web pages (their URLs begin with https)

- The contents of any email message or file encrypted with PGP or similar public-key encryption technology

(((•))) **NOTE**

Even if you close your network through means we describe in Chapter 25, Preventing Access to Your Network, *you may still wind up exposing data to network crackers and others who can penetrate some of the basic methods of preventing access. We talk about securing the contents of what you're sending in Chapter 26,* Securing Data in Transit.

Each item that you might transfer in the clear falls into one of three categories: account access information (user names and passwords), information that could be used to track your online steps, and content related to what you say and do.

We're pretty transparent people (well, not literally), so there isn't much that we would say or do online that we would worry about someone else reading.

We might be embarrassed if the wrong person read the wrong document, but that's it. But what if that document were posted on a widely read mailing list or Web site? Even for us, that could be a problem, and other people might have data that could get them fired, damage their businesses, humiliate them publicly, or cause lawsuits or divorces. You probably have a pretty good sense of whether or not you're at risk from the things you say or do.

Similarly, information that tracks online movement doesn't worry either of us, since as journalists, we can always claim we visited a Web site for research purposes. (That might not work if it's a site we visited 1000 times.) But it doesn't take much imagination to see how the fact that a politician had frequented certain sex sites could ruin his career. Again, you probably have a decent idea of whether your online movements could be in any way damaging.

Last, and most important, is account access information, which, when stolen, presents two types of risk. First, since most people tend to use the same passwords in multiple places, having your email password stolen could compromise a more-sensitive system, like your online banking account. Second, attackers often use a password to one account to break into another account, working their way ever deeper into a computer with the eventual goal of stealing data, causing damage, or using the computer to run an automated program that attacks other computers. In this respect, protecting your passwords isn't something you do just for your own benefit, it's something you do for the benefit of everyone who may be affected if the attacker takes out a server that you use.

 TIP

With the understanding that it's nearly impossible to remember different passwords for every possible service, we recommend using three different passwords. The first should be simple and easily remembered, but used only for Web sites that don't store personal information about you (such as your address, birth date, or credit card number). The second should be harder to type; should include upper- and lowercase letters, numbers, and punctuation; and should be used for accounts where some personal data is at risk. Lastly, everyone should have one highly secure password that is long, hard to type, and essentially impossible to guess. Use that for accounts, like your bank and PayPal, where money is involved. Using a longer password won't prevent it from being stolen via an unprotected wireless transaction, but realistically, most passwords are stolen by being guessed or because someone wrote them on a Post-it note.

In general, because anything you send or receive could be intercepted and read (text) or used (files and programs), you must accept the notion that everything could be examined or stolen if you're in a location where other people might be able to connect to the network you're using.

So what's your liability? Obviously it depends on the data you're transferring, but no one wants their passwords in other people's hands, and we strongly encourage everyone to take some basic precautions that we outline in Chapter 26, *Securing Data in Transit*. And if you're more concerned, that chapter also has solutions for even the most anxious.

Computer Intrusion Liability

The final form of liability you should consider when thinking about security for your wireless network is what happens if someone uses your wireless network to break into your computer.

 NOTE

Protecting computers from intrusion via your wireless network isn't fundamentally different from protecting them from intrusion via your Internet connection. However, many intrusion programs trust computers on the same local network more than computers on the rest of the Internet, and you must make sure your settings reflect your degree of risk.

We see several types of concerns here.

- **Data theft.** If someone can gain remote access to a computer and its files, she could easily steal sensitive files. All it takes is a few minutes of inattention, or a misconfigured setting, for someone to copy files from your computer. Glenn found this out back in 1994, when his Unix server's password file was first stolen (but the passwords weren't cracked, at least). And, more recently, Adam was irritated with himself after his ISP asked if he knew that anyone could see files on one of his Macs via AppleShare.

- **Data damage.** You may never know if someone has stolen files from your computer, but you'll certainly realize if he instead vandalized your system and deleted all your files. Worse, some attacks focus on more subtle destruction or manipulation that you wouldn't notice at all. If someone were to tweak Excel spreadsheets with hundreds of numbers in them, could you tell?

TIP

A package called Tripwire (www.tripwire.org for open source and www.tripwire.com for commercialware) is designed to scan your system and create a cryptographic signature for each file. You're then supposed to store these signatures on unchangeable media, like a CD-ROM. Each time Tripwire runs, it reports on any changed files, which could help you pinpoint compromises.

- **Exploitation.** Some attacks focus on known bugs in software that allow a remote program or person to infiltrate your computer and take control of some of your software or the entire operating system. Once the attacker has established that level of control, he can install software that attacks other computers, turning your computer into what's called a *zombie*. Most attacks are aimed at computers running some version of Microsoft Windows or other software from Microsoft, such as Outlook or Internet Information Server. Over the years, many different bugs have been found that allow attackers to take over a machine; equally as problematic are worms and viruses that may cause damage, replicate themselves, turn the infected computer into a zombie, or all three. Microsoft has patched known holes, but many Windows users don't download and install these security patches, leaving their computers open to further exploitation and infection. Other attacks use a *denial of service* (DoS) approach, where the attacker sends so much data to your computer that it's overwhelmed. DoS attacks don't cause damage, per se, but they prevent normal operation and can be difficult to shut down.

(((•))) **NOTE**

Glenn once had to spend a full day watching his network be saturation-bombed with garbage traffic before he could convince an ISP from whose network the attack was launched that he had a serious problem. Glenn finally, with informal advice from the FBI, suggested he might have to sue the ISP—after which it took action and shut down the offending DSL customer (who was likely the victim of an attack that had turned his computer into a zombie).

The liability for each of these scenarios is fairly severe; but luckily it's easy to take simple precautions that significantly reduce the likelihood of anything bad happening. Chapter 27, *Protecting Your Systems,* offers the necessary advice.

Who Should Worry About What

Let's combine likelihood and liability for a number of sample users to evaluate your real-world risks and determine which chapters in this section are most important for you to read.

- If you're a home user with no immediate neighbors or nearby public spaces, and if you don't believe your data is particularly sensitive, you don't have much to worry about. At most, read Chapter 27, *Protecting Your Systems,* to see if you want to take steps to prevent anyone from attacking your computers over the Internet. Otherwise, just skip the rest of this section.

- If you're a home user in an urban environment, you should definitely read Chapter 25, *Preventing Access to Your Network,* and the discussion of protecting email passwords in Chapter 26, *Securing Data in Transit.* If you're concerned about the sensitivity of your data, read the rest of that chapter as well. It's also worth reading Chapter 27, *Protecting Your Systems*, just in case.

- If you maintain a wireless network in a business, you should read all the chapters in this section, thinking hard about your company's risk factors as you go. In particular, in Chapter 26, *Securing Data in Transit*, consider how far you want to go to protect your company's sensitive data. Also important is Chapter 27, *Protecting Your Systems*, because your data is probably more attractive to electronic thieves than the data of a home user.

- If you regularly use wireless networks while traveling, be sure to read Chapter 26, *Securing Data in Transit*. The more sensitive your data, the more seriously you should consider the approaches in that chapter.

NOTE

There's no easy way to say this. Security, whether you're talking about protecting your car, your home, or your wireless network, is hard, mostly because it's always a battle with another human being. Locking your door with a simple knob lock stops amateur thieves, but keeping more experienced thieves out requires a strong deadbolt. And if you live where burglary is likely, or if you have especially valuable property, you have to think about whether multiple locks, alarm systems, or bars on the windows are also necessary. Unfortunately, the kind of people who break into networks are usually much smarter than garden-variety thieves, and as a result, the security measures you must take to stop them are commensurately more complicated. So, our apologies up front, but the chapters in this section are inherently more technical than much of the rest of the book.

Preventing Access to Your Network

Until mid-2003, the tools available to prevent both crackers and casual passersby from accessing your network and the computers on it ranged from fair to poor. Thankfully, a broad-based industry alliance has brought real security to home and small-office users without increasing complexity, though support for this new, secure standard is still making its way into the marketplace.

We start, however, with two techniques you've heard a lot about, and which companies have tended to emphasize in the past, but which are almost completely useless against anyone with a few simple tools.

We then move to the real security measures: the old techniques, and why they're broken; plus the new method, and how to use it.

Sops to Security

In the real world, people interested in security may remove the street numbers from houses or take the company name off the front door. Still others put up large "No Trespassing!" signs. These approaches don't prevent burglars from breaking in, and they're unfortunately analogous to several common approaches to securing a wireless network.

Closing Your Network

Most wireless access points enable you to "close" your network, which turns off a message with the network's name that the access point otherwise broadcasts continuously. These broadcasts make it easy for wireless adapters to find and connect to networks.

Some access points call this option a "closed network," and others ask if you want to "disable broadcast name." No matter what the terminology, a closed network's name doesn't appear in the list of available networks in ordinary client software (**Figure 25.1**).

Figure 25.1
Closing your network prevents casual users from seeing the network name.

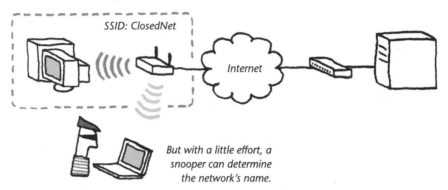

But with a little effort, a snooper can determine the network's name.

Don't be lulled into a false sense of complacency. Although a closed network offers protection from the most casual observer, many programs that can monitor wireless networks—from commercial down to open-source freeware—can easily see the names of closed networks.

In short, if you don't want average people connecting to your network, there's nothing wrong with making it a closed network, but the only people you're keeping out are those who almost certainly weren't a security risk anyway.

Access Control by Network Adapter

There's another mostly useless way to restrict access to a network: allow only specific network adapters to connect (**Figure 25.2**). Like all Ethernet network adapters, a Wi-Fi adapter is identified by its MAC (Media Access Control) address, a unique serial number assigned to every network adapter.

However, as we note in Appendix A, *Networking Basics*, MAC addresses are not immutable and can be spoofed relatively easily. For instance, many gateways and access points let you change their Ethernet adapter's MAC address to simplify connecting to ISPs that lock connections to a specific network adapter. They don't pose a security threat, but it's not much harder to change the MAC address of a wireless network adapter.

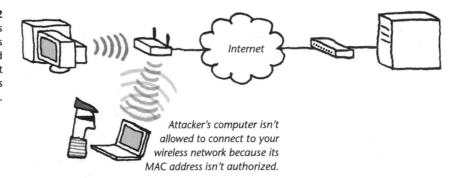

Figure 25.2
Restricting access by MAC address keeps unauthorized computers out of your wireless network.

Attacker's computer isn't allowed to connect to your wireless network because its MAC address isn't authorized.

This flexibility, combined with the fact that MAC addresses are sent in the clear even on encrypted networks, means that a cracker can easily see MAC addresses in use and then assign one of those addresses to her equipment. As with a closed network, restricting access by MAC address will keep honest people honest, but it won't do squat against a determined intruder.

 TIP

Many networks don't even use the MAC address to authenticate, but rather use the DHCP-assigned IP address—which is even easier to guess! Read this disturbing account in New Architect *magazine at* www.newarchitectmag.com/ documents/s=2445/na0902h/.

Encryption and Control

Let's get to the good stuff. While closed networks and adapter address limitations don't do much good, there is hope! Instead of trying to hide or restrict access, you can use technology called WEP (Wired Equivalent Privacy) to require that users enter a password to join a network; that same password is used to scramble all the data passing over the network. Without the password, no one can connect to the network or intercept the data.

This kind of encryption appeared alongside 802.11b back in 1999, but a variety of flaws made it easily crackable. Its replacement is now at hand. We first tell you about WEP, because it's still in wide use, and then about its successor, WPA, which we strongly recommend you upgrade to if you currently use WEP.

WEP Encryption

The developers of 802.11b intended WEP to do precisely what the name itself says: offer an equivalent level of privacy to what could be found on a standard wired network. To compromise a wired network, an attacker generally needs to break in to a room and install a network-sniffing program that watches traffic traveling over the wire.

WEP was designed to act merely as a locked door, to keep intruders from penetrating to the wireless network traffic itself; other measures were supposed to bolster this initial line of defense. WEP basically encrypts all the data that flows over a wireless network, preventing attackers from eavesdropping on network traffic (**Figure 25.3**).

Figure 25.3
Turning on WEP prevents attackers from eavesdropping on network traffic.

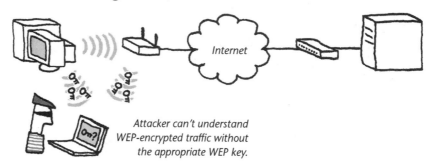

Attacker can't understand WEP-encrypted traffic without the appropriate WEP key.

Unfortunately, even this relatively minimal protection was crippled because of several brain-dead decisions made on the cryptographic front, and because some options were built in but never enabled. Also, even though WEP still offers some level of protection, most people don't turn WEP on because it's a pain to use.

WEP works by using a "shared secret": an encryption key (up to four per network) shared by everyone on the network. Your wireless network adapter uses the encryption key to encode all traffic before it leaves your computer. Then, when the data arrives, the access point uses the key to decode it into its original form.

Users must enter the WEP key manually (and tediously) on every computer that they want to connect to a WEP-protected network. Worse, the key is often expressed in the base-16 hexadecimal numbering system in which the letters A through F represent 10 to 15 as a single digit. Most users haven't the slightest idea of how to deal with hex (reasonably enough—that's what computers are for!). If you combine user confusion with the tedium of inventing (on the access point) and entering strings of hexadecimal numbers, you can see why WEP is annoying to use.

You enable WEP in an access point by inventing a sequence of 10 or 26 hexadecimal digits (corresponding to a 40/56/64-bit key or a 104/128-bit key). Luckily, some access points have a feature in which you type a passphrase and then the access point translates that into hexadecimal digits for you. All adapters and access points must use the same length of key on a single network.

NOTE

Kudos to Microsoft for how it set up its Wireless Base Station: the default walks the user through adding a 128-bit WEP key and storing the backup on a floppy disk.

TIP

See Chapter 17, Setting up a Gateway, for tips on entering WEP keys in access points.

How WEP is Broken

Aside from the usability problems, how is WEP broken from a security standpoint? Here's a quick rundown of WEP's major flaws:

- **Shared secret.** Every computer on a WEP-protected wireless network needs a set of one to four keys that users must typically type and which can sometimes be read as plain text. The complexity of managing keys makes it easy for an attacker to come by a key through social engineering (asking someone for the key), carelessness (the key written on a piece of paper), or disgruntlement (a fired employee). Most keys are never changed after the first time they're entered.

- **Encryption weaknesses.** Because of how WEP generates unique keys by combining the actual WEP key with a 24-bit number known as an initialization vector, the actual key can be extracted relatively easily. The initialization vector isn't used correctly by some manufacturers (who set it to the same number for every packet), or is created in a predictable fashion by others. This results in the reuse of keys, making it easier to break the code, defeating the strengths of the underlying encryption system.

 TIP

Ever wondered why we talk about WEP keys as being 40/56/64-bit and 104/128-bit instead of just 64-bit and 128-bit? Some companies and discussions exclude or incorrectly account for the 24-bit initialization vector as part of the overall key length.

- **Lack of integrity.** While this is usually something that political opponents accuse each other of, integrity in data transmission means that an adapter sending a packet provides some information that allows a receiving station to check that the data that arrived wasn't tampered with in process. WEP's system uses a simple mathematical formula that would allow an intruder to rewrite packets and disrupt a network or corrupt data without detection.

These last two problems may sound obscure, but an attacker needs no special knowledge to exploit them; free automated tools perform all the hard work (see "Extracting WEP Keys," later in this chapter).

 TIP

For more about wireless encryption problems and solutions, see Glenn's regularly updated security status report at http://wifinetnews.com/weak.defense.html.

Despite these faults with WEP, a user with relatively little traffic on his network and/or with little to worry about in terms of interception (passwords but not proprietary data) can generally rely on WEP as the only means of protecting the network. A potential attacker would have to be very determined, scanning a network for perhaps several days or even weeks, to assemble the pieces necessary to break a WEP key.

A Sense of Security

With all these flaws, you'd hope that some of the giant brains that develop wireless networking standards would fix the security system. Your hope has paid off: the IEEE 802.11i task group has been working for years to replace WEP with a forward-thinking, yet backward-compatible, solution that would return WEP to its rightful role as a first line of defense. The first fruits of that work have now appeared in Wi-Fi Protected Access.

Wi-Fi Protected Access and 802.11i

Remember those flaws we mentioned in WEP a few paragraphs above? They're gone. Poof. No more! With 802.11i, phantom security has been replaced with the real thing. As we wrote this edition of the book, 802.11i wasn't finalized, but the Wi-Fi Alliance had taken matters into its own hands by releasing an interim version of 802.11i called Wi-Fi Protected Access (WPA).

WPA is a subset of 802.11i, lacking just a few features that aren't critical to near-term security, and designed to allow upgrades to full 802.11i when the task group finishes its work. If it sounds like the Wi-Fi Alliance was acting high handed, remember that the companies that are members of the trade group are also members of the IEEE committees that develop these standards.

For clarity, we talk about these features as being part of WPA, since it has no unique elements that won't be included in 802.11i.

WPA/802.11i's Fixes

Let's take the fixes point-by-point as we did above:

- **Shared secret.** Like WEP, WPA uses up to four keys that everyone who accesses a network agrees on, but rather than using obscure hexadecimal numbers, the system allows for a plain text password. In WPA, this is called the *pre-shared secret*. Some tools call it the *pre-shared key* or PSK, which isn't quite accurate. Unlike WEP, the pre-shared secret isn't actually the encryption key itself. Instead, the key is mathematically derived from that password. Of course, if someone obtains the pre-shared secret, they can still access your network, but crackers can't extract that password from the network data, as was possible with WEP.

 TIP

Office and academic networks—networks with central user databases, mostly—can bypass the pre-shared secret and have each client assigned a constantly changing key after it logs in. 802.11i will make this task even easier by passing information about who is already logged in among access points, allowing easier roaming across a company. See Chapter 22, Small Office Wi-Fi Networking, for details.

- **Encryption fixes.** WPA introduces a new kind of key using TKIP (Temporal Key Integrity Protocol), which increases the size of the initialization vector to 48 bits, and ensures that the choice of that number isn't predictable. This change vastly increases the complexity of breaking the encryption system—by several orders of magnitude. Engineers estimate that a key won't repeat for over 100 years on a single device. Even more remarkable, each packet will have its own unique key created by mixing the vector with a master key.

NOTE

With the full 802.11i standard, users will also have access to encryption using AES (Advanced Encryption System), which is vastly more secure than even TKIP.

- **Better integrity.** The integrity of packets is now ensured, eliminating the chance of network disruption.

The only gotcha with WPA and 802.11i is that devices that don't use the newer security standard must revert back to WEP, and packets sent between those devices and the access point are susceptible to being broken.

WPA/802.11i Availability

WPA and 802.11i were both designed to allow users to upgrade older hardware to support the new TKIP standard via firmware updates. Newer equipment is required only for more advanced encryption, which isn't strictly necessary for non-military uses right now. (Computation always moves forward, so encryption experts want systems that can't be broken for epochal periods when the usual advances in technology are factored in.)

Unfortunately, to date, we've seen WPA upgrades only for hardware that shipped during 2003, mostly 802.11g devices. Manufacturers made so many promises about fixing security that we fervently hope they will ultimately release firmware upgrades for all existing 802.11a, b, and g devices, but we're still waiting.

Because the Wi-Fi Alliance certifies hardware compliance, by the end of 2003 the WPA standard will become a required part of what manufacturers must support to have hardware certified with the Wi-Fi trademark. Microsoft released client support for Windows XP, 2000, and 2003 in early 2003, while Apple has promised support in Mac OS X 10.3 Panther. See Chapter 6, *Connecting Your Windows PC*, and Chapter 8, *Connecting Your Macintosh*, for instructions on how to configure WPA for each platform.

 TIP

For the latest details on WPA's availability and support, see Glenn's regularly updated security status report at http://wifinetnews.com/ weak.defense.html.

Know Your Enemy

So, who are these people attacking your network and how are they doing it? To paraphrase the *Harry Potter* books, you must learn about dark magic to defend against it.

The tools available to monitor and even break into wireless networks aren't designed with evil intent. For the most part, they were developed to demonstrate that potential weaknesses were in fact security holes. Network administrators need these kinds of tools to understand how to better secure the data that flows over their networks. They're also tremendously useful when searching for open wireless networks when you're out and about, for troubleshooting certain types of network problems on your own network, and for planning a new wireless network.

These tools fall into three categories. Some scan constantly to help you find open or closed wireless networks, reporting signal strength and whether or not WEP/WPA is enabled. Others intercept wireless data and convert it into something you can read. And, in case you didn't believe us when we said it was easy to break WEP keys, there's even a tool that does that with no effort.

$((\bullet))$ **NOTE**

We don't even play lawyers on TV, but we still advise you to consider whether or not it's legal to run any of these tools in your country, state, county, province, canton, city, or town. An increasing number of laws make it illegal to scan networks—even passively—unless you either own the network or have explicit written (on paper, not email) permission.

Stumbling onto Wi-Fi

Most types of wireless client software automatically detect open Wi-Fi networks and present you with a list of possibilities to which you can connect. But few of the programs built into the operating system or provided by Wi-Fi adapter manufacturers go much further than that. For additional information about the wireless networks in your vicinity, turn to one of the *stumbler* programs. These utilities sniff for accessible wireless networks, display those that they find, and present you with additional information about each one.

Data that the stumbler programs can provide includes network name, channel, signal strength, and WEP/WPA encryption status. All are useful for seeing how signal strength for a given Wi-Fi network changes as you move around; some can even provide a graph of signal strength over time, which could be useful for determining how environmental conditions affect a long-range wireless Internet connection.

Here's a list of the main stumbler utilities; note that they tend to work only with specific Wi-Fi adapters, so it's worth checking compatibility before you download. Unfortunately, there aren't any stumbler utilities for the Palm yet.

Windows Stumblers

- **Netstumbler** (www.stumbler.net) is the best known of the stumbler utilities (**Figure 25.4**). It works only in Windows 98/Me, Windows 2000, and Windows XP, and it supports a large number of Wi-Fi adapters, including some 802.11a cards in Windows XP. It set the standard for the basic set of stumbling features, including support for mapping discovered access points with a GPS device, though it can't detect closed networks.

- **ApSniff** (www.bretmounet.com/ApSniff/) is a simple wireless network sniffer that works only with Windows 2000 and Wi-Fi adapters that use the Prism 2 chip set.

- **Aerosol** (www.stolenshoes.net/sniph/aerosol.html) is, like ApSniff, a simple wireless network sniffer for Windows and Wi-Fi adapters that use the Intersil Prism 2 chip set, along with the Orinoco adapters.

Figure 25.4
A Netstumbler screen capture shared on the Internet showing an enormous array of interesting points.

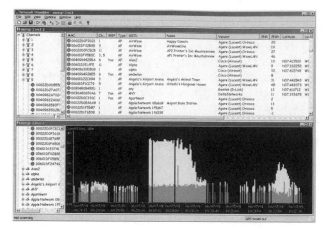

Macintosh Stumblers

- **MacStumbler** (www.macstumbler.com) fills Netstumbler's role as the best known of the Macintosh stumbling utilities (**Figure 25.5**). It offers all the basic features of discovering access points, and with the most recent release, it gained GPS support for mapping the location of discovered access points. It works only with Apple AirPort cards, but since it doesn't work in monitoring mode, it can't detect closed networks.

Figure 25.5
MacStumbler scanning Glenn's network.

- **KisMAC** (www.binaervarianz.de/projekte/programmieren/kismac/) is related to Kismet (see "Unix Stumblers," next) only in name and basic function (**Figure 25.6**). It works only on Mac OS X, and only with Apple AirPort (not AirPort Extreme) cards, along with Orinoco and Cisco Aironet PC Cards. It can do roughly what Kismet can, including the GPS mapping. KisMAC is the only Macintosh stumbler program that puts the AirPort card in monitoring mode, thus enabling it to find closed networks, and all while being completely passive (other programs send out probe requests).

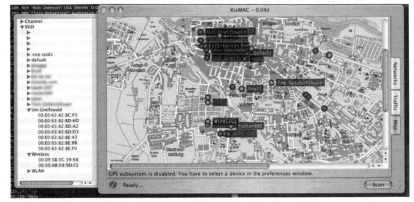

- **iStumbler** (www.istumbler.net) is a free open-source stumbling tool for Mac OS X that provides a clean Aqua interface. It's a young program, so it works only with Apple AirPort cards, has only experimental GPS support, and doesn't yet offer the full feature set of other stumblers. It's pretty, though.

Unix Stumblers

- **dstumbler** (www.dachb0den.com/projects/dstumbler.html) works in BSD-based Unix operating systems. Along with the usual features, dstumbler offers color signal-to-noise graphs that can help you troubleshoot interference, GPS support for mapping the location of discovered access points, audio support for reporting access points, and data logging.

- **Kismet** (www.kismetwireless.net) is a Unix-based wireless network sniffer that can discover closed networks, identify the manufacturers of discovered access points, map access point locations via GPS, crack WEP keys, and much more. It works with a large number of 802.11b cards, and even 802.11a cards using a specific chip set. Kismet is distributed only in source code form; it's not for the technically inexperienced.

Pocket PC Stumblers

- **Ministumbler** (www.stumbler.net) is a port of Netstumbler for use on Pocket PC handhelds running Pocket PC 3.0 and 2002. It's available from the Netstumbler site, but it's almost impossible to find any details about it there. Ministumbler running on a Pocket PC probably makes for a highly portable Wi-Fi detector, though the combination might benefit from an external antenna for picking up weaker networks.

Other Stumblers

- **Red Fang** is the first program that demonstrates how data can be stolen from Bluetooth devices unprotected by default security settings. Of course, since Bluetooth has a rather short range, and since many Bluetooth devices are quite mobile, the real security risks are likely to be quite minimal. Red Fang isn't available for download as far as we've been able to find.

Listening In

Once you're connected to a wireless network, you can listen in to all the traffic on it by placing your network interface in what's called *promiscuous mode*. A computer in promiscuous mode listens to all traffic on the network, not just packets intended for the particular device.

The most graphical approach to listening in is a proof-of-concept Macintosh tool called EtherPEG (www.etherpeg.org), which extracts images as they fly by from Web page viewing and creates a random collage onscreen (**Figure 25.7**). It's a fun tool for a conference where you can watch people become bored and start browsing the Web instead of paying attention to the presentations. The goal of the EtherPEG creators was to demonstrate just how easily someone can listen to your wireless network traffic if you don't take basic precautions like turning on WEP.

Figure 25.7
EtherPEG watching the graphics whizzing by on the wireless network.

Closer to the network level is tcpdump, a command-line utility found in most Unix and Linux distributions, and also available from the Mac OS X command line. The tcpdump utility shows the headers from TCP/IP packets transiting the network. This lets you see which IP numbers are in use and what kinds of traffic network users are engaged in. It's a useful network troubleshooting tool, but isn't easy to use.

The Unix and Windows ntop utility (www.ntop.org) collects data comprehensively, building a database as it works, and then presents a Web interface through which you can examine connections and traffic statistics. As with tcpdump, ntop can prove extremely useful when tracking down network problems.

The War Prefix

You might have read articles—some of them written by Glenn—about wardriving, warflying, warwalking, warcycling, and warchalking. All these terms essentially describe different ways of finding other people's wireless networks. The "war" prefix in these words has nothing to do with actual violent conflict, but is borrowed from *War Games*, a 1983 movie demonstrating the threat of computer-driven nuclear war. *War Games* was one of the first mainstream movies about computer hackers.

In *War Games*, Matthew Broderick's character finds open modem connections by having his computer dial lots of numbers until it hits an answering tone. Once connected, he tries to break into the computer connected to that modem. Hackers call this process "wardialing."

The first takeoff was "wardriving," which is the technique of driving around with Netstumbler or MacStumbler running on a laptop computer in the car. As you drive, the program gathers information about wireless networks that you pass (see "Listening In," next). Warwalking, warcycling, and warflying are all the same idea, varying only by the mode of transportation used.

Warchalking is a sort of second-order derivative word. Matt Jones, a London resident, decided that the hobo chalk language used in the late 1800s and through World War II by itinerants could be adopted to the task of marking information in the physical space about nearby wireless access points (www.warchalking.org).

The media quickly leapt on this—that's when Glenn wrote what he describes as a well-balanced story about it for *The New York Times*—and spun the story quickly that warchalking was used to identify networks that could be cracked. In fact, there is no way to determine how common warchalking is. And, there's no real telling whether it's being used to show community networks, individual access points that people have purposely shared, or networks that were intended to be private and secure (**Figure 25.8**).

At this writing, most warchalking reports come from individuals who chalk their own access points. Some suspect that the media hysteria may be fed by pranksters who warchalk in nonsense locations. We've never seen a mark in the wild, nor has anyone we know throughout an extensive group of Wi-Fi enthusiasts and journalists. Even the picture we show in Chapter 32, *Working on the Road*, was of a mark made by a friend of Matt Jones!

We object to the unfortunate choice of "war," because it lends itself to the public perception of hacker involvement. You can't control the evolution of language, but it's a bad development when legitimate and fun purposes seem malicious because of their names.

Figure 25.8
One view of
warchalking.

They always dreamed of having a home *in* the range.

Finally, although it has other uses as well, the Unix, Mac OS X, and Windows utility ettercap (ettercap.sourceforge.net) is a network traffic sniffer that's optimized for finding passwords from several different protocols, like email and FTP. The best use of ettercap is for convincing people that they should turn on some sort of password protection. At a conference we were at recently, one guy ran ettercap all the time, and would periodically call out things like "If your username is ace, you should change your password and turn on APOP." Our advice is to avoid ettercap, since it's hard to claim you're using it only for legitimate purposes.

Extracting WEP Keys

The Linux utility AirSnort (airsnort.shmoo.com) is a simple tool that listens to several million packets across a network and then produces the WEP key. Yup, it's that easy. Don't do it.

Actually, the reason to run AirSnort is to determine how long it would take for an intruder to capture enough data to break your WEP key. If it would take 30 minutes, you know additional security precautions are essential, but if it would take a week, you know there's much less reason to worry about someone cracking your WEP key.

((•)) **NOTE**

Even though we warned you before, we warn you again: check with a lawyer if you have any questions about the legality of using AirSnort. Check before you suffer the consequences.

Securing Data in Transit

In the last two chapters, we've discussed whether or not you should worry about the security of the data crossing your network, and explained how to prevent people from accessing your wireless network. However, you may still find yourself in circumstances in which you want protection but restricting access to the network won't help:

- You're sharing your local wireless network or using a shared network on which encryption can't be enabled.

- You're using a public wireless network in a coffee shop, hotel, airport, or elsewhere, or a community networking hot spot.

- At least one of your computers can't support WPA (Wi-Fi Protected Access), and the use of WEP (Wired Equivalent Privacy) exposes your whole network to WEP's problems (see the previous chapter).

- Your corporation won't let you use any network except the local one without using some form of encryption.

You do have an alternative: you can encrypt the data before it leaves your machine, and have it decrypted only when it arrives at some destination. By creating end-to-end encryption links using strong, currently unbreakable standards, you can keep your data completely safe from prying network sniffers. Even if people can join your network and reach the Internet—hijacking your link—they still can't see your data. Encrypting your data in transit is a lot more difficult than setting up a closed WEP/WPA-protected network, but it's eminently more sensible.

TIP

An added bonus of encrypting data from end to end is that the data you send and receive becomes completely unreadable not just on your wireless network, but also on every network link between your computer and the destination machine. That's the reason large organizations typically require their employees to use encryption technology.

We look at four popular categories and methods of securing data, ranging from simple password protection up to full network encryption of all data.

Email Password Encryption

Even if you aren't worried that people might read your email, you should worry about protecting your account passwords (**Figure 26.1**).

Figure 26.1
Encrypting email passwords prevents them from being stolen.

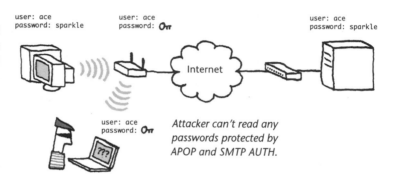

NOTE

Don't forget that many Web sites use user names and passwords merely for identification and thus don't use secure pages when asking for those passwords. Since these passwords are easily stolen, make sure they're different from your email passwords and passwords to sensitive information.

There are two primary methods of encrypting just your password, both of which require support in your mail server, though most modern mail servers have these options. Your ISP or network administrator has probably already enabled them, requiring that you just set an option in your email program.

APOP

APOP (Authenticated POP) protects your password when you retrieve inbound email from a POP (Post Office Protocol) server. Instead of sending your password in the clear, APOP sends a unique, per-session token that the server uses to confirm that your email program knows the correct password. The token can't be reused or reverse engineered.

APOP does not encrypt email messages or do anything other than protect your password. We recommend it as a sensible minimum security precaution; most home users won't need the protection described in the rest of this chapter.

SMTP AUTH

SMTP AUTH (the AUTH part is actually an SMTP command), or Authenticated SMTP, identifies you to your SMTP server when you want to send outgoing messages. Technically, there's no reason to require authentication for sending email, but Authenticated SMTP has become commonplace in this age of spam, because if an SMTP server requires SMTP AUTH, that prevents a spammer from sending spam through that server. SMTP AUTH typically uses the same user name and password that you use for checking mail via POP or IMAP.

 TIP

Another benefit of SMTP AUTH is that it enables you to send email from anywhere on the Internet (such as from a wireless-enabled coffee shop in another city), instead of just from specific network locations that your system administrator has defined. Many WISPs, like Boingo Wireless, offer Authenticated SMTP for outbound email on their networks.

Unfortunately, not all servers that authenticate outbound traffic require encryption to exchange your login information. There's no way to know unless you ask your system administrator or ISP and check that your email program can encrypt SMTP AUTH transactions.

Content Encryption

Although we recommend protecting your passwords, there is a middle ground between encrypting passwords and encrypting all your data—using content encryption on specific files and email messages. This approach lets you protect the pieces of content that you feel are the most sensitive.

Content encryption makes it almost impossible that anyone other than your intended recipient could read the file or email message, even if they obtained access to your machine, a mail server, or the recipient's computer. That's because when you encrypt content manually on your end, it usually requires the recipient to decrypt it with a manual action on the other end.

The most popular software that encrypts the contents of messages or entire files is PGP (Pretty Good Privacy). PGP uses public-key cryptography to secure a message so only the intended recipient can read it (**Figure 26.2**).

Figure 26.2
Encrypting email
messages and
specific files with
PGP prevents
crackers from
reading just those
messages or files.

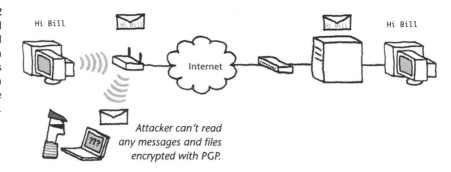

Attacker can't read
any messages and files
encrypted with PGP.

 NOTE

The PGP product was sold by its developers to Network Associates. In 2002, Network Associates sold it back to PGP Corporation (www.pgp.com), which has released new free and commercial versions.

TIP

An open-source alternative to PGP is GPG or GNU Privacy Guard (www. gnupg.org); a Mac version is also in development (http://macgpg.source forge.net). GPG works with most files created by newer versions of PGP and vice versa, but read the GPG FAQ if you plan to use the two together.

How Public-Key Cryptography Works

In public-key cryptography systems, each user generates a pair of keys, one public, one private. Using combinations of those keys, users can sign files or messages to prove that they sent them and can encrypt files or messages so only the intended recipient can open them. The keys work together like puzzle pieces—if someone encrypts something with your public key, only your private key can open it. And, if you sign something with your private key, only your public key can verify that you signed it.

Getting Started

As an example, assume that Glenn and Adam set up PGP so they can exchange encrypted drafts of this book without concern about industrial spies from other publishers sneaking a look before the book is published. (In reality, we're nowhere near that paranoid.)

The first step in public-key cryptography is to generate a public key and a private key. Along with the keys, you must generate a passphrase that enables you to decrypt and unlock your own private key when you want to use it. Adam and Glenn both run through these steps, so they each have public and private keys, and then they share their public keys with each other. Now, here's how they can use their keys.

Adam wants to send Glenn an extremely important email message regarding the book schedule. Adam's not worried about someone else seeing this message, but he does want to make certain that Glenn believes it comes from him, and hasn't been forged by some joker on the Internet. (Email forgery is remarkably simple, though doing it in such a way that it can't be traced easily or identified as a forgery is more difficult.) So Adam signs the message using his private key.

When Glenn receives the message, he can read it with no extra effort, but to verify that it did indeed come from Adam, he uses Adam's public key to check the signature. When they match, Glenn knows that the message is legitimate (**Figure 26.3**). Had someone used any other private key to sign the message, it wouldn't have matched with Adam's public key and the signature verification would have failed.

Figure 26.3
Signing and verifying a message.

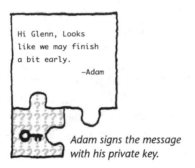

Adam signs the message with his private key.

Glenn uses Adam's public key to verify the message.

Next, assume that Glenn wants to send Adam a draft of the book, but because he's worried that one of his neighbors may be eavesdropping on his wireless network traffic, he decides to encrypt the file before sending it. This time, Glenn uses Adam's public key to encrypt the file, and then sends the file along. When Adam receives the file, he uses his private key to decrypt it (**Figure 26.4**). If someone were to intercept the file and try to decrypt it, she couldn't because only Adam's private key can decrypt files encrypted with his public key.

Figure 26.4
Encrypting and decrypting a document.

Glenn encrypts the file with Adam's public key.

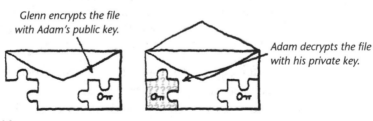

Adam decrypts the file with his private key.

 TIP

You can see from this example how important it is that you keep your private key safe and don't share it with anyone. If someone were to learn your private

key, that person could pretend to be you and could decrypt any encrypted information sent to you. In reality, if your private key were compromised, you'd have to revoke its public key partner.

Distributing Keys

The fact that public keys can be shared without jeopardizing encryption is what makes the public-key cryptography method unique. But sharing public keys is also an Achilles heel: how do you distribute your public key and receive keys from others for the first transaction? You can just send it to people in email; include it in your email signature; put it on your Web site; or post it to a public directory, called a *keyserver* (such as keyserver.pgp.com, which is available from within PGP).

Although these methods all work, none of them are watertight, because someone bent on impersonating you could forge mail from you or post a key to a keyserver while pretending to be you. Once the fake key is out in the wild, revoking it is tricky.

The solution is for people to exchange keys in ways that ensure the other party's identity. For instance, Glenn and Adam could have created their public keys while at lunch together; being able to see the other person across the table is as much verification of identity as is usually necessary. Slightly less sure, but more reasonable, is using a telephone or fax machine; in those cases you don't read out or write the entire public key (which is way too long for accurate transcribing). Instead, you convey a shorter sequence of letters and numbers that verifies to the other person that the public key you've sent them is indeed your public key—the sequence of letters and numbers is called a *fingerprint*. Some people put their fingerprints in their email signatures, assuming that a recipient can email them to verify identity.

 TIP

PGP offers a neat fingerprinting method: it associates unique words with each number from 0 to 255 in hexadecimal to make it easier to read out. Glenn's fingerprint starts "soybean drunken stormy uncut Oakland." Sounds like Beat poetry.

Luckily, although it can be tricky to verify that a public key does indeed belong to a specific person, the worst possible outcome is that someone could distribute a public key under your name, thus bringing documents ostensibly signed by you into question. But when somebody sends you an encrypted file or message that uses this fake public key, you can't decrypt it with your private key. This should alert you to potential problems, but your security is intact.

Once you have a public key for someone and have verified who she is, you can exchange messages for the life of the key. Many public keys are set to expire on a certain date for additional security.

Using PGP

Special software is necessary to sign or encrypt (and verify or decrypt) files and messages using PGP. You can either download free versions or buy a commercial version—both from PGP Corporation (www.pgp.com). (The free version is slightly hidden on the Products page.)

The commercial version comes with various levels of technical support and includes mountable, encrypted disk images and plug-ins for popular email programs, such as Microsoft Entourage for Mac OS X and Lotus Notes for Windows. The Mac OS X-only Mailsmith email client, which Glenn swears by, has built-in PGP support allowing you to automatically sign all outgoing messages, among other shortcuts (**Figure 26.5**).

Figure 26.5
Mailsmith's built-in support for PGP.

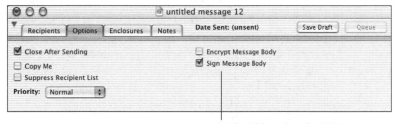

Mailsmith's options for PGP.

Inside any email program that has plug-ins, you can compose a message, select an option, and have the message replaced with its encrypted version before sending. Likewise, you can decrypt an incoming message with a menu selection.

SSH (Secure Shell)

SSH was originally created as a way to establish encrypted terminal sessions that *tunnel*—or create simple end-to-end connections—between a client computer and a server computer (**Figure 26.6**). SSH was necessary because the telnet protocol sent all information in the clear as plain text, allowing any network snooper to grab often critical data.

SSH has expanded far beyond this original purpose. It now lets you create tunnels for any kind of protocol, whether POP and SMTP, FTP, Web, or even Timbuktu Pro. It does this with a trick called *port forwarding*, which connects a local port on your computer with a remote port on a server.

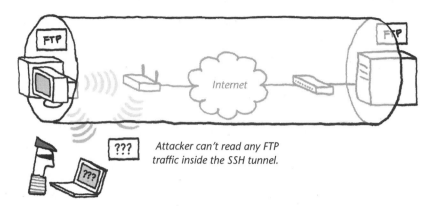

Figure 26.6
Creating a secure
tunnel with SSH
protects data inside
the tunnel.

Attacker can't read any FTP
traffic inside the SSH tunnel.

With SSH, you're protecting both passwords and all the content that you send or receive via the specific Internet services you choose to tunnel.

How SSH Works

SSH encrypts the entire contents of any session, and it's considered highly secure. SSH doesn't, by default, use outside trust: the initial exchange between a server and a client to set up a trusted relationship for future sessions requires either blind faith or the use of a confirmation code, also called a fingerprint.

NOTE

An SSH server generates a fingerprint for its encryption key, and when you connect for the first time from a client, you can double-check that the fingerprint your client sees is identical to the one on the server. If you run your own server, you can retrieve the fingerprint yourself (see the documentation for OpenSSH). Otherwise, ask a system administrator.

NOTE

SSH uses public key encryption, as described above, as the first step of a session. After trust is established by exchanging public keys, a session is started by encrypting a much shorter session key with a public key. The server and client can safely confirm the shorter key. A shorter key speeds encryption for real-time data transfer.

Port forwarding with SSH involves connecting a port on your local computer with a port on a remote machine using an encrypted SSH tunnel as the connector. For instance, if you want to retrieve email via an SSH tunnel, you first set up the tunnel between the POP (Post Office Protocol) port (110) on your computer and the remote server's POP port. Then you configure your email program to retrieve email from IP address 127.0.0.1, which is a generic alias for your local machine, on that same port 110.

The SSH software intercepts requests for connections on that port from your mail program and forwards those connections, securely encrypted, to the mail server you specify; responses pass along the same encrypted tunnel.

The main drawback of SSH is that you must have access to a server that can run SSH on its end of the connection. (It takes two to tango in the SSH tunnel.) You may be able to avoid this problem by running your own SSH-equipped or -capable servers or by working with an ISP or a network administrator willing to set up the connection.

 TIP

If SSH isn't an option on your servers, you can try services such as Anonymizer.com (www.anonymizer.com) that offer for-fee SSH tunneling services as well as what the company calls "private surfing" using SSL encryption described later in this chapter.

SSH Software

Setting up an SSH connection requires additional software for all Windows users and for Macintosh users with versions of the Mac OS before Mac OS X. As with many other types of software, you can either try software from the freeware/shareware world or pay for full-fledged commercial software.

In both cases, the software helps you configure all the ports, hostnames, and other details, after which you click a single connect button to activate the forwarding connection through the graphical interface.

For freeware and shareware, check out the list maintained at www.openssh.com/windows.html. SSH Communications Security offers a non-commercial version of its SSH software for Windows at www.ssh.com/support/downloads/secureshellwks/non-commercial.html. Its commercial offerings can be found at www.ssh.com.

You can also obtain commercial SSH packages from F-Secure (www.f-secure.com) and VanDyke Software (www.vandyke.com).

FTP

Mac OS X users can also use FTP over SSH with Interarchy (www.stairways.com), a shareware file transfer program. Interarchy supports two methods that it calls FTP/SSH and SFTP (SSH FTP), both of which use SSH. Just to be confusing, SSH FTP is sometimes called Secure FTP, but Secure FTP servers may also use SSL instead of SSH: there's seemingly no standard terminology.

There's a similar program for Windows from the open-source world called WinSCP (http://winscp.sourceforge.net/eng/).

TIP

What's the difference between an FTP session encrypted with SSH and one encrypted with SSL? With SSL, the FTP server must talk the SSL lingo. With SSH, an FTP client can try a few methods that don't require special support from the FTP server.

Terminal SSH

Because SSH is part of most Unix and Linux distributions, and it is built into the Mac OS X Unix core, it's frequently invoked from a terminal prompt using a command line.

Setting Up Forwarding

At any prompt, or in a script that you write and then execute, enter the following:

```
ssh -l username -L port:host.domain:port host.domain -f -N -C
```

For instance, if user "billg" had SSH access on his POP (which uses port 110) mail server "mail.example.com", the SSH command would be:

```
ssh -l billg -L 110:mail.example.com:110 mail.example.com -f -N -C
```

NOTE

For the extra-geeky, the command line switches (the parts with a dash, followed by a letter) mean: -l = user, -L = forward ports, -f = don't exit if terminal is closed, -N = don't buffer or wait for output, and -C = compress.

You can put all your port forwarding commands on a single line by simply adding another -L. In this example, we're also forwarding port 25 (SMTP) and port 80 (Web):

```
ssh -l billg -L 110:mail.example.com:110 -L 25:mail.example.com:25 -L 80:
mail.example.com:8080 mail.example.com -f -N -C
```

Note the last item, 80:mail.example.com:8080. It forwards Web requests (port 80) to port 8080 on the far side of the connection where, in this example, a proxy server lives that receives requests, sends them, and returns them to the requesting machine. For additional security, you can forward requests from one port to a completely different port on the remote machine. This can help prevent certain automated attacks.

When you shut down, put your machine to sleep, or change wireless networks, you must reinitiate the SSH connection. You may have to stop the current SSH connections first, however. To accomplish this task, Glenn runs the small Perl script below. Replace hostname.domain with your fully qualified hostname, and substitute your user name for username. Also, add any -L statements you need for ports other than the POP and SMTP ports that we list here.

```perl
#!/usr/bin/perl
@jobs = grep(/ssh -C/, `ps auxw`);
foreach (@jobs) {
        (undef, $job) = split /\s+/;
        `sudo kill -9 $job`;
        print "Killed ssh job $job\n";
}
system("sudo ssh -C -l username hostname.domain \
  -L25:hostname.domain:25 -L110:hostname.domain:110 -p 23 -N -f");
```

TIP

If you've never used Perl before, type the script into a text editor and save it as a text file (not as a Word document or other formatted document) in your home directory with the name tunnel.pl. *At a terminal prompt, type* chmod u+x tunnel. *Then, when you want to execute it, just navigate to the directory that holds the script and type the script's name preceded by a period and a slash:* ./tunnel —*don't type a period or anything after the* l.

Using SCP (Secure Copy)

For just limited file copying, you can use a command line tool called scp or secure copy, which uses SSH behind the scenes to copy files from one computer to another. The syntax for the command is:

```
scp -C localfile user@host.domain:/path
```

The software prompts you for a password after you enter this command. You can also use wildcards to match the localfile, such as *.html to match all files that end with .html.

We recommend including the -C flag, which compresses data before it's sent, thus reducing the time it takes to transmit files.

SSL (Secure Sockets Layer)

SSL was initially developed to secure financial transactions on the Web, but it is now widely used to secure Internet transactions of all kinds.

SSL solves the "shared secret" problem found in WEP by using an expanded version of public-key cryptography (see "Content Encryption" earlier). Instead of requiring that people agree on a secret (the encryption key in WEP) in advance or requiring that public keys be published, an SSL-equipped browser and server use a trusted third party known as a *certificate authority* to agree on each other's identity. (SSH depends on fingerprinting for the same effect, although you can also store public keys on computers that want to create secured tunnels.)

Typically, SSL is used for short session-based interactions, like sending credit card information via a Web form. But it can be used to encrypt email sessions (sending and receiving) including the entire contents of email from the client to the server, for FTP (in a form known as Secure FTP even though some flavors of Secure FTP work only with SSH), and for many other transaction types. SSL works for any Internet service that exchanges data in chunks rather than as a stream of information. (For example, you can use SSL for instant messaging, but not for RealAudio music playback.)

Because SSL can be verified by a third party, you don't have to rely on trust (blind or confirmed) as you do with SSH.

You can also work with SSL where there's no certificate authority, just a *personal certificate* or *self-signed certificate*. This certificate isn't signed by another party, but for certain cases, like a private mail server, it's good enough. Some programs don't like these self-signed certificates, and might cause you grief. Entourage for Mac OS X, for instance, requires that you accept the certificate through Internet Explorer (somehow) before it allows you to send email.

((•)) **NOTE**

SSL is now widely used because the underlying patents expired. Often, the developers replace the name SSL (Netscape's coinage) with TLS or Transport Layer Security. For instance, in EAP-TLS, which is used with 802.1X, an encapsulated authentication protocol message is secured with SSL.

Unlike SSH, in which you can connect any two arbitrary ports through a tunnel (port to port), SSL works from program to program, with the client encrypting data and the server decrypting it (**Figure 26.7**). But, just like SSH, all data sent over that tunnel, including passwords and all sent and received content, is securely encrypted.

How SSL Works

When you connect to an SSL-protected Web page, your Web browser and the remote Web server must negotiate the exchange of keys.

First, your browser sends a message that only the server can read, and the server uses information in that message to package a public-session key along with the certificate. Next, the server sends the public-session key and certificate to your browser, which then verifies that the certificate comes from a trusted

Figure 26.7
Encrypting select transactions with SSL protects just the contents of that transaction.

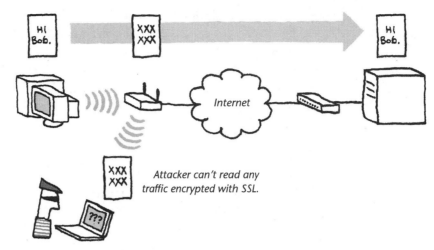

certificate authority and that the server's session key is legitimate. Because this first exchange, when conducted with third-party certificates, is entirely secure and the server's keys are verified independently, the session key can be used with no worries that it was intercepted.

Enabling SSL

In contrast with PGP and SSH, when it comes to SSL, you seldom need to enter a password, run a script, or use a separate program. The client software handles communication and authentication just as it would with an unencrypted connection. With the Web, modern browsers and servers use SSL when necessary (assuming the webmasters have set it up properly). You can tell when you are viewing an SSL-protected Web page because there's often a little closed-lock icon in one of the extreme corners of the window. Also, look for the telltale sign in a URL: instead of the URL starting with http, it starts with https.

Many email programs support SSL, and turning on SSL simply requires that you set an option, often hidden in an advanced configuration dialog. Unfortunately, not all mail servers support SSL, and of those that do, not all handle SSL in the same way. As a result, some SSL-capable mail servers aren't compatible with some SSL-capable email programs. To learn if SSL is an option for protecting your email, check with your ISP or system administrator, or be sure to install a mail server that is compatible with the software you've chosen to use.

 TIP

In the middle of 2003, PGP Corporation released a mail proxy that handles every kind of encrypted connection for every kind of email program. This lets system administrators avoid supporting multiple configurations.

FTP can be secured with SSL by using free and commercial software as long as the FTP server you want to connect to handles SSL connections. On the free side, check out Glub Tech (www.glub.com) to find a Java-based, secure FTP client. On the commercial side, read the article "Secure FTP 101" to find an overview of secure FTP and a list of commercial software (www.intranetjournal.com/articles/200208/se_08_14_02a.html). Also, various software companies have added SSL support to their FTP client software. (Other FTP packages have opted for SSH; see details under "SSH (Secure Shell)," above.)

 TIP

A Unix and Windows package called Stunnel (www.stunnel.org) lets a system administrator add SSL to practically any service by wrapping SSL around existing server software instead of requiring a different FTP or email server.

VPN (Virtual Private Network)

As you've undoubtedly noticed, all the encryption solutions we've discussed so far are specific to a type of Internet service, specific files or messages, or certain software. Why not just encrypt everything? For that you need a VPN, or virtual private network. VPNs are the ultimate solution for securing your data because they create an encrypted pipe, called a tunnel, between your computer and a VPN server. Since the data you send or receive—email, FTP, Web, and anything else—between your computer and the VPN server is encrypted, you don't have to worry about an intruder breaking into your wireless network. Even if someone were to break in, she couldn't decrypt the tunnel that carries all your communications (**Figure 26.8**).

The downside to using a VPN is that setting up a VPN server is not trivial. It requires dedicated hardware, as well as ongoing monitoring and maintenance. Apple's inclusion of VPN server software in its Mac OS X Server 10.3 package—$499 or $999 for 10 or unlimited users, respectively—might ease the cost and difficulty enormously.

Also, at least one quasi-ISP, Boingo Wireless, lets you create a VPN tunnel using its VPN servers. Boingo is a national wireless ISP that aggregates access from other wireless networks, providing a single login account and a single bill, no matter which of their partners' wireless ISP networks you might use (see Chapter 28, *Finding Wi-Fi on the Road*). Boingo's Windows client software features a built-in VPN client. When you connect to a wireless network using this client, the VPN software tunnels all traffic to Boingo's network operations center, at which point it's decrypted to traverse the rest of the Internet.

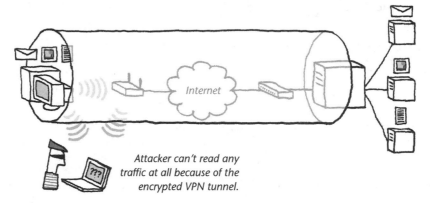

Figure 26.8
Encrypting all traffic inside a VPN tunnel.

Attacker can't read any traffic at all because of the encrypted VPN tunnel.

NOTE

Boingo plans a Mac client as well, and may charge a monthly fee to use its VPN service and authenticated SMTP outbound mail server.

Two popular protocols are used for VPNs: PPTP (Point-to-Point Tunneling Protocol) and IPsec (short for "IP security"). Microsoft developed PPTP, so PPTP client software ships with most versions of Windows. In addition, PPTP is built into Mac OS X 10.2 and later, and PPTP clients are available for Unix and Linux.

Security experts consider IPsec a more robust standard, and IPsec client software is widely available for Windows, as well as built into Mac OS X 10.2 at the command line and into 10.3 in the Internet Connect software (**Figure 26.9**).

NOTE

IPsec used with VPNs is technically called IPsec-over-L2TP, because IPsec is an encryption protocol, while Layer 2 Tunneling Protocol is the method of running IPsec over an Internet connection. We've also seen it called L2TP-over-IPsec for reasons we can't explain.

Graphical clients are generally necessary for IPsec because it is substantially more complicated to configure than SSH, currently requiring a number of configuration files and command-line settings.

VPNs using IPsec often don't work over wireless networks that use NAT because of how the content is encrypted. The VPN server needs to see a specific, public IP address attached to the client, but because NAT rewrites packets to include the IP number of the NAT gateway instead of the actual client, there's a mismatch that disables starting a connection. However, many gateways and access points have been updated in the last year to support IPsec. If your access point doesn't support IPsec, see if the manufacturer offers a firmware upgrade, or buy an access point that can handle it.

Figure 26.9
Connecting to an
IPsec VPN in
Mac OS X 10.3 and
Windows XP.

Our bottom line: if you need to use an existing VPN, your company almost certainly offers internal support to help you configure it. If you want to set up a VPN, you should investigate the options and see if they offer enough benefits to outweigh the initial and ongoing costs; we offer some insight into this in Chapter 22, *Small Office Wi-Fi Networking*.

Most large organizations have adopted VPNs as a comprehensive approach to security for employees connecting from insecure remote locations, such as their home wireless networks.

Protecting Your Systems

One part of security is protecting your data in transit; the other part is protecting your systems—your computers, any Internet servers you run, your wireless gateway, and so on—from online intruders. Because wireless networks potentially expose your systems to attackers who would never have the same kind of access on a wired network—unless they broke into your house or business—you need to exercise greater care when protecting your computers on wireless networks.

NOTE

We could go into great depth here, but this topic takes us far afield from wireless networking itself. Instead, if you're interested in reading more about this topic, we recommend checking out Internet Security for Your Macintosh: A Guide for the Rest of Us *by Alan Oppenheimer and Charles Whitaker. Although the book is full of how-to information for Mac users, the conceptual overviews apply to Mac, Windows, Linux, and Unix.*

You can secure your computers against snooping or attack in two ways: an active firewall or network address translation. You can use them separately or, for additional security, combined. And of course, it's essential to run current anti-virus software, particularly if you use Windows. But first, why worry?

Why Worry?

You might think that you don't need to protect your computers, but, unfortunately, there are seemingly hundreds of thousands of bored, amoral people out there, constantly and automatically scanning large blocks of Internet addresses for weaknesses. These days, it can be only a matter of minutes after a computer first receives a public IP address before the first attack is launched against it. Most of these attacks are entirely automated using scripts deployed by *script kiddies*, or inexperienced crackers who use prefabricated software.

These attacks focus on known bugs in software that allow a remote program or person to infiltrate your computer and take control of some of your software or the entire operating system. Once the attacker has established that level of control, he can either destroy your system or install software that attacks other computers, turning your computer into what's called a *zombie*.

Don't assume that attacks necessarily come from people. It's even more likely that your computer will be attacked by a worm that's already taken over someone else's machine. Worms propagate viruses which in turn propagate worms. The virus may also cause other damage or turn the computer into a zombie for later attacks.

 NOTE

We're not kidding about being infected within minutes of turning on a new computer. Glenn was testing a Windows XP Home laptop in August 2003: he had—no joke—powered the machine up and had just run the browser when the machine was infected and rebooted. He was able to download the Blaster patch on the next go round and fix it. But it had been one or two minutes at most before the infection took place.

Most attacks are aimed at computers running some version of Microsoft Windows or other software from Microsoft, such as Outlook or Internet Information Server. Microsoft has patched known holes, but many Windows users don't download and install these security patches, leaving their computers open to further exploitation and infection.

TIP

If you're using Windows, put this book down right now and use Windows Software Update to install all security patches released by Microsoft! If you're a Mac or Unix user, make sure to encourage all your Windows-using friends and colleagues to do the same. If everyone would just stay current on security patches, most worms would have much less impact.

Although some viruses exist for Macs, the number is a fraction (and a very small fraction, at that) of those aimed at Windows, which reduces the worry for Macintosh users. Also, since Macs are a much smaller percentage of the overall market, most crackers haven't been particularly interested in breaking into Macs. It's also very difficult to force a Mac user to execute an attachment in an email program unintentionally, or to convince a Macintosh email program to execute malicious code attached to an email message, which are two of the primary methods by which Windows viruses spread.

When you combine that lack of interest with the architectural accidents that made Mac OS 9 and earlier highly secure, you can see why Macs haven't suffered much from security concerns. That is changing now that Apple uses Unix underneath Mac OS X; although Unix isn't inherently insecure, it's a more likely target for crackers, and security holes in widely used programs like Apache are regularly reported. But Mac OS X and the various flavors of Unix systems seem to resist spreading disease: attacks generally compromise one box at a time. Like Microsoft, Apple regularly releases security updates via the Software Update utility; we always recommend installing them.

Other attacks use what's called a "denial of service" (DoS) approach, where the attacker sends so much data to your computer that it's overwhelmed. DoS attacks don't cause damage, per se, but they prevent normal operation and can be difficult to shut down. They're unfortunately quite frequent.

$((\bullet))$ **NOTE**

> *A DoS attack once saturated Adam's dedicated Internet connection; only calling his ISP and having it block the offending traffic fixed the problem.*

The entire issue of protecting your computer becomes much more complicated when you're roaming. The wireless networks themselves could be untrustworthy (is the Internet café's resident geek probing your system?) or a cracker at the next table could be probing your computer directly. Remember, if someone can monitor your unencrypted network traffic and steal your passwords, she can often use those passwords to enter your machine itself while it's still on the network.

A little precaution, such as encrypting your passwords and installing a firewall, goes a long way toward preventing an ocean of pain and suffering. Even more important, always back up your data before you take a laptop on the road—even if you're completely safe from crackers, you may drop and break the computer while going through an airport security check or someone may steal it while you're looking the other way. Everyone will lose data at some point, and those with backups will suffer the least because of it.

Anti-Virus Software

There are tens of thousands of viruses that can attack computers running Microsoft Windows, and a few viruses have been reported for computers running the Mac OS and Unix as well. These viruses use a variety of methods of infecting computers, and although many are essentially harmless (perhaps only causing crashes due to poor programming), many others are inherently malevolent, with code that causes them to delete or corrupt files or even erase your hard disk.

Equally as problematic are macro viruses, which live inside documents written with programs that have some sort of scripting—they most commonly infect Microsoft Office documents due to Office's built-in scripting support.

 TIP

Avenues for infection include inserting an infected removable-media disk from a friend into your computer, downloading an infected file from the Internet, receiving and opening an infected attachment via email, being attacked over the Internet by an automated program, and more. There's no way to close every possible way you could be infected (although exercising caution is always worthwhile), which is why anti-virus software that constantly scans your computer is so important.

Put bluntly, if you're using a Windows computer, you will eventually be infected by a virus unless you run anti-virus software and you keep it up to date. Since so many Windows viruses appear every month, makers of anti-virus software always provide an automatic update service that ensures that their software can identify and eradicate newly discovered viruses.

Numerous companies have sprung up to provide anti-virus software, but the two most common packages are Norton AntiVirus from Symantec (www.symantec.com) and McAfee's VirusScan (www.mcafee.com). Our impression is that most anti-virus packages are fairly comparable in terms of basic functions, so you'll want to choose among them based on price, usability, support, and other features. We don't care which you choose, just make sure you run some form of anti-virus software and keep it up to date.

Active Firewalls

An active firewall monitors all data entering and leaving a computer or network. It could be installed on individual computers or on a network gateway or router. Active firewalls examine inbound and outbound data and block particular bits (and sometimes alert you) if the data matches certain criteria. Inside your network, using a firewall so your network's services are open only to local computers is a fine way to discourage ne'er-do-wells from wreaking havoc.

In an active firewall, you can choose to block or pass only certain protocols, only connections that use specific port numbers, or only specific users. In larger networks, you can combine user authentication with a firewall to ensure that only certain people can carry out certain tasks on the network.

More advanced firewall software identifies patterns of data, and when it recognizes an attack pattern in progress, locks out the IP address the data is coming from, and optionally alerts you. Extremely expensive network firewall hardware can recognize thousands of these attack patterns.

Many firewalls also let you set access rules that vary by day of week and time of day. Thus, when you're paying attention to the network, it can operate at a lower level of security. This makes it easier to carry out routine tasks that otherwise might be tedious with the firewall in place.

Practically every gateway we've looked at includes a built-in firewall, although these bundled firewalls tend to be primitive. Refer to your manual for details on how to configure your gateway's firewall.

If you're roaming, or want more granular control, you can install personal firewall software on individual computers. You could try Windows XP's built-in firewall, but we recommend the more full-featured ZoneAlarm Pro (www.zonelabs.com) for Windows, a powerful but easy-to-use package that's cheap and well supported. On the Mac, Glenn swears by Intego's NetBarrier X3 (www.intego.com/netbarrier/). Under Mac OS 9, Adam likes Sustainable Softworks' IPNetSentry (www.sustworks.com/site/prod_ipns_overview.html); in Mac OS X, he uses the built-in firewall or Sustainable Softworks' IPNetSentryX (www.sustworks.com/site/prod_sentryx_overview.html). If you want more control over Mac OS X's built-in firewall, check out the shareware BrickHouse utility at http://personalpages.tds.net/~brian_hill/brickhouse.html.

 NOTE

Zone Labs offers a version of ZoneAlarm that works hand-in-hand with some Linksys gateways, like the EtherFast BEFW11S4 we cover in Chapter 17, Setting up a Gateway. *See Linksys's Web site at* www.linksys.com *for details.*

 TIP

When configuring a firewall, the standard approach is to deny all access, then open specific holes in the firewall. That way, it's much easier to figure out what's happening in an attack, since the set of possible ways through the firewall is small. The only downside is that you must spend time determining which ports to open.

TIP

If you use Dantz Development's Retrospect backup program or Netopia's Timbuktu Pro remote control program, you might go crazy troubleshooting connection problems with certain remote machines. It's almost always because the firewall is on. Read the FAQs at www.dantz.com *and* www.netopia.com *on which ports to open.*

Enabling the Windows XP Firewall

Commercial firewall software may give you more options and a better interface, but the built-in firewall software in Windows XP will do the job.

In Windows XP, follow these directions to set up a firewall:

1. Open Control Panel, and then double-click Network Connections.

2. Select the connection you want to secure (you can repeat this for multiple connections).

3. In the left pane, click Change Settings of This Connection under the Network Tasks area.

4. Click the Advanced button.

5. Check Protect My Computer and Network by Limiting or Preventing Access to This Computer from the Internet.

Enabling the Mac OS X Firewall

In Mac OS X, enabling the firewall is extremely easy. Follow these steps:

1. Open System Preferences, and click Sharing to open the Sharing preferences pane.

2. Click the Firewall tab, and click Start.

3. Select any services that need outside access.

4. Click New or Edit to modify the services listed.

NAT (Network Address Translation)

Running NAT on your gateway eliminates the possibility of many break-ins because NAT addresses are typically private—restricted to the local network—and thus unreachable from the outside world (see Appendix A, *Networking Basics,* and Chapter 16, *Buying a Wireless Gateway,* for more details on NAT). Whenever a computer with a private address on the local network requests a connection with another machine on the Internet, the NAT gateway rewrites the request so it appears to have come from the NAT gateway, which must run on a publicly reachable computer.

If someone tries to attack a network protected by NAT, only the gateway is exposed. A gateway may have some vulnerability, but gateways are typically much more capable of resisting attacks because their software is so simple and they don't have many ports open—possibly none at all. Because gateways don't do that much, it's hard to hijack them.

Some people call NAT a "passive firewall," and many manufacturers that advertise gateways with firewalls are really offering only NAT.

You should be aware that NAT doesn't protect you from other users on the same network, such as in a coffeehouse or hotel.

Taking It on the Road

Using a wireless network at home or in your office is freeing, of course, but you haven't lived until you've opened up your laptop in some random airport or coffee shop and been rewarded with wireless Internet access. Talk about one of life's little victories!

But how do you find wireless networks when you're traveling (or better yet, before you leave)? Turn to Chapter 28, *Finding Wi-Fi on the Road*, for a slew of tips and pointers for where you can find access to an Internet-connected wireless network. Most of those networks aren't free, and the commercial wireless ISPs often provide their own connection software—which is what you learn to use in Chapter 29, *Configuring WISP Software*.

And as much as Wi-Fi is becoming increasingly available almost anywhere you think to travel, cellular phones work in many more places around the world, so in Chapter 30, *Using Cellular Data Networks*, we investigate using your cell phone to check email and browse the Web.

Chapter 31, *Prepping for the Road*, and Chapter 32, *Working on the Road*, distill our years of experience related to accessing and using wireless networks while (and before) traveling. You can make your life a lot easier with some preparation, and once you're actually out on the streets of an unfamiliar city, our tips will help make you as productive as possible.

Finding Wi-Fi on the Road

In this age of the Internet, being out of touch while traveling can be incredibly frustrating. Cell phones help, certainly. But for many of us, email forms the hub for most of our communications. When our customers, clients, colleagues, friends, and family don't realize that we are traveling, they expect us to check our email as frequently as we normally do. For us travelers, the lifeline back to the rest of our lives—our digital lives at least—is increasingly becoming Wi-Fi networks found in public places.

For the most part, using a wireless network while you're on the road is exactly the same as using one at home or at the office. The main difference is that collecting all the information you need to connect to a potentially unknown network successfully can take time, and—in most cases—you must compile the information before you leave.

 TIP

No matter how reliable you believe your wireless connectivity will be during a trip, always make sure you can use the modem in your laptop or low-speed service via your cell phone to connect to an ISP as well. It might be costly to dial long-distance if your ISP doesn't have a local number in your area, and per-megabyte charges with your cell carrier can add up, but even expensive Internet access is better than none at all in some situations.

You may find wireless networks in unlikely and far-flung spots so it's worth taking a few minutes before you leave to determine where you can find wireless networks at your destination.

Free Wireless Networks

Remarkably, there are thousands of places where you can hop on a wireless network to access the Internet for free. There are no service guarantees, of course, and the speed of the connection can range from a trickle at the speed of a 56 Kbps dial-up to a Niagara Falls at the speed of multiple T-1s. But for a quick email check, a free network could be just the ticket.

All that's necessary to access the Internet via one of these free networks is that you select the network name from your list of available signals. A few community networks redirect your first Web browser request to a page that identifies legitimate use of the network and asks you to agree to it before proceeding.

 TIP

If a community network requires you to click through an acceptable use agreement before you are allowed to connect, you can't check email until you launch a Web browser and agree to the acceptable use policy.

Community Wireless Networks

Many communities have small, or even large, collections of loosely aggregated open networks created by individuals in the community. These community networks provide isolated hot spots in most cities, and certain neighborhoods have nearly complete coverage. For instance, several parks in New York City have excellent high-speed service, including locations in Lower Manhattan. These hot spots are generally operated by business districts or NYCwireless (www.nycwireless.net).

Although there's no comprehensive way to find an up-to-date list of all these hot spots nationwide or worldwide, the best approach is to look for a wireless community network where you're going, and then see if its Web site maintains a list of current hot spots. Personal Telco, a Portland, Oregon–based grassroots organization devoted to community-based communications networks, publishes the most extensive list of wireless community networks at http://personaltelco.net/index.cgi/WirelessCommunities.

Libraries

Many communities have added (or plan to add) wireless Internet access to their public libraries. Adam's wife, Tonya, serves on the Tompkins County Public Library Board of Trustees in Ithaca, New York; as we write this book, Adam is helping the library consider what it would take to install and use the necessary access points for wireless Internet access.

Our Top Five Coolest Wi-Fi Locations

Wi-Fi itself is kind of cool, but there are some unique places you can connect to the Internet that provide Wi-Fi–squared. Here's a sampling.

1. **Mount Everest.** Sherpas at the Nepal approach to Mount Everest have built a satellite-linked wireless network that enables expeditions to connect to their homes and institutions, while also providing service to a nearby village that lost phone service and other contact with the rest of the world following an attack by Communist rebels. It's a several-day yak trip (we're not kidding) from Kathmandu to the base camp, and conditions are extreme, but that hasn't stopped the Sherpas. Although the cost will be thousands of dollars per expedition, it's worth it to surf near—but not at—the top of the world.

2. **Aboard a flight**. The Boeing Connexion service went into testing for a single Frankfurt–D.C. Lufthansa flight in 2003, and it was a hit with both passengers and the airline. Starting in 2004, several airlines will offer the several megabits-per-second satellite-based service throughout a plane via Wi-Fi for about $35 for a long international flight. Although downtime is important for any traveler, it's also great to use some of those long empty periods to good effect.

3. **Driving down a highway.** The driver shouldn't attempt this, but passengers might. Using a Bluetooth-enabled cell phone or a PC Card that communicates via cell standards, a laptop plugged into the car's cigarette lighter with a software access point enabled can provide Internet access to other passengers—even those in nearby cars! Several convoys to various geek fests have proven the concept works. As cell networks increase in speed, more Car Area Networks are bound to form.

4. **Pioneer Courthouse Square in Portland, Oregon.** A nearby business helped Personal Telco, a community networking group, offer free Internet access via Wi-Fi all over the heart of Portland's rejuvenated downtown. When that firm relocated its offices in the middle of 2003, a local ISP and a business group with offices on the 10th floor of a nearby building picked up the slack. It's a lovely place to people-watch while surfing the Web and checking email.

5. **San Francisco International Airport.** Starting in March 2003, the San Francisco airport, which is the primary airport for the high-tech denizens of Silicon Valley, finally started to offer wireless network access. By the end of 2003, the whole complex is supposed to be a giant Wi-Fi hot spot. Sit near the heart of the dotcom revolution and keep the cord cut: no more pay phone struggles.

NOTE

Wireless network access has many potential benefits in a library. Adam and Tonya hope that wireless network access in the Tompkins County Public Library will take some of the pressure off the desktop Internet computers, allow patrons to carry laptop-based displays of the online catalog into the shelving areas, and provide more mobility and efficiency to staff operations. Free wireless Internet access could also enhance the ability of the public library to draw more people into the downtown business district.

Adam and Glenn's colleague Neil Bauman, the impresario behind and captain of Geek Cruises, lives within connection range of his local library's wireless network. (Neil also has cable, DSL, and gigabit fiber optic Internet connections thanks to his location in Palo Alto, California. We're so jealous.)

Finding wireless Internet access in a public library when you're on a trip may involve more effort than it's worth, however, unless you know people in the community. Libraries typically don't advertise their services widely, and they may impose login or other access restrictions—although a parking lot or outside bench might be close enough.

More importantly, however, you may not be able to find a public library easily in the places you visit.

Colleges and Universities

It's a pretty good bet that most colleges and universities provide wireless Internet access. If you're attending a conference held at (or near) a university, it's worth checking if it offers public access.

Unfortunately for visitors and travelers, many colleges and universities, such as Cornell University and the University of Washington, use central authentication servers to restrict their wireless networks to students, faculty, and staff, making it difficult to arrange access for a visitor.

On the flip side, institutions like Case Western Reserve University in Cleveland, Ohio, have designed their networks specifically to handle public traffic while securing university business. Case has 1200 access points sprawling across its campus, which intersects with business districts. Read about the OneCleveland project at www.case.edu/its/strategic/OneCleveland.htm.

NOTE

At a landmark conference examining open versus licensed spectrum at Stanford University in early 2003, organizers were slightly embarrassed because many attendees were unable to use the Wi-Fi network. Although the conference organizers had asked for MAC addresses from attendees, a few typos and a lack of response coupled with a weekend event with no techies on site almost derailed access. Fortunately, one audience member ran a company that makes Wi-Fi gateways and had a unit with him. After a little fiddling, he spoofed a legitimate MAC address and provided access to the rest of those present.

Although primary and secondary schools are less likely to have wireless networks installed, they're also less likely to restrict access to them. If you end up at a meeting in a school conference room, open your laptop and see if you can connect to a wireless network.

Free Commercial Locations

We're seeing an increasing number of companies offer free wireless Internet access in exchange for a splash screen and advertising in the neighborhood.

Hot Spot Directories

We've found a number of Web sites that attempt to track the many different hot spots across both the U.S. and the rest of the world. Visit them first in any search for wireless networks at a travel destination.

- **Jiwire** (www.jiwire.com) actually sends scouts out in the field who make sure that Wi-Fi access really exists at the locations that say they have it. The guides also take photos and report on amenities, such as electrical outlets and the kind of food served. Jiwire lists locations they haven't checked, too. The site provides proximity information, so that you can enter a street address and see a list of hot spots, free and for-fee, in order of distance from your location. You can filter by provider, whether a location charges, and other characteristics. (Full disclosure: Glenn is a senior editor at Jiwire, but we would think they were cool anyway.)

- **HotSpotList.com** (www.wi-fihotspotlist. com), **Hotspot-Locations** (www.hotspot-locations.com), **WiFinder** (www.wifinder. com), **EZGoal Hotspots** (www.ezgoal.com/ hotspots/wireless/), and **The Wireless Node Database Project** (www.nodedb.com). These directories have a grab bag of locations, and often show many community nodes—sometimes standalone locations in an apartment or private home.

- **The Wi-Fi FreeSpot Directory** (www.wifi freespot.com) is run by Jim Sullivan, who is generous with his time and effort on behalf of others. It provides a pretty good list of locations that have free Wi-Fi. It's not exhaustive, but it's a great start when you're traveling.

Some hot spot directories accept submissions from users, so if you know about a publicly accessible hot spot, we encourage you to help other wireless travelers by adding it to directories.

- **Apple Stores (nationwide, mostly in upscale shopping districts).** Apple's retail stores (www.apple.com/retail/) offer free Wi-Fi, and Apple doesn't care who knows about it. We have asked if the company has any restrictions on who uses these open AirPort networks, and the answer is no: Apple wants people in the door, doing interesting things, preferably on Macs. From what we can tell, the stores all have T-1 speed lines.

- **Newbury Open.net (Boston).** Michael Oh, founder of Tech Superpowers, (www.techsuperpowers.com) operates Newbury Open.net (www.newburyopen.net), a high-speed Wi-Fi network that uses a series of antennas to shoot service down Boston's famous commercial walk, Newbury Street.

- **St. Louis.** In St. Louis, Missouri, a wireless ISP called O2Connect (www.o2connect.net)—as in "Oh! To connect!"—recently worked with the city to provide free Wi-Fi service across a huge swath of downtown, donating the equipment (about $25,000) and monthly service bills (estimated at $1000) to enhance downtown and promote O2Connect's offerings.

The low cost of broadband Internet connections and the ease of setting up a wireless network has resulted in many public shops providing wireless Internet access as a way of enticing customers to come and spend time (and sample the wares, of course). Some of the companies that manage commercial hot spots for retail stores, in late 2003, started offering a fixed-rate managed service for businesses that want to provide free access, making it even easier.

Over the years, we've found a number of one-off hot spots that offer free service. For instance, the Dana Street Roasting Company in Mountain View, California, has free wireless access because a customer who wanted to surf the Internet while he drank his lattes paid for it (www.live.com/danastreet/). Meanwhile, down the street from Glenn's office, a java joint named Herkimer Coffee (www.herkimercoffee.com) opened with free Wi-Fi, and the buzz (caffeine and otherwise) keeps the place busy even during traditionally slow joe times in the afternoon.

These isolated hot spots may never show up in directories, so the only way to find them ahead of time is to search in Google (www.google.com). For example, to find wireless networks in Rochester, New York, you might search on terms like "wireless Internet access Rochester". Sometimes you may have to wait until you arrive at your destination, find a likely location (coffeehouses are your best bet), and ask.

Our friend and colleague Jeff Carlson once found a coffee shop in his former town of Renton, Washington, that offered free wireless Internet access, but only if you asked someone to turn the network on. Why? The shop didn't want people to park outside and use the network without buying coffee. (More recently, the owners divorced and the Wi-Fi service disappeared entirely—another reason why you may not be able to rely on free service.)

Conferences and Trade Shows

At many conferences and trade shows, particularly those with a technical bent, the conference organizers may set up an area where you can access the Internet wirelessly for free. The only downside is that these areas are often crowded, making the Internet access somewhat poky at times and making it difficult to find a chair in which to sit.

As 2003 comes to a close, we are finding that conference organizers have gotten wise and started to put Wi-Fi everywhere: in seminar rooms, dining areas, and trade show spaces. However, the backlash has also started: the wide use of laptops and Wi-Fi in sessions can make it sound like light sleet is falling while speakers are presenting.

We've also heard disturbing news to the contrary, which is that the companies handling the telecommunications for trade shows and conferences might start charging egregious amounts for access. One firm reportedly plans on charging attendees about $25 a day for 64 Kbps service—roughly the equivalent of cell data rates. Given that cell data is becoming easier to use, it doesn't make sense to charge that much or offer that little.

 TIP

It's always worth checking for nearby ad hoc wireless networks when you're at a conference hotel. Since most hotels that offer high-speed Internet access charge by the day, if someone decides to pay for the connection, he may also decide to run a software access point and make the Internet access available to other wireless users within range. We once saw a "Send beer to room 1471 for password" network at Macworld Expo—meaning if you want the WEP key, send beer to that person's room. Unfortunately, we were receiving the wireless signal from a nearby hotel, so we didn't know where to send the beer!

Commercial Wireless Networks

Free wireless networks are great, but sometimes you get what you pay for. Free networks seldom offer formal tech support if you have trouble connecting, they don't guarantee a certain level of Internet bandwidth (such as a 1.544 Mbps T-1 line or a DSL equivalent that a business would typically offer), and they don't provide much assurance that they will be accessible from one day to the next. If you need to use a VPN to connect to your office, that may not be possible through a free network if it relies on an incompatible NAT gateway. And without a guarantee of some kind on the hot spot, you might be reluctant to make plans around using that location, particularly for sensitive data.

It's not difficult to offer tech support, guarantee a certain throughput, and provide overall reliability—and a number of companies now offer those services to retail stores and business venues and split the incoming revenue—but it is expensive. We've seen estimates that offering commercial services could cost $30 per day when you include the cost of bandwidth and paying off startup costs, while free wireless might cost just $6 per day. Businesses that provide wireless Internet access generally have charges from about $4 to $12 per hour, from $5 to $10 per day, or flat rates for unlimited service from $20 to $50 per month.

The growth rate of commercial hot spots has paralleled an increase in the number of wireless ISPs that offer service in numerous locations. As we write this, the idea of subscribing to one wireless ISP's network and roaming across others, much the way cellular carriers allow other companies' customers to use their networks for a fee, is one whose time has come. Currently, a business traveler must still maintain accounts on several networks to enjoy uninterrupted service throughout much of the United States.

We're also seeing increased interest in and coverage areas for aggregated wireless service resellers like Boingo, iPass, and GRIC. These companies offer accounts that let you access the Internet via dial-up, Wi-Fi, and wired Ethernet in thousands of locations around the world, all for a single fee. We talk about these companies later in this chapter.

 TIP

To connect to a commercial hot spot, either you choose an active network and use a Web browser to log in to a captive portal Web page, or you use special client software that handles the login. We talk more about these special programs in Chapter 29, Configuring WISP Software.

Wireless ISPs

Wireless ISPs, known commonly as WISPs or wISPs (an irritating capitalization style), abound worldwide, offering access for a fee to their wireless networks. Some people also call them *Hot Spot Operators* or HSOs, but the term seems limited mostly to business plans, and isn't one we've heard in common parlance. An increasing number of WISPs offer dozens to hundreds or even thousands of hot spots, but most specialize in a certain kind of venue, like hotels or coffee shops.

Until 2002, a typical WISP ran its networks, sold access directly to customers, and promoted its own brand name. But by 2002, it was clear that no one company could build enough service on its own. Most existing WISPs now resell service to aggregators, which in turn offer customers access to numerous wireless networks worldwide. In fact, newer WISPs, like Cometa, were founded on the notion of building a network to which they only resell service. Other WISPs chose to compete by specializing in particular industries. For instance, STSN is Marriott's preferred hotel provider, offering both wired Ethernet and Wi-Fi in hotels.

Ultimately, many of these WISPs will be like the logos on an automated teller machine that tells you which ATM networks the cash dispenser supports. No one knows or cares what Cirrus is, but you know that if there's a Cirrus logo on your card and on the ATM, you can use that machine. The evolution of that trend has to do with retail stores: a store doesn't want 15 logos on its door for the 15 different networks it partners with.

Pricing

We're sure you'd like to know exactly how much Wi-Fi access will cost, but we've gone to some pains to be vague about details. The reason? Pricing has changed dramatically and non-intuitively in the years we've been watching the wireless ISP market evolve.

At one point, it cost close to $75 per month for unlimited access, and that was only on smaller networks. As the wireless ISPs' networks have grown, and as roaming deals have come into being, cheaper unlimited plans have emerged. Wireless ISPs with larger networks want to sign up as many users as possible, and reducing prices is a necessary part of that goal.

As we write this book, Boingo Wireless offers an unlimited service promotion priced at $21.95 per month for 12 months. After 12 months, Boingo says its price will increase to $34.95 per month (a $40-per-month reduction over pricing a year ago), but we don't see that as likely. To get unlimited Starbucks, Borders, and airport service on T-Mobile's network, you could pay as little as $19.95 per month if you're a T-Mobile cellular customer, or $29.95 per month with a 1-year commitment and a $200 cancellation penalty.

Prices haven't dropped in pay-as-you-go service. Typically, you still pay about $5 to $10 per hour, just like two years ago, or $7 to $10 per day for a 24-hour session.

We expect that by 2004, a single $25-per-month account, probably discounted when bundled with a cellular voice plan, will provide unlimited wireless Internet access across most current networks.

Here's a list of the major WISPs in the U.S. and Canada as we write this. Unless noted otherwise, all these networks resell their access to at least one of the aggregators we discuss next.

- **Airpath Wireless** (www.airpath.com), **NetNearU** (www.netnearu.com), and **Pronto Networks** (www.prontonetworks.com). These three firms handle billing, customer service, and logins for any venue or network that wants to install Wi-Fi service. They can also provide the necessary hardware. Some firms become "virtual WISPs" by signing contracts at venues like a hotel or coffee shop and then using one of these companies to manage accounts and other details. Airpath and NetNearU also provide roaming across many of the hot spots that they manage on behalf of these locations and companies, giving them an interesting patchwork that includes many smaller airports that might have just a single access point in a waiting area or shop. Each company lets individual networks or locations set pricing for service, which can include hourly, daily, monthly, and other options. Airpath has over 350 locations at this writing, and 900 more nearing deployment. Airpath estimates 4500 locations by mid-2004. NetNearU has about 200 locations; Pronto doesn't seem to disclose its network size.

- **Cometa Networks** (www.cometanetworks.com). Cometa was founded with money from AT&T, IBM, and Intel, and had a goal of building out 20,000 hot spot locations within two years. Its plan is only to resell service to wireless providers, mostly cellular and telephone companies that want to run virtual networks. Cometa had a slow start, taking several months to get rolling, but in September of 2003, the company revealed the first major stage in its plan: 250 hot spots in greater Seattle, including two high-end malls (University Village and Bellevue Square), several downtown office buildings, the Tully's coffee store chain, local Barnes & Noble stores, local McDonald's restaurants, and other locations. The CEO of Cometa told Glenn that the company plans to roll out only in major chunks, city by city. The Seattle rollout included announcements that Cometa would resell service to AT&T (the parent company), AT&T Wireless, iPass, and Sprint PCS. We expect the Cometa juggernaut to start rolling by 2004.

- **FatPort** (www.fatport.com). This Vancouver, British Columbia, firm has dozens of its own locations and hundreds more across Canada run by other companies for which FatPort handles billing and support. FatPort offers pay-as-you-go service, prepaid cards, and subscription plans. The company also has roaming agreements and partnerships to extend its territory and user base.

- **Surf and Sip** (www.surfandsip.com). Surf and Sip started in the San Francisco Bay Area with several dozen hot spots, but now has service worldwide, with a pile of locations in the United Kingdom and a rapidly expanding presence in the Czech Republic, Slovakia, and Poland. Surf and Sip offers hourly pay-as-you-go access, prepaid cards, and monthly service plans. Surf and Sip installs some locations itself and sells hardware for setting up a turnkey hot spot.

- **T-Mobile HotSpot** (http://t-mobile.com/hotspot/). T-Mobile USA, a division of Deutsche Telekom and the sixth largest cellular carrier in the U.S., bought the assets of the bankrupt MobileStar service in early 2002. In mid-2002, it relaunched the MobileStar service under the T-Mobile name as a Starbucks partner in over 1200 locations. By late 2003, T-Mobile had over 3000 locations in Starbucks, Borders, and Kinko's stores throughout the U.S., as well as service in San Francisco International Airport. However, T-Mobile doesn't currently share its network with any other WISPs or aggregators, except for the SFO airport location, which T-Mobile is required to share by contract. T-Mobile offers a monthly subscription and two pay-as-you-go plans, with discounts available to its cell phone customers. T-Mobile also plans to provide software that would let you connect either over the company's 2.5G cell data network or via Wi-Fi with a single account.

- **STSN** (www.stsn.com). STSN is Marriott International's preferred network provider partly because Marriott invested in the company (as did Intel Capital, later). STSN has about 500 hotels connected to the Internet with wired broadband in rooms. Most also have Wi-Fi in public spaces. Although STSN resells access, Marriott's pay-as-you-go pricing is way too high: while it charges only $9.95 per night for Internet access coupled with unlimited local and long-distance (domestic) calls, Marriott charges Wi-Fi at a rate of $2.95 for 15 minutes and 25 cents per additional minute. Oddly, Marriott will give away free wired and Wi-Fi Internet service to guests staying in its 1700 budget hotels, and will charge only in its premier Marriott and Renaissance hotels.

- **Wayport** (www.wayport.com). The granddaddy of wireless ISPs, Wayport has over 550 locations installed since 1999, mostly in hotels and airports. In hotels, Wayport typically offers wired broadband in rooms and Wi-Fi in common areas and meeting rooms. Wayport has the biggest collection of airport locations, including exclusive service in Seattle-Tacoma, Minneapolis-St. Paul, LaGuardia (New York), and San Jose and Oakland

(California), and competing service with T-Mobile in Austin and Dallas. Wayport offers day rates, including discounts for buying several connections at once, and monthly service plans. Wayport's network should expand dramatically in 2004, because giant telco SBC has hired them to install thousands of locations.

Roaming Aggregators

It's financially impossible for any single WISP to dominate the hot spot world. There are too many places where people want to connect—even just considering hotels, airports, and conference centers—for a single company to make all the deals. Already, several different WISPs are operating airport locations under long-term leases.

All of this means that subscribing to a single WISP makes little sense for anyone who travels much at all, and that any WISP that doesn't resell access to its locations is forgoing revenue.

Enter the aggregators. A number of companies, including three cell carriers, offer access to many separate networks through a piece of software that controls the login process. Without the software, you cannot use an aggregator's network.

Six companies currently offer some form of aggregation, and we tell you a little about each here. For more about their software, see Chapter 29, *Configuring WISP Software*. We expect many more firms to enter the market after this book goes to press, so you should have an increasing number of subscription choices.

Boingo Wireless

Boingo Wireless (www.boingo.com) is the only aggregator that resells only Wi-Fi access. All the others sell some mix of dial-up, broadband, and Wi-Fi, or cell voice/data and Wi-Fi. Founded by Sky Dayton, the fellow who brought us EarthLink, Boingo has built its system up to over 2600 locations as we write this. Dayton had originally predicted thousands more locations by the end of 2002, but the hot spot world didn't catch up to the scale he predicted until late in 2003.

Boingo prices its service by the connection, a standard unit of broadband measurement: noon to noon in hotels, usually, and midnight to midnight in other locations. If you pay as you go, each connection is $7.95. A monthly plan with unlimited connections is $39.95, but as we write this book, Boingo is offering a 12-month, $21.95/month plan with no cancellation penalty.

The Boingo software includes a VPN client that lets you tunnel all your traffic from your machine to Boingo's network operation center before it's decrypted and sent over the public Internet. (For more about VPNs, see Chapter 26, *Securing Data in Transit*.)

Boingo also includes outbound email service through authenticated SMTP, which requires you to reconfigure your email software temporarily with your

Want to Become a Hot Spot?

If you're interested in launching a hot spot service from your home, business, or community center, you first have to choose whether or not to charge for service. If you want to go the free route, and you're a self-starter, check out http://nocat.net, www.bawug.org, and www.personaltelco.net, all of which have excellent advice and links. We also recommend Rob Flickenger's book, *Building Wireless Community Networks*. You might also look into Sputnik's wireless LAN system (www.sputnik.com) which allows you to manage a network with different classes of users, so you can reserve bandwidth for your own purposes and manage security. Finally, even if you want your network to be free, some WISPs now offer managed services for $50 per month or less plus some setup expense.

If you want to charge a fee for access to your network, we don't recommend putting together your own system, as many companies have solved the problems already. As mentioned in our list of WISPs and aggregators, many offer what's known as OSS (operations support systems): billing, user account management, authentication or login, customer service, technical support, and network management.

You can either buy hardware directly from these companies as a complete turnkey option, or buy certain access point models and then contract with these firms to handle your network. A turnkey access point can cost from $200 to $1000 depending on options and expected usage.

You might also need to purchase business-grade bandwidth. Many ISPs don't let you resell access from basic DSL or cable accounts, requiring more expensive business accounts. Some WISPs and turnkey networks have special arrangements with ISPs to get you a good deal. And Speakeasy (www.speakeasy.net) offers DSL and T-1 service nationwide with no restrictions on reselling access to any of its kinds of accounts, and it doesn't charge fees for excess bandwidth use.

We recommend you find a company that will include your hot spot in a group of frequently used wireless locations, and that allows you to sell service flexibly: by the hour, day, month, and other combinations. Providers offering both benefits include Airpath, NetNearU, Pronto Networks, and Surf and Sip. You can find the latest list of options at Glenn's Wi-Fi Networking News site at www.wifinetnews.com/turnkey_hotspots.html.

Boingo account name and password. This service helps you avoid a whole category of outbound email problems, which we discuss in Chapter 31, *Prepping for the Road*.

Software: Although Boingo's software is currently available only for Windows and Pocket PCs, Boingo is working on a Mac OS X client.

iPass

iPass (www.ipass.com) started as a way to let companies give a roaming road warrior a single account that would allow her access to dial-up Internet service no matter where in the world she landed without setting up individual accounts or paying outrageous prices. With ISP partnerships around the globe—in over 150 countries and with 19,000 points of presence—iPass has met that mark. Dial-up Internet access from iPass costs up to about $15 per hour depending on the amount of service you buy, where in the world you're using the service, whether you're a company or an individual, and whether you're dialing a toll or toll-free number. According to a recent filing when iPass offered its stock to the public, the company still makes 99 percent of its money from dial-up.

But that hasn't stopped iPass from aggressively expanding to include Wi-Fi and wired broadband access. It has over 2500 locations with one or the other, with Wayport and STSN forming a big part of its hotel/wired network at over 1000 locations. iPass's pricing for hot spots is more varied worldwide, with $7 to $20 per 24-hour period being typical. The company charges per minute up to a daily maximum in most locations, which can be cheaper than a daily fee for checking email for just a few minutes.

iPass doesn't sell to individuals directly. Most of the time, it works with corporations that have hundreds or thousands of employees, and it directly connects the company's user login database with iPass's accounts. Employees then use their normal network passwords to use iPass and the company doesn't have to set up individual accounts. Pretty nifty.

However, iPass does work with value-added resellers, who can offer service to individuals and smaller companies. Visit the iPass Web site, click Partners, then click Resellers, and answer the question on location and company size to be directed to individual resellers.

Software: iPassConnect is available for Windows, Macintosh (Mac OS 9 and Mac OS X), and various handhelds. Version 3 of the software is available only for Windows at the time of this writing.

GRIC Communications

GRIC (www.gric.com) offers services similar to iPass, though we were able to find out only that it partners with Airpath and Wayport for wireless Internet access. The company's Web site notes many points of presence, but provides no information on cost or other details.

Software: Available for Windows only.

AT&T Wireless

In the Denver airport, AT&T Wireless operates Wi-Fi service that was originally built by Nokia, which searched for years to find an operator to run the network. AT&T also resells Wayport's service, but doesn't seem to yet have a plan to expand access or build its own network. AT&T Wireless charges are currently egregiously high, but we expect that they'll come in line as AT&T Wireless's cellular brethren start offering Wi-Fi at a more reasonable rate.

Software: AT&T Wireless has said that it will offer a software connection manager, but we're not sure what form it will take.

Sprint PCS

Sprint PCS announced plans in mid-2003 to resell access to Wayport and Airpath locations, and to have Airpath provide the back-end billing and account management as Sprint PCS builds 1300 of its own locations by the end of 2003. (You can check our Web site to see if the company met its goal!)

Sprint PCS hasn't yet announced pricing. The company also said that it won't be able to bill the service on a single bill with cellular fees until late 2003; it's expected that existing Sprint PCS cell customers will get a discount on adding unlimited monthly service.

Software: Sprint PCS uses a custom Windows software client based on the iPass software. You cannot have iPassConnect 3 and the Sprint PCS software installed at the same time on one machine.

Verizon Wireless

Verizon Wireless says it will resell Wayport's network, but little else is known.

Software: Almost certainly Windows only.

Travel Points

Many travelers are increasingly making plans based on where they can find high-speed access. We've both made specific hotel reservations to ensure that we had

Wi-Fi or wired broadband in our rooms or at least nearby. Fortunately, more airports and hotels are providing Wi-Fi (and, less often, wired broadband).

Airports

In the world after the terrorist attacks of September 11, 2001, people who still travel extensively find themselves spending many more hours than before in airports: you arrive early and if passing through security takes only a short time, you end up with nearly two hours on your hands. Plus, some connection times are longer, so you might have a multi-hour layover between flights. Even if you fly only a few times a year, these extra hours add up.

Glenn recently talked with a manager at Booz Allen Hamilton, a business consulting firm with 10,000 employees, 70 percent of whom spend a day a week or more on the road. Surprisingly, they're traveling more than ever in the last two years, and spending much more downtime in airports—and their time is money, since they bill hourly.

It's a natural match, therefore, to provide wireless Internet access in airports, whether in special hot spot locations or cafés, or throughout entire terminals. Unfortunately, the wireless Internet service provider market is littered with bankruptcies, and many of those bankrupt firms had made arrangements with airport authorities to install wireless service. These broken deals, along with early poor revenue figures from airports that did install wireless networks, made some airport authorities wary, and the entire industry slowed down from 2001 to 2003.

Fortunately, with the economy on the slight uptick as we write this, business travel creeping higher, and a demand for Wi-Fi on the rise, several major airports have just lit up wireless networks, including San Francisco and two New York metro airports: LaGuardia and Newark. More major airports are expected soon, as they've just started soliciting bids from WISPs to build Wi-Fi networks.

Also, T-Mobile partnered with American, Delta, and United Airlines to put Wi-Fi in their membership club lounges, most of which will be running by the end of 2003; T-Mobile and its predecessor, MobileStar, has provided Wi-Fi service in American lounges for years. A few scattered network providers like Airpath and NetNearU have limited service in waiting areas or shops, too.

Almost all airport wireless networks are resold by aggregator services. Denver is the largest exception, but service in Seattle-Tacoma, Austin, LaGuardia, and elsewhere can be purchased through any of the aggregators.

NOTE

In several airports, Wayport also runs little slices of heaven called Laptop Lanes (www.wayport.com/laptoplane), which it bought from an early into-and-then-out-of-it wireless ISP's parent company. Laptop Lanes are tiny, self-contained offices, soundproofed and with telephones and wired high-speed Internet connections. You pay a fairly high hourly fee, but it's quiet, calm, and private.

TIP

Because airport terminals are long metal tunnels with cutouts for lounges, you may need to wander around looking for a signal that you can lock onto. Even in airports that provide "100-percent coverage," there are certainly places where no service gets through. See Chapter 18, Wireless Gadgets, for details on portable Wi-Fi finders.

Outside the U.S., you can find wireless access in many airports, including Amsterdam's Schiphol, parts of Heathrow in London, and a number of lounges in airports where Sweden's SAS airline lands. It's well worth searching Google before you leave to find information about wireless Internet access at your intermediate and destination airports.

Hotels

Hotels, recognizing the often-pressing needs of their guests to connect to the Internet (and perhaps admitting the ridiculous nature of the per-minute charges they apply even to local and toll-free telephone calls), increasingly offer some form of broadband Internet access in guest rooms and Wi-Fi in public areas like lounges and lobbies.

Hotels started by wiring each room, which works well, but is an expensive proposition for the hotels and may require that guests bring an Ethernet cable (some hotels provide the necessary cable). More recently, however, some hotels have partnered with a WISP, primarily Wayport, StayOnline, or STSN, to offer in-room wireless Internet access. Hotel analysts tell us that in the future, hotels will almost certainly bypass the expense and complexity of Ethernet for Wi-Fi.

Typically, hotels charge about $10 per day, with a day defined as noon to noon. (Some used to define a day as midnight to midnight, which is ridiculous for a hotel—some still do, so check the fine print!) Many hotels are now trying to avoid customer irritation at niggling charges by bundling unlimited broadband, local calls, and long-distance calls for a single rate. A Westin outpost in Santa Clara, California, charges $15.95 per night for that privilege, while Marriott and Renaissance hotels charge $9.95.

You can also find a remarkable option that's becoming more and more common: entirely free service. It's more likely that you can get free broadband (and often free calls, too) in hotels that cater to the mid-level traveler than in the high-end hotels. The expensive locations have more loyalty, and the cost of communications is less likely to raise an eyebrow when a breakfast of toast and orange juice costs $22. But budget-minded travelers have more options for where to stay, so free service might sway them.

We currently know of two major chains that are in the process of rolling out free service. Marriott International operates 1700 hotels under the names Courtyard, Fairfield Inn, Residence Inn, TownePlace Suites and SpringHill Suites. Marriott says all will provide free Internet access via Wi-Fi in public areas and wired Ethernet in rooms by the end of 2004, with most hooked up before the end of 2003.

Wyndham Hotels and Resorts has several hundred locations, and is seen as just a notch below the high-end hotels. To stand out, the chain provides guests who belong to the ByRequest program with free local and long-distance calls, free broadband, a free beverage on arrival, and a number of other nice touches. The best part? ByRequest is free. However, you must sign up before you arrive to get the goodies on that visit; go to www.wyndham.com and click Join Wyndham ByRequest.

There's another way to get "free" access in a hotel, too, although it's not exactly free. With the cost of purchasing unlimited Wi-Fi service having dropped to as little as $22 per month from an aggregator, it may be most cost effective to use Boingo Wireless or another aggregator and then pick the right hotels and travel hubs to avoid additional charges beyond your monthly subscription.

Retail Chains

Chain stores are adding Wi-Fi service in droves, since they think—rightly or wrongly—that they can fill up non-peak hours with new customers. We're not sure that the cost of providing the scale of Wi-Fi that these locations offer can be repaid through additional customers buying more food, but it is a grand experiment currently being conducted in thousands of locations.

Starbucks

The coffeehouse chain Starbucks will tell you again and again: it's not an Internet café. Rather, Starbucks wants you to bring your expensive laptop in and buy expensive drinks using its, well, slightly expensive network. Starbucks has over 5200 stores in the U.S., and it partnered first with MobileStar, which went bankrupt, and then with T-Mobile to build high-quality, T-1–based hot spots in its U.S. stores and elsewhere.

In mid-2002, Starbucks and T-Mobile announced full wireless Internet access in 1200 stores in a number of cities and metropolitan areas. Over the next year, the pair upped that number to well over 2500 in dozens of cities, including some small towns near metropolitan areas. They're also adding service gradually in Europe.

You can see the latest list at http://locations.hotspot.t-mobile.com/starbucks.htm. The only flaw we've found with so much Wi-Fi coverage is that T-Mobile won't allow any other WISP or aggregator access to its locations. It would be ideal if we could subscribe to one plan and hit Starbucks, the Austin airport, and a McDonald's in New York City. (We hope this has changed by the time you read this.)

McDonald's

"Yes, I *do* want Wi-Fi with that Extra Value Meal!" cries the customer as he stands before the cashier. McDonald's is trying an interesting experiment by deploying Wi-Fi in four test metropolitan areas: Chicago, New York, San Francisco, and Seattle.

McDonald's is experimenting with pricing and providers, too: Wayport runs the San Francisco show, charging $4.95 for two hours; Cometa's WISP partner in New York, AT&T, charges $2.99 a day; and we haven't seen pricing from its partners for Seattle yet. Wayport also gives the service for free to existing Wayport subscribers. In Chicago, Toshiba is operating the network as part of its effort to sell $199 turnkey hot spot kits. Chicago McDonald's stores charge $4.95 per hour or $7.95 per day.

As we write this, the New York metro and San Francisco Bay Area each have 75 stores with Wi-Fi access, and McDonald's hasn't decided whether all 14,000 of its restaurants will have service or not. For more details, visit www.mcdwireless.com.

Schlotzsky's Deli

Schlotzsky's Deli installed free wireless Internet access and several Apple LCD iMac computers in about 20 locations in Texas, Georgia, Ohio, and North Carolina, mostly company-owned outlets (www.cooldeli.com/wireless.html). Schlotzsky's found an enormous emotional response from customers of all ages.

Often, the CEO said at a conference panel Glenn arranged, youth sports teams show up and the kids pile on one computer and the adults pull out laptops. The company hopes to convince its franchisees to buy into this free idea and roll out service nationwide.

Bookstores

Wi-Fi is not just about coffee and burgers. Barnes & Noble and Borders have deals with Cometa and T-Mobile, respectively, to equip hundreds of U.S. stores with Wi-Fi. In many ways, it's a sensible combination because these two chains typically have cafés attached or inside, and plenty of places to sit and work.

Although we don't know when all the Barnes & Noble stores will go live—Seattle outlets are slated to go first—Borders has rolled out T-Mobile's Wi-Fi service to almost all of its 400-plus locations.

You can find Borders stores via its store locator (www.bordersstores.com/locator/locator.jsp) or Barnes & Noble locations by visiting the company's home page (www.bn.com) and entering a ZIP code.

Kinko's

Kinko's and T-Mobile have announced that all Kinko's copy shops in the U.S. will have T-Mobile service by 2004, and while that's a useful addition, we're not entirely sure how it plays out. If you have an unlimited T-Mobile account, can you come in and squat for as long as you want—and where would you set up? Will Kinko's still rent computers at the same rates as it used to?

Kinko's also said that the Wi-Fi service won't connect directly to printers in Kinko's locations initially, but that customers will have to send print jobs via email to the store, even when they're in the store.

Still, it's a natural adjunct for a business traveler, who often needs to print, fax, or copy material while on the road.

Up, Up in the Air

Many business travelers spend enormous amounts of time in airports and on airplanes. As airports have slowly added Wi-Fi service and cell companies have increased data options on the go, airlines picked up on the notion that passengers might want to use some of the many in-transit hours on airplanes to work and entertain themselves on the Internet.

Two services currently offer in-air wireless Internet access, but with entirely different mindsets.

Connexion by Boeing

Boeing's Connexion service (www.connexionbyboeing.com) uses phase-array antennas on each plane. These antennas communicate with satellites to provide an asymmetric 1 Mbps of bandwidth upstream to the Internet and from 5 to 20 Mbps from the Internet back to the plane. Connexion has commitments from Lufthansa and Scandinavian Airlines to equip their 100-odd long-haul planes; ANA (All-Nippon Airlines), JAL (Japan Airlines), and British Airways have agreed to install the service but haven't released their plans at this time.

Connexion's service is distributed on the plane via Wi-Fi or wired connections, depending on the airline. The cost will wind up being about $30 to $35 per flight for eight hours or so, and possibly less for shorter flights.

Tenzing Communications

Tenzing (www.tenzing.com) offers a more affordable, but more bandwidth-limited service—only 128 Kbps per plane—that it's reselling through Verizon Airfone and others.

The Tenzing service allows an unlimited number of emails of up to 2K each per flight for $15.95. Each kilobyte above 2 runs you 10 cents. Most email messages are several kilobytes, but you can usually get the gist of a message in a few hundred words for non-HTML email.

Worse, you must use special Web-based software to access your email, and you must provide the service with your connection details, such as mail server, account name, and password. The server then uses a proxy to retrieve your email while you wait. Travelers who use encrypted connections (virtual private networks, SSH, or SSL) will be unable to use this service.

United Airlines has committed to installing it on all its domestic planes.

Configuring WISP Software

A great advantage of Wi-Fi networks is that using them is so simple: a one-time configuration, maybe a click or two, and you're on. At least that's true of networks that individuals set up in homes and small offices. But when you use public space networks in hot spots, you're forced to navigate through captive portal pages and sign-up screens in which you enter account information, credit card details, or one-time scratch-off usage card codes.

Couldn't it be easier? Sure. But since that account information is necessary, instead of using captive portal pages, you must install software on your laptop or PDA. Several wireless ISPs and service aggregators—see the previous chapter—offer service across many Wi-Fi networks, and they use a software program to establish the connection and provide your account information in the appropriate format.

((•)) NOTE

We expect that the integration of cellular data networks and Wi-Fi may result in you using an identification module that allows you to bypass any login and potentially any special software. Nokia has already demonstrated PC Cards that use the module that GSM phones rely on to activate a phone and bill a user.

A special software program is necessary because the process behind the scenes for billing and authentication (checking that a user name and password are valid) is so incredibly varied among the WISP networks that it's much simpler to build the rules into a program than to set up a complex back-end system that could somehow meet the needs of many WISPs.

A custom program isn't necessarily a consumer benefit; in fact, it increases the hassle factor because you have to learn and manage yet another piece of software. However, the WISPs—the ones who are reselling access to many different networks—like it because they can splash their own logos all over the software, hiding the fact that they don't actually own or run the locations you're connecting to. The trend is for more of these packages to appear, as more companies start reselling Wi-Fi service on hot spot networks that they haven't built.

(((•))) **NOTE**

When these packages are running, they typically disable the operating system's own control over a wireless network. In Windows XP, for instance, expect to see all kinds of System Tray balloons appear when you run, configure, or exit a WISP application.

(((•))) **NOTE**

It's possible to have several of these packages installed at the same time, but some of them conflict: a few firms are writing software for operators, and you can often install only a single version of the underlying software at a time.

Boingo Wireless

Boingo Wireless was the first Wi-Fi–only network aggregator, and as we write this, the company connects its users to over 2500 locations in the U.S. We write more about Boingo and its network in Chapter 28, *Finding Wi-Fi on the Road*.

Boingo's package is optimized around maintaining profiles for different locations, because it assumes that many Wi-Fi–toting travelers will have office, home, friend, colleague, and random connections in addition to the paid network connections that Boingo manages for them.

To get started, download the Boingo client software from www.boingo.com/download.html. You must also set up a Boingo account. At this writing, you can set up an account without paying a setup fee. Because Boingo's profile management is so good, we suggest using Boingo's software instead of Windows XP's built-in client software.

(((•))) **NOTE**

We cover version 1.3 of the Windows 98SE, Me, 2000, and XP software here, but Boingo issues new releases quite frequently. Boingo has promised a Mac OS X client for some time, and the company still expects it to appear in 2003. Check the Boingo Web site for updates.

When you run the Boingo software for the first time, you're prompted for your account information, after which you can start configuring the client.

Setting Up a Connection

You should start with the Boingo client by selecting My Signal Profiles from the Profiles menu. The default setup shows the Boingo network connection, which lets you connect to any Boingo partner, and an Other Signals profile for unconfigured networks—turned off by default (**Figure 29.1**).

Figure 29.1
My Signal Profiles in the Boingo client.

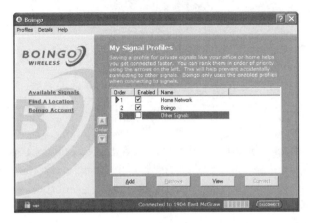

Let's start with adding a profile for your home network.

1. Click Add to open the Profile Editor dialog, which presents you with four tabs.

2. In the Network (SSID) field, enter the name of the network or click Browse to view locally broadcasting networks. If your network is closed, check Does Not Broadcast Its SSID (**Figure 29.2**).

Figure 29.2
Choosing your network in the Profile Editor dialog.

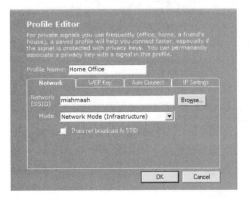

3. If your network is protected, click the WEP Key tab, check WEP Encryption, and click the I Provide the WEP Key Data radio button. Enter the key in the Data field. For more options, such as choosing between ASCII or hexadecimal keys, check Advanced (**Figure 29.3**).

Figure 29.3
Setting WEP options in the Profile Editor dialog.

4. Click the Auto Connect tab, and then select how this profile is activated: as an option (Offer), automatically if you're not connected (Connect), or automatically even if you're connected to another network (Switch). You can also have the Boingo client run a program like a Web browser after connecting (**Figure 29.4**).

Figure 29.4
Configuring connection preferences in the Profile Editor dialog.

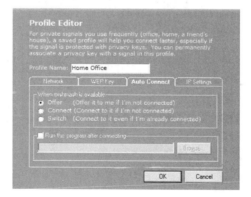

 TIP

For the preset Boingo profile, the only settings you can change are in the Auto Connect tab.

5. In the IP Settings tab, you can choose between using a static IP address or the more common DHCP option (**Figure 29.5**).

6. Click OK to close the Profile Editor dialog and save your changes.

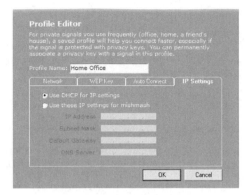

Figure 29.5
Configuring IP
settings in the
Profile Editor dialog.

7. Select a profile and click the up or down Order arrows to choose the order in which the Auto Connect tab's options are carried out.

TIP

If you plan to use Boingo exclusively to manage your wireless connections, select Preferences from the Profiles menu, click Advanced, and check Launch Boingo When My Computer Starts (Figure 29.6).

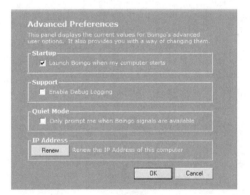

Figure 29.6
Setting the Boingo
client to launch
automatically at
startup.

Connecting and Disconnecting

Click the Available Signals link in the left navigation bar of the main Boingo screen to see any active networks, including those you've configured. You can select one and click Connect to connect to it, depending on your Auto Connect options. Click Disconnect in the lower right corner to sever a network connection.

The Boingo client always displays the signal strength of the connected network at the bottom of the screen, while Available Signals shows the signal strength of all networks in your vicinity.

TIP

You can select Preferences from the Profiles menu and click Advanced, and then click Renew to tell the DHCP server you want a new IP or your current IP's lease extended.

My VPN

Boingo offers a VPN connection that tunnels encrypted traffic leaving and entering your computer all the way to Boingo's network operation center (NOC) far away on the Internet. This VPN protects your data slightly less well than an end-to-end VPN that terminates at your company's network because your traffic is exposed when it leaves Boingo's NOC. It does eliminate local sniffing and snooping, and we consider the likelihood of a malefactor gaining access to your information as it travels from Boingo's NOC to your destination very, very unlikely.

(((•))) **NOTE**

Currently, the My VPN service is free, although Boingo expects to charge a fee for it at some point.

To use My VPN, select My VPN from the Profiles menu. It requires no configuration; you simply click Connect, or check the box beneath the Connect button to always use a VPN at Boingo locations (**Figure 29.7**).

Figure 29.7
Turning on My
VPN.

Other Options

The Boingo client software serves a few other useful functions.

- **Finding Locations.** Boingo frequently adds new locations to its hot spot network, and the Boingo client software can help you find them. Click Find A Location to search Boingo's frequently updated list of locations (**Figure 29.8**).

Figure 29.8
Finding Boingo
locations.

 TIP

Configure Boingo to retrieve directory updates automatically by choosing Preferences from the Profiles menu and confirming that one of the first two options is chosen under Directory Updates.

- **Maintaining Account Information.** If you want to modify your account details, including billing information, click Boingo Account and then log in. Boingo encapsulates a Web page inside its interface; you can also make these changes directly via the company's Web site. In this billing area, you can change your billing address, your payment plan, and your credit card information.

- **Troubleshooting Tools.** The Boingo client's Details menu features four options for troubleshooting. Available Signal Details shows specifics of networks in the area, providing roughly the same features as a stumbler tool. Signal Performance tracks radio strength over time, which might be helpful when tracking down signal strength problems on your own network. Connection History shows when you've connected or failed to connect. And, finally, System Information offers driver and network details.

iPass

iPass calls itself a premium, worldwide, corporate access provider. Translated from marketing-speak, this means that the company uses a network of ISPs to offer a range of Internet services, including dial-up, wired broadband, wireless, and a Japan-specific technology, to huge companies with fleets of roaming users. We describe iPass more specifically in Chapter 28, *Finding Wi-Fi on the Road*.

The basic notion behind iPass is that as you wander this wide globe of ours, you're looking for service in the place you're at—a sensible conclusion. As a result, iPass's client software, iPassConnect, is designed to help you find somewhere you can get Internet access and then make a connection.

NOTE

iPass's client software can vary depending on whether you purchased access through a reseller directly as an individual, and are thus using the generic version of iPassConnect, or you work for a firm that had iPass customize the interface or enforce specific policies via software (such as only 30-minute sessions or "must use a VPN"). In this chapter, we cover the generic edition of iPassConnect 3 for Windows and iPassConnect 2.3 for Mac OS X.

Windows

The Windows version of iPassConnect 3 works under Windows 98SE, Me, NT 4, 2000, and XP.

Connection Settings

Choose Connection Settings from iPassConnect's Settings menu to configure the details for your connections in each of four tabs: General, Dialup, ISDN, and Wireless.

- **General.** Choose programs you want to launch after a connection is made (**Figure 29.9**).

Figure 29.9
iPassConnect's
General settings.

- **Dialup.** Your modem should already be chosen here, and you can configure redial options (**Figure 29.10**). Sure, this is a book about Wi-Fi, but you still might need to use your modem, particularly when traveling in places where Wi-Fi is scarce!

- **ISDN.** To U.S. readers, the idea of connecting to ISDN at an arbitrary location may seem odd, since ISDN in the U.S. requires a special circuit and a special adapter. In places outside North America where high-speed service has lagged until recently, ISDN is more commonly available.

Figure 29.10
iPassConnect's
Dialup settings.

- **Wireless.** Choose your adapter and the power mode. iPassConnect lets you define one non-iPass network, such as your local network, under Personal Wireless Settings (**Figure 29.11**). Enter the usual connection details: SSID and WEP keys if you use encryption.

Figure 29.11
iPassConnect's
Wireless settings.

Making a Connection

iPassConnect's main screen lets you search for locations that are part of the iPass network (**Figure 29.12**).

 TIP

> *Select Login Information from the Settings menu and choose your Default Country to have the search always pre-fill that field.*

In this example, we're traveling to New Hampshire and want to see what's available. Because we didn't narrow the search to a specific city, we can see that iPass offers 144 phone numbers, 73 ISDN numbers, 1 wired broadband location, and 2 wireless hot spots for the entire state.

Figure 29.12
Finding locations in
iPassConnect.

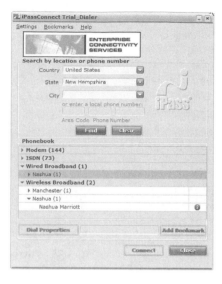

If we drill down to the Nashua Marriott in Nashua, and click the "i" (info) button, iPassConnect provides details about the location, its service, and the SSID for the network (**Figure 29.13**). This information will help you plan trips, to be sure.

Figure 29.13
Drilling down to
see details of a
specific location in
iPassConnect.

If you're actually in a given location, you can simply select the site and click the Connect button. The software handles the rest.

Managing Locations

It's important to keep iPassConnect and its dial-up list up to date. To update the list when you're connected, choose Update iPassConnect from the Settings menu, and then choose either Phonebook to check for new locations or Software to check for a program update.

Whenever you select a location in the Phonebook list, you can click Add Bookmark to make it more easily available.

Macintosh

iPassConnect 2.3 for the Mac works with Mac OS X 10.2 and later. (iPass also makes a version for Mac OS 8.6/9.x that looks quite similar.)

Connection Settings

In Mac OS X 10.2.8, connection settings were unavailable for configuration: choosing Preferences from the iPassConnect menu caused the software to quit in our testing. Since you can configure your AirPort or AirPort Extreme card and your internal modem using the Network preferences pane in Mac OS X, not being able to do so in iPassConnect shouldn't cause any difficulties.

Making a Connection

iPassConnect's main screen is divided into tabs corresponding to the kinds of service offered. Click the Wireless Broadband tab (**Figure 29.14**). In this example, we've searched for locations in New Hampshire. If you want more information about a location, select it and choose Show POP Info from the Edit menu (**Figure 29.15**).

Needless to say, if you can't find any wireless locations where you're going, check the Modem and Wired Broadband tabs for other types of Internet access. It always pays to have backup plans!

TIP

Because locations are frequently added or changed, select Update Phonebook from the iPassConnect menu to download the current list.

To connect to a location you're at, just select it and click Connect.

Figure 29.14
Finding Wi-Fi
hot spots in
iPassConnect.

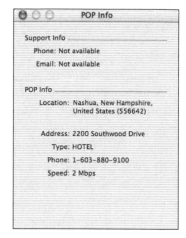

Figure 29.15
Getting more
information about a
location.

GRIC

GRIC, a company much like iPass, didn't respond to a number of requests over
the last couple of years to provide us with its Windows or Mac client software
to write about.

Sprint PCS

Sprint PCS is a large cellular carrier that started offering Wi-Fi service in
September 2003, mostly through locations run by other operators. Sprint PCS's
software is derived from the iPassConnect 3 client, although it has substantially
fewer options. Download the Windows-only software from http://sprint.com/
pcsbusiness/products_services/data/wifi/advantages.html.

 TIP

*When you install PCS Connection Manager, you can choose PCS Wi-Fi Access
as one of the several options in the software; if you're also using or planning on
using Sprint PCS's 2.5G cell data service, you can manage those connections
with PCS Connection Manager as well (**Figure 29.16**).*

The essential operation is straightforward: if there's a network in the area that
Sprint PCS resells access to or operates, you can connect to it. As we write this,
there's a per-connection fee with no unlimited monthly option.

 TIP

*You can set up your service to connect at all times (and thus continuously incur
new fees) by clicking the Menu icon and then choosing PCS Wi-Fi from the
Settings submenu (**Figure 29.17**). Check Keep Buying More Time.*

Figure 29.16
Choosing options
when installing.

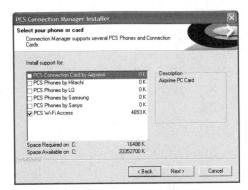

Figure 29.17
Setting the PCS
Connection
Manager to keep
buying more time.

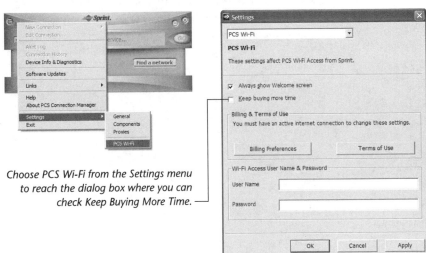

*Choose PCS Wi-Fi from the Settings menu
to reach the dialog box where you can
check Keep Buying More Time.*

To find other locations, click Find a Network in the main PCS Connection
Manager screen. In the Find a Network dialog, enter part of an address,
including city, state, or ZIP code (**Figure 29.18**).

Figure 29.18
Searching for
locations.

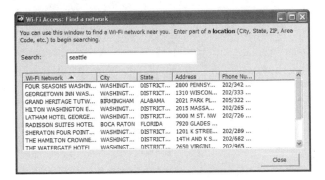

Other WISPs

As we noted at the start of this chapter, other cellular and landline phone companies will soon offer their own custom connection clients. This includes AT&T (the parent company), AT&T Wireless (the cellular company), Verizon Wireless (expected toward the end of 2003), SBC (also by the end of 2003), Cingular (by 2005), and T-Mobile. T-Mobile has licensed Boingo's software.

In most cases, these custom connection programs will allow you to connect not just to Wi-Fi networks, but also to 2.5G and eventually 3G cell data networks. Because hardware makers are creating laptop PC Cards, PDA chips, and cell phones that can handle cell and Wi-Fi in a single slot or device, software that can manage every type of connection will become increasingly useful.

Using Cellular Data Networks

As we noted back in Chapter 4, *Other Wireless Standards*, cellular telephone operators offer (and will continue to offer) a variety of methods to connect to the Internet over a cell network using a PC Card or a cell phone. In that chapter, we discussed the underpinnings and technology that make it up; here, we look at actually using cell data service.

Although dozens of options are available, we examine two popular ones here: connecting to GSM and GPRS networks via a cell phone and using a CDMA2000 network with a laptop and a PC Card.

Before we get started, however, you might be interested in what it currently costs to send and receive cellular data (**Table 30.1**). We expect prices to change constantly, but always in the direction of becoming more affordable.

Connecting with GSM and GPRS

The popular Sony Ericsson T68i cell phone uses both the GSM and GPRS standards, which are common in Europe and increasingly found in the United States. Data calls made over a GSM network run at 9600 bits per second (bps), while over a GPRS network, the speed can range from about 10 to 50 Kbps, depending on the congestion on the network and the local infrastructure.

The easiest way to make a modem call using the T68i is via Bluetooth. In Chapter 11, *Connecting via Bluetooth*, we provide details on how to pair computers and other devices using Bluetooth. As an example, here are the steps for pairing a T68i and a Macintosh:

Table 30.1

Comparison of U.S. cellular data plans as of November 2003

Operator	Plan or Feature Add-On	Flavor	Speed (Kbps)	Monthly Fee	Included MB	Price per Extra MB
AT&T Wireless	Mobile Internet PC Card add-on	GPRS	10–50	$79.99	Unlimited	None
Cingular	Wireless Internet add-on†	GSM	9.6	$3.99	Uses minutes	n/a
	Wireless Internet Express add-on†	GPRS	10–50	None	None	$30
Sprint PCS	PCS Vision	1xRTT	50–70	$40–$100	20 to 300	$2
T-Mobile	T-Mobile Internet add-on	GPRS	10–50	$29.99	Unlimited	None
Verizon Wireless	NationalAccess Megabyte	1xRTT	50–70	$39.99–$59.99	20 to 60	$2–$4
	Unlimited NationalAccess	1xRTT/1xEvDO	50–70	$79.99	Unlimited	None
	Unlimited BroadbandAccess*	1xEvDO	300–500	$79.99	Unlimited	None

†No PC Card required; can work just with cell phone. *Available in only San Diego and Washington, D.C., at this writing, but expected to expand. Includes Unlimited NationalAccess in areas without 1xEvDO.

1. Working on the T68i, press the menu toggle to reach the icon menu.

2. Navigate to the Connection item and select it, or press 8 (**Figure 30.1**).

3. Choose Bluetooth from the Connect menu, or press 3 (**Figure 30.2**).

4. Choose Discoverable from the Bluetooth menu, or press 1 (**Figure 30.3**). The phone shows that it's discoverable by showing a left-pointing-arrow next to the Bluetooth icon on the main screen (**Figure 30.4**).

5. On the Macintosh that will use the phone as a data device, start the discovery and pairing process described in Chapter 11, *Connecting via Bluetooth*. Basically, you run the Bluetooth Setup Assistant, walk through the steps to find the phone, and enter a passphrase. Then you enter that same passphrase on the phone when prompted.

 TIP

We find it difficult to enter letters and symbols in the T68i's passphrase menu, which hides what you're typing. We just use a number sequence instead.

Figure 30.1 to 30.6
Making the
Bluetooth
connection.

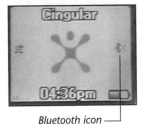

Bluetooth icon

6. Although it's not strictly required, make the T68i phone discover and pair to the computer, too, as it helps if you later want to synchronize or use other advanced features. Working with the phone, return to the Connect menu's Bluetooth menu and choose Discover.

    The phone displays discoverable devices (**Figure 30.5**).

7. Choose your computer and exchange passphrases (**Figure 30.6**).

With the phone and computer paired, you can now set up your computer to make modem calls using the Bluetooth connection. Here's how to set this up and make a connection with Mac OS X:

1. Open System Preferences and click Network to open the Network preferences pane.

2. Choose USB Bluetooth Modem Adaptor *(sic)* from the Show pop-up menu to display the USB Bluetooth Modem Adaptor configuration screen (**Figure 30.7**).

 TIP

If you don't see USB Bluetooth Modem Adaptor as a menu item, choose Network Configurations from the Show pop-up menu and check the box next to that adapter in the list.

 TIP

Mac OS X lists an internal Bluetooth card found in a Power Mac or PowerBook as a USB Bluetooth Modem Adapter.

Figure 30.7
Configuring the
Bluetooth modem
settings.

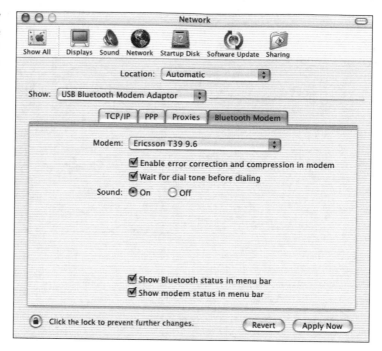

3.   Set up your modem connection just as you would any dial-up connection. For the most part, all you should have to do is enter your account information and ISP's phone number in the PPP tab of the USB Bluetooth Modem Adaptor configuration screen.

4.   To establish a connection, choose Connect from the Phone menu icon (**Figure 30.8**), use the Internet Connect application, or, if you have set the connection to connect automatically on request, just launch an Internet program and connect to an Internet server.

Figure 30.8
Connecting to your
Bluetooth phone.

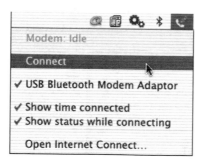

((•)) **NOTE**

Setting up a Windows machine is just as easy—use Dial-Up Networking and treat the Bluetooth connection like any other modem.

With GSM service, you dial into your own ISP: the cell phone acts as a modem relay, letting your computer essentially dial a modem in a cell company's phone closet somewhere—really! With GPRS service, however, the cell company is your ISP and should have provided you with specific numbers (often including asterisks and odd letters and numbers) and account information. Contact the cell company if you've subscribed to a cell data service but lack those details.

NOTE

When you connect to the Internet in this way, you've actually gone wireless in two ways: Bluetooth to the phone and cellular wireless out to the Internet! Talk about wireless goodness.

Connecting with CDMA and CDMA2000

Several U.S. cell operators that rely on the CDMA protocols for their cellular networks offer 1xRTT service that can provide about 50 to 70 Kbps of real throughput in areas of the country that have decent cell service. People traveling the country in RVs have picked up on this because of their lack of proximity to phone lines for making calls or connecting to the Internet.

In Windows XP, we set up a CDMA card from Verizon Wireless: the Sierra Wireless AirCard 555 (**Figure 30.9**). The card supports both the faster 1xRTT service and a GSM-like dial-up service that runs at 14.4 Kbps or slower where 1xRTT isn't available.

Figure 30.9
The Sierra Wireless AirCard 555.

NOTE

Sierra is the dominant provider of CDMA PC Cards, and the company offers only Windows drivers for its PC Cards. There's a cryptic note on the Sierra Web site that says the company could offer Mac OS X support if Apple makes a couple of unspecified changes. Keep your eyes peeled.

Normally, we'd guide you through step-by-step instructions for installing drivers and configuring the unit. However, Sierra has done a fantastic job of providing detailed, useful directions for ensuring its card's drivers work under Windows 95, 98, Me, 2000, and XP, and you should follow its instructions. For Windows XP, in brief:

1. If you have the Venturi Web acceleration package on your machine, uninstall it before proceeding.

2. Install Sierra's software before inserting the AirCard 555.

3. Insert the card and select Sierra's specific drivers from the CD-ROM. We know this sounds a little strange since you've just installed Sierra's software on your hardware, but it's what the company suggests and it works. We're assuming Windows XP picks the wrong driver.

4. Install the Venturi Web acceleration software, which is on the same CD-ROM provided by Sierra.

Once the Sierra software and drivers are installed, launch AirCard 555 Watcher and enter account information provided by Verizon, such as the phone number and an activation number. Choose Activation Wizard from the Tools menu and follow the instructions, which may require calling Verizon Wireless.

With the AirCard 555, you have two options in the Data tab: Express Network (1xRTT) and the slower Quick 2 NetSM (14.4 Kbps). Depending on which service plan you have, you might choose one over the other to reduce costs; also, the faster speed will not always be available.

 TIP

If you've enabled voice calling on the AirCard 555 and plugged a headset into the card's audio jack, you can make calls from your laptop as well. Configure the appropriate options in the Voice tab.

To connect, you simply click Connect in the AirCard 555 Watcher software and the card negotiates the connection (**Figure 30.10**). In our testing of the AirCard 555 and Verizon Wireless's service, we didn't find anything more complex than that Connect button, which changes to Disconnect when a connection is active. When you click Disconnect, Windows XP shows that the connection has been severed (**Figure 30.11**).

Even from Glenn's office, which has a concrete wall on the side that faces where the bulk of Seattle's cell towers are located, service was reliable and fast. He used his ISP's speed connection test to see what kind of throughput he could

Figure 30.10
Connecting
with the AirCard
software.

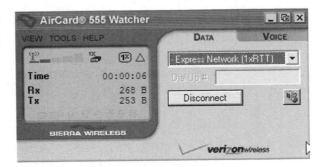

Figure 30.11
Windows alert when
you disconnect.

expect in this poor wireless environment, and discovered that the AirCard 555 offered 46 Kbps for downloads and 61 Kbps for uploads (**Figure 30.12**). You could see better performance with better signal strength: the top speed of the AirCard 555 is theoretically 144 Kbps, but even Verizon Wireless promotes only 50 to 70 Kbps.

Figure 30.12
Checking 1xRTT's
actual performance
in a concrete-lined
room.

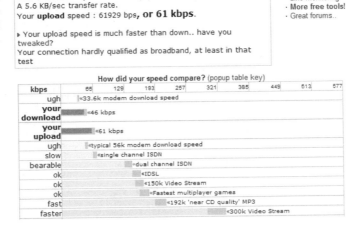

Prepping for the Road

If you want to connect to the Internet wirelessly while traveling, searching for wireless networks that you can use while en route and at your destination is the most important preparation you can do (and we cover the details about that in Chapter 28, *Finding Wi-Fi on the Road*), but you should also gather a number of other pieces of information, which we discuss in this chapter. Plus, you should make sure your laptop is ready to go; we offer some advice on that as well. Failing to prepare ahead of time won't necessarily prevent you from using a wireless Internet connection while you're away, but you may have to spend a long time downloading and configuring software, or fussing with other things when you could be concentrating on the purpose of the trip.

Access Accounts

Most of the for-fee networks we discuss earlier in this section require accounts for even casual access, and a number of them require that you use custom software. Some, such as Boingo, offer a free download of the required software along with free account setup. You pay fees only when you opt into a service session or a subscription plan.

But these downloads are large, and signing up for an account can be annoying when you're trying to make a quick connection to pick up an important email message. We recommend setting everything up in advance: download and install the necessary software, log in and create accounts, and even sign up for service plans if you think you'll need them.

TIP

If you're worried about forgetting your user name and password, write them down, but keep the paper in a safe place. Remember that most passwords are stolen because they were written down.

Email

The most frustrating aspect of email on the road is sending replies and new messages. The frustration stems from the fact that, in order to prevent a spammer from hijacking their outbound mail servers, many companies and ISPs have severely restricted how you can send email through their servers.

Unfortunately, there's little technical difference between what a spammer does to hijack a mail server and what you do when you connect to some random wireless network and then try to send email through your normal outgoing mail server. (In both cases, the action is called *relaying*, and almost all sensibly configured mail servers now refuse to do unrestricted relaying.)

There are a number of ways to work around this problem, all of which you should consider before you hit the road. It's always important to test such changes before you leave.

- **Change your mail server.** One common way that ISPs restrict outgoing mail is by preventing traffic from leaving their network on port 25, which is the standard SMTP port. This doesn't bother the ISP's customers who connect directly to the ISP because they use the ISP's local SMTP server, but it often proves a problem for travelers looking to make a quick connection via a wireless hotspot. One workaround is to reset the outgoing SMTP server setting in your email program to use the hot spot's local mail server (often smtp.example.com, or mail.example.com, where you replace example.com with the ISP's domain). Unfortunately, public hot spots often don't allow access to their SMTP servers at all or even block port 25 on the local network, forcing you to try another option.

- **ISP Web mail.** Many ISPs offer a direct, Web-based email interface that lets you avoid the whole issue on the road. By using a Web mail client to read and/or send your email, you lose the benefit of working in your normal email program, and you can work only when you're connected to the Internet. But because the Web mail program is located on your ISP's computer, it can send email through the ISP's SMTP server with no trouble. One benefit of using an ISP-based Web mail client is that it works on your existing mailbox on the ISP's server, making it easy to integrate what you do in the Web mail client with your main email program when you return.

 NOTE

Most Web mail doesn't use SSL, which means your email is sent in the clear as you read it. If you're concerned about that, read Chapter 26, Securing Data in Transit. Some Web mail allows an SSL sign-in to protect at least your user name and password.

- **Generic Web mail.** A number of independent services let you retrieve your existing email via a Web mail client. These Web mail programs use your POP account information to retrieve the mail behind the scenes, after which they present it to you with a Web interface. Many of these services let you set your return address to your real email address, not the one you use on the service, so replies go to your correct mailbox. Most of these services have free options with severe limits on storage, and they add their own advertisements or taglines; for a small fee, you get more storage and no ads. We highly recommend FastMail (www.fastmail.fm), which offers a secure login using SSL so that (per our note above) your entire session is protected, not just your login.

TIP

If you have mail-forwarding service at your ISP, you could forward your mail directly to your email address at your Web mail service while you're on the road.

- **POP then send.** Some ISPs let you send outbound email only after you've retrieved email from your POP account. Retrieving email via POP opens a window—typically 30 minutes—during which the ISP's mail server will accept email from the network you're using. We've found this approach slightly problematic in practice, because it sometimes requires multiple POP retrievals, and then waiting a few minutes. Although the feature is not universal, and it is on the wane due to spammers figuring out ways to exploit it, many popular email programs support checking a POP account before attempting to send mail.

- **Authenticated SMTP (SMTP AUTH).** An increasing number of mail servers prevent unauthorized people from sending them email via a technique called Authenticated SMTP or SMTP AUTH. To be able to send email, your email program must authenticate itself with a user name and password (not necessarily the same as your POP account), after which you can send email through that server. SMTP AUTH can encrypt your user name and password so it can't be sniffed, and it can encrypt the contents of outgoing email, depending on your client and how the server is configured; see Chapter 26, *Securing Data in Transit*, for more information about SMTP AUTH.

((•)) **NOTE**

Authenticated SMTP is probably the best solution, assuming your mail server and email program both support it. Again, set it up and check before traveling. One problem you can run into is that some ISPs block all traffic from their networks on port 25, the port used by SMTP, which prevents you from sending to any mail server other than their own. A mail administrator can bypass this for roaming users by setting the main or an alternate mail server inbound port to a different port number, either 587, which is standard as a secondary SMTP port, or another port number above 1024.

- **Extended transmit (XTND XMIT).** The POP protocol is used for retrieving mail, but it has an option, called XTND XMIT, that enables you to send mail via POP, too. Although XTND XMIT lets you avoid the problems with sending mail while using random wireless networks, support for XTND XMIT is sporadic both in email programs and in mail servers, so ask your ISP if it supports XTND XMIT, and look in your email program's options for a checkbox to turn it on. We've had erratic results with XTND XMIT, so we recommend that you test it with your setup before you assume it will work while you travel.

- **Secure shell (SSH) tunneling.** If you use the technique we discuss in Chapter 26, *Securing Data in Transit*, to create encrypted SSH tunnels, then you can usually send email directly to your normal mail server. The SSH tunnel fools your mail server into thinking you're from the same machine that's running the mail server, thus bypassing the remote problem entirely.

- **Virtual private network (VPN).** If you're using a VPN client to connect to your office, then you shouldn't have any difficulty sending email. The VPN authenticates you to your home network and encrypts everything you send.

Files

Everyone tries to bring the files they know they'll need—presentations, reports, demonstration software, and so on—when they travel, but at one time or another, everyone finds themselves missing important files, either due to forgetfulness or sheer mischance. Even worse is when something happens to your laptop, or when you arrive and discover that you can neither connect your laptop to a necessary projector nor copy your presentation from your laptop to the computer that can connect to the projector.

Fortunately, with just a little foresight, you can make sure these situations don't leave you fuming in anger. Be sure to test the methods we describe before leaving town, especially from another connection, to ensure that otherwise reasonable security measures don't prevent you from accessing the files you need.

- **IP file servers.** Many file servers, including the built-in file sharing software in Windows, Mac OS 9, and Mac OS X, let you connect to them directly over the Internet. However, system administrators often lock down access to file servers for non-local users, so make sure you have a way in, and if the machine you need to access is behind a NAT gateway, make sure the appropriate port forwarding is in place.

- **FTP, Web, and WebDAV servers.** If you have an ISP account anywhere, or access to local servers, you may be able to upload potentially useful files for later access via FTP, WebDAV, or the Web.

- **Timbuktu Pro.** Both of us use the Timbuktu Pro file exchange and remote control software from Netopia (www.netopia.com) to copy files and check on software running on our local systems while on the road. It works across Mac and Windows. There are also other remote control applications with file transfer capabilities available, though none that work with both the Mac OS and Windows.

- **Online storage.** If you're a Mac user, you can sign up for .Mac (www.mac.com), Apple's paid Web services site, for $100 per year. .Mac includes 100 MB of online storage, which you can access directly from a Mac, or via the Web Folders feature built into recent versions of Windows. (See the iDisk page on .Mac for instructions on accessing an iDisk from different platforms.) Other services offer about 1 GB of storage for roughly $30 per month, including Xdrive (www.xdrive.com), the IBackup division of Pro Softnet (www.ibackup.com), and My Docs Online (www.mydocsonline.com). These services are aimed at Windows but support Mac OS X through WebDAV.

- **Email yourself.** If you use one of the Web mail methods discussed previously in the chapter, consider emailing yourself files you might need. If your mail is accessible via a Web mail client, you can then download them using a Web browser on any other computer.

TIP

If you set your email client to leave messages over a certain size on the server, you can keep files that you've emailed to yourself on the server even if you check email before you need them.

Backing Up

It's easy to create critical new information while on the road, and being away from your regular backup system makes it all too likely that you would lose important data if something were to happen to your laptop.

We recommend:

- **Back up before you leave.** Make a full backup of your laptop and desktop computer right before you leave. That way, even if your laptop is stolen or broken, you can restore files to a new laptop when you return home.

- **Send files home.** All the methods of retrieving files while on the road (discussed earlier in this chapter) are great ways to push files back to a secure place.

- **Burn a CD or DVD.** Many modern laptops have CD or even DVD burners. Pack a few blank discs, and then back up critical new information to them. It's best to store such backup discs in a bag other than your laptop bag, of course, since it's more likely that a thief would steal your laptop bag than your suitcase. You could also bring self-addressed, stamped mailing envelopes with you and send backup discs home via the postal service. That's an especially good idea if you're creating irreplaceable data, as is true with most photos, for instance.

- **Use a USB RAM drive.** You can now buy tiny USB RAM drives that fit on your keychain. They use flash memory and cheaply offer up to 1 GB of space. Better yet, when you plug them into the USB port on either a Mac or a PC, they mount just like hard drives. Since these USB RAM drives are small enough to put in your pocket, even if your laptop disappears while you're not watching, you can still have your critical new (and old) files with you.

- **Use a remote backup program.** Some backup programs, including Dantz Development's powerful Retrospect (www.dantz.com; available for Mac and Windows), let you back up to an FTP server or other remote server.

Better still, for any data that's truly important, make multiple backups using different methods.

VPNs

A VPN (virtual private network) solves a number of these traveling problems by making it seem as though you're always on your company's local network. That's one reason that many business travelers access their company's email and file servers via a VPN. However, you must make sure that you have all the necessary information to connect to your VPN when you're traveling. Most companies offer dial-up access to their VPNs, and although you should always make sure you have the appropriate numbers, it's much nicer if you can use a high-speed wireless Internet connection instead. We strongly recommend that you verify that you can connect to your VPN before leaving on a trip, since many VPNs require special security devices or one-time setups that may not exist until you ask to have them set up for you.

The main bugaboo that can taunt VPN users is that many wireless and other broadband Internet connections use NAT. Some NAT gateways can prevent your VPN software from connecting to the office. This problem is especially common with free community networks.

 TIP

Many wireless gateways have options to enable VPN "pass-through" features, so if you can't establish a VPN connection, it's worth asking the administrator if PPTP and IPsec pass-through are enabled. It's also important to open the correct ports for your VPN; ask your administrator what they are before you leave. See www.smallnetbuilder.com/Sections-article49.php *for more information.*

((•)) **NOTE**

Some managers of public, for-fee hot spots have told us that they use routable, static addresses to avoid this problem on their networks.

Unfortunately, testing VPN connections can be tricky, since you may have no way of knowing the limitations of the network you'll be using. Make sure you have your office's Help Desk phone number and any troubleshooting advice, and find out whether any special access permission or other details need to be settled before you leave town.

Working on the Road

Using a wireless Internet connection while you're on the road isn't particularly different from using it when you're at home or at the office. Nonetheless, we've run into a few quirks over the years and can provide useful advice.

Connect to a Network

To connect to a wireless network, you must find it and have the proper network configuration. If an account is required, you must also authenticate yourself.

Finding a Network

Even if you do your research before leaving and think you know where a wireless network is located, finding the precise spot where you can get access can be more difficult than you'd think. We often run into dead areas in airport terminals that have "full coverage," and we've been known to wander around, dowsing with our laptops for wireless networks near where we think there might be a café with wireless access.

You have four main options for finding a network that you think is nearby, or for investigating whether a network exists:

- **Stumbler tools.** These software programs sniff for local networks in your vicinity, and then tell you the network names, their signal strengths, and if they're protected by WEP or WPA encryption keys. (See "Stumbling onto Wi-Fi" in Chapter 25, *Preventing Access to Your Network*, for a full list and download locations.) You can walk around with your laptop open and see strength increase or decrease, which can help lead you closer to the strongest network signal. Be warned that in some places, use of these tools might freak people out, as they're used both for innocent purposes and by crackers.

- **Detectors.** The Kensington WiFi Finder and the Smart ID WFS-1 are the first two of what we expect will be a plethora of Wi-Fi detectors: they identify only Wi-Fi signals, not general microwave noise, and indicate signal strength. The WFS-1 is fast and directional enough to help you dowse for a signal. We expect this sort of device eventually to have a small LCD screen displaying network names.

- **Warchalk signs.** Warchalking is the act of writing simple, hobo-sign–inspired chalk marks that tell others if a nearby network is available (**Figure 32.1**). Some WISPs have deployed more polished versions of the chalk signs on their store signs; examples include FatPort outlets and Schlotzsky's Deli. For more on warchalking (and an explanation of the name), see the sidebar "The War Prefix" in Chapter 25, *Preventing Access to Your Network*. Neither of us has seen a warchalking sign in the wild, and they're not very persistent.

- **Ask.** We know you're proud; so are we. That's why we put this, the most obvious option, last in the list. But just as with driving directions when you're lost, the better part of valor is to ask someone, perhaps in a coffee shop or copy shop, both of which are relatively likely locations for access. Even if the people you ask don't know, they may be able to point you in the right direction.

Network Setup

The vast majority of wireless networks automatically provide you with an IP address and other network details via DHCP. Because of this, your typical on-the-road network configuration should be set to obtain an IP address automatically.

 TIP

You can find information on configuring your network connection to work with DHCP in Appendix B, Configuring Your Network Settings.

After making sure your laptop is using DHCP, all you have to do is select the wireless network that's in range, and your machine should automatically negotiate an IP address and give you full network access.

Figure 32.1
A warchalking sign.

 TIP

Virtually all public networks are WEP and WPA free to avoid complicated login procedures. Since neither WEP nor WPA protects data from other people who have the same network key, they're useless in public networks, anyway. (With WPA, the key is less obvious, but when shared, just as easy to use to decode the whole network's traffic.)

Login Access

Some public wireless networks require that you navigate past a captive portal page before accessing the network from any Internet-capable application. Fire up a Web browser, try to visit any Web page, and the captive portal page will prompt you for agreement to a contract, your login information, and/or credit card payment details.

In places where you pay by the day, like hotels, figuring out how to pay for access can be tricky. Normally the captive portal page handles the transaction, but in at least one hotel Adam has stayed in (the Paramount, in New York City), you had to call the concierge to get the appropriate user name and password; the fee for using the wireless network was added to his room bill. When in doubt, ask for access instructions at the front desk when you check in. At the Wyndham Hotels and Resorts, access is free if you're a member of the affinity club "ByRequest," but you must enter your number in the captive portal page to avoid paying for broadband.

Working Tips

As we noted at the start of this chapter, once you're connected, using a wireless Internet connection on the road is almost exactly like using a wireless Internet connection at home or in the office. Even so, we can offer a few tips from long experience.

- **Check email whenever you can.** You never know when you'll be able to connect in the future, so any time wireless Internet access presents itself, take advantage of it to keep up to date.

- **Watch your time.** If you're using a commercial WISP or an aggregator, like iPass or GRIC, that charges by the hour or day, pay attention to when you use the wireless connection. Hotels in particular can be a bit snarky about this; at least some we've stayed in assume a day goes from midnight to midnight despite the illogic. So, if you check in late one night, connect to get your email, and then connect again in the morning, you'll be charged for two days. Make sure you know what the charging policies are ahead of time to avoid these unwanted fees.

- **Turn off network cards to save power.** Although today's laptops have improved from the first successful portable computers, short battery life remains a major frustration. Along with other power-saving measures that you may want to take (dim the screen, spin down the hard disk, reduce the processor speed), make sure to turn off your wireless network card if there's no wireless network in the vicinity. That's especially true on airplanes, where you're not supposed to use radio transmitters.

- **Browse offline.** Several Web browsers and other utilities let you store Web pages as a local set of files for later viewing. Adobe Acrobat offers a Web-to-PDF option that can retrieve Web pages and images, including certain kinds of multimedia, and turn them into a self-contained Acrobat PDF file. These features are useful because your Internet access is likely to be sporadic, so by downloading Web pages for later viewing, you can continue to access that information even after you disconnect from the wireless network.

- **Lock your screen.** If you have confidential, sensitive, or embarrassing data on your laptop, consider using options that cause the computer to ask for a password when you wake the machine out of sleep or bring it out of the screensaver. That can prevent casual thieves from accessing your data, even if they were to make off with your computer. And for goodness sake, don't write your password down on a sticky note attached to the computer!

- **Obscure your screen.** "Shoulder surfers" used to refer to people who watched you enter PINs for long distance cards on pay phones in airports. With cell phones abundant and pay phones accepting credit cards, the term has migrated to people who watch your laptop activities while you work on a plane or in other public places. Several inexpensive filters can obscure a laptop screen to anyone viewing at an angle other than direct on. The 3M Notebook Privacy Filter, for instance, comes in many sizes, and costs $40 to $60 (www.3m.com/ergonomics/notebookaccessories.jhtml).

- **Use a security kit.** The problem with extended sessions in a wireless-enabled coffeehouse is that drinking all that coffee often results in needing to use the bathroom. What to do with your laptop? If you're alone, the most secure approach is to pack everything up and bring it with you, at the cost of some time and the risk of losing a good seat. Alternatively, you can do what we do, and use a security kit to lock your laptop and bag to the table. You can buy several kinds of security kits, including ones with alarms so that if a computer is disturbed, a loud noise sounds. We've used and liked security kits from Kensington Technology Group—see www.kensington.com/html/1434.html for the current collection.

VI

Going the Distance

As we near the end of this book, it's time to turn our attention to our geekiest topic yet—long-range wireless networking. After all, there's no inherent reason you need to be within 150 feet or so of an access point, and in fact, with the right equipment, a wireless network can easily span miles. Cool, eh?

We're under no illusion that everyone will want to read these chapters, but you might want to glance through Chapter 33, *Long-Range Wi-Fi Connections,* to see what you can do with a long-range wireless network (it basically comes down to another way to acquire a high-speed Internet connection or a way of connecting multiple remote sites into a single wireless network).

If Chapter 33 piques your interest, read Chapter 34, *Long-Range Antenna Basics,* for all the gory details you need to know in order to set up a long-range wireless network. If you're mostly a computer person, like us, rather than a radio geek, you'll have a lot to learn, but we've enjoyed the process immensely, and you may too.

Long-Range Wi-Fi Connections

You're probably familiar with the caveat on most pieces of Wi-Fi networking gear—something like "maximum performance up to 150 feet" whether that's 11 Mbps or 54 Mbps. And if you've been using wireless networks for any amount of time, you know that 150 feet is often optimistic. Put a wall or two in the way, and the effective range of a wireless network can drop to 30 or 40 feet.

These disclaimers don't mean that there's any particular limitation on the effective range of standard wireless networks. Given the appropriate gear, most notably a *high-gain antenna* that increases the strength of your wireless signal, you can set up a Wi-Fi connection with a range measured not in feet, but in miles.

In fact, with other proprietary wireless network variants that use slower but more robust frequency hopping, those distances can be increased even farther than is possible with 802.11a, b, or g. There's a wireless Internet service provider (WISP) in Maine that typically runs its links 20 to 40 miles using a Wi-Fi–like alternative, including a 22-mile link from the coast to an island with 300 residents.

The residents of this island previously had very slow dial-up connections to the mainland that cost them several cents per minute. With the long-range wireless link, local residents can either connect directly at high speed to the tower on the island, and receive 1 to 3 Mbps of bandwidth; or they can establish dial-up modem connections to the tower by local landline for a fixed monthly rate avoiding long-distance charges. The long-range wireless network connection makes a huge difference for these people.

The Maine WISP's case is particularly apt, because it illustrates the two uses of long-range wireless networking in situations where wires simply may not work: connecting to the Internet and extending an existing network.

We've both done some work in establishing long-range Internet connections and extending networks, and we've learned that every individual situation is different. As such, our aim here is to describe what's possible, talk about which hardware is necessary, and put ideas into your head. We don't offer detailed instructions because it's impossible to anticipate what would be required in your particular situation.

((•)) **NOTE**

Whether you want to connect to the Internet or extend the range of your existing network, it's important to realize up front that a long-range wireless connection links only the remote site and a single device on your side. Don't assume that all your wireless-capable computers will suddenly be able to use the long-range connection, just because you put up a high-gain antenna. Just as with a cable or DSL modem, you must use a gateway to redistribute the connection to the rest of your local network.

Connecting to the Internet

Most people these days have telephones and can connect to an Internet service provider via a standard modem. But modems suffer from long dialing times, slow throughput, and general flakiness, which is one of the reasons that always-on, high-speed Internet connections over phone and cable lines—so-called "consumer broadband connections"—have become so popular.

People who live close enough to an appropriately outfitted telephone company central office or whose cable television companies offer Internet access still make up a relatively small (though growing) percentage of the U.S. (and world) population, though, and it's all too easy to find yourself living in a location where broadband Internet access is either prohibitively expensive or impossible to come by at any price.

The difficulty of finding high-speed Internet access is especially common in lightly populated rural areas, where the chances of a telephone or cable company investing in the necessary back-end equipment for high-speed Internet access are relatively low.

NOTE

Even when high-speed Internet access is available, it's often on a tenuous basis. Friends of Glenn's in small-town Maine were lucky enough to have cable modem service—for a while. A larger Internet service provider's buyout of the local company resulted in the cable modem service becoming unreliable.

In an increasing number of those locations, Internet service providers are turning to long-range wireless networks as a way of bringing Internet connectivity to far-flung customers without dealing with telephone companies or burying miles of wire. With no extra wires to run, the cost of adding a customer is low for both the ISP and the customer, and the standard 1 Mbps throughput (the lowest of 802.11b's speeds) is generally equal to the best DSL and cable modem connections.

NOTE

Some ISPs even partner with the tiny phone companies (the so called "ma-and-pa bells") that still exist in rural areas of the U.S. The ISP brings high-speed Internet to the local exchange via a long-range wireless connection, and then the phone company redistributes it using DSL.

As much as a long-range wireless Internet connection may be the only option for many people, others use them to provide redundant connections. For instance, Internet connectivity is essential for Adam's business of writing and publishing, so when he moved from the outskirts of Seattle, Washington (where he was

802.11b vs. 802.11g for Long-Range Connections

With a long-range connection, does it make any difference whether you use an older (and cheaper) 802.11b-based wireless bridge or client instead of a newer and faster 802.11g model? That's a great question, and not one we have sufficient experience with yet to answer definitively.

Our current understanding is that if you're connecting to a WISP, there's likely no point in bothering with 802.11g, since the WISP's existing industrial-strength equipment is likely to use only 802.11b. In addition, the signal strength for long-range connections isn't likely to be high enough to provide bandwidth above

1 Mbps or so, so 802.11g's maximum throughput of 54 Mbps is likely to go unused.

The situation is perhaps a bit different when you extend your own network, since the distances may be shorter and you're probably buying all the equipment at roughly the same time. WDS (Wireless Distribution System) capabilities also show up only in newer 802.11g equipment, so if you want to use WDS to extend your network instead of using dedicated wireless bridges (see Chapter 20, *Bridging Wireless Networks*, for the tradeoffs), you'll want to buy the newer gear.

considering setting up his own wireless Internet service from his home atop Tiger Mountain), to Ithaca, New York, he signed up for a cable modem Internet connection and also installed a long-range wireless connection to a different ISP. Should something happen to one of the connections, or to one of the ISPs, he can switch his computers to the other connection in a matter of minutes.

Finding a WISP

The first step in setting up a long-range wireless Internet connection is determining if a wireless ISP (WISP) serves your area. Since wireless Internet access is still somewhat unusual, it's not always easy to find, even when it is available. Try these Web sites:

- Broadband Wireless Exchange Magazine (www.bbwexchange.com/wisps/) maintains a WISP directory that includes hundreds of WISPs around the world, although it's undoubtedly not comprehensive, in part because Broadband Wireless Exchange charges WISPs for inclusion.

- The Open Directory Project publishes a list of WISPs at http://dmoz.org/ Business/Telecommunications/Wireless/Service_Providers/Internet/ Fixed_Broadband/. Also be sure to check out The Open Directory Project's list of Regional WISPs at http://dmoz.org/Business/Telecommunications/ Wireless/Service_Providers/Internet/Regional/.

- A standard Google search is always worth trying, although we've found it difficult to come up with search terms that work reliably. Start by searching for "wireless Internet access Seattle WA" (replacing "Seattle WA" with your city and state, of course), and add other terms like "802.11b" and "WISP" if necessary.

We've seen interest in promoting WISP associations from a variety of trade groups, but no one group appears to have hit its stride yet. It's worth checking if any such groups have solidified since we wrote this book, since they would provide lists of their members in your area.

If your area has local Usenet newsgroups or mailing lists, try asking there; all you need is one person to point you in the right direction. Lastly, although it's hard to remember in today's age of the Internet, sometimes the best approach is to revert to traditional methods of finding a business. Check your local Yellow Pages in the telephone book, talk to Internet-savvy friends, and call normal ISPs and ask if they know of anyone offering wireless Internet access in your area. Most ISPs know which other Internet access companies are around, and our experience is that they're not offended at referring customers they can't serve.

TIP

If your search fails to turn up any WISPs and you have no other alternatives for high-speed Internet access, you could try to convince someone who can get high-speed Internet access to host the remote side of a long-range wireless Internet connection. Read "Extending Your Network" later for information on setting up such a connection.

TIP

*If you have a view of the southern sky, satellite-based Internet access from StarBand Communications (*www.starband.com*) or Direcway (*www. direcway.com*) is also a possibility.*

Be Your Own WISP

Assume for a moment that you live in the boonies, but not all that far from where the local telephone company stops providing DSL-based Internet access. You want high-speed Internet access, you don't have a good view of the southern sky to use StarBand or Direcway, but you can see quite a few of your neighbors' roofs. Why not pay for a neighbor to have an Internet connection and use a long-range wireless connection to bring it back to your house?

There's no technical reason you can't do this, but it requires some careful planning and good interpersonal skills, since you must determine ahead of time which of your neighbors' houses is in a location where it can get DSL and provide a line-of-sight wireless connection for your house. That requires some skillful use of binoculars or a telescope, some sleuthing with the local telephone company, and then a persuasive approach for the neighbor you've identified. It's not uncommon to strike out a few times before you find someone who is amenable. Try to find someone who's unlikely to move—she likely won't want to explain the entire situation to potential home buyers,

which could mark an unceremonious end to your Internet connection. Also keep in mind that the ISP from whom you get service may not allow that service to be shared.

There are some disadvantages to this approach. Along with shouldering the monthly cost of the Internet connection, you must also buy two antennas, two wireless Ethernet bridges, and likely a gateway so your Internet host can share the connection as well. (Obviously, if you can find a person or business that already has a high-speed Internet connection and is willing to share, the costs drop significantly.)

You're also probably setting yourself up to provide technical support for your Internet host, and no matter what, you're creating a situation where you're reliant on someone else for your Internet connectivity, including troubleshooting if things go wrong.

Put simply, it's a truly neat idea, but it's not necessarily cheap and may involve you in someone else's life more than you'd like. On the other hand, if it works out, you could be on your way toward starting your very own community wireless network.

Site Check

One huge caveat to long-range wireless Internet connections is that your wireless transceiver must be able to see the WISP's antenna. In the networking world, this is called having *line of sight* to the remote antenna, and it's the main reason more people don't use long-range Internet connections. Depending on the distance, you may not be able to actually see the remote antenna, though you should at least have good reason to believe line of sight might be possible before investigating further. Remember that you might be able to mount your antenna on a mast on your roof to achieve line of sight.

Once you find a WISP and determine that it's conceivable that you have line-of-sight access to the WISP's antenna, the next step is to ask the WISP to perform a site check. WISPs may charge for site checks, since such a check involves bringing a high-gain antenna mounted on a tripod to your location, connecting it to a laptop, and testing to see if there's enough signal strength. A WISP may also have special gear, like a GPS device and a telescope, that can help determine exactly where the remote antenna is located for optimal aiming of your antenna.

Have the site check performed even if you can see the remote antenna, since it should also help you determine what kind of antenna you need. If you get great signal strength, you can buy a smaller, less-obtrusive antenna, whereas if the site check shows that you're on the edge of being able to receive the signal at all, you need a high-gain parabolic antenna. See Chapter 34, *Long-Range Antenna Basics,* for all the details you need to know on antenna types and determining necessary gain.

 TIP

Buy an antenna with more gain than you think is necessary; extra signal strength is always welcome, particularly since climatic conditions can cause signal loss. You have no way of knowing how representative the climatic conditions on the day of the site check are, so leave yourself some margin of error. (Of course, stay within the FCC's limits at all times.)

IP Addresses

After the wireless connection has been made, connecting your computer or network to a WISP is no different from connecting to any other Internet service provider in terms of what you end up with—connectivity provided to one (static or dynamic) or more IP addresses on your local network.

- An ISP usually hands out dynamic IP addresses these days because then its DHCP server can track who is online at any given point and dole out IP addresses from the ISP's block of available addresses. Dynamic addressing is easier for ISPs to manage, and many users don't mind at all because they don't need (or even want) their computers to be available for direct connections from out on the Internet. If you don't want to run Internet servers, dynamic addressing is fine.

TIP

If you can't avoid dynamic addressing, but you still want to run servers, look into dynamic DNS, which enables someone on the Internet to connect to www.example.com, *for instance, and have* www.example.com *map to whatever your dynamic address is at that particular time. See Chapter 16,* Buying a Wireless Gateway, *for more about dynamic DNS.*

- With a static address, you receive a permanent IP address that always maps to your wireless Ethernet bridge or to the computer acting as a bridge. That's ideal if you want to run servers, since your servers are always available at the same IP address (which can in turn be mapped to a domain name). Remember that you'll still need to punch holes through your NAT gateway so your servers can be seen from the outside world. If you want a static IP address, you may have to ask your WISP for one, and it may cost extra.

- If you want multiple static IP addresses, the service will almost certainly cost quite a bit more, you will need a router (though some of the inexpensive wireless gateways can act as routers as well), and your WISP must help you set everything up.

Extending Your Network

Another major use of long-range wireless networking is to extend an existing network to a remote location. Perhaps your company has an office in one building in an office park, and you want to take over offices in another building. The distance may be too great to run Ethernet cable, and the cost of leasing a high-speed digital line from the telephone company may be prohibitive, but for less than $1000 and a few days of work, you can add the new offices to your existing network and never pay recurring costs to the telephone company. Or, you may want to connect a number of houses in your neighborhood in order to share a single Internet connection.

When you set up a long-range wireless Internet connection, you have one big advantage—technicians at the WISP likely know more than you do and are probably willing to help. That's not true if you want to extend your network to a remote location, in which case all the work falls on your shoulders. By "your," we mean multiple people—it's almost impossible to extend a network via a long-range wireless connection without helpers.

Most of what you need to know with respect to extending a network comes in determining where to position the antennas on both sides of the connection; for everything else, read Chapter 20, *Bridging Wireless Networks*.

(((•))) **NOTE**

Even more so than with a long-range wireless Internet connection, the details here depend on your particular network and what you want to accomplish, so necessity forces us to be a bit more general when talking about expanding wireless networks.

Short Distances

If you're connecting two buildings in an office park, for instance, determining the line of sight and where to locate the antennas on either end of the connection is usually fairly easy.

You can estimate line of sight by eye, and then fine-tune the positioning by connecting your antenna to a laptop and using one of the stumbler tools to watch signal strength as you adjust the antenna. The only downside of this approach is that you may need to buy an extra pigtail connector to attach the antenna to your laptop, but it's worth the minimal expense.

Long Distances

The task becomes more difficult as the distance increases, or if you determine that there's simply no way to achieve line of sight without an intermediary antenna in the middle.

When trying to establish both ends of a line-of-sight connection across a long distance, start by looking at detailed topographical maps (**Figure 33.1**). High-quality paper maps are probably the easiest to work with, but you may be able to find the detail you need on a Web site like TopoZone.com at www.topozone.com.

The topographic map only takes you so far, though, because it shows only the elevation of the ground, whereas you care about objects above the ground as well, such as trees and buildings. Once you've identified possible areas for your antennas with the map, it's time to switch to binoculars, or better, telescopes. Here's where you absolutely need a partner, preferably with a cell phone, so you can each relay your location to the other as necessary.

Consider buying some cheap Mylar helium balloons at the grocery store and attaching them to extremely light string (perhaps dental floss) so you can float the balloon up, have the other person find it in the telescope, and then pull it

Figure 33.1
A topographical
map of the area
near Adam's house.

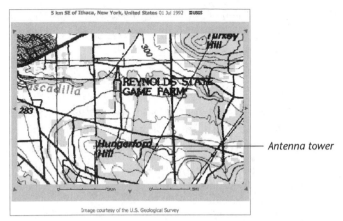

Antenna tower

Image courtesy of the U.S. Geological Survey

down as he watches. Once you've identified a spot that you think might work, mark it with something like a piece of colored plastic that you can easily see from afar and use while mounting the antenna.

 TIP

Pay attention to obstacles that are almost in the way, since the Fresnel effect can cause problems even if you have visual line of sight. Chapter 34, Long-Range Antenna Basics, *has more about the Fresnel zone.*

After you identify antenna locations, it's time to test the locations with actual antennas. Work through the calculations in the next chapter to determine which kind of antennas you're likely to need, since unless you can borrow portable antennas from a WISP or someone else who has extras that aren't mounted, you may as well buy the antennas you think are necessary. Go ahead and install your antennas, but make sure you can still adjust their positioning as necessary.

If you're concerned about buying more gear at this point, the cheapest method of testing is probably to use a pair of laptops with PC Card wireless network adapters and pigtails that connect to your antennas. (You may have to buy an extra pigtail or two, but if the connection simply doesn't work, you won't have purchased the wireless Ethernet bridges unnecessarily.) Set up a simple ad hoc network and see if one laptop can connect to the other's network. Again, having a partner with a cell phone is essential for reporting signal strength and adjusting antenna positions.

On the other hand, if you're not all that worried about cost, go ahead and buy the wireless Ethernet bridges you need on either side of the long-range wireless connection. Install and configure one of them, then use a laptop in the other location to verify that your antennas can receive each other's signals.

Once you've verified that everything works, fasten the antennas down securely, confirm that everything still works, and then run the necessary wiring to tie the two networks together.

Two-Hop Network

Should you give up hope if the topographic maps show that there's no way you could ever find a line of sight between your two locations? It all depends on how badly you want to set up a long-range wireless connection. To solve the problem, you could try building a two-hop connection that uses a pair of antennas in the middle.

The process of determining antenna location for a two-hop connection is roughly the same as for a normal long-range connection, but with the added caveat that you must find a location that can be seen by both of your sites. Topographic maps are essential in this task, as are multiple helpers with cell phones, balloons, and telescopes.

Keep in mind that your intermediate location must have at least power, and ideally, some sort of enclosure where you can put the necessary pair of wireless Ethernet bridges (one for each of the two intermediate antennas and connected by a short Ethernet cable).

Put bluntly, creating a two-hop network is by no means impossible, but it's definitely difficult, expensive, and time-consuming. If the alternative is a high-speed digital connection from the telephone company that costs thousands of dollars per month, the effort of putting in a two-hop network may be worthwhile, but it may also be worth hiring professionals to do the work.

Troubleshooting

In the several years that Adam has run his long-range wireless Internet connection, it's had trouble only a few times. However, if you don't have a great deal of experience with wireless networking, this section should help you figure out what's going wrong and get help.

The first hint that your wireless network is having trouble generally comes when you discover your Internet connection is down. Since there could be numerous reasons that an Internet connection fails that aren't related to the wireless aspect of the network, you must eliminate those Internet-specific variables as well.

 TIP

If you're trying to minimize downtime as much as possible, and you're willing to jump into action as soon as a problem occurs, you can install monitoring

software that continually attempts to connect to a computer on the far side of your Internet connection, warning you in a variety of ways if the connection fails. You can often write a basic form of such software yourself using a standard ping utility, or you can buy powerful software that can check a variety of Internet services. In Windows, check out MonitorMagic from Tools4ever (www.tools4ever.com/products/monitormagic/) or Ipswitch's WhatsUp Gold (www.ipswitch.com/Products/WhatsUp/); on the Mac, the main contenders are Maxum Development's PageSentry (www.maxum.com/ PageSentry/) and James Sentman's Whistle Blower (http://whistleblower. sentman.com/).

Here's what Adam does every time he notices a problem with his long-range Internet connection.

First, he checks the PowerBook he uses to connect to his WISP to make sure it's running and is connected to the WISP's network wirelessly. He also checks to make sure the signal strength is within normal bounds. If anything seems out of the ordinary, he restarts the PowerBook to make sure it isn't the source of the problem (where the problem could be either wireless or TCP/IP). If you were using a wireless bridge like a Linksys WET11 or WET54G, a quick reset would be even easier, and equally as worth doing.

If the PowerBook reports that the wireless connection is either down or not operating at normal signal strength, Adam next checks his antenna and cabling. The cabling has never been a problem since it travels only a relatively short distance, but his antenna bracket allows a small range of motion, and on a couple of occasions, the antenna has been turned from the ideal spot. The more likely it is that something has happened to the antenna or its cable (rain seeping into an antenna connector, a bird knocking the antenna out of alignment, an animal gnawing on your antenna cable), the more carefully you should check your setup when problems occur.

 TIP

For the ultimate in testing a long-range wireless Internet connection, you could try reversing your network so a laptop placed somewhere in front of your antenna could connect to your network (rather than your network connecting to the WISP). This would involve setting up an ad hoc wireless network from whatever you're using as a wireless bridge, or connecting a normal access point to your antenna. It's probably too much work in most cases, but might be helpful in certain situations.

The next part may be difficult. Assuming there are other wireless clients connecting to the same central access point, it's good to find out if those clients are also having trouble. In Adam's case, because he's connecting to a WISP's point-to-multipoint wireless network, he can use a variety of methods of determining if other clients are having trouble with the same point. His WISP publishes a public Web page showing connection information for its wireless links; Adam can use a ping utility to check other wireless clients via his secondary cable modem Internet connection; and lastly, his WISP gave him access to the central access point's management software, so Adam can log in to that via his secondary Internet connection and see if anyone else is having trouble.

In most cases, you probably won't have such flexibility, but you should still think about how you can check to make sure you're not the only person having trouble. If you've set up your own multiple-site extended wireless network, that should be easy, since you can simply visit each remote site and test from there. But if you have a long-range wireless Internet connection with no backup, your only chance at this point may be to call the WISP and ask if others are also experiencing wireless connection problems.

 TIP

We always recommend having some kind of dial-up connection for backup, because otherwise you can wind up disconnected without any alternatives. Many wireless ISPs offer a few hours of free access each month for this purpose.

Contacting the WISP is usually the last thing you do, since it's entirely likely that the problem lies with the central access point or its antenna. For instance, after a horrible ice storm, Adam's long-range wireless connection went offline for a while because water seeped into the antenna cable, and the guys who fixed that sort of thing weren't able to climb the antenna until the ice melted.

 TIP

Make sure you know who to contact at your WISP if something goes wrong. If your WISP primarily offers normal wired Internet connections, it's likely that only a few people within the company will be able to help if your connection goes down.

We hope we haven't sounded alarmist here. A well-engineered long-range wireless network can operate flawlessly for months at a time with no attention whatsoever. Although he hasn't kept detailed records, Adam's impression is that his long-range wireless connection is more robust than his cable modem connection.

Long-Range Antenna Basics

The main piece of hardware that sets a normal home or office wireless network apart from a long-range wireless network is an antenna. All wireless network adapters and access points have antennas built in, but for the most part they're designed for small size rather than for maximum signal strength boost. Most PC Card wireless network adapters cram the entire antenna into the 1-by-2–inch part that juts out from the laptop when the card is plugged in.

((•)) **NOTE**

To be clear, antennas don't actually amplify the signal (that's what amplifiers are for!), they merely concentrate it in specific directions. If you've ever used a flashlight like Mag Instrument's Maglite, which provides a focusing ring for the beam, you can visualize what an antenna does with radio waves. The narrower the beam, the brighter the light in the covered area, even though the flashlight bulb isn't actually producing any more light. And of course, the narrower the beam, the harder it is to aim accurately at a distant target.

For long-range wireless networking, though, built-in antennas will never be sufficient, and you must look to larger external antennas that can be added to some, but not all, wireless network clients. Luckily, thanks to the rise of community wireless networking, it has become significantly easier and cheaper to buy an external antenna. To find a good antenna vendor after reading our discussion of antennas below, visit a community networking site like http://nocat.net and check out the vendors it recommends.

Long-Range Antenna Types

Most old televisions came with rabbit ear antennas that worked acceptably for many people, but those who wanted better television reception would install a large rooftop antenna to pull weak signals. Similarly, you can use a variety of different antenna types when you're setting up a long-range wireless network. Which one you choose depends on two factors:

- Is your network a point-to-point network, where you'd want a highly directional antenna with a narrow beam, or are you creating a point-to-multipoint network where you need to cover a large area with a sector or omnidirectional antenna?

- How much decibel (dB) gain do you need for your connection to work acceptably? Read "Calculating Signal Strength" in this chapter to determine the necessary gain while still staying within the FCC's (Federal Communications Commission) legal limits, and see "Staying Legal" below for more details on the legal restrictions.

((•)) **NOTE**

dB stands for decibels, the unit used for measuring antenna gain, and dBm means decibels relative to a reference level of 1 milliwatt (mW). Roughly speaking, 1 mW equals 0 dBm, and for every doubling of the milliwatts, you add 3 to the dBm. The maximum emitted radiation (called EIRP) from an

Health Concerns

Are there any health concerns related to long-range wireless networking? Yes and no. In most situations, the amount of power involved is far below the amount of radiation emitted by a cell phone, and studies have found no conclusive links between cell phone usage and cancer, even though the cell phone often touches the body.

As we show farther on, the strength of signals transmitted to your antenna is extremely weak, and of course, the fact that you have an antenna doesn't mean you receive any more radio waves than anyone else in your area. We're all constantly bombarded by low-power electro-

magnetic radiation. Further, the intensity of transmitted signals drops enormously when you move just a short distance from an antenna.

That said, if you set up a long-range wireless link that's on the higher end of the allowable power spectrum, exercise some common sense about where you position it so no one spends much time within a few feet of the front of a directional, high-gain antenna.

You can read more about the issues related to electromagnetic fields and health at www.fcc.gov/oet/rfsafety/ and www.fda.gov/cellphones/qa.html#3a.

antenna—which can wind up being much more than the input wattage—that the FCC allows in the U.S. is 1 watt, which is equivalent to 30 dBm. In Europe, it's only 250 mW, or 24 dBm. HyperLink Technologies offers a dBm-to-watts conversion chart at www.hyperlinktech.com/web/dbm.html, and Tim Pozar's white papers at www.lns.com/papers/part15/ explain the restriction in more detail. You'll also see the term dBi, which is decibels relative to an isotropic radiator, or a single point antenna that radiates equally in all directions.

TIP

With some antennas, such as parabolic and panel antennas, it's important to mount them in the proper orientation to match the polarization from the remote antenna. If you're not sure of the appropriate polarization, ask your ISP, and when in doubt, guess at vertical.

Let's look at the different types of antennas that are appropriate for long-range installations. If you're installing an antenna to extend the range of an indoor wireless network, see Chapter 21, *Indoor Antenna Basics*.

Radiation Patterns

All antennas radiate more in some directions than others, and it's important to use the appropriate type of antenna for your intended use. But how can you determine any given antenna's radiation pattern? Antennas radiate in three dimensions, which can be difficult to represent on paper. Many antenna vendors use a modified logarithmic plot to indicate where the antenna concentrates radiation. The graph is circular, with 0° being directly in front of the antenna, and 180° being directly behind it. The concentric circles inside the outer ring mark different gain levels. The closer a plot is to the outer ring, the higher the gain in that direction.

For instance, in **Figure 34.1** (left), which shows the radiation pattern for an omnidirectional antenna, you can see that the antenna radiates most strongly at both 0° and 180°, dropping off at other angles. **Figure 34.1** (right) shows the plot for a highly directional parabolic antenna. It radiates strongly in a narrow beam around 0°, but hardly at all in any other directions.

For more information on how to read radiation patterns, see Joseph Reisert's discussion at `www.astronantennas.com/radiation_pat` `terns.html`.

Figure 34.1
Radiation pattern plot for an omnidirectional (left) and parabolic antenna.

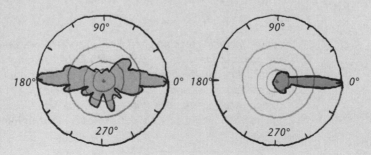

Omnidirectional Antennas

As you can imagine from the name, an omnidirectional antenna—sometimes called a vertical whip antenna—is primarily useful in a location where you want the signal to radiate from the antenna in all directions. That's not quite accurate, because an omnidirectional antenna is usually shaped like a vertical stick, so the signal radiates out to the sides in a circle, but doesn't go up or down much (**Figure 34.2**).

Figure 34.2
An omnidirectional antenna.

For the most part, you use an omnidirectional antenna to create a point-to-multipoint connection—that is, when you want many connections made to your omnidirectional antenna. ISPs often use omnidirectional antennas on their towers to avoid installing a focused-beam antenna for each customer. Another good use for an omnidirectional antenna would be to provide wireless network access for a school or a college campus. Omnidirectional antennas work best in relatively short-range situations where everyone connecting is at roughly the same elevation as the antenna (since the beam doesn't radiate vertically much). Because they don't focus the beam much, omnidirectional antennas max out at about 15 dBi of gain. They're also cheap, easy to install, and durable.

 TIP

If you're mounting an omnidirectional antenna (or any other type of external antenna) outside where it could be struck by lightning, you'd be smart to install a lightning suppressor to protect your access point in the event of a strike. Adam chose not to add lightning suppression to his system because his parabolic antenna is mounted on the wall of his house, under the eaves. Adding a lightning suppressor decreases signal strength slightly.

Sector Antennas

Like omnidirectional antennas, sector antennas are used in point-to-multipoint situations. Unlike omnidirectional antennas, however, sector antennas radiate only in a specific direction, and they're often combined to cover an area. Vendors of sector antennas always describe the spread of the antenna's coverage, usually between 60 degrees and 180 degrees.

The advantage of using multiple sector antennas over an omnidirectional antenna is that you can tilt the sector antennas down to work around the elevation problem that omnidirectional antennas face. They also offer higher gains—as much as 22 dBi. Sector antennas tend to look like thin boxes (**Figure 34.3**).

Figure 34.3
A sector antenna.

Sector antennas cost much more than omnidirectional antennas and since you may need several of them to cover a full 360 degrees, the cost increases even more. They're worth investigating mainly for specific locations where an omnidirectional antenna won't work well.

Panel or Patch Antennas

Panel antennas, sometimes also called patch antennas, are solid flat panels used for focused point-to-point connections, much like yagi and parabolic antennas, which we discuss next. Panel antennas are inexpensive, feature good gain of up to 14 dBi, and can blend in better with their surroundings than large parabolic grid or dish antennas. They don't look like much—just small flat boxes (**Figure 34.4**).

Figure 34.4
A panel antenna.

On the downside, because panel antennas must be pointed at the remote antenna, they often can't be mounted flat on a wall. And if they can't be mounted flat on a wall, strong winds may move them or damage them.

Yagi Antennas

If omnidirectional antennas are easily visualized from their name, yagi antennas are just the opposite. From the outside, a yagi antenna looks like a thick plastic tube, and on the inside, it has a series of metal circles or bars that drop in size as they near the end of the antenna (**Figure 34.5**). A yagi antenna provides a fairly focused beam, along with at most about 21 dBi of gain, with 15 dBi being common. Because of the focused beam, you mount a yagi antenna pointing at the remote location.

Figure 34.5
A yagi antenna.

Yagi antennas are popular because they provide decent gain in a small and unobtrusive package. If you're mounting a yagi on your house, there's little need to worry about paranoid neighbors assuming you're spying on them. Although they're not quite as unobtrusive as panel antennas, yagi antennas suffer much less from the force of the wind (although snow and ice buildup in the winter can interfere with the signal).

Parabolic Antennas

A parabolic antenna is the most powerful you can buy, and it generally looks either like a curved wire grid or like a small satellite dish (**Figure 34.6**). The longer the distance you want to cover, the more likely you are to need a parabolic antenna. With a parabolic antenna, you can enjoy a focused beam and up to 27 dBi of gain. The main downside of parabolic antennas is that they can be big—Adam's 24 dBi parabolic antenna is 2-feet by 3-feet, and 27 dBi antennas are about 6 feet in diameter. Luckily, Adam's wife Tonya thinks a large, white antenna mounted on the side of her house looks pretty slick. The fact that it brings in better Internet connectivity is also a huge plus. Some other spouses may not be so understanding.

Parabolic antennas are quite affordable and those having a grid don't suffer much from either wind load or snow buildup, making them the most appropriate for more extreme situations where high-gain is necessary.

Figure 34.6
Parabolic antennas.

 TIP

If you're unconcerned about the look of your antenna and you don't want to mess around, a high-gain parabolic antenna is probably the safest type to buy.

Dipole Antennas

Although small dipole antennas are not useful for long-range networking (because they have a gain of only about 2.2 dB), they're often built onto access points to increase range indoors (**Figure 34.7**). The main utility of an access point with removable (not all are) dipole antennas is that it's much more likely that you'll be able to add a more powerful external antenna. Life is easier if you don't have to drill holes in your access point or solder connections between your access point and external antenna. See Chapter 21, *Indoor Antenna Basics*, for more on dipole antennas.

((•)) **NOTE**

Dipole antennas are essentially the same as the rabbit ear antennas used for television reception years ago, except dipole antennas used on wireless networking gear are much smaller. They are smaller because 802.11b uses frequencies in the 2.4 GHz (or 2400 MHz) part of the radio spectrum, whereas television uses frequencies in the 100 MHz part of the spectrum. As the frequency increases, the size of the wavelength decreases, and thus the antenna size can also decrease.

Figure 34.7
Dipole antennas.

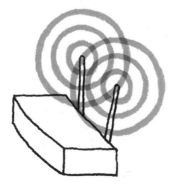

Building Your Own Antenna

No book that talks about long-range wireless networking would be complete without mentioning that, yes, you can actually build an antenna for almost no money at all. The most popular type of antenna to build is the so-called "Pringles can" antenna, which is a yagi type.

TIP

Although the Pringles potato chip can has proven popular for homebrew antennas, people have had better results from other types of cans, with a Nalley's Big Chunk Beef Stew can taking the prize in Greg Rehm's comparison at www.turnpoint.net/wireless/cantennahowto.htm.

Why build your own antenna? Entertainment value ranks high on the list, and although antennas aren't that expensive, building your own from various bits and pieces costs less than buying one.

However, there are also good reasons to buy instead of build. Your self-built antenna is likely to be somewhat random—it could have a higher or lower gain than would be ideal for your situation. If the gain is much higher than expected, it could put you in violation of FCC regulations. It's also likely to spew radio waves in unanticipated directions or on illegal frequencies, which may cause problems for other people in the vicinity. And, of course, decorating with an old can is even less likely to pass spouse muster than a commercial antenna.

For more information about building your own antenna, search on Google or visit Rob Flickenger's explanation of how he built a Pringles can yagi antenna at www.oreillynet.com/pub/wlg/448 (**Figure 34.8**).

NOTE

Rob is also the author of two books: Building Wireless Community Networks, *which is a must read if you're thinking about connecting with your neighbors to make a community network; and* Wireless Hacks, *which is packed full of great ideas for those trying to put together inexpensive hardware and software to great effect.*

Figure 34.8
Rob Flickenger's
Pringles can
antenna.

Antenna Cable & Connectors

For those of us whose experience lies in the world of computers, dealing with antenna cables is a royal pain, because we can use little of our computer-based knowledge. Antenna connections often require multiple, unfamiliar cable types, and in many cases, each cable has a different connector. Cables are often thick and hard to work with (or in the case of pigtails, thin and fragile), and cable length always matters because the longer the cable, the more signal you lose, as we discuss later.

TIP

Our advice? Don't try to build cables yourself unless you're already extremely good at it (or are willing to devote large amounts of time and wire to learning), and try to buy all your cables from the same vendor. Instead of ordering over the Internet, call the vendor and talk to someone to make sure all the pieces you want are appropriate and will connect with one another.

Pigtails

To connect your access point or wireless network adapter to an external antenna, you need a pigtail, which is simply a short piece of thin, flexible wire with appropriate connectors on both ends (**Figure 34.9**). Pigtails exist for three reasons. First, pigtails solve a sizing problem—some wireless network cards have an antenna jack that is extremely small (perhaps a quarter of the diameter of a standard pencil, for instance), making it impossible to connect a much-wider antenna cable (sized at about twice the thickness of a pencil). Second, pigtails can bend—since antenna cable is typically thick and inflexible, the flexibility of a pigtail simplifies making a connection to the thick antenna cable. Third, pigtails can make it easier to work with a variety of equipment with different types of connectors.

As much as pigtails are essential, they have several annoying attributes. They tend to be fairly expensive, ranging from $20 to $60 or more. The price is high

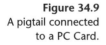

Figure 34.9
A pigtail connected to a PC Card.

in part because the market has no alternative, but also because a good pigtail uses high-quality wire and connectors, and is built carefully. That's important because thin wire doesn't transmit signal well and because every connector you add to an antenna system causes signal loss. Since your goal is always to avoid signal loss, it's worth paying more for a high-quality pigtail.

 TIP

> *To reduce signal loss, buy as short a pigtail as seems reasonable for your installation, generally between 6 and 15 inches.*

The final annoyance with pigtails is that, in order to discourage people from using potentially infringing antennas, FCC regulations require that every manufacturer use a different connector type. Proxim equipment is different from Linksys equipment, for instance, so be careful to order a pigtail that's compatible with your hardware.

Pigtails used to be difficult to find and even more expensive, but the rise of community networking has increased the interest, and thus the supply. For additional information on pigtails, including links to vendors, visit the Seattle Wireless Pigtails page at www.seattlewireless.net/index.cgi/PigTail.

Cable

Although the thin wire used in pigtails is flexible and easy to work with, the signal loss through such thin wire is problematic. As a result, the cable for longer runs from your antenna should be significantly thicker than a pigtail.

You can buy a variety of different gauges of cable that work with external antennas, so the trick is to determine how much money you want to spend in relation to how concerned you are about signal loss. The awkward part of this tradeoff is that the longer your cable needs to be, the more you should worry about signal loss, so your cost increases because of needing more cable and needing a larger gauge cable.

 TIP

> *Measure carefully with string to determine exactly how much cable you need before ordering antenna cable, since there's a downside (extra signal loss) to having more cable than you need.*

The most commonly used type of cable seems to be LMR400, where 400 indicates the gauge of the wire. It provides a good combination of relatively low price, low signal loss, and decent flexibility for ease of installation. Most, if not all, antenna cable is designed to be installed outdoors, so it can withstand the ultraviolet light in sunshine that breaks down the plastic coverings of cables designed for indoor usage. You can also buy antenna cable that's rated for "direct burial," meaning that you can dig a trench in the ground and plop the cable right in without running it through a conduit.

TIP

As with other parts of a long-range wireless system, we recommend researching what you need online and then calling the vendor you've chosen in order to place the order. Ask the salesperson if the pieces you're ordering make sense for your desired use and if they'll all work together. Another reason to ask for help is that some vendors have their own names or descriptions for some parts. For instance, LMR400 cable may go by a proprietary name like Commscope WBC-400—the only way you can be sure it's what you need is by asking.

As with pigtails, finding appropriate cable has become significantly easier than in the past, and most companies that sell antennas and pigtails also sell cable.

Connectors

Even more confusing than pigtails and antenna cable for those of us from the computer world are the many different types of connectors you may see attached to the ends of these cables. We don't discuss every possible type of connector out there; instead we'll focus on the types that you're most likely to use.

TIP

Don't rely on visual comparisons between connectors, as some connectors look identical when, in fact, they have reversed gender or reversed threads. Always verify the cables you're buying have connectors that work with one another.

- N connectors are large, threaded connectors commonly used for connecting antenna cable (particularly LMR400 or larger) to antennas and to pigtails. They have fairly low signal loss and make extremely secure connections, but are simply too large for some smaller cable types.

- TNC connectors are similar to the BNC connectors used for 10Base-2 Ethernet cables (see Appendix A, *Networking Basics,* for a discussion of 10Base-2 and BNC connectors), but with the addition of threads for more secure connections. Signal loss is acceptable, though higher than with N connectors. They're also smaller than N connectors.

- SMA connectors are small, threaded connectors commonly used for cables smaller than LMR400. Less common variants include SMB, which is just a push-on type, rather than a threaded connector, and SMC, which is even smaller.

Visit http://nocat.net/connectors.html for more information on these and other connectors and pictures of the different connectors.

$((\bullet))$ **NOTE**

The N connector and the BNC connector on which the TNC connector is based were both designed during World War II for military applications.

Wireless Accessories

Additional devices that you might want to add to a long-range wireless network setup include an amplifier and a lightning protector.

Amplifiers

As you'll see in "Calculating Signal Strength" in this chapter, the hardest part of setting up a wireless network is making sure you have enough signal strength to transmit a signal to the other side of the network. So why not use an amplifier to add some extra power to the equation? Amplifiers face a number of problems.

- You can add a transmit amplifier to a system to increase the transmitter's power output. However, you will likely need another transmit amplifier on the other end of the network as well, or you risk creating a situation where the other end can hear your amplified signal, but your side can't hear the remote signal.

- It's possible to add a receive "pre-amplifier" to amplify a weak incoming signal, but doing so also adds noise, which is likely to be counter-productive. You may see "bi-directional" amplifiers that combine a transmit amplifier with a receive pre-amplifier.

- Amplifiers require electrical power, which may be difficult to run to the appropriate place in your antenna setup, although there are systems that can run power over the antenna cable itself, eliminating the need for a separate power cable.

- Adding an amplifier to a system inherently means adding at least one connector, which increases signal loss slightly.

Solving these problems is possible, but requires money. As a result, amplifiers aren't cheap. Worse, because amplifiers could easily send you over the FCC's power restrictions, many suppliers won't sell to consumers. For instance, HyperLink Technologies (www.hyperlinktech.com/web/amplifiers.html) offers its amplifiers only for military or international sales, although the company does sell amplified antenna kits that bundle an amplifier with an antenna; adding the amplifier to the kit adds hundreds of dollars to the price. On the upside, many amplifiers do include built-in lightning protection.

For the most part, we don't recommend amplifiers, since you're better off spending your money on a good antenna with low-loss cable and connectors.

Lightning Protectors

As your mother taught you, standing up in a high place during a lightning storm is a really bad idea. But in many cases, that's exactly where you've installed your antenna, which is just asking for trouble, particularly since the cables connected to the antenna could bring any lightning strikes inside your house or office, where they could be deadly.

 NOTE

We're not kidding about the danger here, so to be clear, it's up to you, and only you, to make sure that your installation is safe. We can't be responsible for any damage or injury that may occur if your antenna is struck by lightning.

You can buy relatively inexpensive lightning protectors that attach to your antenna cable and shunt the energy from the lightning strike off to a grounding rod. Honestly, we have little experience with these devices, so we can't say for sure how well they'll work for protecting your equipment in the event of a strike. A slight downside to a lightning protector is that it causes about 0.4 dB of signal loss.

TIP

Make sure you buy a lightning protector with appropriate connectors for your cable.

Nonetheless, since lightning is so incredibly powerful and unpredictable, we recommend adding a lightning protector to your system. They cost between $30 and $100 and are available from the usual suppliers, companies like HyperLink Technologies (www.hyperlinktech.com/web/lightning_protectors.php) and YDI Wireless (www.ydi.com/products/cables-accessories.php).

Proper installation of lightning protection is extremely important, so if you're at all unsure of your abilities, look for a professional installer who will know the best materials to use for the grounding rod, the strap that connects the lightning protector to the grounding rod, and even for the soil that will dissipate the strike.

Calculating Signal Strength

The hardest part of planning a long-range wireless network connection is determining the amount of *gain*, or signal strength improvement, you need from an antenna in order to send and receive signals with the remote location. It's tricky because you must consider a number of variables, some of which aren't easy to determine without already being an antenna expert. Let's walk through a calculation using Adam's long-range wireless Internet connection as an example.

 NOTE

A disclaimer up front here: Both of us are computer geeks, not radio geeks, and we assume that most of you are more familiar with computers than ham radios as well. So our explanations are based on our experience, research, and goal of explaining the topic without delving into the complex physics and math that explain exactly what goes on with a long-range wireless connection.

NOTE

You must run this calculation in both directions because although antennas improve signal strength for both transmitting and receiving, not all radios are as good at receiving data as sending it.

TIP

You can find calculators on the Web that perform this calculation for you, but our experience is that many of them ask for way more information than you could possibly determine, making them far more accurate than our discussion below, but almost entirely useless without all the particulars in hand. See the calculator from Green Bay Professional Packet Radio at http://my.athenet.net/~multiplx/cgi-bin/wireless.main.cgi *for an example of what we mean.*

Transmit Power

The first number to find is the transmit power of the radio transceiver in the device you want to connect to your antenna. Luckily, manufacturers almost always publish that number in the device's technical specifications, so it's easy to find. Adam powers his wireless connection using a Lucent WaveLAN PC Card (cannibalized from an AirPort Base Station) plugged into an Apple PowerBook G3 (**Figure 34.10**). Brief perusal of the AirPort Base Station technical specifications in Apple's online Knowledge Base reveals that it has a transmit power of 15 dBm. Another search on Google (www.google.com) on "Lucent WaveLAN transmit power dBm" found a number of other sources that confirmed the 15 dBm rating.

You must also find out the transmit power of the remote radio, which you can determine either by checking the technical specifications for the hardware, if you know exactly what it is, or by asking your WISP. In Adam's case, his WISP, Lightlink, uses a Cisco AP340, and a quick search reveals that it has a transmit power of 15 dBm as well. If you can't determine this number, guess at 15 dBm, since it's equivalent to a 30 mW transmitter, which is common.

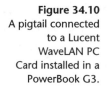

Figure 34.10
A pigtail connected to a Lucent WaveLAN PC Card installed in a PowerBook G3.

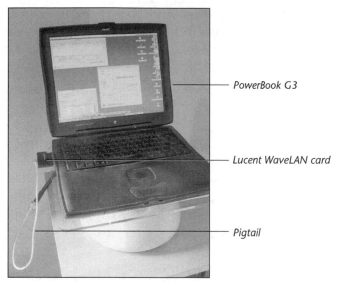

PowerBook G3

Lucent WaveLAN card

Pigtail

It is possible to buy 100 mW and even 250 mW transmitters, but they're less common and more likely to push closer to violating the FCC regulations once you add the antenna.

Signal Loss in Cable

To connect an antenna to a wireless network adapter, you need a *pigtail*, which is a short, thin cable whose purpose is to connect the small jack on your network adapter to the thick coaxial cable from the antenna.

Signal is lost in all cables, and the thinner the cable, the more the signal loss. Since pigtails are always thin, they tend to have a fairly high signal loss; we've seen estimates of 0.4 dB or more per foot. Cable quality can make a huge difference though, so the loss could be higher or lower, depending on the pigtail you buy. The manufacturer may tell you what the signal loss of your pigtail is, but if not, just guess. To be conservative, let's assume that Adam's 15-inch pigtail loses about 1 dB.

Another source of signal loss comes from connectors, so you want to reduce the number of connectors as much as possible. Again, we've seen estimates of between 0.25 dB and 1 dB of loss per connector. Typically, cheap connectors are likely to lose more signal than more expensive connectors. Since Adam has three connectors in his setup—one from the Lucent WaveLAN card to the pigtail, one from the pigtail to the antenna cable, and one from the antenna cable to the antenna—let's assume 3 dB of loss there to be conservative.

The final part of the cable equation comes with the run from the pigtail to the antenna. Cable signal loss varies significantly with the type of cable you buy, but it's something that the manufacturer will either publish or be able to tell you. Adam used 15 feet of LMR400 cable, which loses 6.8 dB per 100 feet, so a quick calculation shows that he loses about 1 dB of signal strength in the cable run.

Add those numbers up—1 dB for the pigtail, 3 dB for the connectors, and 1 dB for the thick antenna cable—and you get a total of 5 dB of signal-strength loss due to the necessary cabling.

Calculating the cable signal loss for the remote side is likely to be a total guess, unfortunately, since only the person who actually installed the equipment is likely to know what types of pigtail and cable were used, and how many connectors were used. If you can't find out easily, guess at 5 dB.

Antenna Gain

The main boost in the system comes from the antenna itself, of course, and it's easy to determine the gain of an antenna because it's one of the two main variables (along with type) that you see when shopping for antennas. As with the other numbers in this calculation, antenna gain is measured in decibels, expressed in this case as dBi, or decibels relative to what's called an "isotropic" antenna.

Some explanation is warranted here. Antennas are useful because they shape the radio signal and focus it in a specific direction. The worst imaginable long-distance antenna would radiate the signal in a perfect sphere, with the antenna a point at the center—that's an isotropic radiator. The design of an antenna enables it to shape and focus the signal in the desired direction, increasing the signal strength in that direction by reducing it in other directions. We discussed different antenna designs earlier; just keep in mind that the design of an antenna directly affects how much it can increase signal strength.

In Adam's case, he first bought a 14 dBi yagi antenna, but when that didn't work, he exchanged it for a 24 dBi parabolic antenna that works perfectly (**Figure 34.11**).

Keep in mind that the other side of the connection also has an antenna, and you must add that into the equation as well—the only way to learn that piece of information is to ask. Adam's WISP's antenna is a 14 dBi omnidirectional.

Free-Space Loss

The easiest part of the signal strength equation to understand, if not to calculate, is the loss of the signal as it travels through the air from your antenna to the

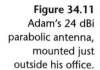

Figure 34.11
Adam's 24 dBi
parabolic antenna,
mounted just
outside his office.

remote antenna. No one has trouble agreeing that the greater the distance between a transmitter and a receiver, the weaker the signal. The reasons for signal loss in free space are that the signal spreads out in a way that's proportional to the square of the distance traveled and some of the energy in the signal is absorbed as it passes through the air, particularly by water droplets on a rainy day.

 NOTE

The Maine WISP Glenn talked to said that the frequent, falling snow in Maine appears to improve signal quality, and Adam once found that his iBook could pick up the remote signal using only its internal antenna during a snow storm. The moral of the story is that precipitation affects signal strength in unpredictable ways, thanks to the reflections of the signal off individual drops of water or flakes of snow.

You can use an online calculator to determine free-space loss (the one at www.comsearch.com/satellite/tools_fsl.jsp is easy to use; others we saw were less so). Or, if it's not available, you can calculate the free-space loss with the following equation:

`-L = C + (20 x log(D)) + (20 x log(F))`

In this equation, -L is the signal loss, C is a constant that's either 36.6 if you measure the distance D in miles or 32.5 if you measure D in kilometers, and F is the frequency in megahertz (2400 MHz for standard 802.11b).

TIP

Don't feel intimidated by all the letters and logarithms in the equation—the equation is easy to solve if you have a calculator or spreadsheet that can calculate the logarithms. However, be careful to multiply the parts inside the parentheses before you add everything together.

The only thing you must determine to solve this equation, then, is the distance between your antenna and the remote antenna. You could get fancy and use a

GPS device to determine your location and the location of the remote antenna, but accuracy isn't that important because using the logarithm of the distance minimizes the effect of the distance on the overall equation.

Adam's house is about 2 miles away from the remote antenna, so the equation for his connection looks like this:

```
-L = 36.6 + (20 x log(2)) + (20 x log(2400))
```

Running the logarithms through a calculator (type the number, then press the log button) gives us this:

```
-L = 36.6 + (20 x .301) + (20 x 3.38)
```

And, solving the multiplication inside the parentheses turns it into:

```
-L = 36.6 + (6.02) + (67.60)
```

Finally, we are left with a simple bit of addition:

```
-L = 110.22 dB
```

So, the distance between Adam's antenna and the remote antenna accounts for about 110 dB of signal loss.

$(((\bullet)))$ **NOTE**

Remember when we said that extreme accuracy in the distance doesn't make all that much difference? If Adam's house were 3 miles away from the remote antenna, the amount of signal loss would increase only to 113 dB. It's not an insignificant jump, but you need more than 3 dB of leeway for a workable connection anyway.

Receive Sensitivity

The above calculation determines the strength of the signal when it arrives, but there's one more detail you must determine before you can tell if your connection is likely to work—the receive sensitivity of both radios. *Receive sensitivity* is a measure of how weak a signal can be at a particular speed before the receiving radio can't decode it. Like transmit power, it's measured in dBm, but the numbers are very small, often around -85 dBm, and the lower the number, the better the receive sensitivity.

For your side, look in the technical specifications of your wireless card or access point. Some wireless networking gear manufacturers include receive sensitivity in their technical specifications, but others omit it. You can also find receive sensitivity numbers for many common networking devices at http://freenetworks.org/moin/index.cgi/ReceiveSensitivity.

Unless you install both ends of the connection, the only way you can determine receive sensitivity for the remote side is to ask your ISP or search for information about the equipment your ISP uses. If you can't find the receive sensitivity numbers, guess at between -75 and -95 dBm.

In Adam's case, searching in Google on "Lucent WaveLAN receive sensitivity dBm" brought up some pages that showed his card has -94 dBm receive sensitivity at 1 Mbps. Another search on "Cisco AP340 receive sensitivity" revealed that the remote radio has a receive sensitivity of -90 dBm at 1 Mbps.

Putting It All Together

Now it's time to put everything together, adding the numbers that represent signal strength and subtracting the numbers that represent signal loss. (There's a nice online calculator at www.retro-city.co.uk/bovistech/wireless/calcs.htm that does these sums for you.) Remember that we must calculate this in both directions: sending information to the remote location and receiving from the remote location. For Adam's long-range connection, we sum the following when sending data out to the WISP (**Table 34.1**).

 TIP

This calculation also includes a margin of 15 dB to account for changes in the weather. If your wireless connection is on the edge of having sufficient signal strength in good weather, a rainstorm or snowstorm may cause it to drop entirely. That's the theory anyway; in the real world, Adam has never seen weather affect the reported signal strength of his network by more than 2 dB.

Since the receive sensitivity of the remote side is -90 dBm, the calculation shows Adam should have 8 dBm of signal strength overhead in the worst weather (the 8 dBm is the difference between the -90 dBm receive sensitivity and the -82 dBm

Table 34.1

Calculating Sending Signal Strength at the Remote Location

Variable	*Gain or Loss*
Local transmit power	+15 dBm
Local cable loss	-5 dB
Local antenna gain	+24 dBi
Free-space loss	-110 dB
Remote antenna gain	+14 dBi
Remote cable loss	-5 dB
Margin for weather	-15 dB
Signal strength at remote location	**-82 dBm**

signal strength we calculate in **Table 34.1**). In good weather, we end up with 23 dBm (that's 8 dBm plus the 15 dBm we kept as a margin for bad weather). If you consider that the transmit power of most wireless networking gear is between 15 and 20 dBm and works fine in short-range situations, being able to send between 8 dBm and 23 dBm to the remote location should work fine.

Now let's run the calculation in reverse, to see how strong a signal Adam receives from his WISP (**Table 34.2**).

Table 34.2

Calculating Receive Signal Strength at the Local Location

Variable	Gain or Loss
Remote transmit power	+15 dBm
Remote cable loss	-5 dB
Remote antenna gain	+14 dBi
Free-space loss	-110 dB
Local antenna gain	+24 dBi
Local cable loss	-5 dB
Margin for weather	-15 dB
Signal strength at local location	**-82 dBm**

Since Adam's equipment has a receive sensitivity of -94 dBm at 1 Mbps, the calculated received signal strength of -82 dBm should be more than sufficient for communication, even in the worst weather, with 27 dBm available under normal conditions.

Changing Variables

In the example of Adam's connection above, we knew or could easily guess at all the numbers because it's an existing connection. But you should perform this calculation before you purchase equipment (and if he'd known then what he knows now, Adam would have done so as well).

Our advice, then, is to set up a simple spreadsheet that looks roughly like the previous tables. Enter all the numbers you can figure out for the remote side (assuming you're not setting up both sides yourself), and then include the free-space loss. Once you've done that, you can plug in values for the equipment you need to buy and see if it all works out.

Had Adam done this calculation before setting up his long-range wireless connection, he might have realized that the 14 dBi yagi antenna he initially bought wouldn't work well because his effective signal strength would have been only -2 dB in bad weather or 13 dB in good weather. Of course, this doesn't explain why the 14 dBi yagi failed to work at all in good weather, since there should have been sufficient signal strength for basic operation. The fact that it didn't work is evidence that the calculation described here is intentionally rough, and if you want to get serious, you must consider many additional variables. Web-based calculators can help you, or you can rely, as Adam did, on a certain amount of trial and error.

Staying Legal

There are legal restrictions on how much power you can transmit from any radio, including a wireless network. These restrictions vary widely by country, and in some countries, long-range wireless connections are completely illegal. If you live outside the U.S., we strongly encourage you to check your local statutes before assuming that you can set up a long-range wireless network.

In the U.S., restrictions on long-range wireless networking are set down by the Federal Communications Commission in what's generally called the "Part 15 Regulations." Part 15 specifies power limits, equipment limitations, certification requirements, and interference handling. You can read the entire Part 15 at www.access.gpo.gov/nara/cfr/waisidx_01/47cfr15_01.html.

For analysis of Part 15 and what it means for setting up long-range wireless connections, we recommend you read Tim Pozar's white papers on the topic, available at www.lns.com/papers/part15/. Though Tim is not a lawyer, he is a long-time broadcast engineer who consults on telecommunications issues, and he is also a founding member of the Bay Area Wireless Users Group (www.bawug.org), one of the pre-eminent wireless users groups in the world.

((•)) **NOTE**

It's up to you to ensure that your wireless network runs within legal power limits, so use what we say here as a guide. If you're truly worried, consult a lawyer familiar with telecommunications law. That said, the FCC isn't likely to come knocking on your door unless you're causing interference for other users and those people complain.

Even Tim's plain-talking discussion can be a bit dense to work through for folks who don't have the necessary deeper understanding of math, physics, and law that inform these principles. Fortunately, in discussions with reader Dr. A. Shiekh of Diné College, we've come up with the following simplifications that should help you determine if your planned installation will be within the FCC regulations.

NOTE

Remember that you must add the effect of any amplifiers to the total power output, but you can also subtract the signal loss due to cable and connectors.

Point-to-Multipoint

For point-to-multipoint 2.4 GHz wireless networks (where you're erecting a central omnidirectional antenna for many clients to connect to), the FCC allows your transmitter to put out up to 30 dBm (1 watt) with a 6 dBi antenna, for a total of 36 dBm (4 watts). If you want to use an antenna with more than 6 dBi of gain, you must reduce the total power output of the transmitter by 1 dB for every 1 dB of antenna gain over 6 dBi.

Since you must lower transmitter power by exactly the same amount as you increase antenna gain, the best approach is probably to pair your transmitter power and antenna gain to provide the maximum allowed power (assuming you need that much—it's always best to use as little power as possible to minimize chances of interference).

See **Table 34.3** for sample possibilities (remember that most wireless networking gear runs at the power outputs listed; consult **Table 34.4** or www.hyperlinktech.com/web/dbm.html if you need to convert a different wattage to dBm).

Point-to-Point

For point-to-point wireless networks (where you're pointing two directional antennas at each other), the FCC is more lenient, because directional antennas minimize interference for other users in the 2.4 GHz band. In a point-to-point network, your transmitter is still capped at 30 dBm (1 watt) with a 6 dBi

Table 34.3

Allowable Power Output/Antenna Gain Combinations in a Point-to-Multipoint Wireless Network

Total Power Output of the Transmitter	Allowable Antenna Gain	Maximum Effective Radiated Power
≤30 dBm (1 watt)	≤6 dBi	36 dBm
≤23 dBm (200 milliwatts)	≤13 dBi	36 dBm
≤20 dBm (100 milliwatts)	≤16 dBi	36 dBm
≤17 dBm (50 milliwatts)	≤19 dBi	36 dBm
≤15 dBm (32 milliwatts)	≤21 dBi	36 dBm

Table 34.4

Allowable Power Output/Antenna Gain Combinations in a 2.4 GHz Point-to-Point Wireless Network

Total Power Output of the Transmitter	Allowable Antenna Gain	Maximum Effective Radiated Power
≤30 dBm (1 watt)	≤6 dBi	36 dBm
≤29 dBm (800 milliwatts)	≤9 dBi	38 dBm
≤28 dBm (630 milliwatts)	≤12 dBi	40 dBm
≤27 dBm (500 milliwatts)	≤15 dBi	42 dBm
≤26 dBm (398 milliwatts)	≤18 dBi	44 dBm
≤25 dBm (316 milliwatts)	≤21 dBi	46 dBm
≤24 dBm (250 milliwatts)	≤24 dBi	48 dBm
≤23 dBm (200 milliwatts)	≤27 dBi	50 dBm
≤22 dBm (158 milliwatts)	≤30 dBi	52 dBm
≤21 dBm (126 milliwatts)	≤33 dBi	54 dBm
≤20 dBm (100 milliwatts)	≤36 dBi	56 dBm
≤19 dBm (79 milliwatts)	≤39 dBi	58 dBm
≤18 dBm (63 milliwatts)	≤42 dBi	60 dBm
≤17 dBm (50 milliwatts)	≤45 dBi	62 dBm
≤16 dBm (40 milliwatts)	≤48 dBi	64 dBm
≤15 dBm (32 milliwatts)	≤51 dBi	66 dBm
≤14 dBm (25 milliwatts)	≤54 dBi	68 dBm
≤13 dBm (20 milliwatts)	≤57 dBi	70 dBm

antenna for a total of 36 dBm (4 watts). However, if you want to use a higher gain antenna, you must reduce the total power output of the transmitter by 1 dB for every 3 dB of antenna gain over 6 dBi.

That means that using a lower power transmitter allows you to use a higher gain antenna that more than makes up for the transmitter power loss. See **Table 34.4** for a range of possibilities.

((•)) NOTE

You might wonder if both sides in a point-to-multipoint network are governed by the more restrictive point-to-multipoint limitations, or if the client side (which uses a directional antenna to talk with the central omnidirectional antenna) is governed instead by the less-restrictive point-to-point limitations. We wonder as well, and Tim Pozar tells us that as far as he's aware, the FCC hasn't made a ruling on this, meaning that it's still open for interpretation. We suspect that as long as your system doesn't cause interference for anyone else, it's not likely to become an issue.

Antenna Installation

When it comes time to install your antenna, you probably don't have all that many options, because there are so many constraints.

Line of Sight

The most important constraint on your antenna installation is that it must have a clear line of sight to the remote antenna. Although the radios used by wireless networking gear are quite sensitive, almost any obstruction—including tree leaves—will block the signal.

802.11a and 5 GHz Wireless Networks

All the discussion of FCC requirements relates primarily to 2.4 GHz wireless networks—802.11b and 802.11g. The FCC's rules are slightly different for wireless networks in the 5 GHz range, including both 802.11a and those using proprietary technologies.

The so-called "5 GHz band" is divided into three sections. The "low" band from 5.15 GHz to 5.25 GHz has a maximum power of 50 milliwatts and is meant to be used only indoors. The "middle" band runs from 5.25 GHz to 5.35 GHz, and has a maximum power limit of 250 milliwatts. Lastly, after a small gap, the "high" band spans 5.725 GHz to 5.825 GHz. The limitations of the 5 GHz band mimic those of 2.4 GHz wireless networks when used in point-to-multipoint networks (30 dBm transmission power with a 6 dBi antenna for a total of 36 dBm).

For point-to-point networks, the situation is a bit different. You can use only the high part of the 5 GHz band, and when you do, the FCC allows a transmitter power of 30 dBm (1 watt) with up to a 23 dBi antenna.

For antennas with gain over 23 dBi, you must reduce the power of the transmitter by 1 dB for each 1 dB of antenna gain, according to 15.407(a)(3) of the FCC regulations. Oddly, 15.247(b)(3)(ii) seems to contradict this, saying that you may use antennas of any gain for point-to-point networks.

Perhaps because of the need to use gear in only the "high" part of 5 GHz band, the equipment for 5 GHz long-range networking seems to be much more expensive. Also, according to Tim Pozar, 802.11a is more resilient to interference than 802.11b, but its higher frequency results in a higher free-space loss. Thus with the same transmitter power and antennas, 802.11a will have only about 18 percent of the signal strength of 802.11b.

Our impression is that 802.11a and 5 GHz long-range wireless networks are primarily for highly specific situations where expensive equipment and installation is worthwhile, rather than in general-purpose installations designed and built by consumers.

TIP

If you're setting up a long-range wireless connection in the winter or spring before the trees leaf out, make sure to take leaf coverage into account or you may find that your connection is seasonal.

In some cases, such as Adam's, it may be easy to determine line of sight because you can see the remote antenna tower with the naked eye (his ISP's antenna is mounted on the WVBR radio tower, which is easy to see). If you can't see the remote antenna, though, try viewing it with binoculars or a high-power telescope.

(((•))) **NOTE**

*Radio waves in the 2.4 and 5 GHz parts of the spectrum aren't focused like a laser beam. Instead, they spread out and occupy an elliptical area on either side of the straight line of sight. This area is called the Fresnel zone, and you actually need a clear shot in the Fresnel zone as well, so trees that don't block the visual line of sight can still interfere with your wireless connection (**Figure 34.12**). Visit* www.solectek.com/techlib/techpapers/techtalk/tt-howhard.html *for a full explanation of the Fresnel effect, and use the calculator at* http://gbppr. dyndns.org/fresnel.main.cgi *to see how much leeway you need to provide for radio line of sight.*

Figure 34.12
The Fresnel zone.

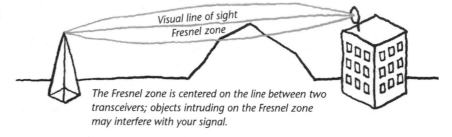

If you simply can't find the remote antenna visually, you may still be able to create a wireless network connection with it, but it's almost certain that you need a high-gain antenna. The only way to know for sure is to test.

In general, elevation helps you achieve radio line of sight, so try to find a location for your antenna that provides added height. Realistically, an antenna usually ends up mounted on a rooftop or even on an antenna mast that rises higher than the roofline of the building.

Cable Runs vs. Easy Access

As you now know, you want to minimize the length of a cable run in order to avoid losing signal strength. That desire has resulted in people figuring out how to place an access point right next to an antenna. The challenge here includes building a waterproof enclosure (try a sprinkler control enclosure from a hardware store), connecting the access point to the rest of your network via an Ethernet cable (or wireless bridge; see Chapter 20, *Bridging Wireless Networks*) and providing power to the access point, perhaps via a Power over Ethernet device (Power over Ethernet is abbreviated PoE and is also known as Active Ethernet).

 NOTE

Power over Ethernet works by running low voltages over unused pairs in standard Ethernet cable. You need an "injector" that puts DC voltage onto unused wires in the Ethernet cable, and unless your access point is already PoE-compatible, you also need a "picker" to deliver the power from the Ethernet cable to the access point. For more information, see www.hyperlinktech.com/ web/what_is_poe.html.

 TIP

Most standard Ethernet cable is not rated for outdoor use and will be broken down by ultraviolet light. Outdoor cable can be hard to find, but if you plan to run Ethernet cable outside, call electronics supply stores and ask for Ethernet cable that's rated for outdoor use or even direct burial.

Some community wireless networking groups have pulled back from trying to reduce cable runs at all costs. It turns out that putting the access point in a waterproof enclosure on a roof makes it significantly more difficult to access in case of trouble (like rebooting it if it crashes), and you don't want to climb a ladder every day to reset the access point in such a situation.

 TIP

Be careful on rooftops! It's all too easy to slip and fall, and it can be a long way down. Our colleague Rob Flickenger had a spill in early 2002, and his comment to Glenn at a conference later that year was, "There's a reason people have two kidneys." Rob recovered and is now a safety advocate. "Spotters, sense, and harnesses," he says.

Our advice is to try to keep the antenna cable as short as possible while placing the access point to which you connect it in a reasonable indoor location.

Durability

The last thing to keep in mind when installing your antenna is that it will be exposed to the elements, day in and day out. Sun, wind, rain, snow, ice, fog, plagues of locusts—you want your antenna to withstand whatever nature throws at it. And keep in mind that by "withstand" we mean, "without moving or failing to operate." If a strong wind turns a panel antenna in a different direction or an ice storm coats a yagi, your network could go down.

We've already discussed how different types of antennas withstand wind load; if your area suffers from high winds at all, check the wind-load rating when buying an antenna. Similarly, when you install it, mount it as securely as possible. If you mount it on a round pole, make sure it can't rotate on the pole—the antenna is more likely to rotate in the wind than to blow over entirely.

Making Long-Range Wireless Connections

We've talked about antennas, cable, pigtails, and connectors, but into what do you plug the pigtail? Whether you're connecting to a WISP or extending your existing network as discussed in the previous chapter, your wireless device must act like a client, that is, like a normal wireless-capable computer connecting to an access point. In fact, if you want to connect only a single computer to a WISP, you can install a wireless network adapter that has an antenna jack and connect it to your pigtail. More difficult is connecting an entire network to a long-range wireless connection, and for that you have two options:

Network server. Connect a wireless network adapter to a computer, attach the antenna (via a pigtail) to the wireless network adapter, and run software on the computer that turns the computer into a gateway. For Windows XP, you can use its built-in capability to share an Internet connection, which we cover in Chapter 19, *Creating a Software Access Point*. For Mac OS X, try using Brian Hill's $25 shareware BrickHouse utility (see http://personalpages. tds.net/~brian_hill/brickhouse.html) to configure Mac OS X's built-in Internet Sharing feature. For Mac OS 9, check out the $89 IPNetRouter from Sustainable Software at www.sustworks.com/site/prod_ipr_ overview.html. Your computer must then connect via normal wired Ethernet to an Ethernet hub, and if you want to provide internal wireless network access as well, instead of a plain hub, use a wireless gateway that integrates an access point and an Ethernet hub. The downside of this approach is that the connection is active only when the computer is on and functioning, so it's a task best handled by a computer that nobody uses for regular work—older computers, particularly space- and power-saving laptops, often work well in this situation.

Wireless Ethernet bridge. Use a wireless Ethernet bridge such as the Linksys WET11 (www.linksys.com/Products/product.asp?grid =22&prid=432) or the smartBridges airBridge (www.smartbridges.com/new/products/ab.php), both of which can accept external antennas and can bridge the long-range wireless connection to a wired Ethernet network. (See Chapter 20, *Bridging Wireless Networks*, for more details.) Again, if you want to provide internal wireless network access, you must also connect the wireless Ethernet bridge to a wireless gateway. (Just because a wireless gateway says it provides bridging between wired and wireless networks does not mean it can bridge a long-range wireless connection. That's because most wireless gateways can run their wireless radios only as access points, where they're acting as a hub for a wireless network, rather than as clients, where they're connecting to another access point.)

In either case, you probably want to run NAT and DHCP to provide private IP addresses for your computers. See Chapter 16, *Buying a Wireless Gateway,* for more information.

Also pay close attention to your cable and connectors. Most antenna cable is designed for outdoor use, and threaded connectors provide much more secure connections than push-on or twist-to-lock connectors. Threaded connectors can be fairly waterproof, but it's still a good idea to wrap them in waterproof tape, since water has a nasty habit of infiltrating even the most secure connections. If the vendor you buy your antenna gear from doesn't carry it, you can find waterproof tape suitable for this task at Radio Shack. If possible, make sure the tape can hold up under ultraviolet radiation, too.

TIP

Several companies sell "ruggedized" enclosures, which are waterproof boxes that resemble the plastic phone company boxes on the outside of your house. You can use these cases for installing wireless networking gear outdoors. Of course, electronics generate heat, so the heat in the box, especially on a hot day, could cause hardware failures.

If you plan to attach your antenna to a building, make sure everything is securely fastened down. In many cases, there may be no obvious place to attach mounting brackets, or you may not have permission to make such modifications to the building. In a situation where you have a flat roof, consider constructing a sturdy sled with a wooden base and supports (**Figure 34.13**). As long as you weigh down the base with concrete blocks or sandbags, the sled should work fine (but make sure it won't damage the roof surface).

Figure 34.13
Simple antenna sled
design.

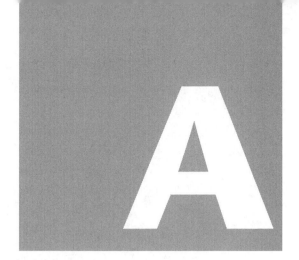

Networking Basics

Although wireless networks are easy to assemble and maintain, they're still networks, and a certain level of comfort with conventional networking can help you understand how your wireless network works. More importantly, most people rarely connect only wireless devices to a network, but must also hook in Ethernet printers and older wired machines, so some additional background in networking serves you well there, too.

When it comes to networking knowledge, we suspect you fall into one of three categories:

- Although you know computers can hook together into networks, you don't know much about 10Base-T Ethernet, never considered the difference between a hub and a gateway, and truly feel lost when contemplating whether or not you should use a crossover cable when connecting two network devices. Don't feel ashamed—we all started somewhere, but you'll want to read this entire appendix carefully. Also, this appendix can act as an ongoing reference if you hit rocky spots while setting up a network.

- You've performed some simple networking before, perhaps connecting a couple of computers to each other via a hub so you could transfer files back and forth and share a high-speed Internet connection. When push comes to shove, you can probably make most network devices work via trial and error, but you're not sure how it all works. We recommend you read this appendix, skipping any sections that cover information you're sure you already know. Refer back as you encounter less familiar concepts in the book: a few minutes of reading can save hours of fruitless experimentation.

- You're a network administrator with lots of certification letters after your name, and we should ask you for help. No need to waste your time here—to quote Obi-Wan Kenobi, these aren't the droids you're looking for, and that's why we've put this information in an appendix.

For those of you in the first two categories, let's start with a real-world analogy so we're all on the same page.

What's a Network?

What's a network? Put simply, networks transport data from one computer to another. When you try to wrap your head around the concept of networks, it can help to think of them in terms of everyday transportation systems, like highways or railroads.

For instance, consider a railroad. It's made up of stations and freight yards connected by tracks. On the tracks, freight trains carry cargo containers; each container is labeled with a description of the container's eventual destination.

Now let's translate our railroad network into a computer network. Our computers are the railroad stations along the tracks, and the tracks are the wires that run from computer to computer. Cargo carried on a freight train travels in containers; data carried on a network—computer files, Web pages, email messages, and so on—travels in *packets*. In the networking world, packets play a key role in moving data around. A packet contains a small chunk of a larger piece of data that's been divided up. Every packet has a *header* that states where it came from and where it's heading, performing the same task as the routing label on each cargo container.

Just as almost all railroads now use the same gauge track for compatibility reasons, adherence to standards in computer networking is essential. For instance, you can't use any old wire to connect computers, and if you mix wire types, you run into exactly the same situation that early railroads of different gauges experienced—workers had to transfer cargo from one train to another, which required a special device like a crane and tended to slow down delivery time. Although you can choose from a variety of acceptable wire types, it's best to stick with one type.

The same principle applies when you connect a wired network to a wireless network. Making the connection is like transferring containers from a railroad car to a cargo plane. The cargo containers remain the same, and their labels still say where they're headed, but you've traded the rigidly constrained world of railroad tracks and stations for wide-open airways and airports.

No matter how a cargo container travels, once it reaches its destination, workers remove and unpack its contents. Here the analogy breaks down a bit, since real-world cargo containers are huge and carry a lot of stuff, whereas network packets are broken-up portions of larger things, such as email messages, Web pages, or spreadsheet files. When network packets reach their destination and are unpacked, their contents must also be combined with the contents of other packets and reassembled into the original file, Web page, or email message.

We could continue this analogy to the point of ridiculousness, comparing policies surrounding what happens when two trains headed in opposite directions meet on the same track to the way Ethernet networks handle packet collisions. But let's not go there; instead, for those of you who are still learning about networks, let's look at what they're good for.

Network Uses

The fact that you're even reading this book means you have some idea of how you can use a network, most likely for sharing an Internet connection or copying files back and forth between computers. Nevertheless, there may be uses you hadn't previously considered, so let's run through the main uses to which we've put our networks over the years.

Internet Sharing

In the age of the Internet, a one-computer-per-connection policy seems bizarre, but most cable and DSL service providers offer practically the same limitations as dial-up networks: each connection comes with a single Internet address, often not a fixed one, and extra addresses are either unavailable or expensive.

Market research shows that a majority of households with one computer have a second, and many have a third or fourth. All these users want to be on the Internet at the same time, which means sharing that one address.

Luckily, sharing an Internet connection requires only inexpensive hardware or software installed on the machine connected to the Internet. And, if you're setting up a wireless network, you almost can't avoid buying a wireless access point that doesn't also share your Internet connection. Using a wireless network to share your Internet connection with a laptop computer is especially compelling, since you can browse the Web, read email, or use instant messaging from anywhere within range of your access point.

Put simply, the Internet is considered standard equipment these days. If you have multiple computers, they should definitely share your Internet connection.

NOTE

Some service providers offer reasonable options for giving each machine on a network a unique, public Internet address, but there are some security reasons to use private addresses via Network Address Translation (NAT) instead. We discuss NAT later in this appendix and in Chapter 27, Protecting Your Systems.

File Sharing and Exchanging Files

File sharing used to be the killer application for networks, and office workers still use it heavily as a means for collaborating and trading files back and forth. Offices typically have file servers—computers that have no responsibility but to provide a place to store files for everyone to access, and to mediate network connections to those files. However, a personal computer running either Windows or the Mac OS can act as a file server with no extra software while still performing its duties as a personal computer, so you can easily share files even in small offices or homes where a dedicated file server would be overkill.

File sharing doesn't necessarily imply copying files between computers, either. For instance, each of us stored a collection of MP3 music files (converted from existing CD collections) on a single computer. Now our families can run music software to play these files over the network, without copying gigabytes of music to their individual computers.

TIP

We help you with the basics of setting up file sharing in Chapter 13, Sharing Files & Printers. *Sharing files between Macs and PCs is slightly trickier, but we offer a few tips on that in Chapter 13 as well.*

After you set up a network, you will find it much easier to share files over the network than to copy them to a floppy disk (especially given that Macs and some PCs no longer have floppy disk drives) or a CD-RW disc.

Printer Sharing

Printers are a part of life, predictions of a paperless office to the contrary. Paper works well for many kinds of tasks, including graphical displays of information and displaying photos, and the latest generation of inkjet printers does a great job with both while costing less than a piece of home stereo equipment.

 NOTE

For a fascinating look at why paper really does work so well, read Malcolm Gladwell's article entitled "The Social Life of Paper" at www.gladwell.com/ 2002/2002_03_25_a_paper.htm.

But even given the low cost and wide utility of current printers, it rarely makes sense for each computer to have its own dedicated output device. Rather, sharing printers across a network, often with different capabilities in each printer (if you have more than one), is a far more sensible approach. Hooking a printer into a computer or a home gateway can let you share even the cheapest of them.

Windows and the Mac OS offer printer sharing features out of the box; the only problem is that each one is good at sharing only among computers running the same operating system. So, if you share a printer via Windows, a Mac won't be able to see it without some extra software called Dave, from Thursby Software Systems (see www.thursby.com/products/dave.html), or the Gimp-Print utilities (http://gimp-print.sourceforge.net/MacOSX.php3). The reverse is also true—a printer shared from a Mac won't be visible to a Windows computer, though Dave helps in that situation as well.

 TIP

Network-based printers typically have several protocols for printing built in, so that computers running the Mac OS or Windows can print directly. Some printers even have IP addresses. You can print to them from anywhere on the Internet.

Backup

Your most important backup was the last one you didn't make—or never made. Most people realize that they should have made copies of important files after losing them, but you're too smart and good-looking for that, right?

Backups are seldom made as frequently as they should be, because most people think backing up files is a tedious operation in which you sit in front of a computer swapping Zip disks or inserting CD-RWs. Every computer you add makes the problem worse, as do today's ridiculously large hard disks, which seem to fill quickly with MP3s, digital video, game software, and huge applications.

Network-based backups can help solve the backup problem. With the appropriate software on each computer and a tape drive or other storage device (removable hard disks make good backup media these days because they're so cheap), you can ensure that all computers on your network back up automatically. We both use and recommend Dantz Development's Retrospect backup software (www.dantz.com) for Macintosh and Windows; it has a Linux client as well. Couple it with a good tape drive or set of removable hard disks, and you have a backup solution that won't let you down.

We don't pretend network backup is appropriate for everyone, nor is it exactly cheap. Unless you're in a household or office with at least a handful of computers, it's probably overkill. But in any situation where important work is done every day, it's a necessity to protect against the day when you will lose data.

(((•))) **NOTE**

Everyone, and we mean everyone, will lose data at some point, and backups are the only protection. It's best to make multiple backup sets and to keep one off-site, as was made clear to a friend when a burglar cleaned out his home office, stealing his computers and his backups.

Network Wiring

As we discussed earlier, the wires of a computer network are like the tracks of a railroad. They connect the different computers—the railroad stations—and carry the data—the cargo. And just like train tracks run in parallel, snake around, and join up in train-switching roundhouses, you can put wires together in different ways when building a network.

Network Topologies

Before we can look at the different types of network wiring, we need to detour briefly into the topic of *network topology*, a fancy term that just means how the network is laid out. For the purposes of this book, there are four main network topologies: star, bus, ring, and mesh.

Star

With a wired star network topology, a central device (called a *hub*) acts like the hub of a wheel. The hub connects to each computer using wires, and the wires resemble spokes on a wheel (**Figure A.1**). Using its internal electronics, the hub connects all of the devices to each other.

Figure A.1
A star network topology.

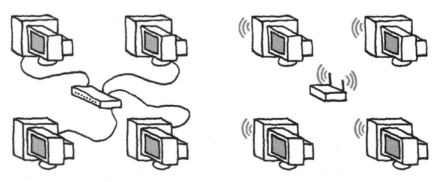

Wired star network   Wireless star network

Star topologies are by far the most common these days because they're used by standard 10Base-T and 100Base-T wired networks (more on those in a minute) and most wireless networks. The beauty of star networks is that if any one of the wire spokes fails, only the computer on the end of that spoke is affected, and the rest of the network continues to work without any troubles. As you'll see, that's not necessarily true of other network topologies.

Networked Computers Listen, Then Talk

All topologies are designed to create *network segments*—physically and logically separate pieces of a network—in which all computers or other devices on the same segment can "hear" each other within the minimum amount of time it takes to transmit a complete short sequence of data called a *frame*.

Even though network signals travel at the speed of electricity in wire (which is near the speed of light), you can still run only a few thousand feet of wire between the two most distant devices. If the segment were longer than that, the most distant computer might not hear the start of the frame before the sending computer finished. That's a problem because all computers on the network have to know when they can start transmitting without interrupting another transmission.

Take this practical example: if Computer A and Computer B are both on the same Ethernet segment, and both start transmitting data at the same time, the only way they know they're interfering with each other's transmission is to hear the other device (after which they stop sending, before they've completed a data frame). This kind of interference is called a *collision*, because the data from different transceivers "collides."

In most types of networks, including Wi-Fi and the several kinds of Ethernet, techniques are built into network adapters to wait for silence, start transmitting, and then halt if they detect an interruption. The devices then stop talking for a short, random period of time, and then try again; if a collision happens again, each device increases the time repeatedly until it can get silence and start without conflict. (Ethernet and Wi-Fi have slightly different approaches, because of how wireless signals are handled, but they wind up working about the same.) The procedure is a bit like the old days of party lines, where an entire neighborhood might share a telephone line, so you had to wait for Betty down the street to finish talking before making a call.

Each network segment essentially has its own party line, so breaking a network into more segments increases the *throughput*, or amount of data you can reliably transmit at any given time over each segment. In the most common networking flavors, 10Base-T and 100Base-T, a hub in the star topology can be passive, which is like a multi-socket electrical adapter, creating one large segment composed of all attached networks; or it can be a switch, which isolates each network segment, and passes data between segments only as needed. You can read more about hubs later in this appendix.

NOTE

The hubs in very large star networks often connect to each other in higher-level stars—many hubs connecting to one massive, high-powered hub—but hubs can also connect in a bus configuration, described next.

Bus

A bus network topology, sometimes called a daisy-chain, uses one long wire, with each computer hanging off the wire (**Figure A.2**). Bus networks are fairly uncommon today for computers (though not for network hubs), although they're easy to set up and were more heavily used in the past. 10Base-5, 10Base-2, LocalTalk/PhoneNet, HomePNA, and HomePlug networks (which we cover later) all use bus topologies.

Figure A.2
A bus network topology.

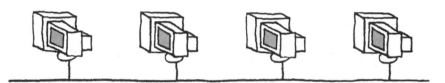

The problem with a bus topology, as you can imagine, is if something cuts the wire in the middle, it's a bit like an errant backhoe chopping your telephone line while you're talking to someone—the line goes dead. Needless to say, network administrators hate tracking down network problems that could be anywhere on the main network wire, so bus networks have fallen out of favor.

 TIP

If you do run into a bus network that seems to be intact but isn't working properly, check for the correct termination on both ends of the network. Without the proper terminator acting as a cap on each end of the main wire, the signals won't travel down a bus network properly.

Ring

Ring network topologies are similar to bus networks, but with the ends of the wire connected to make a ring (**Figure A.3**). Token ring networks offer one solution to the "who's talking" problem; machines pass an electronic token to determine who is allowed to broadcast at any given time. Token ring networks are seldom used today for the same reason bus networks aren't in common use—a single cut in the main network cable, and the entire network comes to a screeching halt.

Figure A.3
A ring network
topology.

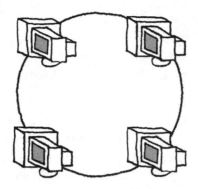

Figure A.3
A ring network
topology.

$((\bullet))$ **NOTE**

The token ring made an unexpected comeback in Wi-Fi in Australia. A community networking group developed a package called "frottle" which, when installed on all the clients and on special gateways, dramatically improved speed by using a token. Of course, this required special hardware and isn't appropriate except for specific networks. For details, see http://wifinetnews. com/archives/002035.html.

$((\bullet))$ **NOTE**

One of Glenn's favorite Dilbert cartoons shows Dilbert telling his pointy-haired boss that his network connection stopped working because the token fell out of the token ring, and the boss needs to look for it.

Mesh

Mesh networks connect opportunistically to any available other device that allows traffic to flow to an ultimate destination (**Figure A.4**). In a wired world, mesh networking makes no sense, because you'd need independent wires running from every device to every other device—the very situation that a star topology solves.

Figure A.4
A mesh network
topology.

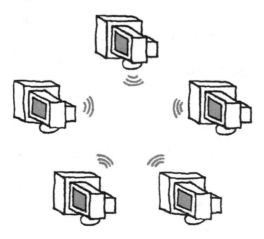

But with a radio-based wireless network, in which many transceivers have a signal path to many other transceivers, mesh networking can entirely replace wired networks while adding the advantages of redundancy—if one connection is blocked, the traffic simply flows around the blockage on other connections.

Although mesh networking is a popular topic, especially among community network enthusiasts, only a few products offer mesh capabilities, and they are affordable now just for companies and service providers. Ultimately, you may find that high-speed, home access to the Internet could be provided by a mesh node on your house, but it's unclear whether the technology will become commercially viable (see Chapter 5, *Wireless of the (Near) Future*).

Ethernet Wiring Types

When it comes to networking, almost every network-enabled computer uses the *Ethernet* networking standard, also known as IEEE 802.3. Ethernet networks can use a variety of physical wires to connect machines, and in fact, wireless networks also use Ethernet, simply replacing the wires with radio waves.

NOTE

The IEEE is key to many of these networking standards, but Ethernet was actually invented by Bob Metcalfe in the 1970s when he was working at the Xerox PARC research lab after he read about Alohanet in Hawaii. The IEEE standardized Ethernet later. Metcalfe's original sketch of how Ethernet could work is available at www.ethermanage.com/ethernet/ethernet.html.

NOTE

You may hear people call wireless networks "wireless Ethernet." That's just fine—the Ethernet standard specifies the way packets are put together, sent, and received; the physical medium can be either wire or radio waves.

For completeness, and in case you ever run into a still-functional network using an older type of physical cable that is compatible with Ethernet networking, we look at Ethernet wiring types in rough chronological order.

10Base-5 or ThickNet

The least common wiring type you may encounter is the thick coaxial cable used for 10Base-5 Ethernet. It looks like a cable used for connecting cable television boxes and is also called thick Ethernet or ThickNet. Its data transfer rate is 10 Mbps, and the maximum segment length—the wires that run between computers—is 500 meters (hence the "5" in 10Base-5). You can't readily buy 10Base-5 networking gear or cables anymore, but you might see it in an old network installation. 10Base-5 networks use a bus topology.

10Base-2 or ThinNet

Whereas 10Base-5 is little used these days, you could conceivably still run into the cabling for the 10Base-2 Ethernet standard, also called thin Ethernet or ThinNet. Like 10Base-5, 10Base-2 runs at 10 Mbps and uses coaxial cables; however, it has a maximum segment length of 185 meters (thus the "2" in 10Base-2, thanks to rounding 185 up to 200). Cables for 10Base-2 are thinner and thus easier to work with, and they use round BNC connectors like those used for cable TV. Like 10Base-5, 10Base-2 requires a bus network topology.

((•)) NOTE

BNC is short for British Naval Connector, Bayonet Nut Connector, or Bayonet Neill Concelman, depending on with whom you're talking. Everyone just calls it BNC.

Adam used a 10Base-2 network in his previous house instead of 10Base-T (covered next), because the cable runs were so long that he would have had to buy an Ethernet hub (discussed later in this appendix) for each location. Today that wouldn't be much of an investment, but at the time, hubs cost around $100 each, and buying four of them felt like overkill. The 10Base-2 network worked fine, and later on, when computers started to include only 10Base-T Ethernet jacks, inexpensive hubs that connected 10Base-2 and 10Base-T wiring types were readily available. (Glenn did the same thing in 1995 in an office: it was cheaper to drill through walls in a run around the office than to bring wire to a central location.)

10Base-T

Thanks to its use of common *twisted pair* wiring and a forgiving star topology, 10Base-T rules the networking world. (The "T" in 10Base-T refers to twisted pair.) Twisted pair wiring is extremely common because it connects most buildings' telephone wiring to the telephone company. The cable you use inside your house to connect a telephone or a modem to the wall jack is not twisted pair; instead, it contains side-by-side wires and is called *silver satin*.

The utility of twisted pair, in which each pair of wires twists together a certain number of times per foot, is that it reduces electromagnetic interference between the signals flowing down each wire. Most twisted pair cables contain several pairs of wires; although only one pair is actually necessary for telephone usage, 10Base-T Ethernet requires two pairs, one for transmitting data and the other for receiving.

TIP

If you attempt to replace a twisted pair cable with a silver satin cable used for telephone cords, the connection won't work because of interference between the two side-by-side wires. Luckily, if you're paying attention to the cables, you're unlikely to attempt such a thing because silver satin cables have standard RJ-11 plugs for RJ-11 telephone jacks (four wire). In contrast, 10Base-T Ethernet cables have the larger RJ-45 plugs (eight wire).

10Base-T networks are limited to a maximum segment length of 100 meters, quite a bit less than the older coaxial-based standards, but more than enough in most situations. Remember that because 10Base-T networks use a star topology, every computer or other device must connect back to the central hub.

Almost any network device you buy today will support at least 10Base-T Ethernet—it's become the least common denominator of networking.

100Base-T or Fast Ethernet

100Base-T, also known as Fast Ethernet, works almost exactly like 10Base-T and uses the same Cat5 twisted pair cable. However, 100Base-T runs at 100 Mbps, which is significantly faster than the 10 Mbps throughput of 10Base-T.

Wire Facts

Twisted pair wiring has many variants. It can be either shielded or unshielded—the shielded variety is used in some business networking situations where the metal shield around the twisted pairs acts as a ground. You're unlikely to see that, though, and normal twisted pair is unshielded, yielding the UTP (unshielded twisted pair) abbreviation you may encounter.

Twisted pair wiring is also rated for different speeds by categories. Although there are categories 1 through 6, by far the most common are Cat3 (as the categories are abbreviated) and Cat5. Only ever buy Cat5 cable—although Cat3 works for 10Base-T, it doesn't cut the mustard for the newer and increasingly common faster standards, 100Base-T or 1000Base-T.

Cat5 works for those standards, though for 1000Base-T, you need four pairs of wires instead of the standard two pairs. Some manufacturers recommend an enhanced kind of Cat5 called Cat5E to ensure maximum throughput (though we've heard from knowledgeable engineers that Cat5E is just a marketing gimmick and doesn't really offer anything beyond Cat5).

Another term you may see associated with Ethernet cable is *plenum-rated*, which means the cable has slow burning, fire-resistant casings that emit little smoke. That's important for cables running through overhead ductwork between rooms, because in a fire, you don't want potentially toxic smoke flowing from a room on fire to one that's still otherwise safe.

Crossover Cables and Uplink Ports

Because twisted-pair Ethernets dedicate certain pairs for receiving and certain pairs for transmitting, any hub has pins (small, rigid, straight wires) in its jacks that match up with the equivalent pins in Ethernet cables. But when you connect certain kinds of devices—like one hub to another hub, or a special device like a DSL modem that's designed to plug straight into a computer—you must switch the transmit and receive wires through a *crossover cable*.

The only difference between a crossover cable and a normal Ethernet cable (more precisely called a *patch cable* because it patches a computer into a hub) is that in a patch cable, the wires go straight through, whereas in a crossover cable the transmit and receive wires are swapped.

Specifically, in a patch cable, pin 1 on one side connects to pin 1 on the other side, pin 2 to pin 2, and so on. In a crossover cable, however, pin 1 connects to pin 3, pin 2 to pin 6, pin 3 to pin 1, and pin 6 to pin 2.

Crossover cables are required for:

- Computer-to-computer connections

- Hub-to-hub connections

- Connecting DSL modems or other special devices to a hub

Almost all hubs come with at least one *uplink* port, which is the equivalent of a crossover cable. Plugging a patch cable into the uplink port gives the effect of crossing the appropriate wires, just as in a crossover cable. Some devices have a separate, labeled port; others, such as the Linksys WET11 wireless bridge, have a manual switch on the side for crossover or straight-through mode.

Other hubs have no dedicated or switchable uplink port, but rather include auto-sensing circuitry known as auto-MDI/MDI-X. Most newer Linksys switches, such as the inexpensive, gigabit workgroup models, include this feature on every port. You can also find auto-sensing on modern Macs and some PCs: if the computer can auto-sense, you can plug either a crossover or a patch cable into any Ethernet port.

Make sure to read the documentation that comes with your hub, since some hubs (notably some older models from Linksys—Adam had one of these) share the connection between the uplink port and the normal port next to it. That means that if you use the uplink port, you cannot use the port next to it for a computer or other network device. The hint, if you can't find your documentation, is that when the uplink port is connected to another hub, the LED for the port next to the uplink port lights up. There are also often printed lines on the back of the hub connecting the uplink port with the one next to it.

It's not a bad idea to have a crossover cable in your network tool kit, but if you get one, make sure you label it clearly. Trying to use a crossover cable in a situation that calls for a patch cable is an exercise in frustration. Adam solved this problem by getting a little connector that, when he plugs two normal patch cables into it, turns the entire resulting cable into a crossover cable. Crossover cables are often yellow, curiously.

Although Fast Ethernet won't make one whit of difference for Internet access (if you don't work in a large organization, you're lucky to have more than a 1 Mbps Internet connection, much less a 100 Mbps connection), you will notice and appreciate the performance improvement whenever you copy files from one computer to another using Fast Ethernet as opposed to 10Base-T. It's remarkably fun, for instance, to drag a 1 GB file from your Desktop to another machine, and then watch it copy in a few minutes.

Fast Ethernet has become sufficiently common and inexpensive that it's worth spending an extra few dollars on networking gear that supports it in addition to 10Base-T. If you opt for 802.11g or 802.11a, both of which operate at 54 Mbps, or want to hook several 802.11b access points (each running at 11 Mbps) into a network, then 100 Mbps becomes even more worthwhile.

Even if your current computers don't support Fast Ethernet, it's impossible that any future computer you would buy wouldn't include it. In fact, several years ago, Apple started shipping Macs with Ethernet ports that support Fast Ethernet as well as 10Base-T (you may see such ports called "10/100 Mbps ports"), and every PC maker and Ethernet card manufacturer followed suit.

We've also found that the switches or hubs that connect twisted-pair networks together now almost uniformly support automatically configured 10/100 Mbps traffic, meaning that you can plug one or the other flavor in without flipping switches. You'll find these kinds of mini-hubs built into many wireless gateways, too.

1000Base-T or Gigabit Ethernet

Lastly, we come to 1000Base-T, more commonly called Gigabit Ethernet because it runs at 1000 Mbps, or roughly 1 Gbps. Since early 2003, the price of Gigabit Ethernet has plummeted: as we write this, you can buy a PCI Card for $100, and Ethernet switches for $20 per port—down from several hundred for a card and $150 to $300 per port in 2002!

Apple now includes Gigabit Ethernet in all of its Power Macs (and has for some time), as well as the 15-inch and 17-inch PowerBooks. Dell offers 1000Base-T as an option with its laptops, and virtually every machine above the consumer level either includes or offers Gigabit Ethernet as a cheap add-on.

Do you need all that speed? It's remarkable to see hundreds of megabytes fly across a network in seconds, but it's not critical unless you're building a new network and need to buy new gear—in which case, spend a few extra dollars to be ready for next-generation video streaming. Gigabit Ethernet is also worthwhile if you routinely transfer enormous files or streaming media, or plan to operate many 802.11g or 802.11a access points across a single small network.

Other Network Types

Ethernet may be the 600-pound gorilla of the networking world, but there's still room for a few chimps, or depending on your attitude, chumps.

LocalTalk/PhoneNet

Although it never took off outside the Macintosh world, for many years the Macintosh standard was a low-speed networking technology called LocalTalk. LocalTalk ran only at 230.4 Kbps, and when it was first released, it required proprietary cables and connectors made by Apple. Workers at Farallon Communications realized quickly that LocalTalk works fine over standard telephone wire (even the silver satin stuff). Farallon's PhoneNet adapters (and clones thereof), used with standard telephone wires, soon supplanted Apple's custom LocalTalk cables and connectors entirely.

LocalTalk and PhoneNet connectors plugged into the serial ports (specifically the printer ports) of older Macs, and they made for extremely tolerant networks. Although they used a bus topology, forgetting to plug a terminator in at either end of the network seldom made a difference, and users quickly realized how easy it was to adapt existing telephone wiring to work with PhoneNet connectors. Since PhoneNet required only a single pair of wires, and since most telephone wiring contained an unused pair, it was simple to add network jacks to in-house telephone wiring.

$((\bullet))$ **NOTE**

To give you an idea of how resilient LocalTalk networks can be, a friend tells a story of a LocalTalk network that used hot and cold water pipes(!) instead of a pair of wires.

No recent Macintosh has serial ports, so LocalTalk networks have been disappearing in favor of wired and wireless Ethernet networks. However, unlike older types of Ethernet cabling, it's not uncommon to find LocalTalk networks still in service, even if only to provide access to one of Apple's early LaserWriter laser printers, which were easily added to networks via LocalTalk. Modern Macs that don't support LocalTalk can still send jobs to those older printers, and many people are understandably loathe to give up these workhorse printers.

Luckily, that's not necessary, since a device called a LocalTalk-to-Ethernet bridge, such as the AsantéTalk Ethernet to LocalTalk Bridge from Asanté Technologies, can connect either a wireless or wired Ethernet network to a LocalTalk network, even if the only device on the LocalTalk network is a laser printer. You can learn more about bridges later in this appendix; the important thing to check when using a LocalTalk-to-Ethernet bridge with a wireless access point is if your access point bridges AppleTalk (more on AppleTalk soon, too). In essence, the question is if the access point can accept an AppleTalk packet (which is just a specific sort of cargo container for data) from a computer on the wireless network and send it on to the LocalTalk network without damaging it in some way. Some access points can keep AppleTalk packets intact, some can't.

HomePNA

More modern than LocalTalk is the HomePNA networking standard, which was developed by an industry group called the Home Phoneline Networking Alliance. Like LocalTalk, HomePNA uses standard telephone wiring on a bus network. Although HomePNA 1.0 was capable of a throughput of only 1 Mbps, HomePNA 2.0 increases that to 10 Mbps, and a just-defined HomePNA 3.0 standard takes a giant leap to 128 Mbps, with optional extensions to 240 Mbps. Of course, as with all networks, those speeds are theoretical, and reports have placed HomePNA 2.0's real throughput at about 4 Mbps, and it remains to be seen how much of HomePNA's 128 Mbps will actually be available.

What's most interesting about HomePNA is that it uses the same wires as your telephone, modem, or fax machine, theoretically without any interference. In theory, you just attach a HomePNA network adapter (available as a PCI card, USB adapter, or Ethernet adapter) to your computer and run some telephone wire from the network adapter to your telephone jacks. You can purchase HomePNA Ethernet bridges that connect HomePNA networks to standard Ethernet networks, and HomePNA support is being built into other network devices as well.

Why would you use HomePNA? You could use it to network all your computers together, but considering that you're reading this book, we're guessing you'd prefer to avoid wires where possible. To us then, HomePNA is potentially useful for connecting computers in different rooms using the telephone wiring that's already in your walls. By attaching a wireless access point to a HomePNA Ethernet bridge in each room (or by buying an access point that also supports HomePNA), you could also extend the range of a wireless network to a portion of a building that was otherwise inaccessible.

If you must run new wires (a process often called *pulling wire* by those in the field), you may as well run Cat5 twisted pair instead of telephone wire, since buying HomePNA adapters for your computers costs a lot more than simply plugging Ethernet cables into your computers' existing Ethernet ports. Plus, if you have modern computers, they probably support Fast Ethernet, which is much faster than HomePNA.

HomePNA faces a number of challenges that may limit its popularity:

- Most homes have relatively few telephone jacks in each room, making it less likely that there will be a jack where you want it.

- Although HomePNA's performance has increased with the 2.0 version, the 4 Mbps real-world throughput isn't particularly impressive. The next version, HomePNA 3.0, promises 128 Mbps of theoretical throughput, though how that will pan out in the real world (watch for products in late 2003) remains to be seen.

- Ethernet is a better choice at home for almost anyone who wants to use the same computer at home and at work—most workplaces use Ethernet.

For more information about HomePNA, visit the HomePNA Web site at www. homepna.org.

HomePlug

Far more common than telephone jacks in most rooms are power plugs, and that's where the HomePlug Powerline Alliance set its sights with the HomePlug networking standard. Instead of plugging a network adapter into a telephone jack or network outlet, you simply plug it into an electrical socket.

(((•))) **NOTE**

Yes, it is truly neat that they've figured out how to transfer data over standard power lines within the home. Researchers have even determined how to provide high-speed Internet access via power lines, though we haven't heard of that being implemented widely anywhere in the world yet. Amateur radio operators are freaked out about power-line networking; they said in mid-2003 that it could interfere with their ability to receive distant signals.

HomePlug runs at 14 Mbps, although its real-world throughput is reportedly between 5 and 6 Mbps. Like HomePNA, HomePlug uses a bus network topology, so you don't need a central hub. In fact, apart from the use of electrical lines instead of telephone wiring, HomePlug is extremely comparable to HomePNA (so just read the previous section again, mentally replacing "HomePNA" with

"HomePlug" as appropriate). HomePlug even reportedly works with other technologies that transmit data over power lines, such as X10 home automation devices.

NOTE

Unfortunately HomePlug works only on 110-volt power systems, making it useless in the many countries that don't use 110-volt power. It also has to be plugged directly into an outlet: power strips need not apply.

If you live in an apartment and decide to set up a HomePlug network, give network security some thought since apartments often share power lines. All HomePlug hardware can encrypt data so your neighbors can't connect to your printer, see shared folders, or eavesdrop on your network communications. If you're worried about security, make sure to turn on the encryption; it's likely off by default.

In mid-2002, we were still asking the questions about whether HomePlug or HomePNA was the best way to extend a wired or wireless network. HomePNA seemed to be an advantage in homes that had older electrical wiring but newer phone wiring. However, equipment maker Siemens changed the whole picture by releasing the SpeedStream Powerline Wireless Access Point (www.speedstream.com). This HomePlug device acts as an extension of your wireless network without needing to add Ethernet hubs or other cabling. For many situations in which you want to extend a wireless network to many rooms in a house or building, the SpeedStream access point saves money and effort. Since the SpeedStream access point first appeared, more well-known network equipment vendors like Linksys, Netgear, Belkin, and IOGear have jumped into the fray with devices that bridge the gap (literally) between HomePlug and Wi-Fi.

NOTE

Glenn's cousin Steven wanted to have cable modem service installed at his house and was nervous about the cable company installer running wire to his upstairs home office. Glenn worked with him to put in a Linksys broadband router next to the cable modem which was in turn connected to a HomePlug adapter. Upstairs, another HomePlug adapter linked to his computer. It worked like a charm the minute it was all plugged in.

Our impression from people who have tried both is that HomePlug is worth checking out for simplicity and the ease of setup, but if you need higher throughput, it might be worth waiting until HomePNA 3.0 devices start appearing.

For more information about HomePlug, visit the HomePlug Web site at www.homeplug.org.

Network Devices

The next step in learning about networking is getting a feel for the different devices with which you build a network. This is easy, but you must keep two things in mind.

- Although the devices noted in this section started out as separate items, it turned out to make sense to combine multiple functions in the same device. For instance, it's simple to buy a device today that combines a 4-port switching hub, wireless access point, firewall software, and wired Ethernet to wireless bridge, all in one.

- Manufacturers tend to play fast and loose with terminology, making it hard at times to determine exactly which functions have been incorporated into any one device.

Nevertheless, follow along with our descriptions below, and a careful reading of the specification for the product you're investigating should reveal which functions it offers.

Network Adapters (NICs)

The easiest piece of a network to understand is the *network adapter*, also frequently called a *network interface card* (*NIC*). Put simply, the network adapter is the piece that connects your computer to the network—nothing can happen without it. To continue our railroad analogy, a network adapter is like a boarding platform at the train station—the station might be there, but it won't be useful without the platform to make it possible for people to travel between the train and the station.

As you might expect, network adapters are specific to a certain type of network, so if you buy a 10Base-T network adapter, you can connect it only to a 10Base-T network. Since the circuitry necessary to support different flavors of Ethernet is pretty much the same, manufacturers sometimes combine support for multiple flavors in a single network adapter. In the old days, when 10Base-2 networks were as common as 10Base-T networks, for instance, network adapters often had both an RJ-45 port for 10Base-T and a BNC jack for 10Base-2. Either (but not both) could be activated at any time, just by connecting the appropriate cable. Nowadays, many network adapters combine 10Base-T and 100Base-T, or even add 1000Base-T to the mix. These cards are frequently labeled "10/100 Mbps" or even "10/100/1000 Mbps."

Types of Network Adapters

Network adapters come in many different shapes and sizes, and an ever-increasing number of computers, including every Macintosh made since the first iMac, have them built in. If your computer has an Ethernet port, that's a built-in network adapter. Examples of other network adapters include:

- PCI cards plug into PCI slots inside many modern desktop computers and are probably the most common type of network adapters. You can buy PCI cards that provide access to both wired and wireless networks. For older computers that came out before PCI was the standard expansion slot, you can probably still find ISA (for PCs) or NuBus (for Macs) network adapter cards for wired networks, but probably not for wireless networks.

- PC Cards fit into PC Card slots in laptop computers. Desktop computers almost never have slots for PC Cards. Many PC Card network adapters for wired Ethernet come with a tiny dongle, which is a small cable that plugs into the credit-card sized PC Card and provides a normal Ethernet jack. Wireless PC Card network adapters typically extend out from the side of the laptop to accommodate their antennas.

 TIP

Old-timers still call PC Cards "PCMCIA cards," the original name given by the industry (it stood for "Personal Computer Memory Card International Association"). If you hear someone spew that many letters, it means they're behind the times.

- USB network adapters plug into the USB ports available on most modern computers. USB network adapters come in both wired and wireless versions.

- Custom solutions aren't unheard of, and even with today's modern computers, you may encounter proprietary cards like Apple's internal AirPort and AirPort Extreme wireless network adapters. Some earlier Macs even had proprietary CommSlot network adapter cards. Finding an old custom network adapter for a wired Ethernet network may require going directly to the company that developed it, though that's not the case with Macintosh peripherals—Apple doesn't make any of them any more (if it ever did).

(((•))) **NOTE**

Before Apple started building standard Ethernet ports into every Mac, it used a generic Ethernet connector called an AAUI (Apple Attachment Unit Interface). The idea was that you could buy an AAUI transceiver for the type of Ethernet network to which you wanted to connect—10Base-5, 10Base-2, or 10Base-

T. Glenn has squirreled away a few 10Base-T AAUI adapters: if the adapter for an older printer or computer dies, he doesn't want to have to replace the entire device.

- Parallel port network adapters plug into parallel ports on PCs. Since parallel ports are extremely slow (not to mention increasingly uncommon these days), a parallel port Ethernet adapter is a last-ditch solution for adding an elderly PC to a wired Ethernet network.

- SCSI Ethernet adapters are a Macintosh-based approach similar to the PC world's parallel port network adapters. SCSI Ethernet adapters plug into the standard SCSI ports on all Macs before the iMac, though realistically, you'd only use a SCSI Ethernet adapter with Macs from the early 1990s since almost all others have better options. No SCSI Ethernet adapters are still sold, and if you buy one used, make sure to get software with it, since most of the companies that made them are dead and gone.

Finding older network adapters can be tricky, but if all else fails, search on the eBay auction site at www.ebay.com—it's a great source for old hardware. Luckily, none of these devices should be particularly expensive.

MAC Addresses

Your computer probably has a serial number, but it's likely printed only on the outside of the case—the computer doesn't know what its serial number is. However, every network adapter—Ethernet or wireless—has a unique serial number called a *MAC address*. MAC stands for Media Access Control; it has nothing to do with Apple's Macintosh computers.

Ethernet works by sending packets to specific MAC addresses on the network. If MAC addresses weren't unique, it would be possible for two computers with the same address to connect to the same network. And if that happened, well, it would be like trying to direct a train to one of two identically named railroad stations. If it were a television sitcom, hilarity would ensue; in the real world, people get extremely angry when things are improperly delivered. The same is true in the computer world.

 TIP

MAC addresses are associated with network adapters, not computers, so if your computer has a built-in Ethernet network adapter and a wireless network adapter, each has its own unique MAC address.

The IP addresses necessary for a computer to communicate on the Internet are associated with MAC addresses using a process called Address Resolution

Protocol (ARP). IP networks span many Ethernet networks, and the association of IP with MAC lets traffic leave a computer, hit a router, transit the Internet, pass a second router to a local network, and reach another machine on the other end. Thanks to ARP, the routers know which IP addresses are connected to which MAC addresses on each local network segment. You can have many IP addresses assigned to a single MAC address, but only one MAC address per IP.

For the most part, you don't need to know anything about MAC addresses. There are three exceptions to that rule, and although we don't go into them in great detail here, we touch on them in other parts of the book, so don't panic if some of this information goes over your head.

- You can tell certain gateways to assign the same IP address to a specific MAC address at all times. This way, you can set your laptop to get an IP address via DHCP (Dynamic Host Configuration Protocol, which we cover later in this appendix) no matter where you may happen to be, and if you're at home or in the office, you can ensure that your computer will always get the same IP address on those networks. When you're traveling, although you won't be able to get the same IP address, you don't have to change your network configuration to receive a dynamically assigned IP address from the remote network's DHCP server.

- You can set up security on a wireless network so only computers with specific MAC addresses are allowed to connect. This approach is fairly secure, but…

- Most network adapters can have their MAC addresses changed either easily or with a bit of elbow grease. When an adapter leaves its assembly line, it must be set to a unique address, which is typically also stamped on a label attached to it. The address is also stored in persistent but changeable memory on the network adapter. There are two reasons you might want to change a MAC address. First, some cable ISPs and universities restrict network connections to registered MAC addresses. Cable companies often allow you to register only one machine. If you want to move computers around or share a connection via a wireless gateway, you must set the new network adapter (the adapter making the connection) to the MAC address of the registered network adapter. Wireless gateways often provide an option in their software to reset the MAC address for this reason. The other reason isn't so nice—if you're a wireless network cracker, cloning the MAC address of a computer that's legitimately allowed on a wireless network is necessary for hijacking network access. Sad but true.

Hubs & Switches

Think back to our discussion of network topologies for a moment. Remember that in a star network topology there's always a central hub, from which all the connections radiate like spokes in a wheel? Well, that's where Ethernet *hubs* come from—they act as the central point to which all the computers on a network connect.

 NOTE

In fact, wireless access points are essentially just hubs for wireless networks. They use radio waves instead of Ethernet cables, of course, but otherwise they work in almost exactly the same way. We talk more about wireless access points in Chapter 3, Wireless Hardware.

Hubs have two or more ports into which you can plug computers (although a 2-port hub may seem fairly pointless, since it lets you connect only two computers; two-port hubs tend to be extremely small and intended for creating quick networks while traveling).

TIP

When deciding how large a hub to buy, buy one with more ports than you think you need. The extra ports always come in handy.

As with network adapters, hubs must support the type of Ethernet your network uses, so if you've installed Fast Ethernet (100Base-T) or Gigabit Ethernet (1000Base-T), make sure your hub supports it if you want to take advantage of that speed. Modern hubs can auto-sense the speed of the network and configure their ports appropriately—there's no problem with mixing and matching 10Base-T devices and Fast Ethernet devices on a single 10/100 auto-sensing hub.

NOTE

Though they're less common now, it used to be easy to find hubs that had not just 10Base-T RJ-45 ports, but also a BNC port for 10Base-2 networks. That made it easy to mix network types; for instance, you could use 10Base-2 coaxial cable for a long cable run and place a hub on either end for devices that could connect only with 10Base-T networks.

Types of Hubs

There are three types of hubs: passive, switching, and intelligent.

- A passive hub does nothing more than act as a conduit for the data from a computer on one spoke of the wheel to a computer on another spoke. You need to know three important facts about passive hubs, since they account for the differences with the other two types. First, passive hubs share all the bandwidth on the network internally. So, let's say that you have eight computers plugged into an 8-port, 10Base-T passive hub. If you're copying files from one computer to another, and copying those files is using 5 Mbps of bandwidth, the other six computers must share the remaining 5 Mbps for whatever else they want to do. That's because when a packet arrives from a computer on one spoke, the passive hub copies it to all the other spokes, even though it's destined only for one particular computer. Contrast that in a moment with a switching hub. Second, with a passive hub, the only feedback you get is an LED that indicates when a computer is attached to the port (the LED is lit) and when traffic is flowing to or from that computer (the LED flashes). Contrast this with an intelligent hub. Third, a passive hub makes an Ethernet network appear to be one segment, which can limit maximum distances and increase collisions.

- A switching hub, also called a *switch*, reads the destination address on every packet and sends it to the correct physical port (rather than to all ports simultaneously, except for special broadcast packets used by DHCP and a few other protocols). This variation on the passive hub provides a significant benefit: because each port is a separate connection between the connected devices, rather than shared, each connection receives the full bandwidth available on that type of network. For instance, let's say our eight-computer network from our passive-hub example is now using a switching hub. When you copy files from one computer to the other, the switching hub makes those two computers (and all the rest on the network) think that those two computers are connected directly to one another. Should two other computers start communicating while the files are copying, the switching hub does the same for them, giving them a virtual direct connection. A switching hub provides improved performance over a passive hub—it makes a network run faster if you regularly have several pairs of computers communicating with one another. Switching hubs are also useful when connecting passive hubs or switching hubs together in larger network configurations. For a very small network, whether you use a passive or a switching hub probably doesn't matter much, but luckily, most hubs are switching hubs these days, thanks to the lowered cost of the necessary circuitry.

- An intelligent hub adds features that let network administrators monitor traffic passing through the hub and configure each port separately. Typically, you use these features via a Web browser connected to a Web server embedded in the hub. A small network doesn't need an intelligent hub.

If you want to connect hubs together that don't have cable auto-sensing, you must either use a crossover cable between normal ports or a patch cable from a normal port on one hub to the uplink port on another hub. See the sidebar "Crossover Cables and Uplink Ports" earlier in this appendix for more details.

What sort of hub should you get, given a choice? We recommend switching hubs, because they're cheap and provide the best performance. Only larger networks have much use for intelligent hubs.

Bridges

The next important piece of networking hardware is the *bridge*. Despite the name, visualizing a real-world bridge won't help you understand a networking bridge. Instead, think about what happens when you want to transfer a cargo container (a packet) from one railroad car to another railroad car on a different, but nearby track. The cargo container itself doesn't change, but you need a device, like an automated conveyer belt, to move the container from one railroad car to another.

In networking terms, that conveyer belt is a bridge. Bridges connect similar network types that use different media or are physically separate in some fashion from one another. To put it more technically: a bridge moves data from one kind of physical medium into another without doing much with the data.

We find bridges pretty neat, because they're inexpensive and solve many tricky networking problems. You need a bridge to connect a wired Ethernet network to a wireless network, connect a LocalTalk network to a wired Ethernet network, connect a HomePNA network to a wireless network, and so on.

Although bridges are often built into other devices, such as wireless access points that also bridge between wired and wireless networks, you can also find them as standalone devices. They're particularly useful when you have an older network, such as a LocalTalk network, that you want to connect to a more modern Ethernet network without buying new network adapters.

Bridges aren't particular about where they send data—they just pass traffic from one network to the other. This makes bridges fast, since they don't look at the data they pass and are usually apathetic about what network protocols are involved. When you need to translate one kind of protocol into another, such as moving from a local area network (LAN) to a wide area network (WAN), like your home network out to the Internet, you need a router, which we describe next.

Routers

In our transportation metaphor, bridges move the same kinds of containers across similar kinds of transportation systems, like cargo containers from one train to another train on another track. Routers, on the other hand, don't just move containers around, but can also open containers and repackage the contents in smaller containers: think of a shipment arriving at a wholesale furniture outlet by train, and then having its dining room sets removed for delivery by truck over the highway system.

A more Internet-oriented example might be to imagine Amazon.com: the company orders thousands of books from a single publisher, which arrive by train or freight truck. The books are unloaded, sorted, put into new packages destined for each recipient, and then loaded into a truck, run by a shipping company such as UPS or Federal Express.

Routers convert address-based protocols that describe how information should get from one place to another. Each packet is inspected and repackaged with the appropriate destination information for the network it's handed off to. In practice, this role often comes down to a router taking Ethernet packets containing Internet-bound data or Internet-arriving data bound for machines on a local wired or wireless network and translating between IP and MAC addresses.

Routers can talk to other routers, too, of course, and traffic routing across the Internet typically goes Ethernet, router, Ethernet, router, Ethernet, as data finds its way up to a high-enough level to "see" its way back down to its destination.

As you might expect, watching and acting on every packet takes processing power and RAM, making routers more expensive devices than simple bridges. And yet, advances in technology have enabled networking gear manufacturers to build routing capabilities into even rather inexpensive devices, such as Linksys gateways, which actually sport full routing capabilities. Of course, they probably wouldn't meet the needs of a large network, but for the small networks where they're usually installed, they do just fine.

That said, if you're interested in a small network, and if your Internet connection comes via cable modem, DSL, or even a standard modem, you probably don't need routing capabilities at all. If they happen to be in the device you want, great, but don't pay extra for them. You can also dragoon older computers to act as routers with the addition of special software—a program called IPNetRouter from Sustainable Softworks (see www.sustworks.com) has become popular because it can turn even an elderly Macintosh into a full-fledged router.

Gateways

We've mentioned that the manufacturers of networking gear tend to play fast and loose with terminology, and nowhere is that more evident than with gateways. Technically speaking, a gateway is the next step above a router—we're talking about networking big iron.

However, the term is far more widely used these days to mean a device that merges most, if not all, of the capabilities of all the devices mentioned here, plus some others—such as standard modems and firewalls—for increasing network security. Plus, gateways frequently offer additional software features, such as a DHCP server and a NAT gateway.

((•)) **NOTE**

A better term would be "home gateway," but we bow to the standard usage today and use just "gateway" when we refer to one of these jack-of-all-trades devices.

In short, you can't assume much when you see the term "gateway." It's a good bet that the manufacturer assumes the device has several helpful features to connect your wired or wireless network to the Internet, but beyond that you must read the specifications carefully to determine which functions it performs.

Network Protocols

In this appendix, we talk in general about transferring data, but a few words are in order about how that actually happens. You don't need to know this information to set up a network, but you may find it handy when you try to make certain things work.

All communication between computers takes place according to a set of agreed-upon rules, called a *protocol,* and often informally (and sometimes inaccurately) called a *standard.* It's exactly the same as communication between people, where the agreed-upon rules are called a language. A network protocol is just that, the language that two computers must speak to understand one another.

((•)) **NOTE**

Standards are agreed upon by standards organizations, whether the organizations are regulatory, consensus-driven engineering, or industry. Anyone can develop a protocol, and it may even become widely used, but without the stamp of approval from a standards body, it isn't a standard.

Just as numerous languages have sprung up around the globe, many network protocols have appeared over time. However, the drive toward common communication has caused many of these protocols to fade away; unlike endangered human languages, there's seldom a movement to keep an unused network protocol from disappearing.

Although this is a bit of an oversimplification, every network protocol typically has a specific function that combines with the functions of other network protocols to make communication over the network possible. Here we look at a select set of protocols you're likely to run into when setting up your network.

Establishing a Connection

PPP (Point-to-Point Protocol) is the reigning champion for dial-up and broadband connection negotiation; the broadband Ethernet version is called PPPoE for PPP over Ethernet.

PPP is a simple way for two devices, after establishing a network link of some kind, to negotiate a login, and then provide network details for the connecting machine.

When a client connects via PPP or PPPoE, it passes its user name and password, among other details; the server end of the connection opens access to the given network or dial-up port once the connection is negotiated.

Negotiating an Address

Once connected to a network, your devices need addresses. Ethernet devices have their hardware MAC addresses by default, and AppleTalk (see later in this appendix) lets a computer assign its own unique address. But in the TCP/IP world (again, see later in this appendix), every device needs an IP address, which must be entered manually (for static networks) or assigned dynamically. It's this latter case that we look at here.

DHCP (Dynamic Host Configuration Protocol), which we discuss in many contexts throughout this book, enables a server to assign an IP address to any machine on the same network that wants one. When a computer with a DHCP client, found in most operating systems, first connects to a network, it broadcasts a message saying, "Hey, give me an address!"

One or more DHCP servers can reply with, "I have this address to offer." The client confirms with the appropriate DHCP server that it has accepted the offered address, after which the client is now a full member of the network, with an address, a gateway, and usually DNS server information.

NAT (Network Address Translation) works with DHCP to translate between the DHCP-assigned private, non-routable addresses that aren't reachable outside of the local area network and the public IP address of the gateway. So, for instance, DHCP might assign an IP address of 192.168.1.20 to a computer, but no one on the Internet can reach that private IP address without NAT acting as the traffic cop. The NAT server intercepts outbound requests leaving the network, and rewrites them so they appear to come from the gateway's public, routable Internet address. It also rewrites the response to these requests and sends them back to the internal machine that made the request.

$((\bullet))$ **NOTE**

If you're interested, there are three kinds of NAT: the kind you find in home gateways maps private addresses to specific ports on the gateway's public address (port address translation). The two others map one static address to another (a private address to a dedicated public address) and handle a many-to-many approach in which a local pool of private addresses is arbitrarily mapped to a pool of public addresses.

Packaging and Addressing Data

The next set of protocols package data into discrete, addressed lumps that can pass across a network. The addressing information helps individual machines on a network or routers connecting to other networks deliver the lumps to their destinations.

In all cases, there's a part of the protocol that deals with packaging (the TCP in TCP/IP), and a part that deals with addressing (the IP part of TCP/IP). These are almost always lumped into a single name or concept. AppleTalk comprises both parts. TCP/IP dominates most network discussions these days, but you should also understand how Microsoft's NetBEUI and Apple's AppleTalk interact with modern wireless networks because they're still sufficiently common.

Ethernet

You may recall from earlier in this appendix that Ethernet is a low-level network protocol which comes in several flavors. Ethernet sends data in lumps called *frames*, and all of the protocols we discuss below—TCP/IP, NetBEUI, and AppleTalk—can be *encapsulated*, or wrapped up in Ethernet frames. Ethernet uses MAC addresses to deliver data.

TCP/IP

TCP/IP is a set of two separate protocols that work together: TCP (Transmission Control Protocol) and IP (Internet Protocol). TCP puts packets together and takes them apart; IP handles addressing. Together they form the basis of most communication on the Internet.

The major advantage of TCP/IP over the other protocols is that it's completely standardized and well supported in computer operating systems. It has other benefits as well, such as excellent performance and scalability to very large networks. Since TCP/IP is everywhere, almost every network-related application communicates via TCP/IP.

Both Macs and Windows computers can speak TCP/IP with no trouble. In Windows Me and earlier, the Network control panel provides the necessary options; the much-improved Network Connections control panel handles it in Windows XP. In Mac OS 9, you use the TCP/IP control panel; in Mac OS X, the Network preferences pane has the controls you need. We look at the steps necessary to configure these different operating systems to use TCP/IP in Appendix B, *Configuring Your Network Settings*.

NetBEUI

NetBEUI (NetBIOS Extended User Interface, pronounced Net-BOO-ee) was developed by IBM for use with its LAN Manager product and subsequently adopted by Microsoft for Windows. Its benefits include high performance and easy discovery of network resources like file servers and printers. NetBEUI remains available in Windows for communicating with other computers running Windows; however, technical limitations ensured that NetBEUI would never be used in large networks, and perhaps in part because of that, it was never used to connect computers of different types.

You can use NetBEUI as the underlying protocol for sharing files and printers in Windows, but it's probably easier at this time to stick with TCP/IP instead, especially since some residential gateways may not bridge NetBEUI from wired to wireless networks.

AppleTalk

AppleTalk is a suite of network protocols developed by Apple for networking Macintosh computers and LaserWriter laser printers together, and when it came out, it was revolutionary. Though AppleTalk isn't a particularly high-speed network protocol, it offers welcome features to users, such as automatic discovery of network devices, so users don't have to know the addresses of computers or printers to which they want to connect.

NOTE

A friend of ours at Apple, Stuart Cheshire, helped lead a working group that developed a standard protocol called ZEROCONF (for zero configuration), an attempt to bring the ease-of-use of AppleTalk to TCP/IP networking. Apple calls the technology Rendezvous and is promoting it heavily to hardware manufacturers; Microsoft has already built part of it into Windows XP, remarkably. Since it's a standard that's in the process of being finalized by the Internet Engineering Task Force (IETF), an Internet standards body, ZEROCONF has a good chance of succeeding. For more information, visit www.zeroconf.org.

Several software products, including Microsoft's own Services for Macintosh in Windows NT/2000 and the free Unix/Linux/BSD Netatalk package, support AppleTalk for other platforms, but AppleTalk never took off for connecting computers other than Macs. Even Apple has been moving away from AppleTalk, instead basing all of its network services on TCP/IP. Because old Macs and old Apple LaserWriters (which communicate via AppleTalk) tend to stick around, though, AppleTalk isn't likely to disappear entirely for some time.

If your Macintosh hardware was purchased in the last few years, you don't have to worry about AppleTalk at all. To keep an old LaserWriter available on your network, however, you need to make sure you have AppleTalk turned on (check the AppleTalk control panel in Mac OS 9 or the Network preferences pane in Mac OS X). If you buy an access point, make sure it can bridge AppleTalk from wired to wireless networks; for instance, Apple's AirPort Base Station can, whereas Linksys's access points cannot.

$((\bullet))$ **NOTE**

Adam worked around this limitation in his Linksys gateway by connecting his LaserWriter to an AsantéTalk Ethernet to LocalTalk Bridge, and then sharing the printer from a server running Mac OS X. He can print to the Mac OS X-based print server using TCP/IP (he uses the Desktop Printer Utility in Mac OS 9, and he created a printer using IP Printing in Mac OS X's Print Center utility); the server then passes the print job to the LaserWriter via AppleTalk and the AsantéTalk Ethernet to LocalTalk Bridge. It's neat that it works at all, and an added benefit is that print jobs can wait on the server until he turns on the printer, even days later.

Applying Networks

Moving up one more level in the scheme of things, you need programs that talk over networks and exchange information. Otherwise, why bother having a network at all? It's likely that you're already familiar with many of the protocols in this category in the TCP/IP world, at least through the applications that implement them.

DNS

Every computer on the Internet must have a unique IP address that identifies it. But IP addresses like 216.168.61.154 aren't easy for humans to remember or type, so the domain name system (DNS) was developed to translate between human-readable names like www.tidbits.com and their associated IP addresses. So, if you visit www.tidbits.com in your Web browser, the browser asks a DNS server what IP address goes with www.tidbits.com. The DNS server checks to see if it knows the IP address for www.tidbits.com already; if not, it queries other DNS servers until it find the appropriate IP address. Then the DNS server returns the IP address, 216.168.61.154, to your Web browser, which proceeds to make the connection to the www.tidbits.com server.

Ports in a Storm

In this appendix, we talk about two different ways addressing can take place—Ethernet MAC addresses and IP addresses. But how does a computer differentiate among the different types of data that come in? What separates an email message from a Web page from an instant message? One word: *ports,* and in this case we're not talking about physical jacks on your computer.

To go back to our railroad analogy, if you consider a computer to be a railroad station, then a port is a loading dock at the station that accepts only one type of cargo. Perishable foods go to one loading dock, heavy equipment to another, and so on. Similarly, every Internet service from email to the Web uses a specific port. Thus, a port is essentially an address refinement—the IP address identifies the destination computer, and the port number identifies what sort of data is being sent to that computer.

Many port numbers have been agreed upon for a long time (and are thus referred to as "well-known" ports), so for instance, SMTP uses port 25, DNS uses port 53, the Web uses port 80, and so on. However, nothing prevents someone from running a server on an otherwise unused port, so you'll sometimes see Web servers running on port 8080. And some protocols, like FTP, may start on one port but switch to another unused port after setting up the connection.

You should know three main facts about ports:

- If a Web site you want to visit is running on an unusual port number, you must build it into the URL you send other people or use on Web pages, as in http://www.example.com:8080/index.html. The port number comes after the domain name and a colon.

- Firewalls usually work by allowing traffic to pass on only a few specific ports. If you try to use an application that requires a port that your firewall has closed, that application won't work.

- Running servers behind a NAT gateway can be problematic, because the NAT gateway won't know where to direct incoming requests. A technique called port mapping helps work around this problem. In your NAT gateway, you simply say that all traffic on port 80, for instance, should be passed to an internal computer that's actually running a Web server. Without this port mapping, the machine acting as the NAT gateway would assume—incorrectly—that it was the intended destination.

(((•))) **NOTE**

IP addresses may change for infrastructure reasons, or when a company moves servers from one hosting facility to another. But because DNS-assigned names can stay constant, they enable DNS to work as a pointer to resources instead of to permanent, fixed addresses.

DNS can be a problem on any network that relies on DHCP and NAT to translate between private internal addresses and a single external IP address. Many Internet service providers offer dynamic IP addresses that can change from day to day; this approach prevents DNS servers on the Internet from knowing your IP address, and thus prevents people from connecting directly to your computer. Luckily, there's a workaround that lets people connect to your computer even when you have a dynamic IP address. A service called *dynamic DNS* enables you to map an unchanging host name to whatever your current IP address may be. See Chapter 16, *Buying a Wireless Gateway*, for more about dynamic DNS.

FTP

FTP (File Transfer Protocol) is an increasingly creaky way to retrieve files from or upload files to a remote server. FTP is most commonly used in conjunction with Web servers, where you use FTP to upload the HTML files that make up a Web site.

FTP is one of the earliest Internet protocols, and it has a behavior that can cause frustration if you use it from behind a NAT gateway and a firewall. When you initiate a normal FTP session, the FTP server responds to an arbitrary port to start the transaction. Unless your firewall and NAT gateway are set up to allow incoming access to any old port, the connection will be blocked.

Passwords in the Stream

FTP sends its passwords as plain text, which should worry you, since a network snooper who managed to steal your password by watching your FTP traffic can use that password to log in to a terminal account on the same machine or upload new files to your Web site.

By default, POP and IMAP also transmit their passwords with no encryption, meaning that someone could read your email. That may not sound dire, but because many Internet services maintain security by sending you confirmation email and requiring that you click a link in that message, making it possible for a snooper to read your email could open you up to a host of other problems.

See Chapter 24, *Wireless Worries*, for advice on evaluating your real risk and Chapter 26, *Securing Data in Transit*, for how to encrypt your passwords and other data while in transit.

Luckily, many FTP clients and most servers support an option called *passive FTP*. Passive FTP starts a connection from the well-known port 21, which is reserved for FTP, and the server replies over the same port.

SMTP, POP, and IMAP

These three protocols are used for sending and receiving email. Mail that you send relies on SMTP (Simple Mail Transfer Protocol), while you receive incoming email via POP (Post Office Protocol) or IMAP (Internet Message Access Protocol). For the most part, there's nothing unusual in how these protocols interact with wired or wireless networks.

HTTP

The most common application protocol in use on the Internet today is HTTP (Hypertext Transfer Protocol). It started as the basic language of the Web, although it's now used for a variety of other functions, including the WebDAV file service (Web-Based Distributed Authoring and Versioning).

Configuring Your Network Settings

Most modern computers default to using network settings that just work as soon as you make some sort of an Internet connection. Achieving this ease of use involves the use of DHCP, which is called *Dynamic* Host Configuration Protocol for a reason. When you use DHCP, your computer picks up all its network settings dynamically from a DHCP server (usually in your wireless gateway), and you don't have to set anything else. We strongly recommend that you use DHCP whenever possible, particularly if you're traveling, since it makes switching among different networks much easier.

In some cases, you may need to enter network settings manually rather than relying on DHCP. If you're working on an existing network, ask the system administrator, or person who set it up, what to enter. If you're connecting directly to an Internet service provider, refer to its documentation, ask its Help Desk, or use the advice in the sidebar "Configuring Your Network Settings Manually."

 TIP

You may need to configure your computer with manual settings briefly when setting up a new wireless gateway, since you can't access a Web-based interface unless your computer can be on the same network (usually 192.168.1.x or 10.1.1.x, where x is any number except 0 and 255) as the gateway. Refer to your gateway's manual for specifics.

Configuring Network Settings in Windows

No matter which version of Windows you're using, you must install your wireless network adapter and configure the network settings appropriately before you can use any of the instructions in Chapter 6, *Connecting Your Windows PC*, to configure your wireless client software. Follow these steps to configure your network settings:

 NOTE

If your Wi-Fi network adapter is already installed and working, skip to the step 4 below that corresponds to your version of Windows.

1. Install the drivers for your network card using the CD-ROM or floppy disk that came with it, or using an installer you downloaded from the manufacturer's Web site.

2. Shut the computer down, and connect your network adapter to the computer. Power up again.

TIP

Shutting down isn't essential for PC Card or USB wireless network adapters, but it is for PCI cards or other internal cards, and starting from scratch is always a good idea.

3. If all goes well, Windows identifies your new wireless network adapter, loads the driver you installed, and creates an entry in the Network (95/98/Me/NT) or Network Connections (XP/2000) control panel corresponding to the hardware (**Figure B.1**).

Figure B.1
Windows recognizes
new hardware and
configures it.

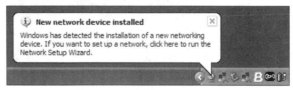

 **NOTE**

If Windows does not automatically detect and configure your new wireless network adapter, you should refer to Appendix C, How to Troubleshoot, *and Chapter 14,* Troubleshooting Your Connection, *for troubleshooting tactics and solutions.*

Here's where the steps diverge, splitting into instructions for earlier versions of Windows (95, 98, Me, and NT) and for more recent versions (2000 and XP).

Windows 95/98/Me/NT

4. Open the Network control panel, and in the Configuration tab check that you have TCP/IP mapped to the new device (**Figure B.2**). For instance, if your card is identified in Windows as "Linksys WPC11 Wireless Network Adapter," you should see an entry that says "TCP/IP->Linksys WPC11..."

5. If you need additional networking protocols (many people don't), click Add, choose Protocol, scroll to Microsoft or other companies on the left, and select NetBEUI or whichever other protocol you want or need.

If you're using dynamic addressing with a DHCP server, which we recommend because it's the easiest, you can leave the default settings alone and skip to step 8, where our instructions converge again for all versions of Windows.

Configuring Your Network Settings Manually

If you're connecting to your own access point and have decided not to use DHCP, no one can tell you what network numbers to enter. That's usually not as bad as it sounds, because if you're the type of person who wants to use a manual configuration, you generally know what to enter. In that situation, here's a brief rundown of the necessary bits of information to enter.

- **IP address.** This is the IP address for your computer. It must be in the same private network range as your access point, usually 192.168.1.x or 10.1.1.x, where *x* is any number except 0 and 255 (which are reserved for special purposes). The number must be unique on the local private network.

- **Subnet mask.** This setting indicates the size of your network, and if you're using an IP

address in one of the two ranges above, you should enter 255.255.255.0 for subnet mask.

- **Gateway or router address.** This is the internal IP address of your access point, and it's probably an IP address in your private range, like 192.168.1.1. (We always make our gateways one of the first addresses in the IP range, skip nine addresses, and then start assigning IP addresses to computers. The gateway usually ends up being 192.168.1.1, for instance, and the computers start at 192.168.1.10.) Microsoft uses the term *gateway*; Apple calls the same thing a *router*.

- **DNS server addresses.** For these numbers, enter the addresses—there will usually be at least two—given to you by your ISP.

Figure B.2
Network
control panel's
Configuration tab.

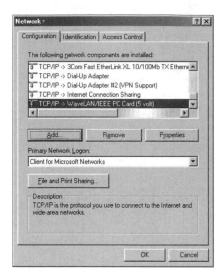

6. Select TCP/IP->*device* (where your particular adapter's name appears instead of *device*) from the list and click Properties (**Figure B.3**).

7. In each of three tabs—DNS Configuration, Gateway, and IP Address—click the radio buttons for enabling DNS and specifying an IP address, after which you can enter the necessary IP address, subnet mask, gateway address, and DNS server addresses.

TIP

Where do you get these settings? See the sidebar "Configuring Your Network Settings Manually" in this appendix.

Figure B.3
TCP/IP Properties.

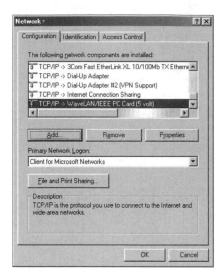

Windows XP/2000

4. Open the Control Panel directory (accessible from the Start menu in Windows XP, and from the Settings menu in the Start menu in Windows 2000), and then open Network Connections in Windows XP (**Figure B.4**) or Network and Dial-up Connections in Windows 2000.

Figure B.4
Windows XP
Network
Connections
window.

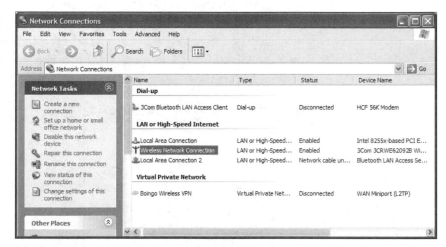

5. Right-click the icon named Wireless Network Connection and choose Properties from the shortcut menu to open the Properties dialog for the connection (**Figure B.5**). If no item named Wireless Network Connection is in the list, then the adapter isn't installed correctly, and you should walk through the steps to install the network adapter again, or read our troubleshooting advice in Chapter 14, *Troubleshooting Your Connection*.

Figure B.5
Windows XP
Wireless Network
Connection
Properties dialog.

Each wireless connection is numbered separately, so if you remove and add many wireless adapters, you may find yourself with connections labeled "Wireless Network Connection 12," as Glenn did on a machine used for testing wireless network cards.

6. Select Internet Protocol (TCP/IP) from the list. If there's no checkmark in the box next to its name, check that box. (If TCP/IP or other protocols you need aren't listed, click Install, and select them from the Protocols list or Clients list.) Click the Properties button to open the TCP/IP Properties dialog (**Figure B.6**).

Figure B.6
Windows XP TCP/IP
Properties dialog.

7. If you're using dynamic addressing with a DHCP server, then you can leave the default settings alone and skip to step 8.

    Otherwise, select Use the Following IP Address and Use the Following DNS Server Addresses radio buttons and enter the appropriate values for your IP address and DNS servers. (See the "Configuring Your Network Settings Manually" sidebar earlier for where to get these numbers.)

All Windows versions

8. Click OK twice: once to close the TCP/IP Properties dialog and a second time to close the Network control panel or Wireless Network Connection Properties dialog.

9. Restart your computer when (or if) Windows prompts you to do so.

Configuring Network Settings in Mac OS 8.6/9.x

To configure your network settings in Mac OS 8.6 and 9.x, you work in the TCP/IP and AppleTalk control panels. Follow these steps to configure your network settings. After that, you can return to the instructions in Chapter 8, *Connecting Your Macintosh*, to configure your AirPort software:

1. From the hierarchical Control Panels menu in the Apple menu, choose TCP/IP to open the TCP/IP control panel.

2. From the File menu, choose Configurations to open the Configurations dialog and display the different configurations you may have (**Figure B.7**).

Figure B.7
Creating a new AirPort configuration.

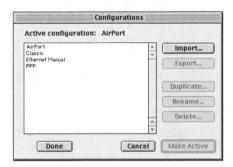

3. If there is a configuration called AirPort, select it and click Make Active. Otherwise, select any other configuration, click Duplicate, and name the configuration "AirPort" (or whatever you want—the name isn't important). Then select your new AirPort configuration and click Make Active.

4. Back in the TCP/IP control panel's main window, choose AirPort from the Connect Via pop-up menu (**Figure B.8**).

5. Assuming you're connecting to an AirPort Base Station or other access point that has DHCP turned on, choose Using DHCP Server from the

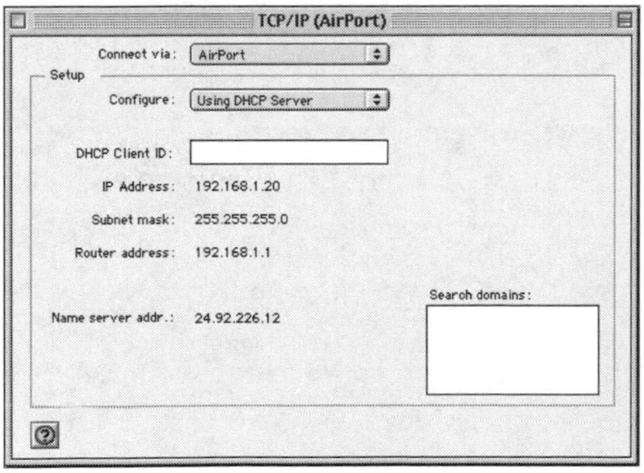

Figure B.8
Configuring the TCP/IP control panel for use with AirPort.

Configure pop-up menu. If you instead want to use a static IP address, choose Manually from the Configure pop-up menu and enter the appropriate IP address, subnet mask, router address, and DNS server addresses (Apple labels this field "Name server addr"). If you're not sure what to enter here, refer to the "Configuring Your Network Settings Manually" sidebar near the start of this appendix.

6. Close the TCP/IP control panel, and save the settings when prompted.

7. From the hierarchical Control Panels menu in the Apple menu, choose AppleTalk to open the AppleTalk control panel.

8. Follow steps 2 and 3 again to select or create a new AirPort configuration.

9. From the Connect Via pop-up menu, choose AirPort (**Figure B.9**).

10. Close the AppleTalk control panel, and save the settings when prompted.

Figure B.9
Configuring the AppleTalk control panel for use with AirPort.

Configuring Network Settings in Mac OS X

In Mac OS X, you change network settings in the Network preferences pane in System Preferences. Follow these steps to configure your network settings. After that, you can return to the instructions in Chapter 8, *Connecting Your Macintosh*, to configure your AirPort software:

1. Choose System Preferences from the Apple menu, or click its icon on the Dock, and once System Preferences opens, click the Network icon to display the Network preferences pane.

2. Choose AirPort from the Show pop-up menu.

   If AirPort doesn't appear in the menu, choose Network Port Configurations, select the On checkbox next to AirPort, and choose AirPort from the Show pop-up menu.

The display changes back to the AirPort configuration screen.

3. Click the TCP/IP tab, and from the Configure menu, choose Using DHCP if your address is assigned dynamically by a DHCP server. If you want to enter a static IP address instead, choose Manually and enter your IP address, subnet mask, router, and DNS servers (**Figure B.10**). If you're not sure what to enter here, refer to the "Configuring Your Network Settings Manually" sidebar near the start of this appendix.

Figure B.10
Configuring TCP/IP
for use with AirPort.

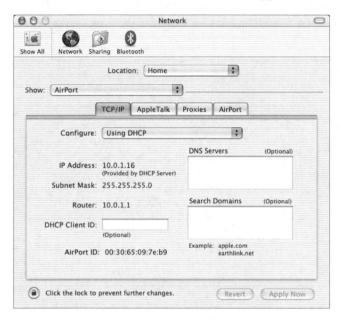

4. Click the AppleTalk tab, and check Make AppleTalk Active to let AppleTalk pass over your wireless network along with TCP/IP (**Figure B.11**).

 TIP

With AirPort and another networking method active, like Ethernet, Mac OS X warns you that AppleTalk can work over only one of the networks.

5. Click the Apply Now button to activate your changes.

 TIP

If you travel regularly and find that you need to change your settings often, you can instead create multiple locations using the New Location item in the Location menu at the top of the Network preferences panel. Each location can have its own AirPort configuration, and you can easily switch among them using the Location menu.

Figure B.11
Configuring
AppleTalk for use
with AirPort.

How to Troubleshoot

Most people have little trouble noticing problems. But we've noticed—and as usability expert Don Norman has frequently said—that new users assume that it's them behaving incorrectly rather than a computer-related fault that can (and should) be eliminated. If you find yourself routinely performing the same set of steps to work around some problem, we recommend taking a few moments to work through these steps to see if you can solve the problem and simplify your life.

((•)) **NOTE**

Sometimes workarounds do reflect absences in a program or operating system. Determining whether it's a bug, a misunderstanding, or an absence is key to troubleshooting.

The most important piece of advice we can give in this appendix is: be methodical. If you start trying solutions to a problem without thinking about what caused the problem and what the effect of any given solution may be, you just complicate the entire situation. The best way to encourage a methodical approach is to get a notebook and take notes about what you see (especially any error messages), what you do, and the effects of what you do. There's no need to be truly obsessive about taking notes, but make sure you at least describe the order of events, just in case you need to refer back later.

Follow this five-step process to get to the bottom of any problem.

1. Describe the Problem

The first step is to identify the problem and gather information about it. That sounds simple, and it usually is, because most problems aren't particularly subtle. Perhaps you can't send email, or your one wired computer isn't visible to the computers on your wireless network.

It's important to determine if the problem is reproducible or intermittent. Although an intermittent problem may be less annoying than a reproducible problem, since you may be able to keep working through it, intermittent problems are much harder to track down, because one of the variables is related to some time- or state-related fact. Reproducible problems beg to be solved, because you generally can't keep working until you've solved the problem.

Also pay attention to any visible indicators that might give more information about the problem. For instance, most network adapters have LEDs that indicate when they're powered up and flash when traffic is flowing. If those LEDs aren't working the way you expect, that's an important piece of information to add to the description.

Finally, be on the lookout for any error messages when something fails—or even the fact that no error message appears. Write these down exactly as you see them or take screen captures, since every digit or letter in an error number can be important.

2. Break the System Apart

Once you have a firm grasp on the problem you're trying to solve, you need to start breaking the system related to the problem into discrete steps or pieces. Then you can start analyzing different parts of the whole. The hard part here is that you may not realize what the different parts of the system are, making it difficult to understand how one could fail.

For instance, take the example of a wireless network that also has one computer connected via an Ethernet cable. In this sample network, the one wired computer is used as an informal file server. You're using one of the wireless computers, and you suddenly can't connect to a shared folder. What are the variables involved here? Let's determine what must be true for the situation to work properly, after which we can start testing each of the components. Here's what must be true:

- On your computer, you need properly installed file sharing client software.

- Your computer must have a working connection to the access point.

- The access point must allow you to see a computer connected via wired Ethernet.

- The wired Ethernet computer must have a working connection to the access point.

- File sharing server software must be running on the wired Ethernet computer.

- A folder must explicitly be shared on the wired Ethernet computer.

You could certainly break these pieces into even smaller pieces, but this should be sufficient to get started.

Keep in mind that what we've just described is only one working system, which is important, because if there are other working systems—other wireless computers that can see the file server—that helps us isolate the problem more quickly.

Note all these variables briefly in your notebook, and if you're a picture person, consider drawing yourself a diagram of how it all fits together; diagrams can come in handy if you need to break the system apart by disconnecting cables or rearranging equipment.

3. Ask Yourself Questions

Now that you've identified all the parts of a system, it's time to look carefully at each part, making up a possible reason why a failure at that point could be responsible for the whole problem. In our example, let's take each variable and analyze it, asking questions that lead to tests:

- File sharing client software is of course necessary, but since you were able to connect previously, it's a good assumption that it's installed. Is it turned on? Has anything changed since you last connected successfully that might provide a clue? Have you restarted? (It's always worth trying.) What about other computers? Can their file sharing client software see the wired computer?

- Are you connected to the access point? Is it working for other network-related tasks at the same time you can't connect to the wired computer?

- Is the access point configured correctly so wireless computers can see the wired computer? Since it worked properly before, this likely isn't the source of the problem. Has anything changed on the access point since you last connected that could be related?

- Can the wired computer connect to the access point via Ethernet? Never underestimate the trouble a broken, loose, or flaky cable can cause.

- Is file sharing on the wired computer turned on and configured properly? Has anything changed on that computer that might have resulted in file sharing being turned off or reconfigured? Have you restarted the wired computer recently?

- Is the shared folder still shared? Could someone have changed which folders were shared? Has the folder been moved or renamed or otherwise modified in some way that might have changed its state?

We mentioned the difference between reproducible and intermittent problems above; if you have an intermittent problem connecting to the wired Ethernet computer, that generates additional questions.

- Does the problem happen at all times of day? Does it happen right after you've done something else? Is it related to the presence or absence of any other computers on the network?

Jot these questions down in your notebook, numbering them so you can easily refer back to them when you start answering the questions through testing.

4. Answer Questions

Once you have your list of questions, revisit it and think about a test you must perform to answer each question. Separate your questions roughly into easy, moderate, and hard categories (you might write an E, M, or H next to each question's number in the margin).

Also give your intuition a chance to work. If you have a nagging feeling that your spouse might have let your 4-year-old nephew play a game on the wired Ethernet computer, start with that machine. Or, if you just had to reset the access point to factory default settings for another reason, start there.

Wherever you choose to start, begin with tests that eliminate the easiest questions first. For instance, it's trivial to check if your nephew kicked the Ethernet cable out of the jack; there's no reason to consider reinstalling the entire operating system on that machine until you've exhausted every easier option.

((•)) **NOTE**

Glenn knows about reinstalling the operating system at this point: he once went through the pain of reinstalling Windows XP Professional before being told that a single, obscure system service needed to be reset. Oy.

Working methodically is essential in this step, and if you change something in a way that significantly changes your variables, it's best (if possible) to put it back so the situation stays the same as when you analyzed the problem. For instance, if you had been thinking about installing a new access point that you'd just bought, don't do that in the middle of the troubleshooting process or you risk confusing everything.

Make sure to check off each question you answer in your notebook, and note any interesting things that happened when you performed the test. We don't suggest you do this because you're going to forget what you've done while you're troubleshooting, but because you may have forgotten by the next time the problem happens. Plus, if you end up wanting to ask someone else for help, you can say authoritatively that you had indeed tried a particular test with negative results.

In most situations, the solution to your problem will make itself clear during this process of answering questions. Perhaps it's summer, and the reinstallation of your screen door is blocking the wireless network signal, or perhaps your spouse configured the computer in an unusual way for your nephew's game. Maybe your access point lost track of the wireless-to-wired Ethernet bridge settings, or maybe your computer just needed to be restarted.

5. Get Expert Help

But what if, after all these steps, you still haven't solved the problem? Failure to solve a problem on your own is no cause for surrender, because you usually just don't understand the system well enough to break it into appropriate chunks. Or perhaps you simply didn't think of the necessary tests.

For instance, in our example, if you didn't realize that all the network traffic had to pass through the access point, and a factory default reset (perhaps caused by a lightning strike-driven power surge) had turned off wireless-to-wired Ethernet bridging, you could easily have tested everything else without realizing what you were missing.

That's where experts come in. Sometimes they may have solved so many problems that they automatically know the solution to your problem based on your description. But more often they can simply break the problem down into more chunks, one of which usually turns out to be the problem.

Here's where intermittent problems can drive you crazy. Although an expert can offer suggestions about where to look, if you have a system that works some of the time, it's difficult to determine whether you were testing the wrong variables or if you were testing the right variables at the wrong time or in combination with the wrong set of other variables.

Where to Turn

So you need help. Where should you turn first? Give the order in which you jump from expert to expert some thought, since your goal should be to find a solution to your problem with the least effort and cost, not to mention the least irritation to your collection of experts.

Before anything else, try searching on the Web, both in company support databases and in Google (www.google.com). The only hard part is coming up with appropriate search terms, but it's often worth five minutes of searching in Google. You wouldn't believe the number of questions we've received over the years whose answers were easily found in Google (since that's where we look first, too).

If you have any books or magazines that touch on the topic, it's worth looking in them as well, although we usually prefer to search the Web first, since it's faster than flipping through an index or scanning multiple issues of a magazine.

 NOTE

Of course, for problems with wireless networking, Chapter 14, Troubleshooting Your Connection, *and Chapter 23,* Troubleshooting Your Wireless Network, *are required reading. There's little that's more annoying to a book author than someone asking for help without having read the appropriate sections of his or her book first.*

If a Web search doesn't turn up an answer, or at least some new tests to try, the fastest, cheapest, and easiest person to ask for help is an expert friend. If you have such a friend, we recommend asking that person for help next. Be careful, though, because overusing a friend's willingness to answer your technical questions or fix your problems can strain otherwise solid friendships. And if the friend is really more of an acquaintance, even more care is warranted to avoid causing irritation.

If possible, try to perform roughly equivalent favors for the friend helping you so she doesn't feel exploited. Adam and his wife even have a personal "friend consulting rate" for computer help: dinner. That way, the event changes from a consulting visit into a social event with friends, and everyone feels appropriately rewarded. Glenn has traded consulting for a sushi lunch and a new cell phone.

TIP

If you're ever confused about what sort of hardware to buy, even to the point of deciding between a Mac and PC, one way of breaking the deadlock is to pick the option already chosen by your best expert friend. In other words, figure out who you can call at 9 p.m. on a Saturday night for help, and buy either what that person owns or recommends. Of course, that friend might recommend the opposite platform if she knows what she's getting into.

If you don't have an expert friend, the next best option is to contact the technical support department run by the manufacturer of the device in question. If you haven't already done so, visit its Web site and search quickly to see if it has an online database of problems and solutions that can solve your problem instantly, along with often-essential firmware updates that you can download and install.

 TIP

Adam was recently testing an Asanté wireless gateway that was having huge problems picking up and keeping a DHCP-assigned IP address from his cable ISP. He looked for a firmware update on Asanté's Web site, but because they categorized the wireless gateway under "Routers," and not also under "Wireless," his searches all failed. Once he called tech support and was told how to search the support site, he was able to download and install the firmware update that solved all of his problems.

If the Web site doesn't help, send email or call. Company tech support engineers are likely to know more about the products you're using than anyone else, and it's their job to help you if you're a customer (but that doesn't mean you should ever be snotty to them, as we explain later). Contacting tech support is often your best option for getting fast, accurate help.

That's not to say company tech support works in all situations. Tech support engineers are often paid poorly, so turnover is high, meaning that it's not uncommon to get a tech support engineer who knows less than you do. (In that case, ask politely if your problem can be escalated to second-level support.)

Some companies charge for support, and even when support is free, the calls are seldom toll-free any more. That wouldn't be bad, but it's all too common to wait on hold for 30 minutes before you even talk to a person, and there's little that is more frustrating than knowing that your phone bill is increasing 10 cents per minute while you sit there, not getting your work done.

Finally, some tech support engineers may know their products well, but if the problem stems from an interaction between several products, they may not see the bigger picture, or they may try to pass the blame on to another company (which will, in the most annoying cases, pass it back).

 TIP

Figuring that Sony technical support would have one less excuse to make in the event of a problem, Glenn once recommended that a friend buy a Sony Vaio-branded version of the Orinoco PC Card for the friend's Vaio laptop.

Assuming tech support fails you or isn't worth contacting because of usurious charges or ridiculous phone wait times, the next place to look for help is an appropriate Internet forum. The hard part here is identifying the right place to ask, since so many different groups exist. Check for appropriate mailing lists, Usenet newsgroups, Web-based support forums, and even IRC channels. When we say "appropriate," we mean it. Watch the forum briefly before posting your question to make sure that what you plan to ask fits in with the kinds of discussions that go on, because posting an off-topic request for help will irritate people unnecessarily and won't provide you with the solution you need. Plus, it wastes your precious time.

 TIP

Don't be greedy when it comes to asking for help in Internet forums. They work only because individuals are willing to donate their time and knowledge to the public good, so if you want the forum to thrive, be a sport and help others when you can.

If all other avenues have failed, or if you have no time or patience for any of the previous approaches, consider hiring a consultant. Going the consultant route costs the most and isn't necessarily quick, depending on the consultant's schedule and how familiar he already is with your situation. But if the problem is sufficiently severe or annoying, the time and money will be well spent.

How to Report Problems

When it comes time to report your problems to someone else, your notes are invaluable, because without them, you find yourself repeating tests just to verify the results one more time. Obviously, how you report a problem varies depending on to whom you're reporting it, but this approach should work in most situations.

First, create a profile of your computer that lists:

- Your model of computer, how much memory it has, and which operating system you're using, with its major version number (like Windows XP Pro) and any patches (such as the .8 in Mac OS X 10.2.8 or Service Pack 1 for Windows XP).

- Any recent changes to the system, such as upgrading the operating system itself or installing new drivers.

- Special extensions or add-ins installed, like a third-party firewall or, in Mac OS 9, system extensions.

- Any relevant add-on devices like a second monitor, third-party video card, SCSI card, audio/video hardware, scanner, and so on.

- Version numbers for software or drivers that are relevant to the problem. Often, outdated or too-new drivers cause problems.

TIP

In Windows, look for a program called System Information (it's generally in the System Tools folder inside your Accessories folder), and on the Mac, look for Apple System Profiler either in your Apple menu in Mac OS 9, or in your Utilities folder in Mac OS X. These utilities can generate profiles of your computer that you can save and send along with your problem report.

Once you've developed a profile that you can make available if asked, it's time to report the actual problem. Outline your problem and note that you've done standard troubleshooting. Then briefly relate what you've tried already, but don't go into detail right away, since the mere fact that you're asking for help means that what you tested wasn't helpful. How you continue to proceed depends on how interactive the support medium is.

For support situations that lend themselves to fast interaction (such as in person, via the phone, or instant messaging), let the support person ask questions and guide you through the process, since he likely has ideas about where the problem

Be Nice!

Actually, there is something worse than providing incomplete answers to questions, and it's a little hard to say this, but don't be a jerk! You wouldn't believe how many people assume that the problem is somehow the tech support person's fault. Yes, you're frustrated, and possibly even angry, because of having bought a piece of hardware or software that just isn't working. But, you're far more likely to get help if you're nice, or at least polite and professional, when talking with the tech support person.

Although most people are more polite when they're asking for help in an independent mailing list or other online forum, there's still a tendency to whine or threaten never to buy products from the company again. Bad idea, because the people who are most likely to be able to help you probably like the company and its products, and the more you rant and rail, the less interested they become in responding to you. Further, if you are sufficiently annoying, they may prefer that you turn to another company's products instead of continuing to harass them.

Put bluntly, there's a time and a place for complaints, and complaints should be separated from requests for help. That way you get the maximum effect from your complaint and stand the best chance of receiving help.

is. If you launch into a detailed retelling of what you've tried right off, you may overwhelm him with unnecessary trivia. Don't be offended if he asks whether lights are lit or the device is plugged in. It can be irritating, but it's his version of methodical problem-solving.

When you're asking for help in a situation where interaction is slow (such as direct email, mailing list posting, Usenet news posting, or a Web support forum posting), follow your brief summary of what you tried with a more detailed list of the tests you performed and your system configuration. There's no need to explain what happened with tests that failed to shed any light on the situation, but it is helpful to list them all so people trying to help don't ask about tests you've already performed. (In these slow-interaction forms of communication, a back-and-forth interchange can take a day or two, so you want to keep the number of messages as small as possible.)

In either situation, try to answer questions from the experts as quickly and completely as possible. From our perspective of helping people over the years, there's nothing worse than getting incomplete answers to questions, forcing us to ask the same questions in slightly different ways and stringing out the entire interchange.

Dealing with the Insolvable

We'd like to pretend that if you just follow all the steps outlined above you can solve any problem. Unfortunately, there are a small number of problems that will resist your best efforts, and the best efforts of every expert you can bring to bear. That's because everything you try takes time and effort, and there's a limit to how much energy and money you should invest to solve a given problem. Sometimes the better part of valor is to give up and buy new hardware or software that eliminates the problem entirely. The hope is, of course, that you realize you're heading down this path before you've wasted too much time and effort.

Don't let the fact that some problems can't be solved with a reasonable amount of effort prevent you from trying. In the vast majority of cases, working methodically through the steps we've outlined will result in success.

Glossary

Use this glossary to look up short definitions for terms related to wireless networking. For more detailed information, refer to the chapters indicated at the end of each definition.

1000Base-T   See *Gigabit Ethernet*.

100Base-T   An increasingly common Ethernet wiring standard that works almost exactly like 10Base-T, but increases the maximum throughput to 100 Mbps. 100Base-T is often called "Fast Ethernet." (Appendix A)

10Base-2   An Ethernet wiring standard that uses thin coaxial cable, has a maximum segment length of 185 meters, runs at 10 Mbps, uses a bus network topology, and isn't in common use any more. 10Base-2 is also called "ThinNet." (Appendix A)

10Base-5   An Ethernet wiring standard that uses thick coaxial cable, has a maximum segment length of 500 meters, uses a bus network topology, runs at 10 Mbps, and isn't in common use any more. 10Base-5 is also called "ThickNet." (Appendix A)

10Base-T   The most common Ethernet wiring standard. 10Base-T uses twisted pair wiring that's used to connect buildings' telephone wire to the telephone company, runs at 10 Mbps, uses a star network topology, and is limited to a maximum segment length of 100 meters. (Appendix A)

1x   A prefix for cellular data technology that indicates that only 1.25 MHz of spectrum are in use. (Chapter 4)

1xEV-DO   An upcoming third-generation cellular data technology for CDMA networks in testing by Verizon Wireless. EV-DO stands for Evolution Data Optimized (but is sometimes referred to as Evolution Data Only). (Chapters 4, 30)

1xEV-DV	An upcoming third-generation cellular data technology for CDMA networks in testing by Sprint PCS and AT&T Wire-less. EV-DV stands for Evolution Data/Voice. (Chapter 4)
1xRTT	A cellular data technology for CDMA networks. RTT stands for Radio Transmission Technology. 1xRTT has a theoretical maximum of 144 Kbps of bandwidth, but achieves a practical throughput of only 50 to 70 Kbps in the real world. (Chapters 4, 30)
3x	A prefix for a future third-generation CDMA cellular network that will use 5 MHz of spectrum, or 3 times the 1x spectrum use. (Chapter 4)
802.11 specifications	A family of specifications related to wireless networking. There are too many 802.11 specifications to list here, so see the referenced chapters for full descriptions. (Chapters 2, 4)
802.11a	One of three wireless networking specifications under the Wi-Fi rubric. 802.11a uses the 5 GHz band and runs at 54 Mbps. 802.11a is little used outside specific business situations. (Introduction, Chapter 2)
802.11b	The most common of the three wireless networking specifications included in the Wi-Fi certification mark. 802.11b uses the 2.4 GHz band and runs at 11 Mbps. (Introduction, Chapter 2)
802.11g	The newest of the three Wi-Fi specifications. 802.11g is backward compatible with 802.11b, thanks in part to its use of the 2.4 GHz band, and it runs at the 54 Mbps speed of 802.11a. Most new equipment uses 802.11g. (Introduction, Chapter 2)
802.16	The technical name for WiMax. 802.16 and a subset, 802.16a, are used for long-haul and backhaul connections. (Chapter 4)
802.1X	An authentication specification that allows a client to connect to a wireless access point or wired switch but prevents the client from gaining access to the Internet until it provides credentials, like a user name and password, that are verified by a separate server. In 802.1X, there are three roles: the supplicant (client), authenticator (switch or access point), and authentication server. (Chapters 6, 16, 22)
access point	The hub of a wireless network. Wireless clients connect to the access point, and traffic between two clients must travel through the access point. Access points are often abbreviated to AP in industry literature, and you may also see them referred to as "wireless routers," "wireless gateways," and "base stations." We prefer to use "access point" when discussing true access points that don't also share Internet connections or bridge between wired and wireless networks. (Chapters 3, 14, 16, 17, 19)
ad hoc connections	Spur-of-the-moment connections made for a specific reason and then shut down. Most uses of infrared communications are for ad hoc connections. (Chapters 1, 12)
ad hoc mode	An informal way of creating a wireless network between two or more computers without the need for a centralized access point. (Chapters 12, 19)

ad hoc network   A short-term wireless network created between two or more wireless network adapters without going through an access point. Ad hoc networks are handy for quickly trading files when you have no other way of connecting two or more computers. (Chapters 3, 12, 19)

AES   An extremely strong encryption standard that's just starting to become available. AES stands for Advanced Encryption System. (Chapter 22)

aggregator   A company that resells access to other companies' wireless networks. (Chapters 28, 29)

AirPort Extreme   Apple's marketing name for its 802.11g wireless networking technology. (Chapters 2, 8)

AirPort   Apple's marketing name for its 802.11b wireless networking technology. (Chapters 2, 8)

amplifier   A device you can connect to your antenna to increase the signal strength and amplify weak incoming signals. (Chapter 34)

antenna   A device connected to a wireless transceiver that concentrates transmitted and received radio waves to increase signal strength and thus the effective range of a wireless network. To accept an antenna, a device must have an appropriate antenna jack. (Chapters 3, 14, 16, 21, 23, 33, 34)

APOP   A protocol for protecting email passwords used with POP. APOP stands for Authenticated Post Office Protocol. (Chapter 26)

AppleTalk   A network protocol used primarily by older Macs and LaserWriter printers. If you have such hardware, you must ensure that any access points you buy support AppleTalk. (Chapter 16, Appendix A, Appendix B)

authenticate   The process of confirming the identify of someone connecting to a network. (Chapters 3, 22)

authentication server   A back-end database server that confirms the identify of a supplicant to an authenticator in an 802.1X-authenticated network. (Chapter 22)

authenticator   The gatekeeper role in an 802.1X-authenticated network. You can think of the authenticator as a gatekeeper; access points and Ethernet switches can act as authenticators. (Chapter 22)

backhaul   Connecting Internet access to a location over long or short distances. Traditionally, wired networks have been necessary for backhaul, but with 802.16, also known as WiMax, backhaul via wireless will become even more common than it is with Wi-Fi. (Chapter 4)

band   Another term for spectrum used to indicate a particular set of frequencies. Wireless networking protocols work in either the 2.4 GHz or the 5 GHz bands. (Chapters 1, 2, and 4)

bandwidth	See *throughput*.
base station	See *wireless gateway*.
Bluetooth	A short-range wireless cable replacement technology. (Chapters 4, 11, 18)
bridge	A device that passes traffic between two networks that use different media or are physically separate, but which use similar network standards. Common uses for bridges include connecting wired and wireless networks, connecting a HomePlug network to a wireless network, and connecting distant wireless networks (with the aid of antennas). (Chapters 20, 33, 34, Appendix A)
bridging	The act of connecting two networks via a bridge. (Chapters 20, 33)
bus network	A network topology in which all the computers connect to a single wire. Bus networks are also sometimes called "daisy-chain" networks, and they aren't commonly used any more. (Appendix A)
captive portal	A Web page that appears automatically when you try to access any URL when first connected to some public wireless networks. On the captive portal page, you must enter login information or agree to acceptable use policies before you can use the wireless network to do anything else. (Chapter 32)
Cat5	The only type of twisted pair wire you should buy for Ethernet networks. Cat3 isn't rated for 100 Mbps. (Appendix A)
CDMA	The type of digital cellular phone network used throughout most of the United States, but rare elsewhere in the world. CDMA stands for Code Division Multiple Access, and CDMA2000 is the third-generation, or 3G, extension to which CDMA cellular operators are gradually upgrading their networks. (Chapters 4, 30)
Centrino	A marketing name developed and promoted by Intel for laptops that use the Pentium-M processor, an Intel Pro/Wireless mini-PCI adapter, and some of Intel's support chips. Intel also requires some compatibility testing before manufacturers can use the Centrino name. (Chapter 7)
certificate authority	A trusted third party that can assure the identity of others when using security systems like SSL. A certificate authority registers the digital identity of a site or individual, and lets you confirm manually or automatically that someone you're interacting with—say, over a secure Web connection—is who he appears to be. (Chapter 26)
certificate	An instantiation of a digital identity. Certificates are typically signed by other people or certificate authorities to guarantee their authenticity. (Chapter 26)
channel	A specific portion of the radio spectrum; for example, the channels allotted to one of the wireless networking protocols. 802.11b and 802.11g use 14 channels in the 2.4 GHz band, only 3 of which don't overlap (1, 6, and 11). In the 5 GHz band, 802.11a uses 8 channels for indoor use and 4 others for outdoor use, and none of them overlap. (Chapters 2, 6, 15)

circuit-switched network	A network in which a virtual circuit is set up for each connection in order to simulate having a physical wire between two points. The telephone system is a circuit-switched network. Circuit-switched networks are generally considered less efficient than packet-switched networks like the Internet because the circuit remains reserved even when no data is being transferred (i.e. when no one is talking). (Chapter 4)
clear text	Sensitive information like passwords sent across a network without encryption. Clear text is also commonly referred to as "in the clear." (Chapter 24)
client association	The process by which a wireless client—like a laptop computer—connects to an access point. (Chapter 3)
cloning	The act of replicating one device's MAC address onto another to work around restrictions that prevent only particular MAC addresses from connecting to a network. Also sometimes called "spoofing." (Chapter 16)
closed network	A wireless network that doesn't advertise its network name. (Chapters 3, 6, 17, 25)
collision	The interference that results when two devices on a network start transmitting at the same time.
computer-to-computer network	See *ad hoc network*.
crossover cable	Ethernet cable that has the transmit and receive pins switched. You use a crossover cable to connect certain kinds of network devices, like hubs. (Appendix A)
daisy-chain network	See *bus network*.
decibels	The unit used for measuring antenna gain. Decibels are abbreviated as dB, and you may also see dBm (decibels relative to a reference level of 1 milliwatt) and dBi (decibels relative to an isotropic radiator, or a single point antenna). (Chapters 3, 21, and 34)
DHCP	A protocol by which a server automatically assigns IP addresses to clients so users doesn't have to configure them manually. DHCP stands for Dynamic Host Configuration Protocol. (Chapters 16, 17, 23, 33, Appendix A, Appendix B)
dipole antenna	An antenna type that offers omnidirectional coverage, but not much gain. Access points usually have one or two dipole antennas to increase their gain slightly. (Chapters 21, 34)
direct sequence spread spectrum	One of two approaches (with frequency hopping spread spectrum) for sorting out overlapping data signals transmitted via radio waves. Direct sequence spread spectrum is commonly abbreviated to DSSS or DS. 802.11b uses direct sequence spread spectrum. (Chapter 1)

discoverable	The state in which a Bluetooth device must be to be seen by another Bluetooth device for pairing. (Chapters 4, 11)
discovery	The act in Bluetooth of finding a discoverable device within range for pairing.
DMZ	A feature in a NAT gateway that lets you expose a machine on your internal network to the outside Internet. DMZ nominally stands for *demilitarized zone,* and is sometimes also called "virtual server." It's basically port mapping for all available ports. (Chapter 17)
DNS	An Internet protocol for mapping cryptic IP addresses (like 205.232.177.122) to human-readable domain names (like macaroni.tidbits.com). DNS stands for Domain Name Service. (Chapter 16, Appendix A, Appendix B)
DSL	A common form of broadband Internet connection. DSL stands for Digital Subscriber Line (Introduction)
dynamic DNS	A technique that lets people connect a permanent domain name to an ever-charging IP address. (Chapters 16, 17, Appendix A)
EAP	A standard form of generic messaging used in 802.1X, among other places. EAP stands for Extensible Authentication Protocol. (Chapter 22)
EAP-TLS	Used to create a secured connection for 802.1X by pre-installing a digital certificate on the client computer. EAP-TLS stands for Extensible Authentication Protocol-Translation Layer Security. (Chapters 6, 26*)*
EDGE	An upcoming cellular data technology for GSM networks. EDGE atands for Enhanced Data GSM Environment and should provide more than 100 Kbps of bandwidth. (Chapter 4)
encapsulated	A way of wrapping protocols such as TCP/IP, AppleTalk, and NetBEUI in Ethernet frames so they can traverse an Ethernet network and be unwrapped when they reach the destination computer. (Appendix A)
ESSID	Extended Service Set Identifier. See *network name.*
Ethernet backbone	The wired Ethernet network you use to connect access points in a roaming network. (Chapters 15, 20)
Ethernet	The most common networking standard in the world, formally known as IEEE 802.3. (Appendix A)
Faraday cage	An electromagnetic shield, which may be simulated in a house by chicken wire supporting plaster on the walls. (Chapter 1)
Fast Ethernet	See *100Base-T.*
fast handoff	A way that access points can let authenticated users roam among different access points without losing authentication. Fast handoff also makes voice-over-IP possible. Fast handoff will be made possible with the 802.11f specification. (Chapter 4)

fingerprint A short sequence of characters you can send someone so she can verify that a specific public key is actually your public key. (Chapter 26)

firewall A network program that blocks malevolent traffic that might endanger the computers on your network. (Chapters 16, 17, 27)

firmware The internal software that runs dedicated hardware devices. Upgrades to firmware are often necessary to fix problems. (Chapters 2, 14, 16, 23)

frame bursting An approach to increasing the speed of 802.11g-based wireless networks by unwrapping short 802.11g packets and rebundling them into a larger packet to reduce the impact of mandatory gaps between packets. Frame bursting is sometimes called "packet bursting." (Chapters 2, 4)

frame A packet encapsulated to travel on a physical medium, like Ethernet or Wi-Fi. A packet is like a shipping container; a frame is the boat on which the shipping container is loaded. (Appendix A)

frequency hopping spread spectrum One of two approaches (with direct sequence spread spectrum) for sorting out overlapping data signals transmitted via radio waves. Frequency hopping spread spectrum is commonly abbreviated to FHSS or FH. Bluetooth uses frequency hopping spread spectrum. (Chapter 1)

Fresnel zone An elliptical area on either side of the straight line of sight that must also be clear for a long-range wireless network to work. (Chapter 34)

FTP A common way of transferring files on the Internet, though it's primarily used for uploading these days. FTP stands for File Transfer Protocol. (Appendix A)

gain The amount by which an antenna concentrates signal strength in a wireless network. (Chapters 3, 21, and 34)

gateway See *wireless gateway*.

Gigabit Ethernet An up-and-coming Ethernet wiring standard that works almost exactly like 10Base-T, but increases the maximum throughput to 1000 Mbps, or roughly 1 Gbps. Gigabit Ethernet is more technically known as "1000Base-T." (Appendix A)

GPRS A cellular data technology for GSM networks. GPRS stands for General Packet Radio Service and provides between 10 and 50 Kbps of bandwidth. (Chapters 4, 30)

GSM The primary type of digital cellular phone network used throughout most of the world outside the United States, and a growing standard in the U.S. GSM stands for Global System for Mobile Communications. GSM provides a very slow (9600 bps) cellular data service. (Chapters 4, 30)

header Address information on packets that says where it should go. (Appendix A)

high-gain antenna An antenna that significantly increases signal strength. High-gain antennas are necessary for long-range wireless networks. (Chapters 33, 34)

home gateway	See *wireless gateway.*
HomePlug	A networking standard that uses standard electrical wiring. HomePlug is primarily useful for bridging wireless networks across obstacles (like brick walls) that block radio waves. HomePlug runs at 14 Mbps. (Chapter 15, Appendix A)
HomePNA	A networking standard that uses standard telephone wiring. HomePNA is primarily useful for bridging wireless networks across obstacles (like brick walls) that block radio waves. HomePNA 2.0 runs at 10 Mbps, and the just-defined HomePNA 3.0 runs at 128 Mbps, in theory. (Appendix A)
HomeRF	A now-defunct competitor to Wi-Fi that integrated voice, data, and streaming media into a single wireless signal. (Chapter 2)
hot spot	A place where you can connect to a public wireless network. (Chapters 28, 29)
HTTP	The network protocol used by the Web, although it's also now used for many other services. HTTP stands for Hypertext Transfer Protocol. (Appendix A)
hub	The central device in a star network, whether wired or wireless. Wireless access points act as hubs in wireless networks. (Appendix A)
IEEE	The Institute of Electrical and Electronics Engineers. The IEEE is a non-profit, technical trade association that develops consensus-based technical standards for electronics in several industries. (Chapter 2)
IMAP	An increasingly common way of receiving email from a mail server on the Internet. IMAP defaults to storing mail on a server, in contrast to POP, which stores mail on your computer. IMAP stands for Internet Message Access Protocol. (Appendix A)
infrastructure mode	The most common way of creating a wireless network in which clients associate with an access point. (Chapters 6, 12, 19)
IP address	The numeric address (like 192.168.1.1) that identifies each device in a TCP/IP network. (Chapters 17, 33, Appendix A, Appendix B)
IPsec	One of two protocols (with PPTP) used for VPNs. IPsec stands for *IP security.* (Chapter 26)
key server	An Internet-based server that lets you look up other people's public keys. (Chapter 26)
latency	The length of time between a packet being sent and the response to that packet being returned. (Chapter 5)
line of sight	A clear line from one antenna to another in a long-range wireless network. A line of sight is necessary for a long-range network to connect. (Chapters 1, 33, 34)
local area network	The computers at your site, connected via Ethernet or Wi-Fi. Local area network is often abbreviated to LAN. Compare local area networks with wide area networks. (Chapter 3, Appendix A)

LocalTalk	An old networking standard used by Macs. LocalTalk runs at 230.4 Kbps. (Appendix A)
long haul	The transmission of data over long distances, potentially many miles. Traditionally, wired networks have been necessary for long haul, but with 802.16, also known as WiMax, long haul via wireless will become more feasible. (Chapter 4)
MAC address	The unique address assigned to every wireless and wired Ethernet network adapter. MAC stands for Media Access Control. Despite the fact that MAC addresses are all unique, it's possible to assign one device's MAC address to another device. (Chapters 16, 25, Appendix A)
master access point	The primary access point in a wireless network that uses WDS to extend range. The master access point shares the Internet connection with the rest of the remote, or relay access points, along with all the wireless clients. (Chapter 20)
mesh networking	A network topology in which every device can communicate with any other device that's within range. Mesh networking is particularly interesting for bringing wireless network access to an entire neighborhood. (Chapter 5, Appendix A)
NAT	A network service that makes it possible to share a single IP address with a network of many computers. NAT stands for Network Address Translation. Since a NAT gateway exposes only a single IP address to the outside Internet, it's useful for security, and some manufacturers may call it, somewhat incorrectly, a "firewall." (Chapters 16, 27, Appendix A)
NetBEUI	An older networking standard developed by IBM for LAN Manager and adopted for use in Microsoft Windows. NetBEUI stands for NetBIOS Extended User Interface. (Appendix A)
network adapter	The card or built-in hardware used in a computer or handheld device to connect to a network, whether wired or wireless. (Chapters 3, 14, Appendix A)
network diagram	A rough picture of a proposed or existing network. Network diagrams are extremely useful for planning new networks and for troubleshooting problems with existing networks.
network interface card	Commonly abbreviated to NIC. See *network adapter.*
network name	The name you give to your network; it's what shows up when a wireless client displays available networks. Many manufacturers use the terms "SSID" or "ESSID" in place of network name. (Chapters 6, 15, 17)
network segments	Physically and logically separate sections of a network. Breaking a network into segments increases bandwidth by reducing the amount of traffic that each device must listen to. (Appendix A)
network topology	The specific layout of a network. (Appendix A)

omnidirectional antenna	An antenna type that radiates more or less evenly in all horizontal directions. Omnidirectional antennas are sometimes called "vertical whip antennas." (Chapters 21, 34)
open network	A wireless network that is broadcasting its name. (Chapter 3)
packet bursting	See *frame bursting*.
packet	A discrete chunk of data, being transferred on a TCP/IP or other addressable network. (Appendix A)
packet-switched network	A network in which data is transferred in discrete chunks, called packets. The Internet is a packet-switched network. Packet-switched networks are generally considered more efficient than circuit-switched networks like the telephone system because multiple connections can use the same network simultaneously. (Chapter 4)
pairing	The act of introducing two Bluetooth devices to each other so they can communicate. (Chapters 4, 11)
panel antenna	An antenna type that radiates in only a specific direction. Panel antennas are commonly used for point-to-point situations. You may also see them called "patch antennas." (Chapters 21, 34)
parabolic antenna	An antenna type that radiates a very narrow beam in a specific direction. Parabolic antennas offer the highest gain for long-range point-to-point situations. (Chapter 34)
passive FTP	An option in FTP in which a connection starts from port 21 and the server replies using port 21 as well, instead of a higher numbered port, as it would normally. (Appendix A)
passphrase	One or more words you must enter to authenticate both sides of the connection when pairing Bluetooth devices. Some manufacturers may use the terms "password" or "passkey" instead. More generically, you may see passphrase used in place of "password" to indicate that you can enter more than a single word. (Chapters 11, 30)
pass-through	See *port mapping*.
patch antenna	See *panel antenna*.
patch cable	A normal Ethernet cable, as opposed to a crossover cable. (Appendix A)
personal certificate	A certificate you generate for use with SSL that doesn't have a certificate authority behind it. Personal certificates, also known as "self-signed certificates," aren't secure, but they're good enough in cases where you're working with your own SSL-enabled systems. (Chapter 26)
PEAP	A method of securing an 802.1X session within an encrypted tunnel to protect credentials used for logging in. PEAP stands for Protected Extensible Authentication Protocol. (Chapters 6, 22)

PGP	A technology and set of programs for encrypting data. PGP stands for Pretty Good Privacy. (Chapter 26)
PhoneNet	An adapter that enabled LocalTalk networks to operate over standard silver-satin telephone wiring, rather than Apple's proprietary LocalTalk cables. (Appendix A)
pigtail	A thin cable that connects an antenna to a wireless network adapter, usually converting between plug types in the process. (Chapters 3, 21, 33, 34)
plain text	See *clear text*.
plenum-rated	A term used describe Ethernet cable that has slow-burning, fire-resistant casing that emits little smoke. Plenum-rated Ethernet cable is used in overhead ductwork. (Appendix A)
point-to-multipoint	A wireless network in which one point (the access point) serves multiple other points around it. Indoor wireless networks are all point-to-multipoint, and long-range wireless networks that serve multiple clients usually employ either a single omnidirectional antenna or multiple sector antennas. (Chapter 34)
point-to-point	A long-range wireless network between two points. Point-to-point wireless networks use directional antennas. (Chapter 34)
POP	The most common way of receiving email from a mail server on the Internet. POP defaults to storing mail on your computer, in contrast to IMAP, which stores mail on the server. POP stands for Post Office Protocol. (Chapter 31, Appendix A)
port forwarding	See *port mapping*.
port mapping	The act of mapping a port on an Internet-accessible NAT gateway to another port on a machine on your internal network. Port mapping enables you to run a public Internet service on a machine that is otherwise hidden from the Internet by your NAT gateway. Other names for port mapping include "port forwarding," "pass-through," and "punch-through." (Chapters 16, 17, 26)
port	Either a physical jack on a network device or a way of identifying the type of data being sent in an Internet connection. Every Internet service has its own port number. (Appendix A)
Power over Ethernet	A wiring scheme that lets you run electrical power to an access point or wireless bridge over the same Ethernet cable that connects the device to your network. Power over Ethernet is often abbreviated to PoE. (Chapters 15, 34)
PPP	A network protocol that handles dial-up Internet connections. PPP stands for Point-to-Point Protocol. (Appendix A)
PPPoE	A technology that enables an ISP to require users to log in to an always-on Internet connection, something that wouldn't otherwise be necessary. PPPoE stands for PPP over Ethernet. (Chapters 16, 17, Appendix A)

PPTP	One of two protocols (with IPsec) used for VPNs. PPTP stands for Point-to-Point Tunneling Protocol. (Chapter 26)
pre-shared key	A TKIP passphrase used to protect your network traffic in WPA. Some manufacturers use the term "pre-shared secret" instead. (Chapter 22)
pre-shared secret	See *pre-shared key*.
private key	The key you keep secret in public-key cryptography systems. You use your private key to decrypt encrypted data sent to you by other people, who used your public key to encrypt it. You also use your private key to sign email messages; your recipients then use your public key to verify your signature. (Chapter 26)
promiscuous mode	A state of a wireless network adapter in which it listens to all the traffic on a wireless network rather than just the traffic addressed to your computer. (Chapter 25)
protocol	See *specification*.
public key	The key you give out to the world in public-key cryptography systems. Other people use your public key when sending you encrypted data, which you can then decrypt with your private key. You also use other people's public keys to verify the authenticity of mail messages they've signed with their private keys. (Chapter 26)
pulling wire	The act of running network cabling from one location to another. Wireless networks generally obviate the need to pull wire, which is one of their great attractions. HomePlug and Home-PNA can also help you avoid pulling wire. (Appendix A)
punch-through	See *port mapping*.
receive sensitivity	The capability of a radio transceiver to receive weak signals. The lower the receive sensitivity, the more capable the transceiver is of understanding weak signals. (Chapters 3, 5, 34)
relay access point	See *remote access point*.
relaying	The act of sending email through your mail server when you're not connected to your local network. Spammers take advantage of mail servers that allow unrestricted relaying. (Chapter 31)
remote access point	One of a number of secondary access points in a wireless network that uses WDS to extend its range. Remote access points, sometimes also called "relay access points," connect to a master access point. (Chapter 20)
ring network	A network topology similar to a bus network, but with the ends of the wire connected to form a ring. Ring networks are uncommon today. (Appendix A)
RJ-11	A plug type used by telephones. Don't confuse it with the larger RJ-45 plug type used in Ethernet networks. (Appendix A)

RJ-45	A plug type used in Ethernet networks. Don't confuse it with the smaller RJ-11 plugs used for phone cables. (Appendix A)
roaming	The act of seamlessly moving your wireless connection from one access point to another as you walk around. To enable roaming between access points, connect them to the same wired Ethernet network, give them the same network name, and set them to use different, non-overlapping channels (1, 6, and 11). (Chapters 15, 20)
router	An intelligent network device that goes one step beyond bridging by converting address-based protocols that describe how packets move from one place to another. In practice, this generally comes down to translating between IP addresses and MAC addresses for data flowing between your local network and the Internet. Many people use the term interchangeably with "gateway." You must enter the IP address of your router when configuring network settings manually. (Appendix A, Appendix B)
script kiddies	Wanna-be crackers who don't have the technical skills to break into computers on their own, so they use canned cracking software. (Chapter 27)
sector antenna	An antenna type that radiates in only a specific direction. Multiple sector antennas are commonly used in point-to-multipoint situations. (Chapter 34)
self-signed certificate	See *personal certificate*.
signal diversity	A process by which two small dipole antennas are used to send and receive, combining their results for better effect. (Chapter 21)
signal loss	The amount of signal strength that's lost in antenna cable, connectors, and free space. Signal loss is measured in decibels. (Chapter 34)
signal strength	The strength of the radio waves in a wireless network. (Chapters 5, 34)
silver satin	A wiring type in which pairs of wires run side-by-side. Silver satin is used for plugging in telephones; don't use it for networking. (Appendix A)
SMTP AUTH	A command in the SMTP protocol that requires identification before an SMTP server will accept outgoing mail from you. SMTP AUTH is essentially authenticated SMTP. (Chapters 26, 31)
SMTP	The protocol for sending email on the Internet. SMTP stands for Simple Mail Transfer Protocol. (Chapter 31, Appendix A)
software access point	A wireless-enabled computer running special software that enables it to act exactly like an wireless access point. (Chapters 12, 19)
specification	In the networking world, a formal language used by different devices to communicate. Agreed-upon specifications become standards. Specification is generally interchangeable with the term "protocol." (Chapter 2)

spectrum   A range of electromagnetic frequencies. (Chapter 1)

SSH   A security system that lets you create encrypted tunnels for any Internet protocol via port forwarding. SSH stands for Secure Shell. (Chapters 26, 31)

SSID   Service Set Identifier. See *network name*.

SSL   A security protocol that secures Internet transactions at the program level. SSL, which stands for Secure Sockets Layer, is widely used in Web browsers to protect credit card transactions, for instance. SSL is a component in EAP-TLS (Extensible Authentication Protocol-Transport Layer Security). (Chapter 26)

standard   A specification that has been agreed-upon by enough parties or given a stamp of approval by an industry body. (Chapter 2)

star network   A network topology in which all traffic goes through a central hub. Most wireless networks are star networks. (Appendix A)

stumbler   A software program that looks for available wireless networks in range and reports information about them. (Chapters 15, 21, 25, 28, 32)

subnet mask   A network setting that indicates the size of the network you're on. (Appendix B)

supplicant   The client role in an 802.1X-authenticated network. (Chapter 22)

switch   A specific type of hub that isolates the communications between any two computers from the rest of the network, thus increasing throughput. Switches are also called "switching hubs." (Appendix A)

TCP/IP   The primary communication protocol of the Internet. Actually a pair of cooperating protocols, TCP/IP stands for Transmission Control Protocol/Internet Protocol. (Chapter 16, Appendix A)

ThickNet   See *10Base-5*.

ThinNet   See *10Base-2*.

throughput   The amount of data that can be transmitted in a given amount of time. Throughput is commonly measured in bits per second. (Although throughput is not really a measurement of speed, most people, including us, use the word "speed" when talking about a high-throughput network.) (Appendix A)

TKIP   An encryption key that's part of WPA. TKIP stands for Temporal Key Integrity Protocol. It's nominally weaker than the government-grade AES, but in the real world, TKIP is more than strong enough. (Chapter 22)

TLS   Transport Layer Security. See *SSL*.

transmit power   The amount of power used by a radio transceiver to send the signal out. Transmit power is generally measured in milliwatts, which you can convert to dBm. (Chapter 34)

trigger

A special form of port mapping in which outgoing traffic on a specific port alerts a NAT gateway to allow incoming traffic on other ports. Triggers are used for network gaming. (Chapter 16)

twisted pair

A wiring type in which each pair of wires twists in a certain way to reduce electromagnetic interference. 10Base-T, 100Base-T, and Gigabit Ethernet all use twisted pair wires. Compare twisted pair to silver-satin telephone wire, in which the pairs don't twist, and which thus cannot be used for networking. (Appendix A)

Ultra Wideband

A wireless networking approach that broadcasts millions of tiny pulses at trillionth-of-second intervals using very low power over enormous swaths of spectrum. In comparison, traditional radios broadcast continuously on tiny bits of spectrum. Ultra Wideband is commonly abbreviated to UWB. (Chapter 5)

unshielded twisted pair

The most common type of twisted pair wiring. Unshielded twisted pair lacks a shield to act as a ground. Unshielded twisted pair is often abbreviated to UTP. (Appendix A)

uplink port

A special port on a hub or switch that has the transmit and receive pins switched, so you can use a normal patch cable instead of a crossover cable to connect it to other hubs. Many hubs now come with ports that you can switch between normal and uplink status, and others can automatically sense whether they should switch from normal to uplink status, depending on which device is connected to them. (Appendix A)

voice-over-IP

A way of making telephone calls over a packet-switched network like the Internet. Voice-over-IP requires special telephones and software. Voice-over-IP is commonly abbreviated to VoIP. (Chapters 4, 18)

VPN

A method of creating an encrypted tunnel through which all traffic passes, preventing anyone from snooping through transmitted and received data. VPN stands for *virtual private network*. (Chapters 10, 16, 26, 31)

warchalking

The act of making hobo-inspired chalk marks on walls or sidewalks to indicate the presence of wireless networks. Warchalking is more media hype than reality. (Chapters 25, 32)

wardriving

The act of driving around with your laptop open, looking to see if you can connect to open wireless networks as you drive. Change the mode of transportation and you get "warwalking," "warcycling," and "warflying." (Chapters 25, 32)

WDS

A technology that enables access points to communicate with one another in order to extend the range of a wireless network. WDS is appearing in 802.11g-based access points, and it stands for Wireless Distribution System. (Chapters 16, 17, 20, 23)

WEP

An encryption system for preventing eavesdropping on wireless network traffic. WEP stands for Wired Equivalent Privacy. WEP is easily broken, and is in the process of being replaced by WPA. (Chapters 6, 8, 10, 14, 16, 17, 23, 25)

wide area network	A collection of local area networks connected by a variety of physical means. The Internet is the largest and most well-known wide area network. Wide area network is generally abbreviated to WAN. (Chapter 3, Appendix A)
Wi-Fi	A certification mark managed by a trade group called the Wi-Fi Alliance. Wi-Fi certification encompasses numerous different standards, including 802.11a, 802.11b, 802.11g, WPA, and more, and equipment must pass compatibility testing to receive the Wi-Fi mark (Introduction, Chapter 2)
WiMax	Another name for the 802.16 wireless networking specification used for long-haul and backhaul connections. (Chapter 4)
wireless access point	See *access point*.
wireless gateway	A somewhat generic term that we use to differentiate between an access point and a more-capable device that can share an Internet connection, serve DHCP, and bridge between wired and wireless networks. You may also see the term "wireless router," or "base station." (Chapters 3, 16, 17, 19 and Appendix A)
wireless ISP	A company that provides wireless Internet access. The term is often abbreviated to WISP. (Chapters 28, 29, 33)
wireless network adapter	See *network adapter*.
wireless router	See *wireless gateway*.
WPA	A modern encryption system for preventing eavesdropping on wireless network traffic that solves the problems that plagued WEP. WPA stands for Wi-Fi Protected Access. (Chapters 6, 8, 14, 16, 17, 23, 25)
XTND XMIT	An extension to POP that lets you send email via POP instead of just receiving via POP. XTND XMIT isn't particularly reliable. (Chapter 31)
yagi antenna	An antenna type that radiates in only a specific direction. Yagi antennas are used only in point-to-point situations. (Chapter 34)
zombie	A computer that has been taken over by a malevolent program that uses it to attack other computers. (Chapter 27)

Index

G

H

Special offer to readers of
The Wireless Networking Starter Kit:

One FREE Month of Boingo Wireless™

The easiest way to get started with Wi-Fi...

Get started with Wi-Fi the easy way – with Boingo Wireless. Now you can take advantage of Boingo's™ instant, convenient, award-winning, one-click access to thousands of popular Hot Spots worldwide, so you can get more done whenever you travel.

Try it free right now with no risk. All you need to get started is your Wi-Fi enabled laptop (or Pocket PC) and a Boingo account. All it takes is a few minutes to sign up to get insanely fast, high-speed Internet connections at hotels, airports, restaurants and more.

Log on to the easiest to use Wi-Fi Network Today!
Visit www.boingo.com/partners/peachpit or call 1-800-U-BOINGO

Not sure you're ready to sign up? *Download our free Wi-Fi Utility now.*
The Boingo Wi-Fi Signal Detector makes it easy to search for, and connect to Wi-Fi signals, at home, at the office and on the road. With a built-in location directory, this free software helps you locate Hot Spots, manage your connections, and move seamlessly from network to network. Just visit www.boingo.com/download.